10th SIGHAN Workshop on Chinese Language Processing (SIGHAN-10 2024)

Bangkok, Thailand
16 August 2024

ISBN: 979-8-3313-0175-0

Printed from e-media with permission by:

Curran Associates, Inc.
57 Morehouse Lane
Red Hook, NY 12571

proceedings.com

Some format issues inherent in the e-media version may also appear in this print version.

Printed with permission by Curran Associates, Inc. (2025)

Association for Computational Linguistics
209 N. Eighth Street
Stroudsburg, Pennsylvania 18360

Phone: 1-570-476-8006
Fax: 1-570-476-0860

acl@aclweb.org

Additional copies of this publication are available from:

Curran Associates, Inc.
57 Morehouse Lane
Red Hook, NY 12571 USA
Phone: 845-758-0400
Fax: 845-758-2633
Email: curran@proceedings.com
Web: www.proceedings.com

SIGHAN-10 2024

The 10th SIGHAN Workshop on Chinese Language Processing

Proceedings of the Workshop

August 16, 2024

Association for Computational Linguistics (ACL)
317 Sidney Baker St. S
Suite 400 - 134
Kerrville, TX 78028
USA
Tel: +1-855-225-1962
acl@aclweb.org

Introduction

We are excited to welcome you to SIGHAN-10, the 10th SIGHAN workshop on Chinese language processing. This year, the 10th SIGHAN workshop returned and co-located with the 62nd Annual Meeting of the Association for Computational Linguistics (ACL-2024) in Bangkok, Thailand on August 11–16, 2024. Furthermore, SIGHAN 10 provides a shared task, namely Chinese Dimensional Aspect-Based Sentiment Analysis, dimABSA.

In an increasingly interconnected world, the importance of Chinese language processing cannot be overstated. As one of the most widely spoken languages, Chinese presents unique challenges and opportunities in the current research of artificial intelligence. Effective processing of the Chinese language opens doors to vast markets and cultural exchanges, fostering global collaboration and understanding. It serves as a critical tool in bridging linguistic divides and unlocking the rich textual heritage and contemporary content in Chinese. The focus of this workshop delves into the challenges in processing of the Chinese language, especially within the technology explosion of large language model, to explore how the Chinese specific tasks can be optimised to effectively understand as well as generating Chinese text.

We received 29 submissions this year, comprising 21 papers from the main workshop, and 8 papers from the shared task (dimABSA). We had two Area Chair (AC) members for the main workshop and one AC for the shared task, guiding the discussion process and writing a meta-review. For the main workshop, we accepted 10 papers. The acceptance rate for main workshop papers is 47.6%.

This year, SIGHAN-10 held in a hybrid format. Kang Liu from Institute of Automation, Chinese Academy of Sciences presents a keynote on "Beyond Facts: Understanding and Inducing Rule-based Knowledge in LLMs". Further, there are also several oral sessions, including five oral papers from the main workshop and three oral papers from the shared task.

We thank our Program Committee members and all reviewers. We specially thank our three Area Chairs: Runcong Zhao (King's College London), Bin Liang (The Chinese University of Hong Kong), and Lung-Hao Lee (National Yang Ming Chiao Tung University). They did an excellent job in reviewing the submitted papers, and we thank them for their essential role in selecting the accepted papers and helping produce a high-quality program for the conference.

We extend special thanks to all authors who have submitted papers this year and those who have shown interest in SIGHAN-10. We also thank all attendees for their participation and support.

Kam-Fai Wong and Min Zhang
General Chairs
Ruifeng Xu and Lin Gui
Program Co-Chairs

Organizing Committee

General Chair

Kam-Fai Wong, The Chinese University of Hong Kong, China
Min Zhang, Harbin Institute of Technology, Shenzhen, China

Program Co-Chair

Ruifeng Xu, Harbin Institute of Technology, Shenzhen, China
Lin Gui, King's College London, UK

Program Committee

Program Chairs

Kam-Fai Wong, The Chinese University of Hong Kong
Min Zhang, Harbin Institute of Technology, Shenzhen
Ruifeng Xu, Harbin Institute of Technology
Lin Gui, King's College London, University of London

Area Chairs

Lung-Hao Lee, National Yang Ming Chiao Tung University
Bin Liang, The Chinese University of Hong Kong
Runcong Zhao, King's College London, University of London

Reviewers

Jianzhu Bao

Lei Chen, Shiwei Chen

Keyang Ding

Zhe Hu, Shijue Huang

Xianming LI, Yuhang Lai, Lung-Hao Lee, Taishan Li, Jian Liao, Shujun Liu, Zhuohan Long

Xintong Song, Yang Sun

Hanzhuo Tan, Geng Tu

Bingbing Wang, Qianlong Wang, Suge Wang

Yanzheng Xiang, Hainiu Xu, Luo Xuan

Erxin Yu, Liang-Chih Yu

Han Zhang, Wenjia Zhang, Yice Zhang, Libo Zhao

Keynote Talk

Beyond Facts: Understanding and Inducing Rule-based Knowledge in LLMs

Kang Liu
Institute of Automation, Chinese Academy of Sciences
2024-08-16 09:30:00 – Room: **TBD**

Abstract: Large language models (LLM) have been proven to be able to learn knowledge from massive data. Most research currently discusses the relationship between implicit knowledge in LLMs and symbolic factual knowledge in Knowledge Graphs. Besides facts, human knowledge contains more types, such as rules. How does a LLM understand a rule and promote reasoning ability? Whether a LLM induce new rules from the given data? This talk will introduce our latest research work on these questions.

Bio: Kang Liu is a full professor at Institute of Automation, Chinese Academy of Sciences. He is also a youth scientist of Beijing Academy of Artificial Intelligence and a professor of University of Chinese Academy of Sciences. His research interests include Knowledge Graphs, Information Extraction, Question Answering and Large Language Models. He has published over 80 research papers in AI conferences and journals, like ACL, EMNLP, NAACL, COLING, et al. His work has over 20,000 citations on Google Scholar. He received the Best Paper Award at COLING-2014, Best PosterDemo Award at ISWC-2023, and the Google Focused Research Award in 2015 and 2016.

Table of Contents

Automatic Quote Attribution in Literary Works

Xingxing Yang
Division of Emerging Interdisciplinary Areas
Hong Kong University of Science and Technology
China
xyangbx@connect.ust.hk

Yu Wang
Department of Computing Science
University of Alberta
Canada
wang.yu@ualberta.ca

Abstract

In fiction, quote attribution pertains to the process of extracting dialogues and identifying the speakers involved. This encompasses quotation and speaker annotation. To accomplish this, we have developed a pipeline for quote attribution that incorporates classification, extractive question answering (QA), multi-choice QA, and coreference resolution. Additionally, we evaluated our model's performance by employing various models to predict both explicit and implicit speakers.

1 Introduction

Quote attribution, within the realm of literature and textual analysis, plays a pivotal role in enhancing the clarity and understanding of dialogues. It involves the extraction of dialogues from a text and the subsequent identification of the speakers involved. By assigning the appropriate speakers to their respective utterances, quote attribution enables readers to follow the flow of conversation and comprehend the nuances of a narrative. While manual quote attribution has been the traditional approach, advancements in natural language processing and machine learning have opened up exciting possibilities for automating this process. In this article, we explore the challenges and techniques associated with quote attribution, as well as the significance of automated methods in facilitating efficient and accurate analysis of dialogues in various literary contexts.

We leverage an annotated dataset consisting of 1991 modern Chinese novels as the foundation of our research. While our primary focus is on modern Chinese literature, our methodology can be seamlessly applied to other languages as well, despite potential language differences. Initially, our approach revolves around treating quote attribution as an extractive question-answering (QA) problem. To accomplish this, we fine-tune a pre-trained BERT model specifically for dialogues within fictional texts.

As we delve deeper into the complexities of quote attribution, we address more intricate scenarios, such as anaphora and the continuity of conversational threads(Muzny et al., 2017). To effectively handle the resolution of conversational threads, we employ a pre-trained BERT model designed for multi-choice QA. Furthermore, we utilize co-reference resolution techniques to tackle anaphoric references within the dialogues.

In order to distinguish between crowds, soliloquies, and dialogues, we employ a combination of rule-based filtering and a BERT-based classifier. This hybrid approach enables us to accurately identify and categorize different speech patterns and formats within the text.

Our research encompasses several contributions, which can be summarized as follows:

1. We conduct a thorough analysis of the intricate complexities and nuances associated with accurately attributing quotes.

2. We introduce a comprehensive pipeline for quote attribution, comprising multiple stages including classification, extractive question answering (QA), multi-choice QA, and coreference resolution. This pipeline serves as a systematic framework for effectively and efficiently handling quote attribution tasks.

2 Background/Related Work

To perform quote attribution, a dataset containing quoted speech from literary texts is essential for training, evaluation, and testing models. Several studies have focused primarily on creating datasets specifically for quote attribution. There are some open-source datasets available in this field, most of which are English literature works. Muzny, et al. developed an annotation tool for quotation annotation and created the QuoteLi3 dataset with speaker

Proceedings of the 10th SIGHAN Workshop on Chinese Language Processing (SIGHAN-10), pages 1–9
August 16, 2024

and quotation annotations in 3 novels (Muzny et al., 2017). Similarly, Sims, Matthew, et al. presented datasets for speaker attribution, comprised of 1,765 quotations linked to their speakers in 100 different literary texts (Sims et al., 2019), which is now part of the LitBank corpus. The PNDC project has undertaken similar work (Vishnubhotla et al., 2022). Notably, in these datasets, coreference information is also annotated.

As a crucial first step for quote attribution, quotes need to be extracted from the main text. According to the findings by O'Keefe et al., utilizing regular expressions for quote detection can achieve an accuracy exceeding 99% on clean English language data (O'Keefe et al., 2012).

Concerning quote attribution, multiple approaches have been explored in the existing literature. Earlier works typically employed rule-based methods with grammatical rules, complemented by some machine learning techniques, which could be complex due to the need for defining extensive rules (Elson and McKeown, 2010; Krug, 2020). In Pan et al.'s novel understanding system in 2021, they treated speaker identification of dialogues (SID) as a GBDT-based ranking task. It involved first identifying characters using NER, then feeding input features of the candidate speaker and the target dialogue, such as position, distance, etc., into a model for classification to determine the final speaker from the candidates (Pan et al., 2021). To resolve coreferences, they split names into name clusters with primary and candidate names, extracted features like gender, overlapping, personal pronouns, etc., and used a GBDT-based model with name candidates for coreference resolution. LG Pang employed BERT and CRF (Conditional Random Field), framing the task as question answering, for speaker extraction of quotations[1]. Yoder, Michael Miller, et al. and Vishnubhotla, Krishnapriya, et al. approached quotation attribution as a set of sequential sub-tasks: character identification, coreference resolution, quotation identification, and speaker attribution (Vishnubhotla et al., 2023; Yoder et al., 2021).

In contrast to the recent work by Vishnubhotla, Krishnapriya, et al., we propose an additional module for classifying crowds, soliloquies, and dialogues. We omit the character identification module. Instead, we employ a question-answering (QA) approach for quote attribution, which directly predicts the name of the character speaking the quote.

3 Dataset

We utilize a dataset that we refer to as CLD, comprising 1,991 modern Chinese novels annotated by literature practitioners from the audiobook industry, ensuring high accuracy and validation. The original dataset includes information about the main characters and annotated novel texts, with each quote attributed to a specific character. For every character, we have access to their gender information and a brief description.

4 Quote Attribution

Our primary objective is to correctly attribute each quote to the appropriate speaker within the novel. The process begins with quote extraction, where quotes are identified and extracted from the text. Subsequently, we aim to assign the extracted quotes to their corresponding speakers accurately.

We identify several key challenges in this task:

1. Coreference: Characters in literary texts usually appear in three formats: proper names (e.g., "夏洛克·荷马(Sherlock Holmes)"), pronouns (e.g., "他(He)"), and nominal anaphoric noun phrases referring to characters (e.g., "侦探(The consulting detective)") (Labatut and Bost, 2019). The first-person pronoun "我" (I/My) also frequently appears in some first-person novels.

2. Crowds/System/Sound Effects: There are occasions when the quotes are not spoken by a specific individual but rather by crowds, a "system" (which frequently occurs in certain Chinese time-travel novels), or represent audio effects rather than human speech.

3. Following Conversational Threads: Dialogues often follow an "ABAB" pattern, where A denotes one speaker and B denotes another. Many times, there may be no explicit names or references to the speakers within the paragraph, with only the utterances themselves present.

4. Long Soliloquies: Multiple continuous utterances may be given by a single speaker.

We list examples of different cases in quote attribution in Table 1.

To address the above-mentioned challenges, we employ multiple methods within our proposed pipeline, which can be outlined as follows:

[1] https://gitlab.com/snowhitiger/speakerextraction

Table 1: Different cases in quote attribution

Regular	“好好，还需要什么？”杨建国连忙问。 "Alright, what else do you need?" **Yang Jianguo** asked quickly.
Co-reference	大家都幸灾乐祸地望着叶君临，等待他的回复。 他只得笑笑，断然拒绝：“假酒伤身，我喝不了！” Everyone looked at **Ye Junlin** with schadenfreude and waited for **his** response. **He** could only smile and firmly refuse: "Fake alcohol is harmful to the body, I can't drink it!"
Sound effects	“咚咚咚……” 就在这时，门外传来一阵清脆的敲门声。 "Dong dong dong..." Just then, **a crisp knocking sound** came from outside the door.
Following conversational threads	“活啥呀，都死九年了，我看咱们是活见鬼！”杨建国哆嗦着说。 “别瞎说，今晚那个玉瑶，不还施法救咱儿子呢吗，谁听说过鬼还捉鬼哩？” 杨妻白了杨建国一眼。 “怪呀，怪呀。不过不管她是啥，咱们都该感谢人家。” “是呀，我还听那小姑娘，管咱家儿子叫小老公……” “要是能再见到这个玉瑶就好了，一定要问问清楚。” 夫妻二人没想到，迷一样的玉瑶，第二天竟然又出现了。 "What kind of life is this? He's been dead for nine years. I think we're seeing ghosts!" **Yang Jianguo** shuddered. "Don't talk nonsense. Didn't that Yu Yao use magic to save our son tonight? Who's ever heard of ghosts catching ghosts?" **Yang's wife** gave **Yang Jianguo** a glare. "It's strange, it's strange. But no matter who she is, we should be grateful to her." "Yes, and I heard that little girl calling our son 'little husband'..." "If we could see this Yu Yao again, it would be great. We have to ask her some questions." The couple didn't expect that the mysterious Yu Yao would appear again the next day.
Crowds	一掌镇压！而对此，凌风微微抬头，神色风轻云淡，在所有人不可思议的注视下，一根手指缓缓的点出，看上去轻柔而无力。 “这小子在干吗，等死吗？” “我估计是傻了，孟超然师兄可是施展了一品神通，镇山掌。” “狂徒而已，这样轻柔的手指，我上去都可随意灭他，何况孟师兄。” 议论澎湃，只当凌风为小丑。只是，在所有人声音落下的瞬间，前方的一幕，却是让得他们立刻紧闭上了嘴巴，身体剧烈的颤抖起来。 With a single palm strike, Ling Feng suppressed his opponent. However, he lifted his head slightly, his expression calm and relaxed. In the midst of everyone's incredulous gaze, he slowly pointed a finger, appearing gentle and powerless. "What is the buddy doing, waiting to die?" "I think he's gone crazy. Senior Meng Chaoran used a first-grade divine technique, the Mountain Suppression Palm." "He's just a madman. I could easily kill him with a gentle finger like that, let alone Senior Meng." There was **a heated discussion**, and they all thought Ling Feng was a clown. However, in the instant when everyone's voices fell, the scene in front of them caused them to immediately shut their mouths and their bodies trembled violently.
Long Soliloquy	病床很快推到了病房，这层是高级vip病房区，院长亲自过问，整个楼层都被清空，就安排了颜汐、颜清和还有已经能下地行走的顾念风住。祁愿没有跟进去，而是放手站在了门外，他凝眸看着病房许久，才缓缓道： “祁承，走吧。” “调动人手来守住这里，没有我的同意，连只苍蝇也不准放进来！” “联系国外势力，给他们一天时间，我要颜允之毫发无伤地回到华国！” “放弃攻击颜氏集团，控制舆论消除对颜家的负面影响。傅家霍家那些人谁有意见让他们直接来见我。”…… The hospital bed was quickly pushed into the ward. This floor was the high-level VIP ward area, and the hospital dean personally inquired about the situation. The entire floor was cleared, and Yan Xi, Yan Qing, and Gu Nianfeng, who was already able to walk, were accommodated. **Qi Yuan** did not follow them in, but let go and stood outside the door. **He** stared at the ward for a long time before slowly saying: "Qi Cheng, let's go." "Arrange manpower to guard this place. Without my permission, not even a fly is allowed in!" "Contact foreign forces and give them one day to ensure that Yan Yunzhi returns to Hualand unharmed!" "Give up attacking the Yan family's group, control public opinion, and eliminate the negative impact on the Yan family. If anyone from the Fu family or the Huo family has any opinions, let them come see me directly."...

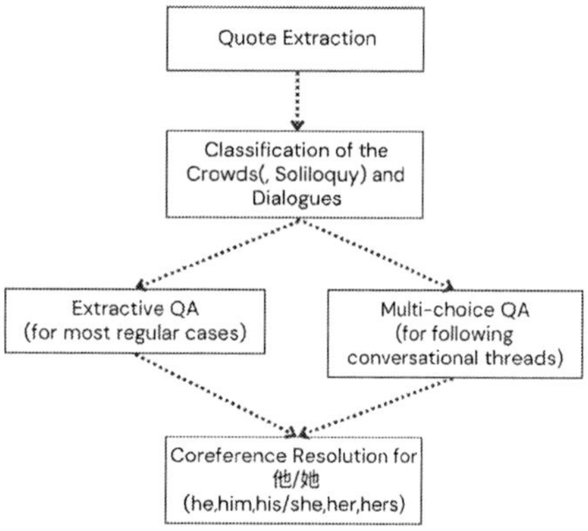

4.1 Quote Extraction

As an initial approach, we employ regular expressions, as described by (O'Keefe et al., 2012), for quote extraction. It's important to note that not all authors follow the conventional practice of enclosing speech within quotation marks. However, this method proves effective for the majority of novels in our dataset, and we currently exclude edge cases from our research scope. Consequently, we utilize regular expressions to extract quotes enclosed within symbols such as "", “”, and ‘’, which are commonly used in Chinese fiction.

In some cases, quotes in Chinese novels may represent sound effects, such as "呼呼" (Huhu), which signifies the sound of wind blowing. These sound effect quotes often occur within the same sentence and are typically followed by the word "声" (sound). To identify and filter out these sound effect quotes, we have developed a specific rule. According to this rule, if a quote is less than 10 characters long and has "声" as a suffix, or if it is less than 10 characters and contains no punctuation marks within the quote itself or before and after the quotation marks, it is considered a sound effect quote. However, it's important to note that while this rule successfully handles most cases, it may not cover all possible scenarios.

4.2 QA-based Quote Attribution

For the task of quote attribution, we employ an extractive question-answering (QA) approach. The method is relatively simple yet effective. We construct each data entry in our dataset following the format outlined in Table 2.

When constructing our extractive QA dataset for fine-tuning, we first extract context and speaker pairs with labeled names that have appeared in the given context. This allows the extractive QA model to identify and extract the explicit names along with their start and end indices within the context.

For first-person novels, we treat them as a special case during our dataset preprocessing. Specifically, we consider the pronoun "我" (I) as a character name. This approach is taken because "我" (I) typically refers to the same person throughout the entire novel, even if a specific name is assigned to the character. Resolving the coreference of "我" (I) using name-based resolution can be challenging, as the assigned name often appears only in the initial chapters of the novel.

Moreover, we have observed a performance decrease when the context contains pronouns such as "他" (he) or "她" (she). It is common for these pronouns to be prevalent in certain novels, with the actual character name being distant from the quoted text. To mitigate this issue, we randomly replace character names with "他" (he) or "她" (she) during dataset preprocessing. This approach makes it easier for the model to identify and resolve instances of "他" (he) or "她" (she). Consequently, when handling contexts containing numerous occurrences of these pronouns, we first extract them as names and subsequently apply coreference resolution.

After completing all the previous steps, we proceed to fine-tune a pre-trained RoBERTa model using our prepared dataset.

4.3 MC-based Quote Attribution

The model exhibits performance degradation on extended conversational threads following an ABAB pattern. This is attributed to limitations of the underlying base model in handling longer text sequences. To mitigate this issue, we introduce a supplementary multi-choice model. The underlying assumption is that by restricting the response space to a predefined set of options, we can enhance the accuracy of answer selection.

To improve the model's ability to handle conversational threads, we built a specific training dataset. We prioritized quotes lacking context, focusing on those within a single paragraph. We then expanded by including nearby paragraphs until the speaker was identified. This ensures the dataset captures complete conversational exchanges, empowering the new multi-choice BERT model to handle them effectively.

After constructing each data pair in the format shown in Table 3, we fine-tune the multi-choice BERT model for improved performance.

Table 2: QA-based quote attribution

Context:	见许念念一脸呆滞，杨翠花哭得更伤心，一把鼻涕一把眼泪的抱着她，肥胖的身体哭得不停颤抖。 "孩子她爹，我们念念要是不行，我也不活了......我苦命的儿啊......" 许念念是被这最后的尖锐声音给刺激回神的。 Seeing Xu Nian Nian's dull face, **Yang Cuihua** cried even more sadly, hugging Niannian with snot, with tears streaming down her plump body that were trembling with non-stop sobs. **"Child's dad, if Nian Nian dies, I won't be able to live either... my poor child..."** Xu Nian Nian was brought back to reality by the sharp last sentence.
Question:	"孩子她爹，我们念念要是不行，我也不活了......我苦命的儿啊......"是谁说的? Who said "Child's dad, if Nian Nian dies, I won't be able to live either... my poor child..."?
Answer:	杨翠花 Yang Cuihua

Table 3: MC-based quote attribution

Context:	说着，杨天明就把骨头扔了出去。 铁柱打了个激灵："你不说这是龙坟吗？" "猜的......" 铁柱无语："现在咋整？" "走吧，天也快黑了，最好赶在天黑之前下山，大人们都说潜山上闹鬼的。" 铁柱快哭了："来之前你可没这么说。" "我也是才想起来的嘛。"杨天明无辜地摊了摊手。 After speaking, **Yang Tianming** threw the bone out. Tie Zhu shuddered: "Don't you say this is the Dragon Tomb?" "Guess..." Tie Zhu didn't know what to say: "What's going on now?" **"Let's go, it's getting dark soon Now, it's best to go down the mountain before dark, the adults said that the hidden mountain was haunted."** Tie Zhu was about to cry: "You didn't say that before we came here." "I just remembered it too. "Yang Tianming spread his hands innocently.
Question:	"走吧，天也快黑了，最好赶在天黑之前下山，大人们都说潜山上闹鬼的。"是谁说的? Who said "Let's go. It's getting dark. It's best to get down the mountain before it gets too dark. The adults all say that there are ghosts on the mountain,"?
Choices:	[杨天明，铁柱] [Yang Tianming, Tiezhu]
Answer:	杨天明 Yang Tianming

4.4 Co-reference Resolution

Novels use many references to connect ideas and characters. In our case, as we're focused on who said what (quote attribution), we only care about references that identify speakers within quotes.

Co-reference resolution in fiction faces unique challenges. First, references can span long passages, making it difficult to keep track of who is being referred to. Second, pronouns can shift between characters within a limited context, further confusing the interpretation. These factors contribute to the difficulty, even for humans, of identifying the correct referent. Table 4 showcases some common scenarios where co-reference becomes ambiguous.

We construct our gender pronoun resolution dataset through a combination of automation and human validation. We begin by automatically extracting quote paragraphs containing relevant pronouns. We then enrich the context by including surrounding paragraphs until the speaker is identified. Utilizing character information, we assign the closest speaker of the same gender to the pronoun. However, to ensure accuracy, human validators meticulously review and refine the automatically generated labels, guaranteeing a high-quality dataset for our task.

Our goal is to link pronouns within quotes to the speaker's name, directly in the original text. To achieve this, we fine-tune a co-reference resolution model. By improving this model's accuracy, we can precisely connect pronouns to speakers, enabling a smoother integration with our existing extractive question answering approach.

We specifically leverage the method in Fast-

Table 4: Different Cases in Co-reference Resolution

Easily recognizable context	但凌天并没有任何恐惧，毕竟，他小时候跟着吴中胤没少来了这个地方。 他不免叫了一声："青青姐，你在这儿吗？" But $LingTian_1$ didn't have any fear. After all, he_1 followed Wu Zhongyin to this place a lot of times when he_1 was a child. He_1 couldn't help calling: "Sister Qingqing, are you here?"
Multiple referees for a single pronoun	刚接过来，上官香放到了桌上，迫不及待地就吃了起来，小桃看着她狼吞虎咽的模样，担心她会噎着，叮嘱她慢点吃。 "这是我应该做的，公主。"念念不忘慕容夫人对她的叮嘱，要照顾好上官香，千万不能让她饿着。 Just as she_1 received it, $ShangguanXiang_1$ placed the pastry on the table and eagerly began to eat. $Xiaotao_2$ watched her_1 wolfing it down and worried that she_1 might choke, so she_2 advised her_1 to eat slowly. "It's what I should do, Your Highness," she_2 said, remembering Lady Murong's instructions to take care of $ShangguanXiang_1$ and not let her_1 go hungry.
Unrecognizable context by human	冥心大帝目光深邃，盯着不断轮动的画面，掌心里多出一件奇特的物件，开口道："差不多了。" "什么？"司无涯生出一种不太好的感觉。 他语气一沉，继续道，"此物名为天道大璋，蕴含天地规则……是勾连十大规则的关键至宝。" 接着…… $EmperorMingxin_1$ gazed deeply at the constantly rotating screen, there was a strange object in his palm, and said: "It's almost there." "What?" $SiWuya_2$ had a bad feeling. $His_?$ tone sank, and $he_?$ continued, "This thing is called Tiandao Dazhang, and it contains the rules of heaven and earth... It is the key treasure that connects the ten rules." Then……

coref[2](Toshniwal et al., 2020a), which employs a bounded memory approach to prioritize the most crucial parts of a document and disregard irrelevant information. It's important to distinguish our approach from prior work in other languages; we replace the original pre-trained Longformer model with its Chinese counterpart and incorporate Chinese word segmentation for task compatibility.

4.5 Classifying the Crowds, Soliloquy, and Dialogues

We've identified three common scenarios where continuous utterances are likely to occur: crowds, soliloquies (internal monologues), and dialogues with multiple speakers. For the case of crowds, these "group quotes" often appear as a series of continuous utterances containing keywords like "everyone," "several people," or "the whole class".

We first extract such cases using our annotated data. In our annotated data, crowds are usually labeled with "龙套"(others). It usually comes in the format of at least 3 continuous utterances.

We compared the performance of rule-based method and the BERT method for classification of the crowds, soliloquy and dialogues.

[2] https://github.com/shtoshni/fast-coref

4.5.1 Rule-based Method for Classifying the Crowds

To address such cases, we implement a rule-based approach that involves maintaining a predefined list of keywords for filtering out irrelevant content. These keywords are derived through data analysis. In our annotated dataset, utterances attributed to crowds are typically labeled as "龙套" (others). For analysis purposes, we extract data consisting of a minimum of three consecutive utterances, each containing only a quotation without any accompanying context, and all labeled as "龙套" (others). This dataset subset allows us to perform detailed analysis and further refine our keyword list for effective filtering.

Based on our analysis, we compile a list of keywords that includes terms like "议论" (discussion), "众人" (the crowds), and others. During the inference phase, we extract a minimum of three consecutive utterances with the closest context and examine the surrounding context (excluding the utterances themselves) for the presence of any of the keywords. This approach helps us identify passages that are likely attributed to crowd dialogue.

4.5.2 BERT Classification

In addition to the rule-based method, we also incorporate a BERT-based approach for comparison. In this approach, we consider the identification of continuous utterances as a three-category classification problem: crowds, soliloquies, and dialogues. Similar to the rule-based method, we extract data for these three cases. The construction of the dataset follows a similar process, with the distinction that we do not rely on predefined keywords for filtering purposes. Instead, the BERT-based method leverages the power of the model to learn and classify utterances based on their contextual information.

Furthermore, we conduct a comparison between the results of binary classification, where the focus is on distinguishing between the two-category classification approach and the three-category one.

5 Experimental Setup

5.1 Text Preprocessing

We construct our data for QA-based quote attribution as shown in Table 2, for MC-based quote attribution as shown in Table 3, and for co-reference resolution as shown in Table 4.

5.2 Training

In all experiments, we use the same original dataset which contains 1991 novels. For each separate task, we correspondingly pre-process the dataset.

To perform QA-based quote attribution, we finetune a Roberta-based QA model using the QA pipeline in the UER (Universal Encoder Representations) toolkit[3](Zhao et al., 2019). In this process, we utilize approximately 16,000 records and structure our data according to the format presented in Table 2. To ensure comprehensive evaluation, we conduct separate experiments for both single-paragraph and mixed-paragraph contexts. For the mixed paragraph context, we take care to ensure diversity by including 60% single-paragraph instances and 40% multi-paragraph instances in our dataset. This approach allows us to assess the model's performance under different contextual scenarios.

To facilitate MC-based quote attribution, we finetune an MC model using the UniMC framework using the fenshen framework[4](Wang et al., 2022). When constructing our dataset, we follow the format outlined in Table 3. This approach allows us to train the model using multiple-choice questions and corresponding answer options, enabling it to effectively attribute quotes.

For co-reference resolution, we use fast-coref[5] (Toshniwal et al., 2021, 2020b) and replace the English base model with the Chinese pre-trained Longformer model[6] and used Jieba[7] for Chinese word segmentation. We use around 7000 records.

To perform classification tasks for crowds, soliloquies, and dialogues, we employ BERT (Bidirectional Encoder Representations from Transformers)[8] (Devlin et al., 2018) as our classification model. For each category, we utilize a dataset consisting of 2000 records to train the model.

6 Results and Discussion

To evaluate the performance of these models, we randomly extract 10% of the dataset for evaluation for each model. Here are our results.

Table 5: Results of extractive QA for quote attribution

Case	F-score	EM
Single-paragraph	95.1794	93.1452
Mixed(Single- & Multi-paragraph)	88.2331	86.3062

Table 6: Results of MC for quote attribution

Model	Accuracy
UniMC	0.9259

Table 7: Results of co-reference resolution

Model	F-score
Fast-coref	95.4

The results indicate that individual modules achieve high performance, showcasing the promising accuracy for quote attribution. We didn't conduct a full test on the whole novels in our dataset because there might be cases of characters annotated as 龙套(the crowds) even if there's a character name in the paragraph or characters that are only annotated with one name but has multiple

[3] https://huggingface.co/uer/roberta-base-chinese-extractive-qa

[4] https://github.com/IDEA-CCNL/Fengshenbang-LM

[5] https://github.com/shtoshni/fast-coref

[6] https://huggingface.co/schen/longformer-chinese-base-4096

[7] https://github.com/fxsjy/jieba

[8] https://huggingface.co/bert-base-chinese

Table 8: Results of classifying the crowds, soliloquy, and dialogues

Method	Accuracy
Rule-based Method (Only for the crowds)	0.6308
BERT classification (Only for the crowds)	**0.8458**
BERT classification	0.72

co-references, so it will take a large effort to re-annotate the novels. But it can be inferred that by using a combination of these models, we can do quote attribution in literary works.

There are still certain challenges that need to be addressed to improve accuracy and robustness further. These challenges include:

1. Longer context for accuracy and co-reference: The pipeline demonstrates a performance drop when dealing with longer contexts, as highlighted in Table 5. This drop is partly attributed to the base model's performance limitations. Additionally, resolving co-reference for names that span across long paragraphs or even chapters, such as "李玉瑶" (Li, Yuyao) and "小瑶" (Xiao Yao), remains unexplored. Instances like these are prevalent in many novels, presenting a complex challenge for accurate co-reference resolution.

2. Eliminating a long chain of models: Due to the diverse range of cases involved in quote attribution, including regular names, sound effects, and crowds, our current approach relies on a long chain of models. However, this has the drawback of previous incorrect predictions affecting subsequent ones. For instance, if the initial BERT classification for crowds and dialogues yields incorrect predictions, subsequent extractive QA processes will also be influenced by these erroneous predictions.

Efforts should be focused on resolving these issues to achieve higher accuracy and enhance the robustness of the quote attribution system.

Limitations

We neglect edge cases for irregular speech content without quotes in Chinese novels in our research. For audio effects, since they only occupy a small portion of the whole novel, we only exclude them by simply defining rules, while there are still a lot of times the rules do not apply.

Our study is only done in modern Chinese literature works. Though the proposed method may be applied to other languages, there might be some language differences that should be taken into account.

7 Future Work

We recognize this work as a stepping stone towards a more comprehensive solution. Here are some promising avenues for further exploration within the domain of automated quote attribution in literary works:

1. Building a Robust Annotated Dataset: A key focus for future work will be the development of a comprehensive and well-annotated dataset specifically designed for quote attribution tasks in fiction. This dataset should encompass a diverse range of writing styles, genres, and complexities to ensure the model generalizes well to unseen data.

2. Unveiling the Potential of Large Language Models (LLMs): LLMs, with their advanced capabilities, including longer context handling and superior understanding, in natural language processing, hold immense potential for quote attribution. Future research will involve exploring the integration of LLMs with quote attribution, potentially leading to a more direct and more accurate result of speaker identification without the combination of multiple models as proposed in this paper. Additionally, the ability of LLMs to parse results in user-defined formats can be a valuable asset, allowing researchers to tailor the output to their specific needs.

These future directions have the potential to significantly improve the accuracy and efficiency of quote attribution in literary analysis. By continuously refining the methodology and exploring new avenues, we can pave the way for a fully automated quote attribution system that empowers researchers and enriches our understanding of literary works.

8 Conclusion

This paper explored the application of machine learning for quote attribution in literary works. By leveraging AI-powered algorithms, we aim to empower literature annotators with faster and more accurate identification of quoted speech sources, ultimately enhancing analysis of fictional works. While writing styles may vary across novels, a significant portion of literary works can benefit from this approach.

References

Jacob Devlin, Ming-Wei Chang, Kenton Lee, and Kristina Toutanova. 2018. Bert: Pre-training of deep bidirectional transformers for language understanding. *arXiv preprint arXiv:1810.04805*.

David Elson and Kathleen McKeown. 2010. Automatic attribution of quoted speech in literary narrative. In *Proceedings of the AAAI Conference on Artificial Intelligence*, volume 24, pages 1013–1019.

Markus Krug. 2020. *Techniques for the Automatic Extraction of Character Networks in German Historic Novels*. Bayerische Julius-Maximilians-Universitaet Wuerzburg (Germany).

Vincent Labatut and Xavier Bost. 2019. Extraction and analysis of fictional character networks: A survey. *ACM Computing Surveys (CSUR)*, 52(5):1–40.

Grace Muzny, Michael Fang, Angel Chang, and Dan Jurafsky. 2017. A two-stage sieve approach for quote attribution. In *Proceedings of the 15th Conference of the European Chapter of the Association for Computational Linguistics: Volume 1, Long Papers*, pages 460–470.

Tim O'Keefe, Silvia Pareti, James R Curran, Irena Koprinska, and Matthew Honnibal. 2012. A sequence labelling approach to quote attribution. In *Proceedings of the 2012 Joint Conference on Empirical Methods in Natural Language Processing and Computational Natural Language Learning*, pages 790–799.

Junjie Pan, Lin Wu, Xiang Yin, Pengfei Wu, Chenchang Xu, and Zejun Ma. 2021. A chapter-wise understanding system for text-to-speech in chinese novels. In *ICASSP 2021-2021 IEEE International Conference on Acoustics, Speech and Signal Processing (ICASSP)*, pages 6069–6073. IEEE.

Matthew Sims, Jong Ho Park, and David Bamman. 2019. Literary event detection. In *Proceedings of the 57th Annual Meeting of the Association for Computational Linguistics*, pages 3623–3634.

Shubham Toshniwal, Sam Wiseman, Allyson Ettinger, Karen Livescu, and Kevin Gimpel. 2020a. Learning to ignore: Long document coreference with bounded memory neural networks. *arXiv preprint arXiv:2010.02807*.

Shubham Toshniwal, Sam Wiseman, Allyson Ettinger, Karen Livescu, and Kevin Gimpel. 2020b. Learning to Ignore: Long Document Coreference with Bounded Memory Neural Networks. In *EMNLP*.

Shubham Toshniwal, Patrick Xia, Sam Wiseman, Karen Livescu, and Kevin Gimpel. 2021. On Generalization in Coreference Resolution. In *CRAC (EMNLP)*.

Krishnapriya Vishnubhotla, Adam Hammond, and Graeme Hirst. 2022. The project dialogism novel corpus: A dataset for quotation attribution in literary texts. In *Proceedings of the Thirteenth Language Resources and Evaluation Conference*, pages 5838–5848.

Krishnapriya Vishnubhotla, Frank Rudzicz, Graeme Hirst, and Adam Hammond. 2023. Improving automatic quotation attribution in literary novels. *arXiv preprint arXiv:2307.03734*.

Junjie Wang, Yuxiang Zhang, Lin Zhang, Ping Yang, Xinyu Gao, Ziwei Wu, Xiaoqun Dong, Junqing He, Jianheng Zhuo, Qi Yang, Yongfeng Huang, Xiayu Li, Yanghan Wu, Junyu Lu, Xinyu Zhu, Weifeng Chen, Ting Han, Kunhao Pan, Rui Wang, Hao Wang, Xiaojun Wu, Zhongshen Zeng, Chongpei Chen, Ruyi Gan, and Jiaxing Zhang. 2022. Fengshenbang 1.0: Being the foundation of chinese cognitive intelligence. *CoRR*, abs/2209.02970.

Michael Miller Yoder, Sopan Khosla, Qinlan Shen, Aakanksha Naik, Huiming Jin, Hariharan Muralidharan, and Carolyn P Rosé. 2021. Fanfictionnlp: A text processing pipeline for fanfiction. In *The 3rd Workshop on Narrative Understanding*.

Zhe Zhao, Hui Chen, Jinbin Zhang, Xin Zhao, Tao Liu, Wei Lu, Xi Chen, Haotang Deng, Qi Ju, and Xiaoyong Du. 2019. Uer: An open-source toolkit for pre-training models. *EMNLP-IJCNLP 2019*, page 241.

TeleChat: An Open-source Billingual Large Language Model

Zihan Wang[*]**, XinZhang Liu**[*]**, Shixuan Liu**[*]**, Yitong Yao**[*]**, Yuyao Huang**[*]**,**
Mengxiang Li, Zhongjiang He, Yongxiang Li, Luwen Pu, Huinan Xu,
Chao Wang[†]**, Shuangyong Song**[†]
Institute of Artificial Intelligence(TeleAI),
China Telecom Corp Ltd
{wangzh54,liuxz,liusx14,yaoyt2,huangyy121,hezj,
liyx25,pulw,xuhn,wangc17,songshy}@chinatelecom.cn

Abstract

In this paper, we present **TeleChat**, a collection of large language models (LLMs) with parameters of 7 billion and 12 billion. TeleChat is initially pretrained on an extensive corpus containing a diverse collection of texts from both English and Chinese languages, encompassing trillions of tokens. Subsequently, the model undergoes fine-tuning to align with human preferences, following a detailed methodology that we describe. We evaluate the performance of TeleChat on various tasks, including general dialogue generation, language understanding, mathematics, reasoning, code generation, and knowledge-based question answering. Our findings indicate that TeleChat achieves state-of-the-art performance to other open-source models of similar size across a wide range of public benchmarks. To support future research and applications utilizing LLMs, we release the fine-tuned model checkpoints of TeleChat-7B and TeleChat-12B, along with code and a portion of our filtered high-quality pretraining data, to the public community[1].

1 Introduction

The research community has witnessed substantial proliferation of open large language models (LLMs). Following the introduction of ChatGPT(OpenAI, 2022), there have been thrilling advancements and applications of LLMs, but the majority of prominent LLMs, such as GPT-4(OpenAI, 2023) and PaLM-2(Anil et al., 2023), are restrictive in their technological sharing. In contrast, a steady stream of openly accessible text-based LLMs has emerged, including OPT(Zhang et al., 2022), BLOOM(Scao et al., 2022), LLAMA(Touvron et al., 2023a), LLAMA 2(Touvron et al., 2023b), etc. Furthermore, there exist various other LLMs that have been designed with a focus on Chinese-English bilingual language generation, including models such as Baichuan-2(Yang et al., 2023), Qwen(Bai et al., 2023), InternLM(InternLM_Team, 2023) and SkyWork(Wei et al., 2023). While these models offer comprehensive details about their pretraining strategies, they often lack transparency in their instruction finetuning processes for chat models, including limited disclosure of the finetuning data composition, methods for concatenating multi-turn dialog data, and techniques employed to enhance conversational performance.

To encourage reproducibility of fine-tuned LLMs and foster responsible development of LLMs, we release TeleChat, a collection of pretrained language models and chat models that have been fine-tuned using human alignment techniques including supervised fine-tuning and reinforcement learning. In particular, we provide a comprehensive explanation of our model architecture and the approach we used to extend TeleChat's context window to 96k in Section 2. Furthermore, in Section 3, we delve into the specifics of our pretraining dataset and cleaning techniques. We then discuss alignment with human preferences in Section 4 and 5. Additionally, in Section 6, we conduct a thorough analysis of the model's performance on standard benchmark tasks and general dialogue generation. Throughout the development of TeleChat, we gain insights regarding mitigating hallucination with a knowledge graph, which is discussed in Section 7. Furthermore, we describe our parallel computing method in Section 8. Our contribution are listed as follows:

- We release TeleChat, a suite of pretrained and fine-tuned large language models with parameter sizes of 7 billion and 12 billion. We release model checkpoints and code to the public community.
- We present our comprehensive data cleaning workflow, and release a portion of our high-quality training corpus, comprising more than

[*]These authors contributed equally to this work.
[†]Corresponding Authors.
[1]https://github.com/Tele-AI/Telechat

Proceedings of the 10th SIGHAN Workshop on Chinese Language Processing (SIGHAN-10), pages 10–20
August 16, 2024

1TB of text data and exceeding 160 billion tokens. To the best of our knowledge, this marks the largest open Chinese corpus for language model pre-training to the date.

- We disclose a comprehensive description of our supervised fine-tuning methodology, an aspect that is frequently overlooked in reports of other publicly available models. Furthermore, TeleChat stands out with its longest context length among open-source large language models.

2 Model Design

2.1 Model Architecture

TeleChat is an autoregressive transformer model that employs a stack of transformer-decoder layers, whose architecture largely follows that of GPT-3(Brown et al., 2020). However, TeleChat deviates from the original transformer model in several notable ways, drawing inspiration from influential language models such as LLaMA(Touvron et al., 2023a) and BLOOM(Scao et al., 2022). The key parameters of the architecture are summarized in Table 1.

Rotary Position Embedding. We use Rotary Positional Embedding (RoPE(Su et al., 2022)) to encode absolute positions with explicit integration of relative position dependencies. To further optimize computational efficiency and minimize memory usage, we implement Flash Attention v2 in the attention modules(Dao, 2023).

Normalizations. To ensure robust training, we incorporate an additional layer normalization step after the initial embedding layer for TeleChat, drawing inspiration from the methodology employed in BLOOM(Scao et al., 2022). However, we diverge from BLOOM by replacing conventional layer normalization with RMSNorm(Zhang and Sennrich, 2019), which has been shown to enhance the stability and performance of transformer models. Additionally, we adopt pre-normalization in each layer instead of post-normalization, a design choice that has been found to improve the training stability of transformer models.

Activations We utilize the SwiGLU activation function(Shazeer, 2020) in the feed forward network (FFN) of TeleChat, and diminish the FFN feed-forward dimension to less than four times the hidden size, adhering to established conventions in prior research(Touvron et al., 2023a)(Wei et al., 2023).

2.2 Extending Context Window

Large language models (LLMs) often encounter input contexts with a significant number of tokens in different scenarios. Hence, it is crucial for LLMs to have long-range capabilities and efficiently handle context lengths that exceed their initial pre-training limitations.

In our approach, we utilize NTK-aware interpolation techniques (bloc97, 2023) to redistribute the interpolation pressure across multiple dimensions. Additionally, we address performance degradation caused by fluctuations in context length during multiple forward-passes by employing a Dynamic NTK-aware interpolation mechanism, in which the interpolation scaling factor is designed as a continuous variable and is updated according to real-time context length.

To enhance TeleChat's long-context capabilities, we employ Multi-stage Long-context Training during supervised finetuning and attention-Scaling techniques(Peng et al., 2023) during the inference stage. Multi-stage Long-context Training periodically extends the context length during training, while attention-Scaling adjusts the attention mechanism by rescaling the dot product relative to the context-to-training length ratio. This ensures stable attention entropy as the context length increases. For a detailed description of Multi-stage Long-context Training, please refer to section 4.2.3. Experimental results demonstrate that these techniques enable TeleChat to extend its context window to over 96k tokens successfully, which achieves longest context length among open-source large language models.

3 Pretraining Stage

During pretraining stage, we train the model from scratch using a substantial amount of data. In this section, we introduce our data collection and cleaning method (Section 3.1 and 3.2), training details (Section 3.3), and tokenizer (Section 3.4).

3.1 Data Collection

TeleChat's pretraining corpus is curated from a wide range of data sources, including both general-purpose and domain-specific data. The general-purpose data comprises a vast range of sources, such as web pages, social platforms, encyclopedias, books, academic papers, code repositories, and

Models	layer num	attention heads	hidden size	FFN hidden size	vocab size
TeleChat-7B	30	32	4096	12288	160256
TeleChat-12B	38	32	5120	12288	160256

Table 1: Detailed model architecture parameters for TeleChat's 7B and 12B models.

Datasets	Percentage%
web page	22
books	11
community QA	7
social sharing	8
documents and reports	13
paper	2
code repository	12
chat data	13
others	12
Chinese	45
English	35
Code	11
Math	9

Table 2: The distribution of various categories of TeleChat's pretraining data.

more. In terms of domain-specific data, we gather corpus from twenty distinct sectors, including finance, construction, health and social work, aligning with national industry classifications[2]. Furthermore, we consistently gather and accumulate real-time data to ensure comprehensive coverage of the most up-to-date information. During the data collection stage, we acquire diverse and extensive pre-training data on a petabyte scale. The distribution of our pretraining data is displayed in Table 2.

3.2 Data Preprocessing

We devise a comprehensive data cleaning procedure to ensure the quality of our pretraining data. Our data clean procedure consists of rule-based filtering, deduplication, high-quality data selection, and data security filtering.

Rule-based Filtering. Heuristic rules are applied to clean the text efficiently and effectively. For instance, we filter out extremely short or low-information texts, discard texts with excessive or minimal punctuation, and replace HTML tags with natural language. Additionally, we exclude data in languages other than Chinese and English, as well as non-text multimodal data.

Deduplication. Performing global deduplication on a large amount of data is unacceptably slow, therefore we perform a hierarchical deduplication method. First, we eliminate duplicate data from similar sources within groups using URL deduplication, which removes approximately half of the duplicate data. Next, we utilize a 128-bit SimHash algorithm for Document-level Deduplication that removes duplicate articles. Finally, we employ Minhash and Jaccard similarity methods to perform Paragraph-level Deduplication, filtering out a large number of homogeneous advertisements and other heavily redundant texts.

High-quality Selection We utilize a 5-gram Kneser-Ney model, as implemented in the KenLM library(Heafield, 2011), to train on existing high-quality corpora and subsequently compute the perplexity of each paragraph. Instead of simply discard texts with high perplexity, we split the data into three even parts: *head*, *middle*, and *tail* based on the perplexity score. The *head* part will be sampled more frequently, while the *tail* part will be sampled less.

Security Filtering. To ensure the security of our dataset, we employ a multi-model classification approach that identifies and removes pornography, advertising, violent, and politically sensitive content. Moreover, we utilize obfuscation techniques to protect personal privacy data.

3.3 Training Details

Batch Generation. To generate data batches, we employ a process of shuffling and concatenating the corpus obtained from the same source, ensuring consistency in the data. Furthermore, to align with the specified context lengths (e.g., 4096), the data is truncated and concatenated with other data samples.

Training Objectives. The method utilized in the pretraining stage is known as autoregressive language modeling, which involves iteratively predicting the probability of the subsequent token in the sequence. We represent the joint probability of

[2]https://www.stats.gov.cn/english/NewsEvents/200306/t20030619_25521.html

tokens in a text as:

$$p(\mathbf{x}) = p(x_1, \cdots, x_T) = \sum_{t=1}^{T} p(x_t | x_{<t}) \quad (1)$$

Where $\mathbf{x}$ is a sequence of tokens, and we calculate the probability of each token x_t based on the tokens that come before it, denoted as $x_{<t}$. The model is trained to optimize this probability across the entire training corpus.

Optimizer. We utilize the widely used Adam(Kingma and Ba, 2017) optimizer for pretraining optimization. We employ a cosine learning rate schedule, where the peak learning rate is specified for each model size. The learning rate gradually decays until it reaches a minimum learning rate of 10% of the peak value. The hyperparameters are set as follows: $\beta_1 = 0.9$, $\beta_2 = 0.95$, and $\epsilon = 10^{-5}$. A weight decay of 10^{-4} is applied to all model parameters except for bias.

Ramp-up Batch. In order to enable the model to converge faster at the very beginning of pretraining, we employ a technique called ramp-up batch size, which involves starting with a small batch size and gradually increasing it linearly to the maximum batch size over a certain number of steps.

Precision. The use of the float16 data type has been recognized as a potential contributing factor to training divergences in LLMs. To address this, we pretrain all models using bfloat16(Wang and Kanwar, 2019), a data type that shares the same dynamic range as float32. Additionally, we employ mixed-precision training, wherein precision-sensitive operations like gradient accumulation, softmax, and weight updating are performed with float32 precision, while the remaining operations are carried out with bfloat16 precision.

The specific hyperparameters are presented in Table 3.

3.4 Tokenizer

We utilize Hugging Face's tokenizers to implement the BBPE algorithm, training the tokenizer on a diverse dataset comprising Chinese, English, code, and mathematical data. This process results in a tokenizer with a vocabulary size of 160,130, which is subsequently padded to 160,256. Additionally, we use special tokens to differentiate dialogue roles and turns, and also incorporate specific designs to mitigate potential injection attacks.

HyperParams	TeleChat-7B	TeleChat-12B
Peak lr	3e-4	1.5e-4
ramp-up batch size	288/72/1,500,000	240/80/2,000,000
batch size	16M	16M
warm up fraction	0.01	0.01
# training tokens	1.0T	1.2T

Table 3: The hyperparameter details utilized during the pretraining stage of TeleChat's 7B and 12B variants. The ramp-up batch size is expressed in the format of <start batch size >/<batch size increment>/<ramp-up samples>. For example, 240/80/2,000,000 indicates that the training begins with a batch size of 240 and increments by 80 for each time. The total ramp-up phase encompasses 2,000,000 samples.

4 Supervised Fine-Tuning Stage

We employ supervised fine-tuning (SFT) stage after the pretraining stage to effectively accomplish various real-world tasks. In this section, we provide detailed information about our data collection and annotation method in Section 4.1, followed by an in-depth discussion of our methodology and experimental details in Section 4.2 and Section 4.3.

4.1 Human Data Collection

We brought together a team of annotators to carry out the manual data annotation process. Our annotators are all native Chinese speakers, boasting a range of academic backgrounds including Computer Science, Law, Chinese language and literature, and other related fields. We ask the human annotators to label varied prompts and organize them into conversations, harnessing our annotation platform for efficient and high-quality annotations. We work closely with the labelers, providing them with clear instructions for each task and addressing their questions promptly.

We collect over 100,000 supervised fine-tuning samples using the aforementioned annotation strategies and train our model accordingly. The statistics of the top 30 categories in our supervised-finetuning data is displayed in Supplement Material Section A.

4.2 Training Methodology

In this section, we present a comprehensive explanation of our training approach during the supervised fine-tuning stage, an aspect that is frequently overlooked in reports of other open-sourced models.

4.2.1 Data Organization

Our dataset spans various domains, such as General Q&A, creative writing, machine translation, code generation, math & reasoning, and more. To ensure that each domain is represented appropriately, we assign respective resampling weights to each dataset based on their importance. Then, we sample single-round and multi-round conversations from each dataset using their corresponding resampling weights. The sampled conversations are then shuffled and concatenated, followed by pre-padding them to a predetermined length (e.g., 4096 or 8192) to ensure consistent input length. We use special tokens <_user>, <_bot>, and <_end> to denote the beginning of a question, the start of an answer, and the end of an answer respectively. To ensure diversity in the combination of data, the datasets are resampled and re-shuffled for each training epoch. We fine-tuned the model in a supervised manner based on this carefully curated instruction dataset.

4.2.2 Noisy Embedding Fine Tuning

In this section, we introduce our method for enhancing the answer quality of large language models (LLMs) through noisy embedding fine-tuning (NEFTUNE), inspired by the work of(Jain et al., 2023). Specifically, NEFTune modifies the input embeddings by adding a random noise vector to them. The noise is generated by sampling independent and identically distributed (i.i.d) uniform entries, each in the range $[-1, 1]$, and then scaling the entire noise vector by a factor of $\alpha/\sqrt{Ld}$, where L is the sequence length, d is the embedding dimension, and α is a tunable hyperparameter.

We observe that while NEFTune enhance the model's performance in scenarios with limited training data, its benefits diminish as the size of the training dataset increases. This is likely due to the model's reduced tendency to overfit on larger datasets. To investigate this further, we conduct experiments using TeleChat-7B fine-tuned models with and without the implementation of NEFTune. Our findings reveal that when the model is trained on the 10,000 samples, NEFTune achieves a 55% win rate against its counterpart without NEFTune, as determined by human evaluators. Some examples are shown in Supplement Material Section B. However, when the model is trained on the entire dataset consisting of 40,000 samples, NEFTune loses its advantage, resulting in only a 48% win rate against its counterpart without NEFTune.

4.2.3 Multi-stage Long-context Training.

During the supervised fine-tuning stage, we gradually increase the training length, enabling the model to activate and strengthen its ability to understand extensive dependencies while preserving its foundational skills. Specifically, we initiate the training with a sequence length of 8,192, building upon the foundation model trained on a sequence length of 4,096. At the 3/4 mark of the training procedure, we transit to a training sequence length of 16,384. Note that we employ the ntk-aware extrapolation method when working with sequence lengths of 8,192 and 16,384. This approach helps us mitigate the difficulties encountered during the transition, allowing for a smooth adjustment in the training sequence length for the model. Training details for TeleChat-7B's multi-stage long-context training is shown in Table 4, and experiment results is displayed in Table 5

4.3 Training Details

Similar to the pretraining phase, we employ next-token prediction as the training task. However, we introduce loss masks for system information and user input questions to ensure that the loss is exclusively calculated for the output answer.

The model undergoes a total of 40,000 steps, with the first 30,000 steps involving training with a sequence length of 8,192, and the remaining 10,000 steps involving training with a sequence length of 16,384, as illustrated in section 4.2.3. In the training process, we utilize the same optimizer as in the pretraining stage, as described in section 3.3.

5 Reinforcement Learning

In this section, we introduce reinforcement learning to align chat models with human preference, aiming to make model outputs consistent with safety and norms.

5.1 Reward Model

When collecting prompts of reward dataset, a consensus is that high-quality and diverse prompts are conducive to the training stage of reinforcement learning.

We collect a large number of prompts, including data from both human annotation and internal user testing phases. The final prompt dataset consists of a total of 300 categories. To further get the high quality prompts, we use clustering and centroid selection to select representative prompts.

sequence length	training steps	peak lr	batch size	tensor parallel	pipeline parallel
8,192	30,000	3e-5	8M	2	4
16,384	10,000	4e-5	8M	2	8

Table 4: Training details for TeleChat-7B's multi-stage long-context training. Note that training with a sequence length of 16,384 demands significantly more GPU memory compared to training with 8,192. As a result, it is necessary to increase the pipeline parallel size to 8, and requires 2 nodes to train.

Method	sequence length						
	2048	4096	8192	16384	32768	65536	98304
baseline	4.8122	4.6562	39.3099	98.3102	155.2708	487.3398	447.6295
NTK-aware (8k)	4.8122	4.6562	5.1904	4.7155	8.6351	77.7478	79.9256
NTK-aware+logN (8k)	4.8122	4.6562	5.1904	4.0353	4.1408	9.4080	7.9711
NTK-aware (16k)	7.6916	7.9900	7.9580	5.1217	4.7932	10.5444	10.3614
NTK-aware+logN (16k)	7.6916	7.9900	7.9580	5.1217	4.7195	8.9751	7.6822

Table 5: Our experiments with TeleChat-7B's long-context inferences illustrate the effectiveness of employing techniques such as NTK-aware extrapolation, attention scaling, and multi-stage long-context training. These approaches result in a significant reduction in perplexity as the context length increases and enable our model to achieve a low perplexity when extrapolating to 96K tokens.

All prompts are firstly convert to embeddings using bge-large-zh [3]. Then we employ elbow clustering algorithms within each categories that aims to find the ideal number of clusters. The closest prompt to each cluster centroid will be selected. In addition, we randomly sampled the prompts in the cluster (except the closest prompt) to ensure the diversity of reward dataset, while the remain is used for reinforcement learning. The responses are collected from TeleChat models of different training stages and reasoning strategies, allowing sampling rich responses for annotation.

Moreover, for improving the accuracy and reducing the difficulty of annotations, we simplify the task of ranking responses with human annotation. A straightforward classification task is introduced, where responses can be categorized under three distinct labels: good, medium, and bad. The basic criteria of this assessment includes but is not limited to safety, factuality, fluency, normality, etc. By evaluating the responses through these aspects, annotators can rank responses consistently. The responses between each pair of distinct labels under the same prompt can be combined with each other to form ranked pairs for subsequent training.

During the training stage, we use the same training objectives as LLaMA2, adding margin in the loss function to teach the reward model to assign more difference scores to response pairs with more difference. The training data distribution, adding margin size and test accuracy of Reward Model on three types of data pairs are shown in Table 6.

[3]https://huggingface.co/BAAI/bge-large-zh-v1.5

5.2 Proximal Policy Optimization

Proximal Policy Optimization (PPO) (Schulman et al., 2017) is widely used for LLM alignment and its mechanism is collaboratively working including four models: actor model, critic model, reference model and reward model. From the experience of (Yang et al., 2023) and (Bai et al., 2023), the critic model updates 50 steps firstly before actor model. The KL divergence coefficient is setting to 0.1 and apply a normalization process to the rewards, which accounts for the moving average. The learning rates for our actor and critic models are configured at $5 \times 10 - 6$ and $3 \times 10 - 6$ respectively through experiments. We get the chat model eventually after training for 400 steps.

6 Experiment

6.1 Evaluation on Standard Benchmarks

In this chapter, we evaluate the zero-shot and few-shot capabilities of TeleChat from various perspectives using standard benchmarks. We select a list of open source models as baselines, including LLaMA 2-Chat (7B, 13B), InternLM-Chat (7B), Belle-LLaMA-2 (13B), Baichuan 2 (7B, 13B), ChatGLM 2-6B, ChatGLM 3-6B, Qwen-Chat (7B, 14B).

Type of data	good & bad	medium & bad	good & medium
Distribution	18.2%	21.1%	65.7%
Margin	1	2/3	1/3
Test Accuracy	70.1%	66.0%	86.4%

Table 6: Training data distribution, adding margin and test accuracy of Reward Model on different type of data pairs.

Model	MMLU (5-shot)	C-Eval (5-shot)	CMMLU (5-shot)	AGIEval (zero-shot)	GAOKAO (zero-shot)	CSL (zero-shot)	CHID (zero-shot)	EPRSTMT (zero-shot)	GSM8K (4-shot)	MATH (4-shot)	HumanEval (zero-shot)
LLaMA2-7B-chat	46.2	31.9	31.5	28.5	16.1	58.8	44.1	57.5	26.3	3.9	12.2
LLaMA2-13B-chat	54.6	36.2	38.7	32.3	18.6	61.2	48	59.4	29.6	5.0	18.9
ChatGLM2-6B-chat	45.9	52.6	49.3	39	46.4	61.2	57.9	71.2	28.8	6.5	11
ChatGLM3-6B-chat	51.9	53.8	54	38.9	49.3	65.6	63.4	85	56.7	18.7	61
InternLM-7B-chat	52	54.1	52.6	43.7	45.8	70	79.7	88.8	34.6	5.6	12.8
Baichuan2-7B-chat	52.8	55.6	54	35.3	39.7	60	75.2	87.5	32.8	6	13.4
Baichuan2-13B-chat	57	56.7	58.4	40	51.4	63.1	78.2	87.5	55.3	8.6	17.7
Qwen-7B-chat	56.6	59.3	59.5	41.3	63.3	63.1	72.3	88.8	52.5	10.3	26.2
Qwen-14B-chat	66.4	71.7	70.0	47.3	76.5	55.6	72.3	91.2	61.0	26.8	36.6
TeleChat-7B-chat	54.4	63.1	64.3	46.8	57.7	66.8	88.0	87.5	36.7	10.3	14.6
TeleChat-12B-chat	73.3	66.6	74.2	51.7	53.1	60.6	83.2	86.3	57.2	16.0	22.0

Table 7: Results of TeleChat compared with other large language models on eleven general benchmarks.

Model	General Q&A	Safety Task	Hallucination Task
GPT3.5	66.3	73.9	**72.2**
Qwen(14B)	66.4	70.7	64.2
BaiChuan2(7B)	59.1	71.9	40.2
TeleChat-12B	**71.4**	**75.4**	66.2

Table 8: The evaluation results of TeleChat and other models on general dialogue Q&A, safety task and hallucination task. The best results are shown in **bold**.

6.1.1 Overall Performance

We evaluate TeleChat on multiple challenging benchmarks. The detailed information of test benchmarks is as follows:

- MMLU(Hendrycks et al., 2021a): An English benchmark covering 57 tasks, which are mostly college level.
- CMMLU(Li et al., 2023): A Chinese benchmark to evaluate a LLM's knowledge and reasoning ability.
- C-Eval(Huang et al., 2023): A comprehensive Chinese benchmark, containing more than 10 thousands questions and four difficulty levels.
- GAOKAO-Bench(Zhang et al., 2023): A Chinese evaluation benchmark utilizing Chinese college entrance examination questions.
- AGIEVAL(Zhong et al., 2023): A bilingual evaluation dataset encompassing standardized test questions.
- CSL(Li et al., 2022): A dataset containing multiple Chinese papers, which requires to checks the match between Chinese academic abstracts and their keywords.
- EPRSTMT(Xu et al., 2021): EPRSTMT is a sentiment analysis datasets based on comments on e-commerce websites.
- CHID(Zheng et al., 2019): A reading comprehension benchmark, which requires the model to select the most appropriate idiom to fill in the blanks within the text.
- GSM8K(Cobbe et al., 2021): GSM8K is a dataset of 8.5K high-quality, linguistically diverse, human-written elementary math problems.
- Math(Hendrycks et al., 2021b): A dataset containing 12.5K challenging competition math problems.
- HumanEval(Chen et al., 2021): A code test dataset provided by OpenAI, which consists of 164 programming questions that measure the correctness of code.

We record the detailed experiment results in Table 7. To standardize the evaluation method, we employ the assessment technique provided by OpenCompass to obtain the results on most of the benchmarks. The referenced model results all originate from the open leaderboard of OpenCompass. We observe that TeleChat exhibits superior performance compared to models of the same size. Particularly in terms of the results on the

MMLU, AGIEVAL, CMMLU and CHID datasets, TeleChat's performance surpasses that of other models of equivalent size.

6.2 Evaluation on General Dialogue Tasks

We assess TeleChat's ability to deliver helpful, truthful, and secure responses to user input, using a specific set of prompts that are distinct from our training data. Our test data is categorized into general dialogue generation tasks, safety tasks, and hallucination tasks. We compare TeleChat's output with other models, using GPT-4 as an automatic referee, and then ask human labelers to review and revise the results of GPT-4. The human evaluation process is conducted in a blind manner. Examples of our evaluation dataset is shown in Supplement Material Section C.

The results, presented in Table 8, demonstrate that TeleChat-12B achieves a 99.3% performance level compared to GPT3.5 and outperforms other opensource models of similar sizes. We also showcase TeleChat's capability to address real-world inquiries in Supplement Material Section D.

7 Alleviating Hallucination with Knowledge Graph

Hallucination problems are frequently observed in LLMs, where there is a tendency to generate text that appears coherent and meaningful but lacks real-world existence. In this paper, we address the first type of hallucinations by utilizing structured information representation provided by Knowledge Graphs (KG).

When a query comes, candidate entities are firstly retrieved based on n-gram similarity with query. Subsequently, a random walk of n steps is conducted within the graph, starting from these candidate entities. Finally, all paths obtained through the random walk are sorted based on their relevance to the user's query. The top-k paths are then returned as the final result of the knowledge graph retrieval process. By combining this retrieved knowledge with a prompt, the large language model can process the augmented query, taking into consideration the background knowledge provided by the knowledge graph. We evaluated the TeleChat's ability to answer factual questions in the China Conference on Knowledge Graph and Semantic Computing (CCKS) 2020 Knowledge Graph based Q&A task[4]. Without the introduction of the knowledge graph, the accuracy of TeleChat on this task is recorded at 0.19. However, after incorporating the relevant knowledge by adding the top 10 relevant paths from the knowledge graph, the accuracy significantly improves to 0.69. This demonstrates the effectiveness of integrating the knowledge graph in enhancing the TeleChat's ability to provide accurate answers to factual questions.

[4]https://sigkg.cn/ccks2020/?page_id=69

8 Engineering

8.1 Hardware

TeleChat is trained on a total of 80 nodes, each having 8 Nvidia A100 Sxm 40GB GPUs. Each node is equipped with 2x Intel 6348 (28 Cores, 2.60 GHz) CPUs, 8x NVLink A100 GPUs, 512GB of RAM, and a 2GB cache RAID card. All nodes are interconnected using InfiniBand (IB) for networking. To enhance data transmission speed and mitigate bandwidth constraints, we employ NVIDIA's GPUDirect RDMA (GRDMA) and utilize the Scalable Hierarchical Aggregation and Reduction Protocol (SHARP).

8.2 Parallel Computing

TeleChat is trained using the Megatron-DeepSpeed framework (Smith et al., 2022) for large-scale distributed training. TeleChat successfully leverages 3D parallelism, which integrates tensor parallelism, pipeline parallelism, and data parallelism to enable efficient distributed training. We scale our system to utilize hundreds of GPUs with extensive GPU utilization, achieving a peak performance of 180 TFLOPs using A100 GPUs, which accounts for 57.6% of the theoretical peak performance of 312 TFLOPs.

9 Conclusions

In this paper, we introduced TeleChat, a collection of large language models (LLMs) with 7 billion and 12 billion parameters. We detailed the pretraining process, supervised fine-tuning, reinforcement learning, and the integration of a knowledge graph to enhance the model's performance. We evaluated TeleChat on various benchmarks and compared its performance with other open-source models, TeleChat demonstrates superior performance in general dialogue tasks, knowledge-based question answering, and various other benchmarks, showcasing its potential for diverse real-world applications. We release model checkpoints, code, and a portion of our filtered high-quality pretraining data totaling 160 billion tokens to the public community.

Limitations

While TeleChat demonstrates impressive performance across various language tasks, there are several limitations to consider. Firstly, the extensive computational resources required for training and inference may also pose challenges for wider adoption and accessibility. Additionally, the integration of knowledge graphs, while effective in reducing hallucination, may introduce biases or inaccuracies if the underlying knowledge graph data is incomplete or outdated. Furthermore, the evaluation of TeleChat's performance, while comprehensive, may not fully capture its real-world applicability and potential limitations in specific domains or scenarios. Addressing these limitations will be crucial for the responsible and ethical deployment of TeleChat in real-world applications.

Ethics Statement

The development and evaluation of TeleChat prioritize ethical considerations. We prioritize privacy, consent, and fairness in data usage, and have made model checkpoints, code, and a portion of the training data publicly available for transparency and reproducibility. We are committed to addressing ethical concerns such as bias, privacy, and misinformation, and will continue to monitor and improve TeleChat's behavior in alignment with societal values.

References

Rohan Anil, Andrew M. Dai, Orhan Firat, Melvin Johnson, Dmitry Lepikhin, Alexandre Passos, Siamak Shakeri, Emanuel Taropa, Paige Bailey, Zhifeng Chen, Eric Chu, Jonathan H. Clark, Laurent El Shafey, Yanping Huang, Kathy Meier-Hellstern, Gaurav Mishra, Erica Moreira, Mark Omernick, Kevin Robinson, Sebastian Ruder, Yi Tay, Kefan Xiao, Yuanzhong Xu, Yujing Zhang, Gustavo Hernandez Abrego, Junwhan Ahn, Jacob Austin, Paul Barham, Jan Botha, James Bradbury, Siddhartha Brahma, Kevin Brooks, Michele Catasta, Yong Cheng, Colin Cherry, Christopher A. Choquette-Choo, Aakanksha Chowdhery, Clément Crepy, Shachi Dave, Mostafa Dehghani, Sunipa Dev, Jacob Devlin, Mark Díaz, Nan Du, Ethan Dyer, Vlad Feinberg, Fangxiaoyu Feng, Vlad Fienber, Markus Freitag, Xavier Garcia, Sebastian Gehrmann, Lucas Gonzalez, Guy Gur-Ari, Steven Hand, Hadi Hashemi, Le Hou, Joshua Howland, Andrea Hu, Jeffrey Hui, Jeremy Hurwitz, Michael Isard, Abe Ittycheriah, Matthew Jagielski, Wenhao Jia, Kathleen Kenealy, Maxim Krikun, Sneha Kudugunta, Chang Lan, Katherine Lee, Benjamin Lee, Eric Li, Music Li, Wei Li, YaGuang Li, Jian Li, Hyeontaek Lim, Hanzhao Lin, Zhongtao Liu, Frederick Liu, Marcello Maggioni, Aroma Mahendru, Joshua Maynez, Vedant Misra, Maysam Moussalem, Zachary Nado, John Nham, Eric Ni, Andrew Nystrom, Alicia Parrish, Marie Pellat, Martin Polacek, Alex Polozov, Reiner Pope, Siyuan Qiao, Emily Reif, Bryan Richter, Parker Riley, Alex Castro Ros, Aurko Roy, Brennan Saeta, Rajkumar Samuel, Renee Shelby, Ambrose Slone, Daniel Smilkov, David R. So, Daniel Sohn, Simon Tokumine, Dasha Valter, Vijay Vasudevan, Kiran Vodrahalli, Xuezhi Wang, Pidong Wang, Zirui Wang, Tao Wang, John Wieting, Yuhuai Wu, Kelvin Xu, Yunhan Xu, Linting Xue, Pengcheng Yin, Jiahui Yu, Qiao Zhang, Steven Zheng, Ce Zheng, Weikang Zhou, Denny Zhou, Slav Petrov, and Yonghui Wu. 2023. Palm 2 technical report. *arXiv preprint arXiv:2305.10403*.

Jinze Bai, Shuai Bai, Yunfei Chu, Zeyu Cui, Kai Dang, Xiaodong Deng, Yang Fan, Wenbin Ge, Yu Han, Fei Huang, Binyuan Hui, Luo Ji, Mei Li, Junyang Lin, Runji Lin, Dayiheng Liu, Gao Liu, Chengqiang Lu, Keming Lu, Jianxin Ma, Rui Men, Xingzhang Ren, Xuancheng Ren, Chuanqi Tan, Sinan Tan, Jianhong Tu, Peng Wang, Shijie Wang, Wei Wang, Shengguang Wu, Benfeng Xu, Jin Xu, An Yang, Hao Yang, Jian Yang, Shusheng Yang, Yang Yao, Bowen Yu, Hongyi Yuan, Zheng Yuan, Jianwei Zhang, Xingxuan Zhang, Yichang Zhang, Zhenru Zhang, Chang Zhou, Jingren Zhou, Xiaohuan Zhou, and Tianhang Zhu. 2023. Qwen technical report. *arXiv preprint arXiv:2309.16609*.

bloc97. 2023. Ntk-aware scaled rope allows llama models to have extended (8k+) context size without any fine-tuning and minimal perplexity degradation.

Tom Brown, Benjamin Mann, Nick Ryder, Melanie Subbiah, Jared Kaplan, Prafulla Dhariwal, Arvind Neelakantan, Pranav Shyam, Girish Sastry, Amanda Askell, Sandhini Agarwal, Ariel Herbert-Voss, Gretchen Krueger, Tom Henighan, Rewon Child, Aditya Ramesh, Daniel Ziegler, Jeffrey Wu, Clemens Winter, and Dario Amodei. 2020. Language models are few-shot learners. *arXiv preprint arXiv:2005.14165*.

Mark Chen, Jerry Tworek, Heewoo Jun, Qiming Yuan, Henrique Ponde de Oliveira Pinto, Jared Kaplan, Harri Edwards, Yuri Burda, Nicholas Joseph, Greg Brockman, Alex Ray, Raul Puri, Gretchen Krueger, Michael Petrov, Heidy Khlaaf, Girish Sastry, Pamela Mishkin, Brooke Chan, Scott Gray, Nick Ryder, Mikhail Pavlov, Alethea Power, Lukasz Kaiser, Mohammad Bavarian, Clemens Winter, Philippe Tillet, Felipe Petroski Such, Dave Cummings, Matthias Plappert, Fotios Chantzis, Elizabeth Barnes, Ariel Herbert-Voss, William Hebgen Guss, Alex Nichol, Alex Paino, Nikolas Tezak, Jie Tang, Igor Babuschkin, Suchir Balaji, Shantanu Jain, William Saunders, Christopher Hesse, Andrew N.

Carr, Jan Leike, Josh Achiam, Vedant Misra, Evan Morikawa, Alec Radford, Matthew Knight, Miles Brundage, Mira Murati, Katie Mayer, Peter Welinder, Bob McGrew, Dario Amodei, Sam McCandlish, Ilya Sutskever, and Wojciech Zaremba. 2021. Evaluating large language models trained on code.

Karl Cobbe, Vineet Kosaraju, Mohammad Bavarian, Mark Chen, Heewoo Jun, Lukasz Kaiser, Matthias Plappert, Jerry Tworek, Jacob Hilton, Reiichiro Nakano, Christopher Hesse, and John Schulman. 2021. Training verifiers to solve math word problems. *arXiv preprint arXiv:2110.14168*.

Tri Dao. 2023. Flashattention-2: Faster attention with better parallelism and work partitioning. *arXiv preprint arXiv:2307.08691*.

Kenneth Heafield. 2011. KenLM: Faster and smaller language model queries. In *Proceedings of the Sixth Workshop on Statistical Machine Translation*, pages 187–197, Edinburgh, Scotland. Association for Computational Linguistics.

Dan Hendrycks, Collin Burns, Steven Basart, Andy Zou, Mantas Mazeika, Dawn Song, and Jacob Steinhardt. 2021a. Measuring massive multitask language understanding. *Proceedings of the International Conference on Learning Representations (ICLR)*.

Dan Hendrycks, Collin Burns, Saurav Kadavath, Akul Arora, Steven Basart, Eric Tang, Dawn Song, and Jacob Steinhardt. 2021b. Measuring mathematical problem solving with the math dataset. *NeurIPS*.

Yuzhen Huang, Yuzhuo Bai, Zhihao Zhu, Junlei Zhang, Jinghan Zhang, Tangjun Su, Junteng Liu, Chuancheng Lv, Yikai Zhang, Jiayi Lei, Yao Fu, Maosong Sun, and Junxian He. 2023. C-eval: A multi-level multi-discipline chinese evaluation suite for foundation models. *arXiv preprint arXiv:2305.08322*.

InternLM_Team. 2023. Internlm: A multilingual language model with progressively enhanced capabilities.

Neel Jain, Ping yeh Chiang, Yuxin Wen, John Kirchenbauer, Hong-Min Chu, Gowthami Somepalli, Brian R. Bartoldson, Bhavya Kailkhura, Avi Schwarzschild, Aniruddha Saha, Micah Goldblum, Jonas Geiping, and Tom Goldstein. 2023. Neftune: Noisy embeddings improve instruction finetuning. *arXiv preprint arXiv:2310.05914*.

Diederik P. Kingma and Jimmy Ba. 2017. Adam: A method for stochastic optimization. *arXiv preprint arXiv:1412.6980*.

Haonan Li, Yixuan Zhang, Fajri Koto, Yifei Yang, Hai Zhao, Yeyun Gong, Nan Duan, and Timothy Baldwin. 2023. Cmmlu: Measuring massive multitask language understanding in chinese.

Yudong Li, Yuqing Zhang, Zhe Zhao, Linlin Shen, Weijie Liu, Weiquan Mao, and Hui Zhang. 2022. Csl: A large-scale chinese scientific literature dataset. *arXiv preprint arXiv:2209.05034*.

OpenAI. 2022. Introducing chatgpt.

OpenAI. 2023. Gpt-4 technical report. *arXiv preprint arXiv:2303.08774*.

Bowen Peng, Jeffrey Quesnelle, Honglu Fan, and Enrico Shippole. 2023. Yarn: Efficient context window extension of large language models. *arXiv preprint arXiv:2309.00071*.

Teven Scao, Angela Fan, Christopher Akiki, Ellie Pavlick, Suzana Ilić, Daniel Hesslow, Roman Castagné, Alexandra Luccioni, François Yvon, Matthias Gallé, Jonathan Tow, Alexander Rush, Stella Biderman, Albert Webson, Pawan Ammanamanchi, Thomas Wang, Benoît Sagot, Niklas Muennighoff, Albert Moral, and Thomas Wolf. 2022. Bloom: A 176b-parameter open-access multilingual language model. *arXiv preprint arXiv:2211.05100*.

John Schulman, Filip Wolski, Prafulla Dhariwal, Alec Radford, and Oleg Klimov. 2017. Proximal policy optimization algorithms. *arXiv preprint arXiv:1707.06347*.

Noam Shazeer. 2020. Glu variants improve transformer. *arXiv preprint arXiv:2002.05202*.

Shaden Smith, Md. Mostofa Ali Patwary, Brandon Norick, Patrick Legresley, Samyam Rajbhandari, Jared Casper, Zhun Liu, Shrimai Prabhumoye, George Zerveas, Vijay Korthikanti, Elton Zhang, Rewon Child, Reza Aminabadi, Julie Bernauer, Xia Song, Mohammad Shoeybi, Yuxiong He, Michael Houston, Saurabh Tiwary, and Bryan Catanzaro. 2022. Using deepspeed and megatron to train megatron-turing nlg 530b, a large-scale generative language model. *arXiv preprint arXiv:2201.11990*.

Jianlin Su, Yu Lu, Shengfeng Pan, Ahmed Murtadha, Bo Wen, and Yunfeng Liu. 2022. Roformer: Enhanced transformer with rotary position embedding. *arXiv preprint arXiv:2104.09864*.

Hugo Touvron, Thibaut Lavril, Gautier Izacard, Xavier Martinet, Marie-Anne Lachaux, Timothée Lacroix, Baptiste Rozière, Naman Goyal, Eric Hambro, Faisal Azhar, Aurelien Rodriguez, Armand Joulin, Edouard Grave, and Guillaume Lample. 2023a. Llama: Open and efficient foundation language models. *arXiv preprint arXiv:2302.13971*.

Hugo Touvron, Louis Martin, Kevin Stone, Peter Albert, Amjad Almahairi, Yasmine Babaei, Nikolay Bashlykov, Soumya Batra, Prajjwal Bhargava, Shruti Bhosale, Dan Bikel, Lukas Blecher, Cristian Ferrer, Moya Chen, Guillem Cucurull, David Esiobu, Jude Fernandes, Jeremy Fu, Wenyin Fu, and Thomas Scialom. 2023b. Llama 2: Open foundation and fine-tuned chat models. *arXiv preprint arXiv:2307.09288*.

Shibo Wang and Pankaj Kanwar. 2019. Bfloat16: The secret to high performance on cloud tpus, 2019.

Tianwen Wei, Liang Zhao, Lichang Zhang, Bo Zhu, Lijie Wang, Haihua Yang, Biye Li, Cheng Cheng, Weiwei Lü, Rui Hu, Chenxia Li, Liu Yang, Xilin Luo, Xuejie Wu, Lunan Liu, Wenjun Cheng, Peng Cheng, Jianhao Zhang, Xiaoyu Zhang, Lei Lin, Xiaokun Wang, Yutuan Ma, Chuanhai Dong, Yanqi Sun, Yifu Chen, Yongyi Peng, Xiaojuan Liang, Shuicheng Yan, Han Fang, and Yahui Zhou. 2023. Skywork: A more open bilingual foundation model. *arXiv preprint arXiv:2310.19341*.

Liang Xu, Xiaojing Lu, Chenyang Yuan, Xuanwei Zhang, Huilin Xu, Hu Yuan, Guoao Wei, Xiang Pan, Xin Tian, Libo Qin, et al. 2021. Fewclue: A chinese few-shot learning evaluation benchmark. *arXiv preprint arXiv:2107.07498*.

Aiyuan Yang, Bin Xiao, Bingning Wang, Borong Zhang, Ce Bian, Chao Yin, Chenxu Lv, Da Pan, Dian Wang, Dong Yan, Fan Yang, Fei Deng, Feng Wang, Feng Liu, Guangwei Ai, Guosheng Dong, Haizhou Zhao, Hang Xu, Haoze Sun, Hongda Zhang, Hui Liu, Jiaming Ji, Jian Xie, JunTao Dai, Kun Fang, Lei Su, Liang Song, Lifeng Liu, Liyun Ru, Luyao Ma, Mang Wang, Mickel Liu, MingAn Lin, Nuolan Nie, Peidong Guo, Ruiyang Sun, Tao Zhang, Tianpeng Li, Tianyu Li, Wei Cheng, Weipeng Chen, Xiangrong Zeng, Xiaochuan Wang, Xiaoxi Chen, Xin Men, Xin Yu, Xuehai Pan, Yanjun Shen, Yiding Wang, Yiyu Li, Youxin Jiang, Yuchen Gao, Yupeng Zhang, Zenan Zhou, and Zhiying Wu. 2023. Baichuan 2: Open large-scale language models. *arXiv preprint arXiv:2309.10305*.

Biao Zhang and Rico Sennrich. 2019. Root mean square layer normalization. *arXiv preprint arXiv:1910.07467*.

Susan Zhang, Stephen Roller, Naman Goyal, Mikel Artetxe, Moya Chen, Shuohui Chen, Christopher Dewan, Mona Diab, Xian Li, Xi Victoria Lin, Todor Mihaylov, Myle Ott, Sam Shleifer, Kurt Shuster, Daniel Simig, Punit Singh Koura, Anjali Sridhar, Tianlu Wang, and Luke Zettlemoyer. 2022. Opt: Open pretrained transformer language models. *arXiv preprint arXiv:2205.01068*.

Xiaotian Zhang, Chunyang Li, Yi Zong, Zhengyu Ying, Liang He, and Xipeng Qiu. 2023. Evaluating the performance of large language models on gaokao benchmark.

Chujie Zheng, Minlie Huang, and Aixin Sun. 2019. ChID: A large-scale Chinese IDiom dataset for cloze test. In *Proceedings of the 57th Annual Meeting of the Association for Computational Linguistics*, pages 778–787, Florence, Italy. Association for Computational Linguistics.

Wanjun Zhong, Ruixiang Cui, Yiduo Guo, Yaobo Liang, Shuai Lu, Yanlin Wang, Amin Saied, Weizhu Chen, and Nan Duan. 2023. Agieval: A human-centric benchmark for evaluating foundation models.

Few-shot Question Generation for Reading Comprehension

Yin Poon,
John S. Y. Lee
Dept. of Linguistics and Translation
City University of Hong Kong
{yinpoon2,jsylee}@cityu.edu.hk

Yu Yan Lam, Wing Lam Suen,
Elsie Li Chen Ong, Samuel Kai Wah Chu
School of Nursing and Health Studies
Hong Kong Metropolitan University
{yuylam,wlsuen,
eong,skwchu}@hkmu.edu.hk

Abstract

According to the internationally recognized PIRLS (Progress in International Reading Literacy Study) assessment standards, reading comprehension questions should require not only information retrieval, but also higher-order processes such as inferencing, interpreting and evaluation. However, these kinds of questions are often not available in large quantities for training question generation models. This paper investigates whether pre-trained Large Language Models (LLMs) can produce higher-order questions. Human assessment on a Chinese dataset shows that few-shot LLM prompting generates more usable and higher-order questions than two competitive neural baselines.

1 Introduction

Given the importance of asking questions for effective learning (Dillon, 2006; Etemadzadeh et al., 2013; Kurdi et al., 2020), there has been extensive effort in developing automatic Question Generation (QG) models to produce high-quality questions for reading materials in educational systems (Heilman and Smith, 2010; Lindberg et al., 2013). Through automatic creation of pedagogical and assessment material, QG benefits teachers by reducing their workload. It also levels the playing field for students, providing them with instant and free access to questions for review and practice.

According to PIRLS (Progress in International Reading Literacy Study), reading comprehension questions should require not only information retrieval, but also higher-order processes such as inferencing, interpreting and evaluation (Mullis and Martin, 2019). However, existing QG benchmarks such as SQuAD (Rajpurkar et al., 2016) mostly focus on factoid short-answer questions. There is therefore a dearth of publicly available training data for the more challenging types of questions (Mulla and Gharpure, 2023) — those requiring inference, synthesis and critique — especially for languages other than English.

Process	Description
Retrieval	Focus on and Retrieve Explicitly Stated Information
Inferencing	Make Straightforward Inferences
Integrating	Interpret and Integrate Ideas and Information
Evaluation	Evaluate and Critique Content and Textual Elements

Table 1: Comprehension processes in reading according to PIRLS (Mullis and Martin, 2019). The italicized processes are those required by *higher-order* questions.

This paper investigates the generation of these higher-order questions with few or no training samples. Our contribution is two-fold. First, we report the first QG evaluation based on PIRLS, an internationally recognized standard for reading comprehension assessment, and demonstrate a high level of human agreement on PIRLS question type classification (Table 1). Second, in experiments on a Chinese dataset, we show that existing QG neural models generate predominantly information-retrieval questions, while few-shot prompting of a Large Language Model (LLM) can generate higher proportions of higher-order questions. The LLM-based approach can therefore produce a balanced set of questions that is desirable in the education setting with minimal supervision.

2 Previous work

Early QG approaches mostly relied on heuristics, linguistic templates and rules (Labutov et al., 2015; Mostow et al., 2016). With the availability of large-scale datasets, QG began to be formulated as a sequence-to-sequence generation task. An encoder-decoder architecture with a global attention mechanism was found to be ef-

Proceedings of the 10th SIGHAN Workshop on Chinese Language Processing (SIGHAN-10), pages 21–27
August 16, 2024

Excerpt of input passage (in Chinese):
太阳和地球虽然相距1.5亿公里，但它却会提供光和热。除此以外，它还会给地球带来意想不到的“礼物”呢！其实太阳的表面常常发生爆炸，在最活跃的时候，更会把表面的物质抛射出去，形成太阳风暴。当太阳风暴经过地球时，不但会损毁人造卫星，干扰无线电通讯，...

Even though the Sun is 150 million kilometers away from Earth, it provides light and heat. Besides, it also gives a surprising ‘gift’ to Earth! There are frequent explosions on the surface of the Sun ... forming solar storms. When a solar storm passes by the Earth, it not only destroys satellites and interfere with wireless communication, ...

Type	Example Question
Retrieval: word-match	太阳和地球虽然相距一亿五千万公里，但它却会提供什么? Even though the Sun is 150 million kilometers away from Earth, What does it provide?
Retrieval: paraphrase	文章提到太阳和地球之间的距离是多少? What is the distance between the sun and the Earth, as mentioned in the passage?
Inferencing	根据文章，太阳爆炸造成的“太阳风暴”会对地球造成哪些影响? How is the Earth affected by the solar storms caused by explosions on the Sun?
Integrating	文章中提到太阳常常发生爆炸会带来什么「礼物」？ According to the passage, what ‘gift’ is brought by the frequent explosions at the Sun?
Evaluation	作者认为太阳的影响对地球有什么优势和缺陷 What does the author think are the Sun’s positive and negative impact on the Earth?

Table 2: Example input passage and output questions of each PIRLS question type (Section 3.2)

fective (Du et al., 2017; Kim et al., 2019), but can be further improved with transformer-based approaches (Scialom et al., 2019), and fully fine-tuned language models (LM) (Xiao et al., 2021). Answer-agnostic QG can be performed via joint Question and Answer Generation (QAG) (Lewis et al., 2021). A QAG model based on fine-tuning encoder-decoder LMs produces high-quality questions (Ushio et al., 2022), but has not been evaluated in terms of question type.

There have been a few QG studies on LLMs in the education setting. On a textbook dataset, few-shot prompting with GPT-3 was able to generate human-like questions ready for classroom use (Wang et al., 2022). A similar approach with InstructGPT achieved an adherence rate between 67% and 69% for generating 9 question types (Elkins et al., 2023). A fine-tuned version of ChatGPT was able to generate questions that are competitive with human ones in terms of readability, correctness, coherence and engagement (Xiao et al., 2023). It remains unknown how these approaches compare to off-the-shelf neural QG models in terms of generating higher-order questions.

3 Evaluation metric

To accurately evaluate the utility and nature of the generated questions, manual assessment is necessary since automatic methods cannot yet reliably determine usability and PIRLS question types.

3.1 Usability

The human assessor assesses the quality of the question on the following three-point scale:

Usable without revision The question can be used as is: it is grammatical, fluent, and relevant for the input passage.

Usable with minor revision The question is relevant for the input passage, but requires improvement in its linguistic quality, e.g., correction of grammatical errors, better vocabulary choice or phrasing.

Unusable The question is irrelevant for the passage, or cannot be understood.

A question classified as one of the first two categories is said to be “***usable***”. Only usable questions are further analyzed on their question type.

3.2 PIRLS question type

According to the International Association for the Evaluation of Educational Achievement, a reading comprehension question should address one of four comprehension processes, as defined in the PIRLS standards (Table 1):

Retrieval The answer is explicitly given in a text span in the passage.

Inferencing Answering the question requires inferences about ideas or information that is not explicitly stated.

Integrating Answering the question "requires comprehension of the entire text, or at least significant portions of it." (Mullis and Martin, 2019)

Evaluation The answer "involves a judgement about some aspect of the text", and is not necessarily found in the passage.

Example questions can be found in Table 2.[1] A question classified as Inferencing, Integrating or Evaluation is considered as "***higher order***". For pedagogical purposes, a well-balanced set of questions should include not only Retrieval questions but also higher-order ones (Mullis and Martin, 2019).

4 Approach

We adopted the answer-agnostic setting for QG, since the target answer is not always found within the input text. The input is a Chinese text without any specified answer span.

4.1 Baseline: pipeline model

We used the DuReader pipeline QG model (Li et al., 2021), a publicly available QG system for Chinese. It performs two subtasks in sequence: answer generation[2] using an extractor trained in the Universal IE framework (Lu et al., 2022)[3]; followed by question generation[4] with a base model fine-tuned with UNIMO (Li et al., 2021).[5]

4.2 Baseline: Seq2seq model

A seq2seq model, trained directly to generate a question-answer pair from a passage, serves as a second baseline. It has been found to be robust in comparison with the pipeline and multitask approach, and computationally less intensive (Ushio et al., 2023).[6] We used the Chinese version of their publicly available end-to-end QAG model.[7]

Model	Unusable	Usable w/ minor rev.	Usable wo/ rev.
Zero-shot	31.5%	6.0%	62.5%
Few-shot	22.0%	7.0%	**71.0%**
Pipeline	46.5%	**18.5%**	35.0%
Seq2seq	**54.0%**	11.0%	35.0%

Table 3: Evaluation results on usability

4.3 LLM: Zero-shot

We used the Chinese version of Stanford Alpaca (Cui et al., 2023)[8], a LLaMA Model that can comprehend and execute instructions (Touvron et al., 2023).[9] We are not aware of any published research on prompt engineering for Chinese QG. Six candidate prompts, with varied keywords on inference, reasoning, and word usage were informally evaluated on a small set of passages randomly taken from Chinese-language public examinations.[10] As shown in Table 7 (Appendix B), the following prompt produced the largest number of usable and non-word-matching questions:

> 基于给定的文章，生成一个需要推断的简答题。你的输出应该包含一个简答问题和这个问题的对应的答案。文章:<input>

[Translation: "Based on the given passage, generate a short-answer question that requires deduction. Your output should include a question and its answer. Passage: <input>]

4.4 LLM: Few-shot

In the few-shot approach, the prompt above is accompanied with N sample pairs of input passage and question, according to the template in Table 8 (Appendix B). We set $N = 5$, with all five sample passage-question pairs taken from the public examination papers mentioned above.

5 Dataset

Our evaluation data was drawn from the dev set of `DuReader_robust` (Tang et al., 2021), a widely used Chinese Q&A dataset[11]. Due to its filtering step, the pipeline model in Section 4.1 may not

[1] The Chinese passage is taken from a Chinese-language public examinations at https://www.hkeaa.edu.hk/en/sa_tsa/

[2] https://github.com/PaddlePaddle/PaddleNLP/tree/develop/applications/question_answering/unsupervised_qa

[3] We used the extractor `uie-base-answer-extractor` and the filter `uie-base-qa-filter`

[4] https://github.com/PaddlePaddle/Research/tree/master/NLP/UNIMO

[5] `unimo-text-1.0-question-generation`

[6] https://github.com/asahi417/lm-question-generation/

[7] `mt5-small-zhquad-qag`

[8] `Chinese-Alpaca-2-7B`

[9] https://github.com/tatsu-lab/stanford_alpaca

[10] https://www.hkeaa.edu.hk/en/sa_tsa/

[11] https://github.com/baidu/DuReader

Model	Unusable	Retrieval	Higher-order			Total
			Inferencing	Integrating	Evaluation	higher-order
Zero-shot	31.5%	39.0%	15.5%	9.0%	**5.0%**	29.5%
Few-shot	22.0%	**46.5%**	**16.5%**	**13.5%**	1.5%	**31.5%**
Pipeline	46.5%	45.5%	6.0%	2.0%	0%	8.0%
Seq2seq	**54.0%**	39.5%	4.5%	2.0%	0%	6.5%

Table 4: Evaluation results on PIRLS question types (first 5 columns add to 100%)

generate any question for some passages. Our test set consists of the first 200 passages for which the pipeline model successfully produced an output.

Two human assessors, both native speakers of Chinese with a Bachelor's degree, independently evaluated the questions generated for each of these 200 passages in terms of their usability (Section 3.1) and question type (Section 3.2). A third assessor, a native speaker of Chinese with a Master's degree, adjudicated in case of disagreement.

6 Agreement

The two assessors agreed 85.0% of the time in the 3-way classification on usability (Section 3.1), leading to a Kappa of 0.739, a "substantial" level of agreement (Landis and Koch, 1977).

In terms of question types, the two human assessors agreed in 93.5% of the cases, yielding a Kappa of 0.861, at the "Almost perfect" level of agreement (Landis and Koch, 1977) The most common disagreement (19 cases) is between Retrieval and Inferencing, typically in judging whether a paraphrase deviates sufficiently from the original expression to require inference. The two assessors also disagreed in 9 cases on whether the answer must be derived from different parts of the passage (Integrating) or from just a single sentence (Inferencing).

7 Results

7.1 Usability

The LLM-based approaches attained higher usability rates (Table 3). Among questions generated by zero-shot prompting, 62.5% can be used without revision. Few-shot prompting, with only five example passage-question pairs, produced a significant boost, with 71% ready for use without revision. The pipeline and Seq2seq neural models yielded substantially more unusable questions and fewer questions that are immediately ready (35.0%). The amount of unlabeled language data used in training — an order of magnitude larger in LLMs than the

	Retrieval	Infer.	Integr.	Eval.
Retrieval	334	13	3	0
Infer.	6	66	1	0
Integr.	1	8	47	0
Eval.	0	0	0	13

Table 5: Confusion matrix of the two human annotators on PIRLS question types

neural models — likely contributed to the grammaticality and fluency of the generated questions.

7.2 PIRLS question types

Both neural QG models produced very limited number of higher-order questions, likely because there were few such questions in the training samples. Despite the lack of such samples, zero-shot LLM produces substantially more higher-order questions (29.5%), and few-shot prompting further increases the proportion (31.5%) (Table 4). It appears that Alpaca was able to learn the characteristics of higher-order questions even with only five samples.

8 Conclusion

Higher-order questions are important for assessment in reading comprehension. However, there is a lack of publicly available datasets of these challenging questions in languages other than English. This paper has presented the first study on automatic question generation (QG) for reading comprehension based on PIRLS, assuming no or minimal supervision. Experiments on Chinese passages show that zero-shot LLM produces more usable and more higher-order questions than two competitive off-the-shelf neural QG models, and few-shot prompting further improves the performance.

In future work, we plan to investigate tailored prompts for producing the different PIRLS question types, and to construct a Chinese dataset of higher-order questions for fine-tuning an LLM.

Limitations

The evaluation has focused on the quality of the questions, but cannot show their pedagogical impact on the students. At the time of system deployment, users should be clearly informed that the automatically generated questions should be viewed only as a first draft, to minimize the risk that the teacher may fail to edit an unusable question and pass it to students.

Acknowledgements

We gratefully acknowledge support from the e-Learning Ancillary Facilities Programme of the Quality Education Fund (Project "Knowledge Overlord - A Self-sustaining AI Game-based Online Platform to Enhance Student's Literacy Ability and 21st Century Skills"); and from a Teaching Development Grant at City University of Hong Kong (project 6000834).

References

Yiming Cui, Ziqing Yang, and Xin Yao. 2023. Efficient and Effective Text Encoding for Chinese LLaMA and Alpaca. In *arXiv:2304.08177*.

James T. Dillon. 2006. Effect of questions in education and other enterprises. In *Rethinking schooling*, page 145–174. Routledge.

Xinya Du, Junru Shao, and Claire Cardie. 2017. Learning to Ask: Neural Question Generation for Reading Comprehension. In *Proceedings of the 55th Annual Meeting of the Association for Computational Linguistics (ACL)*.

Sabina Elkins, Ekaterina Kochmar, Iulian Serban, and Jackie C. K. Cheung. 2023. How Useful Are Educational Questions Generated by Large Language Models? *AIED 2023, CCIS*, 1831:536–542.

Atika Etemadzadeh, Samira Seifi, and Hamid Roohbakhsh Far. 2013. The role of questioning technique in developing thinking skills: The ongoing effect on writing skill. *Procedia-Social and Behavioral Sciences*, 70:1024–1031.

Michael Heilman and Noah A. Smith. 2010. Good Question! Statistical Ranking for Question Generation. In *Proc. Human Language Technologies: The 2010 Annual Conference of the North American Chapter of the ACL (HLT-NAACL)*, page 609–617.

Yanghoon Kim, Hwanhee Lee, Joongbo Shin, and Kyomin Jung. 2019. Improving Neural Question Generation Using Answer Separation. In *Proc. 33rd AAAI Conference on Artificial Intelligence (AAAI-19)*.

Ghader Kurdi, Jared Leo, Bijan Parsia, Uli Sattler, and Salam Al-Emari. 2020. A systematic review of automatic question generation for educational purposes. *International Journal of Artificial Intelligence in Education*, 30:121–204.

I. Labutov, S. Basu, and L. Vanderwende. 2015. Deep questions without deep understanding. In *Proc. ACL*.

J. Richard Landis and Gary G. Koch. 1977. The Measurement of Observer Agreement for Categorical Data. *Biometrics*, 33:159–174.

Patrick Lewis, Yuxiang Wu, Linqing Liu, Pasquale Minervini, Heinrich Küttler, Aleksandra Piktus, Pontus Stenetorp, and Sebastian Riedel. 2021. PAQ: 65 million probably-asked questions and what you can do with them. *Transactions of the Association for Computational Linguistics*, 9:1098–1115.

Wei Li, Can Gao, Guocheng Niu, Xinyan Xiao, Hao Liu, Jiachen Liu, Hua Wu, and Haifeng Wang. 2021. UNIMO: Towards Unified-Modal Understanding and Generation via Cross-Modal Contrastive Learning. In *Proceedings of the 59th Annual Meeting of the Association for Computational Linguistics and the 11th International Joint Conference on Natural Language Processing (Volume 1: Long Papers)*, page 2592–2607.

David Lindberg, Fred Popowich, John Nesbit, and Phil Winne. 2013. Generating natural language questions to support learning on-line. In *Proceedings of the 14th European Workshop on Natural Language Generation*, page 105–114.

Yaojie Lu, Qing Liu, Dai Dai, Xinyan Xiao, Hongyu Lin, Xianpei Han, Le Sun, and Hua Wu. 2022. Unified Structure Generation for Universal Information Extraction. In *Proceedings of the 60th Annual Meeting of the Association for Computational Linguistics (ACL)*, page 5755–5772.

Jack Mostow, Yi ting Huang, Hyeju Jang, Anders Weinstein, Joe Valeri, and Donna Gates. 2016. Developing, evaluating, and refining an automatic generator of diagnostic multiple choice cloze questions to assess children's comprehension while reading. *Natural Language Engineering*, 23(2):245–294.

N. Mulla and P. Gharpure. 2023. Automatic question generation: a review of methodologies, datasets, evaluation metrics, and applications. *Progress in Artificial Intelligence*, 12:1–32.

Ina V. S. Mullis and Michael O. Martin. 2019. *PIRLS 2021 Assessment Frameworks*. International Association for the Evaluation of Educational Achievement.

Pranav Rajpurkar, Jian Zhang, Konstantin Lopyrev, and Percy Liang. 2016. SQuAD: 100,000+ Questions for Machine Comprehension of Text. In *Proc. Conference on Empirical Methods in Natural Language Processing (EMNLP)*, page 2383–2392.

Thomas Scialom, Benjamin Piwowarski, and Jacopo Staiano. 2019. Self-Attention Architectures for Answer-Agnostic Neural Question Generation. In *Proceedings of the 57th Annual Meeting of the Association for Computational Linguistics*, page 6027–6032.

Hongxuan Tang, Hongyu Li, Jing Liu, Yu Hong, Hua Wu, and Haifeng Wang. 2021. DuReader_robust: A Chinese Dataset Towards Evaluating Robustness and Generalization of Machine Reading Comprehension in Real-World Applications. In *Proceedings of the 59th Annual Meeting of the Association for Computational Linguistics and the 11th International Joint Conference on Natural Language Processing (Volume 2: Short Papers)*, page 955–963.

Hugo Touvron, Thibaut Lavril, Gautier Izacard, Xavier Martinet, Marie-Anne Lachaux, Timothée Lacroix, Baptiste Rozière, Naman Goyal, Eric Hambro, Faisal Azhar, Aurelien Rodriguez, Armand Joulin, Edouard Grave, and Guillaume Lample. 2023. LLaMA: Open and efficient foundation language models. In *https://arxiv.org/abs/2302.13971*.

Asahi Ushio, Fernando Alva-Manchego, and Jose Camacho-Collados. 2022. Generative Language Models for Paragraph-Level Question Generation. In *Proceedings of the 2022 Conference on Empirical Methods in Natural Language Processing*, page 670–688.

Asahi Ushio, Fernando Alva-Manchego, and Jose Camacho-Collados. 2023. An Empirical Comparison of LM-based Question and Answer Generation Methods. In *Findings of the Association for Computational Linguistics: ACL 2023*, page 14262–14272.

Z. Wang, J. Valdez, D. Basu Mallick, and R. G. Baraniuk. 2022. Towards Human-Like Educational Question Generation with Large Language Models. *Artificial Intelligence in Education. AIED 2022. Lecture Notes in Computer Science*, 13355.

Changrong Xiao, Sean Xin Xu, Kunpeng Zhang, Yufang Wang, and Lei Xia. 2023. Evaluating reading comprehension exercises generated by llms: A showcase of chatgpt in education applications. In *Proc. 18th Workshop on Innovative Use of NLP for Building Educational Applications*, page 610–625.

Dongling Xiao, Han Zhang, Yukun Li, Yu Sun, Hao Tian, Hua Wu, and Haifeng Wang. 2021. Ernie-gen: an enhanced multi-flow pre-training and fine-tuning framework for natural language generation. In *Proceedings of the Twenty-Ninth International Conference on International Joint Conferences on Artificial Intelligence*, page 3997–4003.

A Appendix: Instruction to Human Assessors

The human assessors gave consent to the data collection and were informed that the results would remain anonymous. They were shown the following instructions:

```
<passage>
<question>
```

1. Is the question understandable and relevant for the passage?
2. Does the language quality of the question need to be improved?
3. If the answer to #1 is "Yes", choose one of the categories for the question:
   - Retrieval (Focus on and Retrieve Explicitly Stated Information)
   - Inferencing (Make Straightforward Inferences)
   - Integrating (Interpret and Integrate Ideas and Information)
   - Evaluation (Evaluate and Critique Content Textual Elements)

B Appendix: Prompt selection and implementation

Table 6 lists the six prompts that were evaluated. The top of Table 7 shows zero-shot evaluation results on a set of 42 passages randomly chosen from public examinations on the Chinese-language subject in Hong Kong.[12] "Creative" refers to the parameter values {temperature=0.8, top_p=1}. Prompt #3 was found to produce the highest proportion of usable questions and questions that are not word-matching in nature.

The bottom of Table 7 shows the tuning of the temperature and top_p values. "Conservative" refers to the values {temperature=0.5, top_p=0.5}; "Less Creative" refers to the values {temperature=0.6, top_p=0.9}. We empirically set the temperature and top_p values at 0.6 and 0.9 in the rest of the experiments since they produced more usable and non-word-matching questions than the other values.

The few-shot template is shown in Table 8.

[12]https://www.hkeaa.edu.hk/en/sa_tsa/

ID	Prompt (in Chinese)	Keywords
0	基于给定的文章，你需要提炼出一个答案，并以此答案为基础 构建一个问题。你的输出应该包含问题和答案。 文章:{input}	none
1	基于给定的文章，提炼出一个答案，然后根据这个答案创造一个 需要推理的问题。确保你的输出包含这个需要推理的问题和 对应的答案。 文章:{input}	reasoning
2	基于给定的文章，提炼出一个答案，然后根据这个答案生成一个 新的简答题，也就是说，新的简答题需要使用与上下文不同的 词语来表达相同的含义。你的输出应该包含那个简答问题和 对应的答案。输出格式如下所示: 问题: 答案: 文章:{input}	vocabulary
3	基于给定的文章，生成一个需要推断的简答题。你的输出应该 包含一个简答问题和这个问题的对应的答案。 文章:{input}	deduction
4	请根据文章内容，生成一个需要推理的简答题。你的输出格式 应如下所示: 问题: 答案: 文章:{input}	reasoning
5	根据文章，生成一个需要推断的问题。问题措辞需要与上下文 不会完全一样。你的输出应该包含问题和答案。 文章:{input}	deduction; vocabulary

Table 6: Candidate prompts (in Chinese) for LLM-based question generation with keywords specifying deduction (*tuiduan*), reasoning (*tuili*), and varied vocabulary (keywords are underlined in this table for clarity but not in the experiments)

ID	Parameters	% Usable	% Non-word-matching
0	Creative	47.62	40.48
1		57.14	57.14
2		59.52	45.24
3		**66.67**	**61.9**
4		61.9	59.52
5		54.76	52.38
3	Conservative	**73.81**	61.9
3	Less Creative	**73.81**	**66.67**
3	Creative	66.67	61.9

Table 7: Evaluation results for prompt selection and parameter tuning (the prompt corresponding to each ID can be found in Table 6)

文章: {example passage 1}
简答题: {example question 1}
答案: {example answer 1}
...
文章: {example passage 5}
简答题: {example answer 5}
答案: {example question 5}

基于给定的文章，生成一个需要
推断的简答题。你的输出应该包含
一个简答问题和这个问题的对应的答案。
文章: <input>
简答题:
答案:

Table 8: Prompt template for few-shot question generation [Translation: "Based on the given passage, generate a short-answer question that requires inference. Your output should include a question and its answer. Passage: <input>]

Adversarial Learning for Multi-Lingual Entity Linking

Bingbing Wang[1], **Bin Liang**[2*], **Zhixin Bai**[3], **Yongzhuo Ma**[1]
[1] Harbin Institute of Technology, Shenzhen, China
[2] The Chinese University of Hong Kong, Hong Kong, China
[3] Harbin Institute of Technology, Harbin, China
{bingbing.wang,baizhixin,yanagichiaki}@stu.hit.edu.cn,
bin.liang.cuhk.edu.hk

Abstract

Entity linking aims to identify mentions from the text and link them to a knowledge base. Further, Multi-lingual Entity Linking (MEL) is a more challenging task, where the language-specific mentions need to be linked to a multilingual knowledge base. To tackle the MEL task, we propose a novel model that employs the merit of adversarial learning and few-shot learning to generalize the learning ability across languages. Specifically, we first randomly select a fraction of language-agnostic unlabeled data as the language signal to construct the language discriminator. Based on it, we devise a simple and effective adversarial learning framework with two characteristic branches, including an entity classifier and a language discriminator with adversarial training. Experimental results on two benchmark datasets indicate the excellent performance in few-shot learning and the effectiveness of the proposed adversarial learning framework.

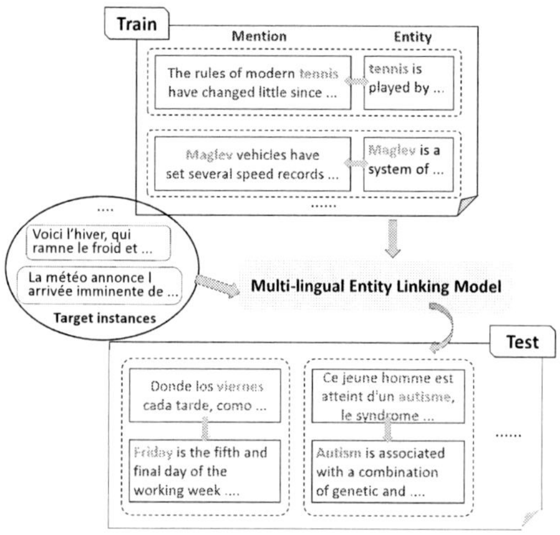

Figure 1: Multi-lingual entity linking task: training and test example of the source text in English and target text in French.

1 Introduction

Entity linking (EL), a process of disambiguating entity mentions with a target knowledge base (KB), is one of the tasks in information retrieval (Joko et al., 2021) and real applications involving information extraction (Phan and Sun, 2018) and question answering (Li et al., 2020), etc. Many state-of-the-art studies generally pay attention to English KB and do not put enough energy into the low-resource and challenging languages, such as Persian. In addition, the vast majority of low-resource languages are only provided with a limited annotated text, even without labeled data. Therefore, the cross-lingual entity linking (XEL) task was proposed for several pairs of source text and KB languages (McNamee et al., 2011; Tsai and Roth, 2016; Sil et al., 2018; Upadhyay et al., 2018a), where mentions expressed in a language are linked to a KB delivered in another.

However, XEL restricted the scope of EL to some extent since this popular method generally relies on the hypothesis of one single pivotal KB language as well as one limited KB. Subsequently, Multi-lingual entity linking (MEL) has gained attention as the generalization of XEL and some datasets (Joko et al., 2021; Botha et al., 2020b; Ji et al., 2015) have been collected for it. Compared to TAC-KBP 2014, TAC-KBP 2015 (Ji et al., 2015) was broadened from monolingual to trilingual coverage in three languages. Recently, Mewsli-9 (Botha et al., 2020b) was introduced as a large dataset featuring all entities to numerous cross-lingual systems with almost 300,000 mentions through 9 kinds of languages.

Given a text and entity mentions, there are two primary steps for multi-lingual entity linking: (1) Candidate Generation, possible entities are engendered for the mention, and (2) Entity Ranking, a score between the representation of mention and a candidate entity is computed. In this work, we con-

*Corresponding Authors

Proceedings of the 10th SIGHAN Workshop on Chinese Language Processing (SIGHAN-10), pages 28–35
August 16, 2024 ©2024 Association for Computational Linguistics

sider the multi-lingual entity linking task illustrated in Figure 1 that mainly takes Entity Ranking into consideration, and adopts a language-adversarial training approach to improve the performance.

First, a multi-lingual pre-trained transformer model XLM-Roberta (XLM-R) (Conneau et al., 2020) which builds robust representations of text in a wide range of languages, is utilized to build a single representation of mention including surrounding context and name of mention, and entity with description. The abundant source languages are leveraged to compute the similarity between mention and entity.

Second, we design a dedicated and simple adversarial learning approach to construct a language discriminator, which cleverly selects a small part from the test data (excluded during testing) and effectively generalizes to unseen languages for better robustness. In addition, previous studies (Arjovsky et al., 2017) contended that an adversarial training network could be regarded as a way that minimizes the Jensen-Shannon (JS) divergence between two distributions, in our case the feature distributions of the source language and target language. For the discontinuities of JS divergence, Wasserstein distance was proposed to enhance the stability of hyperparameter selection. Furthermore, a gradient penalty is introduced in our adversarial training approach to optimize the discriminator loss that hopes to enlarge the difference between source and target language as much as possible.

The main contributions of our work are summarized as follows:

- A novel adversarial learning framework for the multi-lingual entity linking task in few shot learning is proposed with the purpose of English bias reduction and generalization improvement.

- We introduce a simple but effective adversarial training approach that randomly selects a certain proportion of test data, and optimizes the feature distributions between source and target languages by minimizing the Wasserstein distance with an additional gradient penalty.

- State-of-the-art results of the experiment on few-shot learning reveal the robustness of our model in the multi-lingual entity linking task.

2 Related Work

2.1 Entity Linking

A series of previous works paid attention to entity linking which develops a model to link textual mentions to entities in KB. (De Cao et al., 2020) proposed a system that retrieves entities by generating their unique names in an autoregressive manner, processing each token sequentially from left to right while conditioning on the given context. (Liu et al., 2022) introduced a scalable and effective BERT-based entity linking model that balances accuracy and speed. Their two-stage zero-shot linking algorithm defines each entity with only a short textual description, and they provide an extensive evaluation of the model's performance. (Botha et al., 2020a) developed a dual encoder model that significantly enhances feature representation, incorporates negative mining, and includes an auxiliary entity-pairing task. This approach resulted in a single-entity retrieval model capable of handling over 100 languages and 20 million entities.

2.2 Multi-lingual Entity Linking

Building on this foundation, researchers gradually shifted their focus to Cross-Language Entity Linking (XEL). (Upadhyay et al., 2018b) devised the first XEL approach that integrates supervision from multiple languages. This method enhances the limited supervision in the target language with additional supervision from a high-resource language, allowing for the training of a single entity linking model across multiple languages. (Zhou et al., 2019a) examined the impact of resource availability on the quality of existing XEL systems and quantified this effect. They proposed three improvements to entity candidate generation and disambiguation, which optimize the use of limited data in resource-scarce scenarios. (De Cao et al., 2022) designed a sequence-to-sequence approach for multilingual entity linking that enhances the interaction between mention strings and entity names. This method cross-encodes mentions and entity names, capturing more complex interactions than the traditional dot product between mention and entity vectors.

3 Methodology

3.1 Task Definition and Overview

Multi-lingual entity linking is a task that links an entity mention in some context languages to the corresponding entity in a language-agnostic KB.

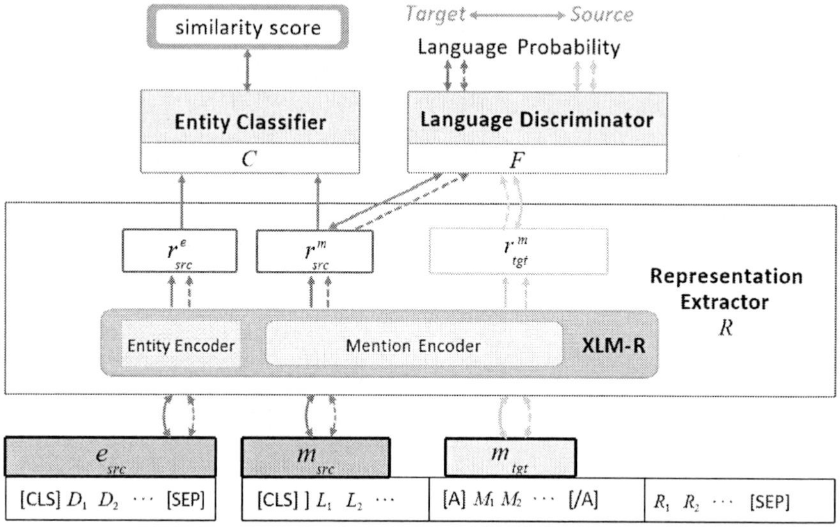

Figure 2: Proposed adversarial learning framework. Blue lines show the flow of source texts and the yellow ones are of target texts. The parameters of R and C are updated and shown as solid lines. The parameters of F are updated and demonstrated as dotted lines.

On this foundation, we employ a few-shot multilingual entity linking task aiming at reducing English bias in EL and improving the generalization for unseen entity set in KBs.

As illustrated in Figure 2, there are three primary components: Representation Extractor R that attains feature representations, Entity Classifier C that aims to compute similarity scores of entity-mention pairs, and Language Discriminator F that identifies whether the input text is from source or target language. Going forward, we assume that if the well-trained language discriminator F can't distinguish the language of the given representation extracted by pre-trained transformer model, these representations can be regarded as language-invariant. That's the motivation we introduce adversarial F to achieve better performance of representation extraction and effectiveness of language invariance.

A representation extractor is designed for the labeled source text T_{src} and unlabeled target text T_{tgt} given as input data. We then conduct a two-step training procedure in each training iteration. First, a small amount of unlabeled source (blue lines) and unlabeled target data (yellow lines) treated by representation extractor R, pass through a language discriminator F for adversarial training. And the labeled source data are put into C to calculate the similarity of mention and entity.

3.2 Representations Extractor

To extract the representation of mention and entity respectively, XLM-Roberta (XLM-R) (Conneau et al., 2020), a transformer representation model that is well-performed in the multi-lingual task is applied as the encoder to represent text into hidden representations. Mention-entity pair in source language is defined as $(m_{src}, e_{src}) \in T_{src}$, while $m_{tgt} \in T_{tgt}$ in target language. m_{src} and m_{tgt} are the combination of local context (the mention span M_i separated by [A] and [/A] markers , left of the mention L_i, right of the mention R_i). The source entity e_{src} is simply the entity description.

Mention in source text m_{src} is fed into XLM-R, and we use max pooling to create a single representation r^m_{src}. A similar method is used for entity in source text and mention in target text to obtain representation r^e_{src} and r^m_{tgt} respectively. Furthermore, r^m_{src} and r^e_{src} are then fed into entity classifier C to produce a score using cosine similarity shown in Eq. 1, while the language discriminator F is exposed to both r^m_{src} and r^m_{tgt}.

$$s(m_{src}, e_i) = \cos(r^m_{src}, r^e_i) = \frac{r^m_{src} \cdot r^e_i}{\|r^m_{src}\| \cdot \|r^e_i\|} \quad (1)$$

where the mention representation r^m_{src} is compared with candidate entity representation $r^e_i (i = 1, 2, ..., k)$ in source text.

3.3 Adversarial Training

In order to aid the training model to learn representations preferably fitted for transferring to unseen languages, we further investigate a simple but effective adversarial training approach, which randomly selects test data (excluded during testing) as target instances according to a proportion of 1%, 5%, 10%. And the distribution of the representation extractor for both source and target instances are defined as below:

$$Y_R^{src} \triangleq Y(r_{src}^m = R(x)|x \in m_{src})$$

$$Y_R^{tgt} \triangleq Y(r_{tgt}^m = R(x)|x \in m_{tgt})$$

Our goal is to make these two distributions as close as possible to get better multi-lingual generalization. Traditional adversarial approaches suffer from convergence and unstable min-max game originating from the discontinuous JS divergence. To settle down this problem, Wasserstein Generative Adversarial Networks (WGAN) (Arjovsky et al., 2017) using Wasserstein distance is proposed. Enlightened by this, we minimize the Wasserstein distance W between Y_R^{src} and Y_R^{tgt} based on Kantorovich-Rubinstein duality (Villani, 2009).

$$W(Y_F^{src}, Y_F^{tgt}) = \sup_{||t||_L \leq 1} \mathop{\mathbb{E}}_{r_{src}^m \sim Y_R^{src}} [t(r_{src}^m)] - \mathop{\mathbb{E}}_{r_{tgt}^m \sim Y_R^{tgt}} [t(r_{tgt}^m)] \quad (2)$$

where the supremum is over all the set of 1-Lipschitz functions t. For convenience, we instead the function as the language discriminator F. The adversarial loss is given as:

$$L_{adv} = \mathop{\mathbb{E}}_{r_{tgt}^m \sim Y_R^{tgt}} [F(r_{tgt}^m)] - \mathop{\mathbb{E}}_{r_{src}^m \sim Y_R^{src}} [F(r_{src}^m)] + \lambda_p L_p \quad (3)$$

where λ_p is the gradient penalty coefficient. The intuition is that F should output the scores of the source language much higher than the target one. Moreover, WGAN also proposes weight clipping to meet the requirement that the discriminator must lie within the space of 1-Lipschitz functions. Unfortunately, it's exactly what leads to optimization difficulties of gradient vanishing and explosion. A gradient penalty is hence introduced to the optimization function and constrains the output relative to the gradient norm of the input:

$$L_p = \mathop{\mathbb{E}}_{\tilde{r} \sim Y_R'} [(||\nabla_{\tilde{r}} F(\tilde{r})||_2 - 1)^2] \quad (4)$$

$$\tilde{r} = \mu r_{src}^m + (1-\mu) r_{tgt}^m, \quad \mu \sim U[0,1] \quad (5)$$

Where $\tilde{r}$ is obtained by sampling from the sample space of the Y_R' distribution, which is implicitly defined sampling randomly along straight lines between a pair of points sampled in the source and target distribution of the mention representation.

3.4 The whole training process

We adopt the original cross-entropy loss expressed as $L_{CE}(\tilde{z}, z)$, where $\tilde{z}$ and z represent the predicted label distribution and the corresponding true label. Finally, combined with entity classifier and the adversarial training, the entire training loss that should be minimized, is given as:

$$L = L_{CE} + \lambda(\mathop{\mathbb{E}}_{r_{tgt}^m \sim Y_R^{tgt}} [F(r_{tgt}^m)] - \mathop{\mathbb{E}}_{r_{src}^m \sim Y_R^{src}} [F(r_{src}^m)]) \quad (6)$$

where λ is the balance factor. The training process of our proposed adversarial learning framework is illustrated in the Algorithm 1.

Algorithm 1 The training process of our proposed adversarial learning framework

Require: Labeled source text T_{src} (mention m_{src}, entity description e_{src}), unlabeled target text T_{tgt} (mention m_{tgt}), gradient penalty coefficient λ_p, hyper-parameter $\lambda > 0$ number of critic iterations per generator n_{critic}, maximum number of iterations n_{epoch}, and number of batches n_{batch}.

```
for t = 0 to n_epoch do
    for i = 0 to n_batch do
        for j = 0 to n_critic do
            Sample unlabeled source data m_src from T_src
            Sample unlabeled target data m_tgt from T_tgt
            A random number μ ~ U[0, 1]
            r^m_src = R(m_src)
            r^m_tgt = R(m_tgt)
            r̃ = μ r^m_src + (1 − μ) r^m_tgt
            ▷ Calculate loss
            L_p = E[(||∇_r̃ F(r̃)||_2 − 1)^2]
            L_adv = −E[F(r^m_src)] + E[F(r^m_tgt)] + λ_p L_p
        end for
        Update F parameters with Adam to minimize L_adv
    end for
    ▷ Main iterations
    Sample labeled source data m_src and e_src from T_src
    Sample unlabeled target data m_tgt from T_tgt
    r^m_src = R(m_src)
    r^m_tgt = R(m_tgt)
    ▷ Calculate loss
    L = L_CE(C(r^m_src); e_src) + λ(E[F(r^m_src)] − E[F(r^m_tgt)])
    Updata R parameters with Adam to minimize loss.
end for
```

Table 1: Accuracy (acc), precision (p), recall (r), and F1 of four languages in three few-shot of 1%, 5%, and 10%.

	es				zh				de			
Split	acc	p	r	F1	acc	p	r	F1	acc	p	r	F1
1%	85.6	92.4	67.9	78.3	90.0	87.8	76.5	81.8	66.1	80.2	86.1	83.0
5%	86.3	93.2	66.8	77.8	91.5	90.3	84.9	87.5	68.4	82.3	86.7	84.4
10%	88.9	93.8	68.2	79.0	92.4	93.5	88.6	91.0	70.1	82.5	87.2	84.8

4 Experiment

4.1 Datasets and Settings

We conduct our evaluation on two well-known entity linking datasets.

- **TAC-KBP 2015**(Ji et al., 2015): following (Sil et al., 2018), we use Spanish and Chinese on TAC-KBP 2015 Tri-Lingual Entity Linking Track, which contains 166 Chinese documents (82 discussion forum articles and 84 news) and 167 Spanish documents (83 discussion forum articles and 84 news).
- **TR 2016**^{hard}(Tsai and Roth, 2016): is a cross-lingual dataset based on Wikipedia. It's constructed to contain difficult mention-entity pairs and removed the mention overlapping between training and test data.

In our experiment, the balance factor in Eq. 3 and Eq. 6 are set to 1. For all the experiments on each language, R and C are optimized by Adam (Kingma and Ba, 2015) with a learning rate of 0.0005, while F is trained through different Adam optimizers with the same learning rate. In order to present the effectiveness of the language discriminator F intuitively, our model using the adversarial approach is referred to as Model X^+, and the model without the adversarial approach is described as Model X. Except for training data, the target instances were selected randomly from test data to implement adversarial training at a small amount proportion of 1%, 5%, and 10% respectively. As for entity candidates, we use FAISS (Johnson et al., 2021) IndexFlatIP index type to obtain the top 100 entity candidates.

4.2 Main results

We first explore the performance of the English training model in an unseen language. This result presents the challenge of solving the entity linking task with a few examples per language. We carry out three settings used in few-shot learning (Gao et al., 2021): taking 1%, 5% and 10% test data as target instances. For each language in two datasets - Spanish (es) and Chinese (zh) in TAC-KBP 2015, German (de) in TR 2016^{hard}, we train our proposed model and demonstrate four indicators including accuracy (acc), precision (p), recall (r), and F1 in difference few-shot settings shown in Table 1. As we can see, with the increase in the few-shot examples, indicators show an upward trend more or less.

Table 2: Accuracy (%) results of ablation study in four languages under the circumstance of 10% few-shot setting. AT represents adversarial learning.

Model	es	zh	de
BERT	78.4	80.3	59.2
BERT + AT	81.2	86.8	65.4
XLM-R	83.5	89.2	64.6
XLM-R + AT	**88.9**	**92.4**	**70.1**

4.3 Ablation study

We launched an ablation study to explore the impact of different components in the proposed adversarial learning framework, and the results are reported in Table 2. From two components between the pre-trained model and whether there is an adversarial training approach or not, we additionally introduce a BERT pre-trained model (Vaswani et al., 2017; Devlin et al., 2019) initialized by Botha et al. (Botha et al., 2020b) using the first 4 layers. Note that XLM-R pre-trained model which can extract robust representations in a wide range of languages, performs better than BERT. Moreover, the removal of the adversarial training approach leads to performance degradation. This implies that the proposed adversarial learning framework with XLM-R pre-trained model and adversarial training advances the performance.

Table 3: Accuracy (%) on TAC-KBP 2015 and TR 2016^{hard}

Model	TAC-KBP2015		TR2016^{hard}			
	es	zh	de	es	fr	it
Sil et al.(Sil et al., 2018)	82.3	84.4	-	-	-	-
Upadhyay et al.(Upadhyay et al., 2018a)	84.4	86.0	55.2	56.8	51.0	52.3
Zhou et al.(Zhou et al., 2019b)	85.5	83.3	-	-	-	-
Botha et al.(Botha et al., 2020b)	-	-	62.0	58.0	54.0	56.0
Model X	84.6	87.2	61.2	58.3	55.2	55.5
Model X^+	**85.5**	**89.3**	**65.3**	**63.4**	**63.9**	**64.2**

4.4 Influence of Adversarial Training Approach

Many recent researchers fix their attention on the zero-shot setting that no mention is available during inference. Therefore, we conduct the following experiment based on a zero-shot setting. On this foundation, we investigate the influence of the adversarial training approach. From Table 2, it's concluded that the adversarial training approach helps better performance. More concretely, this section compares our model with the recent study in zero-shot setting, and the results are reported in Table 3 for TAC-KBP 2015 and TR 2016^{hard} using Model X and Model X^+. We can observe that our Model X^+ consistently outperforms all compared models at the same time. For the model proposed by Upadhyay et al (Upadhyay et al., 2018a), the best-improved results of TAC-KBP 2015 and TR 2016^{hard}respectively are 3.3% and 12.9%.

4.5 Visualization

To qualitatively demonstrate how our proposed adversarial learning framework affects the distribution between English and Chinese instances, we present a t-SNE (Van der Maaten and Hinton, 2008) visualization analysis of feature representations with 10 random mention texts from English and Chinese validation set respectively in Figure 3. Figure 3a shows representation distributions without adversarial training. Note that the two languages mention texts are not translations of each other. To shed light on the effect of our architecture, a significant reduction after adversarial training is presented in Figure 3b where we can see a more mixed distribution of representation between English and Chinese instances. This further indicates that our proposed adversarial learning framework effectively narrows the distance of representation distribution in different languages using the adversarial training approach.

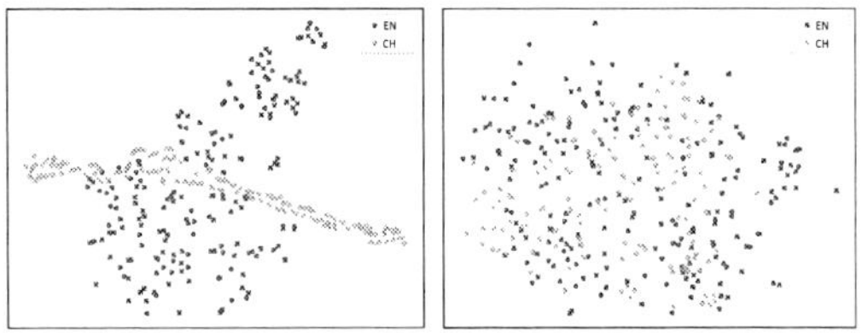

Figure 3: Results of t-SNE visualization. (a) The distribution of representation between English and Chinese instances without adversarial training presents a language gap. (b) A more mixed distribution of representation between English and Chinese instance with adversarial training at the end of the representation extractor shows a smaller language gap.

5 Conclusion

In this paper, we propose a novel model that applies adversarial learning and few-shot learning method to better generalize the learning ability across languages for the multi-lingual entity linking task. To be more exact, a fraction of language-agnostic unlabeled data are selected randomly as the language signal to build the language discriminator. Moreover, we design a simple and effective adversarial learning framework with two branches of an entity classifier and a language discriminator. Experimental results on two benchmark datasets empirically illustrate that the proposed adversarial learning framework is significantly effective.

Limitations

The current exploration, while demonstrating promising advancements, has areas for potential enhancement. Firstly, the study's focus on a limited number of languages may not fully capture the breadth of linguistic diversity, potentially affecting the model's adaptability in multilingual scenarios. Secondly, variations in data quality could impact the robustness of the model's generalization capabilities.

Acknowledgements

This work was partially supported by the National Natural Science Foundation of China (62176076), the Natural Science Foundation of Guangdong (2023A1515012922), the Shenzhen Foundational Research Funding (JCYJ20220818102415032), and the Guangdong Provincial Key Laboratory of Novel Security Intelligence Technologies (2022B1212010005).

References

Martin Arjovsky, Soumith Chintala, and Léon Bottou. 2017. Wasserstein generative adversarial networks. In *Proceedings of the 34th International Conference on Machine Learning*, volume 70 of *Proceedings of Machine Learning Research*, pages 214–223, Sydney Australia. PMLR.

Jan A Botha, Zifei Shan, and Dan Gillick. 2020a. Entity linking in 100 languages. In *Proceedings of the 2020 Conference on Empirical Methods in Natural Language Processing (EMNLP)*, pages 7833–7845.

Jan A. Botha, Zifei Shan, and Daniel Gillick. 2020b. Entity Linking in 100 Languages. In *Proceedings of the 2020 Conference on Empirical Methods in Natural Language Processing (EMNLP)*, pages 7833–7845, Online. Association for Computational Linguistics.

Alexis Conneau, Kartikay Khandelwal, Naman Goyal, Vishrav Chaudhary, Guillaume Wenzek, Francisco Guzmán, Edouard Grave, Myle Ott, Luke Zettlemoyer, and Veselin Stoyanov. 2020. Unsupervised cross-lingual representation learning at scale. In *Proceedings of the 58th Annual Meeting of the Association for Computational Linguistics*, pages 8440–8451, Online. Association for Computational Linguistics.

Nicola De Cao, Gautier Izacard, Sebastian Riedel, and Fabio Petroni. 2020. Autoregressive entity retrieval. *arXiv preprint arXiv:2010.00904*.

Nicola De Cao, Ledell Wu, Kashyap Popat, Mikel Artetxe, Naman Goyal, Mikhail Plekhanov, Luke Zettlemoyer, Nicola Cancedda, Sebastian Riedel, and Fabio Petroni. 2022. Multilingual autoregressive entity linking. *Transactions of the Association for Computational Linguistics*, 10:274–290.

Jacob Devlin, Ming-Wei Chang, Kenton Lee, and Kristina Toutanova. 2019. BERT: Pre-training of deep bidirectional transformers for language understanding. In *Proceedings of the 2019 Conference of the North American Chapter of the Association for Computational Linguistics: Human Language Technologies, Volume 1 (Long and Short Papers)*, pages 4171–4186, Minneapolis, Minnesota. Association for Computational Linguistics.

Tianyu Gao, Adam Fisch, and Danqi Chen. 2021. Making pre-trained language models better few-shot learners. In *Proceedings of the 59th Annual Meeting of the Association for Computational Linguistics and the 11th International Joint Conference on Natural Language Processing (Volume 1: Long Papers)*, pages 3816–3830, Online. Association for Computational Linguistics.

Heng Ji, Joel Nothman, Ben Hachey, and Radu Florian. 2015. Overview of tac-kbp 2015 tri-lingual entity discovery and linking. In *Proceedings of Eighth Text Analysis Conference (TAC 2015)*, Maryland, USA. National Institute of Standards and Technology.

Jeff Johnson, Matthijs Douze, and Hervé Jégou. 2021. Billion-scale similarity search with gpus. *IEEE Transactions on Big Data*, 7(3):535–547.

Hideaki Joko, Faegheh Hasibi, Krisztian Balog, and Arjen P. de Vries. 2021. *Conversational Entity Linking: Problem Definition and Datasets*, page 2390–2397. Association for Computing Machinery, New York, NY, USA.

Diederik P Kingma and JL Ba. 2015. Adam: A method for stochastic optimization. In *Conference Track Proceedings*, San Diego, CA, USA. 3rd International Conference on Learning Representations, {ICLR} 2015.

Belinda Z. Li, Sewon Min, Srinivasan Iyer, Yashar Mehdad, and Wen-tau Yih. 2020. Efficient one-pass end-to-end entity linking for questions. In *Proceedings of the 2020 Conference on Empirical Methods in Natural Language Processing (EMNLP)*, pages 6433–6441, Online. Association for Computational Linguistics.

Shengzhe Liu, Xin Zhang, and Jufeng Yang. 2022. Ser30k: A large-scale dataset for sticker emotion recognition. In *Proceedings of the 30th ACM International Conference on Multimedia*, pages 33–41.

Paul McNamee, James Mayfield, Dawn Lawrie, Douglas Oard, and David Doermann. 2011. Cross-language entity linking. In *Proceedings of 5th International Joint Conference on Natural Language Processing*, pages 255–263, Chiang Mai, Thailand. Asian Federation of Natural Language Processing.

Minh C. Phan and Aixin Sun. 2018. Conerel: Collective information extraction in news articles. In *The 41st International ACM SIGIR Conference on Research & Development in Information Retrieval*, SIGIR '18, page 1273–1276, New York, NY, USA. Association for Computing Machinery.

Avirup Sil, Gourab Kundu, Radu Florian, and Wael Hamza. 2018. Neural cross-lingual entity linking. In

Thirty-Second AAAI Conference on Artificial Intelligence, Louisiana, USA. Association for the Advancement of Artificial Intelligence.

Chen-Tse Tsai and Dan Roth. 2016. Cross-lingual wikification using multilingual embeddings. In *Proceedings of the 2016 Conference of the North American Chapter of the Association for Computational Linguistics: Human Language Technologies*, pages 589–598, San Diego, California. Association for Computational Linguistics.

Shyam Upadhyay, Nitish Gupta, and Dan Roth. 2018a. Joint multilingual supervision for cross-lingual entity linking. In *Proceedings of the 2018 Conference on Empirical Methods in Natural Language Processing*, pages 2486–2495, Brussels, Belgium. Association for Computational Linguistics.

Shyam Upadhyay, Nitish Gupta, and Dan Roth. 2018b. Joint multilingual supervision for cross-lingual entity linking. In *Proceedings of the 2018 Conference on Empirical Methods in Natural Language Processing*, pages 2486–2495.

Laurens Van der Maaten and Geoffrey Hinton. 2008. Visualizing data using t-sne. *Journal of machine learning research*, 9(11).

Ashish Vaswani, Noam Shazeer, Niki Parmar, Jakob Uszkoreit, Llion Jones, Aidan N Gomez, Ł ukasz Kaiser, and Illia Polosukhin. 2017. Attention is all you need. In *Advances in Neural Information Processing Systems*, volume 30, pages 5998,6009, Long Beach, CA, USA. Curran Associates, Inc.

Cédric Villani. 2009. *Optimal transport: old and new*, volume 338. Springer.

Shuyan Zhou, Shruti Rijhwani, and Graham Neubig. 2019a. Towards zero-resource cross-lingual entity linking. *EMNLP-IJCNLP 2019*, page 243.

Shuyan Zhou, Shruti Rijhwani, and Graham Neubig. 2019b. Towards zero-resource cross-lingual entity linking. In *Proceedings of the 2nd Workshop on Deep Learning Approaches for Low-Resource NLP (DeepLo 2019)*, pages 243–252, Hong Kong, China. Association for Computational Linguistics.

Incremental pre-training from smaller language models

Han Zhang[1,2], **Hui Wang**[2,*], **and Ruifeng Xu**[1,2,3*]
[1] Harbin Institute of Technology, Shenzhen, China
[2] Peng Cheng Laboratory, Shenzhen, China
[3] Guangdong Provincial Key Laboratory of Novel Security Intelligence Technologies
hanlardresearch@gmail.com, wangh06@pcl.ac.cn, xuruifeng@hit.edu.cn

Abstract

Large language models have recently become a new learning paradigm and led to state-of-the-art performance across a range of tasks. As explosive open-source pre-trained models are available, it is worth investigating how to better utilize existing models. We propose a simple yet effective method, Incr-Pretrain, for incrementally pre-training language models from smaller well-trained source models. Different layer-wise transfer strategies were introduced for model augmentation including parameter copying, initial value padding, and model distillation. Experiments on multiple zero-shot learning tasks demonstrate satisfying inference performance upon transferring and promising training efficiency during continuing pre-training. Compared to training from scratch, Incr-Pretrain can save up to half the training time to get a similar testing loss.

1 Introduction

Large language models have led to state-of-the-art accuracies across a range of tasks and have demonstrated strong performances with few-shot in-context learning (Zhang et al., 2020b; Zeng et al., 2021; Brown et al., 2020). From GPT (Radford et al., 2018) to Switch-Transformer (Fedus et al., 2021), the number of parameters grows from 125 million to 1.6 trillion at an exponential rate. The study of GPT3 (Brown et al., 2020) shows that a large language model (up to 175 billion) can have strong context learning ability, and obtains comparable performances with state-of-the-art finetune style methods even without any parameter updating. An empirical scaling law (Kaplan et al., 2020) shows that the larger models with wider and deeper architecture are significantly more sample-efficient on a relatively modest amount of data. Furthermore, as the model size increases, there is still room for performance improvement.

However, training large language models from scratch always costs huge computing resources and time. For instance, NVIDIA leveraged their Selene supercomputer to perform scaling studies and used up to 3,072 A100 GPUs for training the largest Megatron (Shoeybi et al., 2019) model (1 trillion parameters). OpenAI spent 355 GPU-years for training GPT-3 (Brown et al., 2020), and the total costs are more than ten million dollars. Most existing model transfer methods aim at improving the performance of downstream tasks, e.g. transfer learning (Zhuang et al., 2019) or speeding up the inference process, e.g. knowledge distillation (Gou et al., 2020), but studies for accelerating model pre-training from scratch remain limited. To our knowledge, no research on how to transfer a small pre-trained model to a large model has been done.

We introduce Incr-Pretrain to augment a smaller source Transformer model to a larger target model and make them have comparable performances, both upon transferring and after continuing pre-training. Different layer-wise transfer strategies are introduced for model augmentation including parameter copying, padding and model distillation. Specifically, we propose a KL-divergence-based approximation method to distill the LayerNorm layer to address a mathematically intractable issue during transferring. We tested our method's performance on zero-shot tasks of BERT-base and GPT-2, and the results show that the augmented models obtain satisfying performances. When incrementally training a dialogue-GPT model on different scales, the training and testing losses can continue declining from the values before transferring. The total training time can be saved up to half compared with that training from scratch.

To the best of our knowledge, this is the first parameter-based method for incrementally pre-training language models. Our method can help reduce the heavy resource cost of training large language models from scratch and can be applied

* R. Xu and H. Wang are corresponding authors.

Proceedings of the 10th SIGHAN Workshop on Chinese Language Processing (SIGHAN-10), pages 36–44
August 16, 2024

to almost any open-source pre-trained model in the Transformers library (Wolf et al., 2020). The proposed method is also compatible with mainstream parallel training techniques. We summarize our contributions as follows: 1) We prove that it is feasible to train a larger language model from smaller Transformer models without training from scratch; 2) We propose a distillation-based method to transfer the LayerNorm parameters.

2 Method

We present the implementation of Incr-Pretrain in the scenarios of both widening and deepening a Transformer model. For widening the model, we use parameter copying and padding to transfer the embedding, attention and MLP layers and a distillation-based method to adjust the LayerNorm's parameters to the new input distribution due to the changed input dimension problem. For deepening the model, we initialize the deeper layers with small parameter values, the noise of which could be overwritten by the residual connection setting and have less adverse impact on the entire model. The overall framework is shown in Figure 1.

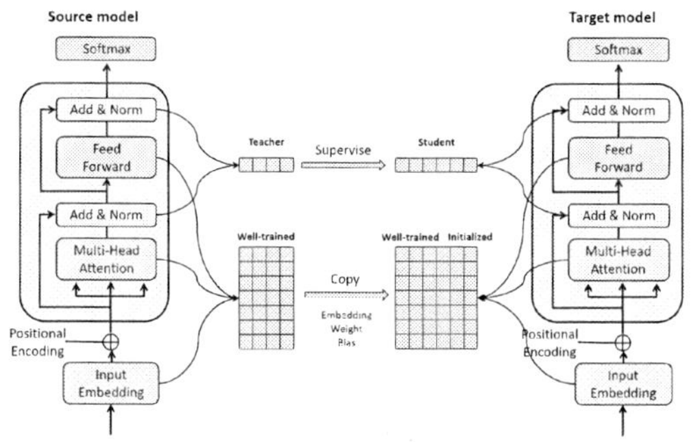

Figure 1: The Incr-Pretrain framework

2.1 Widen the model

Linear transformation is the basic operator that exists in both the multi-head attention and feed-forward layer. Incr-Pretrain transfers a smaller-size matrix of the linear transformation from the source model to a bigger matrix in the target model. As shown in Figure 2, by padding small random values or zeros at the tail of the source matrix, both vertically and horizontally, the result of the matrix multiplication is approximate to that by directly doing matrix multiplication on the source matrix. This is ensured by the block matrix multiplication rule. We also prove that if we pad random values $\theta \sim N(0, \sigma^2)$ to the dense layer, the changes on the output can be controlled in $O(\sigma^2)$ (Appendix). Especially, if σ reduces to zero, the nonzero values in the matrix multiplication result will be unchanged.

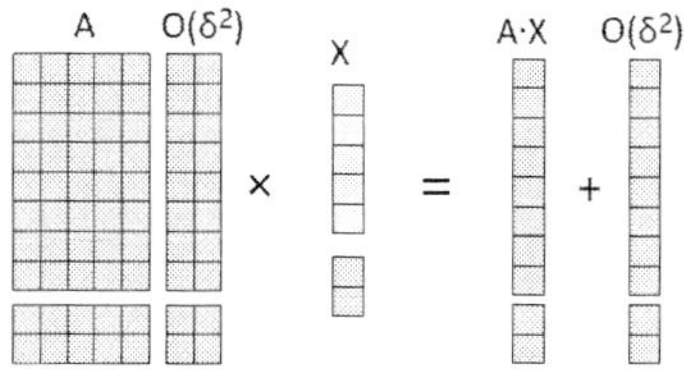

Figure 2: Block matrix multiplication

In the multi-head attention layer, parameters are the weights and biases in linear transformation for queries, keys, and values. So we can also apply the above method to the attention layer. To ensure the attention score of each head is valid, we can keep each attention head dimension fixed and only increase the head number, or keep the head number and pad values to each attention head, either combination is feasible. In the embedding layer, we directly pad small random values or zeros to the source embeddings. According to the block matrix multiplication rule, the inner product similarity of any two-word vectors will not change much, which is critical to the attention layer.

2.2 Transfer LayerNorm

LayerNorm is a technique to normalize the distributions of intermediate layers. It enables smoother gradients and faster training by re-centering and re-scaling both inputs and weight matrix. However, both re-centering and re-scaling operations are related to the hidden size, which would change after transferring. Mathematical inequivalence will affect the performance of the target model, but the scaling weight and bias can be updated fast after training several steps to adjust new model parameters.

We introduce a distillation-based method for transferring the LayerNorm layer. Let input $x \in \mathbb{R}^H$, LayerNorm re-centers and re-scales x as $h_i = g_i \cdot N(x_i) + b_i$, where $N(x_i) = (x_i - \mu)/\sigma$, $\mu = (\sum_{i=1}^{H} x_i)/H$, $\sigma = (\sum_{i=1}^{H}(x_i - \mu)^2/H)^{1/2}$. h is the output of the LayerNorm layer, $(\cdot)_i$ is the scalar value of the i-th dimension, and μ and σ are the mean and standard deviation of the input. The bias b and gain g are parameters with the same dimension H.

Let $\hat{x} = (x_1, x_2, \ldots, x_H, \theta_1, \ldots, \theta_{D-H})$ be the input e.g. padded word embeddings, $\hat{x} \in \mathbb{R}^D$. Since we padded *D-H* values to the input, the mean and variance were changed. We define $\hat{h_i} = \hat{g_i} \cdot \hat{N(x_i)} + \hat{b_i}$, $\hat{N(x_i)} = \frac{\hat{x_i} - \hat{\mu}}{\hat{\sigma}}$, $\hat{\mu} = (\sum_{i=1}^{H} x_i + \sum_{i=1}^{D-H} \theta_i)/D$, $\hat{\sigma} = ((\sum_{i=1}^{H}(x_i - \hat{\mu})^2 + \sum_{i=1}^{D-H}(\theta_i - \hat{\mu})^2)/D)^{1/2}$. To make the outputs of source and target LayerNorm equal, for every integer i in section $[1, H]$, we need to let

$$g_i \cdot N(x_i) + b_i = \hat{g_i} \cdot \hat{N(x_i)} + \hat{b_i}, \quad \forall i \in [1, H] \cap \mathbb{N} \tag{1}$$

So we established a equation where the variables are $\hat{g_i}$ and $\hat{b_i}, i \in [1, H] \cap \mathbb{N}$. We need to find a set of solutions to Eq. 1 which are viable for $\forall (x_1, x_2, \ldots, x_H)$. In particular, for any word index $k \in [1, |Vocab|] \cap \mathbb{N}$, the equation k is

$$\begin{pmatrix} \hat{N^k}, & \mathbf{E} \end{pmatrix} \begin{pmatrix} \hat{\mathbf{g}} \\ \hat{\mathbf{b}} \end{pmatrix} = \mathbf{h}^k \tag{2}$$

where $\mathbf{E}$ is the unit matrix, $\hat{N^k} = Diag(\hat{N(x_1^k)}, \hat{N(x_2^k)}, \ldots, \hat{N(x_H^k)})$. Unfortunately, we found that Eq. 2 is intractable, the proof is presented in Appendix.

The gain and bias are parameters that can be updated based on gradient, so we construct a loss function to train the LayerNorm parameters in the target model by calculating the KL-divergence between the outputs from the target and source. The loss function L is defined as

$$L = D_{KL}(P(x|\theta_{source}), P(x|\theta_{target})) \tag{3}$$

By minimizing the loss, the target and source LayerNorm outputs are converging.

2.3 Deepen the model

Deepening the neural network is the most common way to increase the model size. When we transfer a source model with few layers to a deeper target model, the parameters in deeper layers need to be initialized with small values. In both self-attention and MLP layers, the small parameters θ will result in small layer output $layer(x|\theta)$, so the output through residual connection $layer(x|\theta) + x$ approximates to x. It enables the deeper layers will not change the output distribution of shallow layers much, so a deeper target model can have similar output distributions to the source model.

3 Experiments

We conducted extensive experiments on inference upon transferring and continuing pre-training. We tested BERT on the cloze tasks and GPT on the next word prediction tasks, which are corresponding objectives at their stages of pre-training. To validate the time efficiency of using Incr-Pretrain, we continued to pre-train the target model and compared the loss curve with that of training from scratch.

3.1 Inference upon transferring

We tested BERT on the LAMA (Petroni et al., 2020) dataset and GPT-2 on the Lambada (Paperno et al., 2016), ClozeStory (Bugert et al., 2017), and HellaSwag (Zellers et al., 2019) datasets with a zero-shot method without any continuing pre-training.

Datasets BERT is a masked language model whose primary pre-training task is mask filling (cloze), so the performance on the cloze task is the most effective indicator. The language model tested on LAMA needs to understand the whole sentence and predict the masked keyword. Considering that some samples are too difficult to BERT in zero-shot tasks, to reduce the impact of randomness, we let BERT predict 5 times for each sample, and if any time the correct answer is predicted, we consider it correct.

GPT is a causal language model (CLM) that is pre-trained by predicting the next word with only one side of the text visible. LAMBADA, storyCloze, and HellaSwag are all datasets that aims to predict the ending text piece(s), so they are consistent with the pre-training process of the causal language model. In this task, we let GPT predict only one time on the test part of LAMBADA, the test part of StoryCloze, and the dev part of HellaSwag. On StoryCloze and HellaSwag datasets, the inference method is the same as the perplexity-based method (Zeng et al., 2021).

Configuration We compared three types of models on both datasets. The *Source* models exist as open-resource models, i.e. BERT and GPT-2. The *Target* models are the basic enlarged versions in which parameters of each layer are directly copied from the Source models with padded values. For attention, we let the number of heads increase but the dimension of each head is unchanged. We set σ as zero to make the calculation as equivalent as possible and also reduced the impact of randomness on the experiment. Compared to the target models, the *Target-LN* models further transfer the LayerNorm parameters using the distillation-based method training on only 2,425 short dialogues (Eric and Manning, 2017).

The results of the inference tasks are shown in Table 1. We observe that after transferring, the performances of the Target models drop dramatically compared with the Source models. This is likely due to the LayerNorm part, which is not mathematically equivalent when transferring. In comparison, the Target-LN (Both GPT and BERT) models are comparable with the Source models, which shows that the distillation-based approximation method is effective.

Table 1: Results on zero-shot tasks. All datasets are evaluated by accuracy, and perplexity(PPL) is evaluated on LAMBADA. ***Target-LN** uses the distillation-based method to adjust the LayerNorm parameters of target model.

Model	Dataset	Source	Target	Target-LN
BERT	ConceptNet	26.00	15.24	22.66
BERT	Squad	15.89	10.26	15.89
BERT	Google_RE	5.06	4.29	5.23
BERT	TREx	19.45	11.22	17.49
GPT	PPL	80.37	214.1	95.56
GPT	LAMBADA	20.28	16.83	20.88
GPT	StoryCloze	59.40	53.10	59.20
GPT	HellaSwag	21.65	22.87	23.08

3.2 Continuing pre-training

We pre-trained three sizes of Dialog-GPT models on a benchmark dialog corpus (Zhang et al., 2020a) to validate our incremental pre-training method, including small, medium, and large versions. We conducted transfers between models of different sizes and the model configuration details are shown in Appendix. We pre-trained the three GPT models for 14.5k steps with the batch size 32, and performed the model transfer from the checkpoints of the 5,000th steps. The testing losses of different models are shown in Figure 3. In general, the loss values can continue declining from a smaller value after transferring. We did not use the distillation-based method to transfer LayerNorm parameters since it is no longer needed to make the model converge to the source model during continuing pre-training. As shown in Table 2, training GPT-m using Incr-Pretrain only costs 7.05k steps to reach a testing loss value comparable with that of 14.5k steps training from scratch. This shows that our method saves about 51% of the training time. However, as more parameters are padded, e.g. from small to large, the amount of training time that can be saved declines, which is likely due to pre-training larger models needing more computation. (Kaplan et al., 2020).

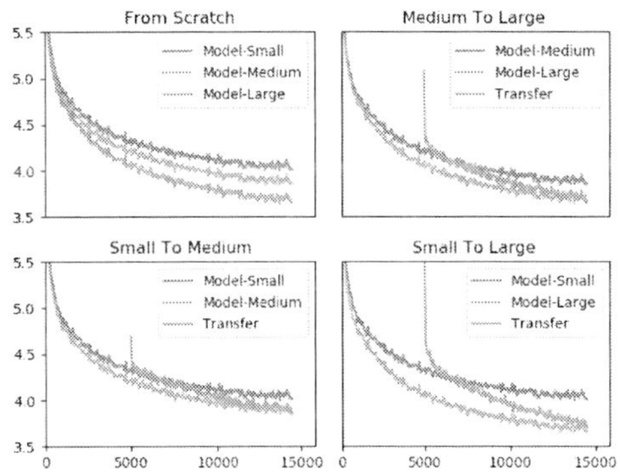

Figure 3: Testing Loss

Table 2: Pre-training time saved. Pre-training steps number when reaching the same loss. ECPN: enlargement coefficient of parameters number, PPTS: percentage of pre-training time saved.

Train Mode	Steps	ECPN	PPTS
GPT-S/M/L from scratch	14.5k	-	-
GPT-S to GPT-M	7.05k	2	51%
GPT-M to GPT-L	8.50k	3	41%
GPT-S to GPT-L	9.50k	6	34%

Further experiments showed that using our transfer method, the amount of pre-training time saved depends on not only the enlargement of the number of parameters but also the padding values. When padding zeros, the testing loss can decline starting from near to the loss value of the source model but converging slowly. Considering previous work (Glorot and Bengio, 2010; He et al., 2015) on parameter initialization, we padded smaller random values instead of zeros, and the convergence can accelerate much. More experimental details are presented in the Appendix.

4 Conclusion

We propose a transfer strategy that can incrementally pre-train language models with acceptable performance decreases. The inference performances show that the target models are comparable with the source models. The continuing pre-training experiment demonstrates that the transfer method is computationally efficient compared to pre-training a large model from scratch. Our future directions will be transferring with different parallel styles and exploring the influence of padding values.

Limitations

During the process of incremental pre-training, although this method effectively reduces training time and achieves test losses close to those obtained by training from scratch, the percentage of pre-training time saved gradually decreases as the number of model parameters increases. For instance, transitioning from a small to a medium-sized model can save approximately 51% of training time, but extending from a small directly to a large model reduces the saving to 34%. This indicates a diminishing marginal return in pre-training efficiency as the model scale expands.

Acknowledgements

This research was supported in part by the Major Key Proiect of PCL (NO.PCL2023A09 and NO.PCL2023AS7-1), the National Key Research and Development Program of China (2021ZD0112905), the National Natural Science Foundation of China (62176076), the Guangdong Provincial Key Laboratory of Novel Security Intelligence Technologies(2022B1212010005), Natural Science Foundation of Guangdong (2023A1515012922), and Shenzhen Foundational Research Funding (JCYJ20220818102415032).

References

Tom B. Brown, Benjamin Mann, Nick Ryder, Melanie Subbiah, Jared Kaplan, Prafulla Dhariwal, Arvind Neelakantan, Pranav Shyam, Girish Sastry, Amanda Askell, Sandhini Agarwal, Ariel Herbert-Voss, Gretchen Krueger, Tom Henighan, Rewon Child, Aditya Ramesh, Daniel M. Ziegler, Jeffrey Wu, Clemens Winter, Christopher Hesse, Mark Chen, Eric Sigler, Mateusz Litwin, Scott Gray, Benjamin Chess, Jack Clark, Christopher Berner, Sam McCandlish, Alec Radford, Ilya Sutskever, and Dario Amodei. 2020. Language models are few-shot learners.

Michael Bugert, Yevgeniy Puzikov, Andreas Rücklé, Judith Eckle-Kohler, Teresa Martin, Eugenio Martinez Camara, Daniil Sorokin, Maxime Peyrard, and Iryna Gurevych. 2017. LSDSem 2017: Exploring Data Generation Methods for the Story Cloze Test. In *Proceedings of the 2nd Workshop on Linking Models of Lexical, Sentential and Discourse-level Semantics (LSDSem)*, pages 56–61, Valencia, Spain. Association for Computational Linguistics.

Mihail Eric and Christopher D. Manning. 2017. Key-value retrieval networks for task-oriented dialogue.

William Fedus, Barret Zoph, and Noam Shazeer. 2021. Switch transformers: Scaling to trillion parameter models with simple and efficient sparsity.

X. Glorot and Y. Bengio. 2010. Understanding the difficulty of training deep feedforward neural networks. *Journal of Machine Learning Research*, 9:249–256.

J. Gou, B. Yu, S. J. Maybank, and D. Tao. 2020. Knowledge distillation: A survey.

Kaiming He, Xiangyu Zhang, Shaoqing Ren, and Jian Sun. 2015. Delving deep into rectifiers: Surpassing human-level performance on imagenet classification.

Jared Kaplan, Sam McCandlish, Tom Henighan, Tom B. Brown, Benjamin Chess, Rewon Child, Scott Gray, Alec Radford, Jeffrey Wu, and Dario Amodei. 2020. Scaling laws for neural language models.

Denis Paperno, Germán Kruszewski, Angeliki Lazaridou, Quan Ngoc Pham, Raffaella Bernardi, Sandro Pezzelle, Marco Baroni, Gemma Boleda, and Raquel Fernández. 2016. The lambada dataset: Word prediction requiring a broad discourse context.

Fabio Petroni, Patrick Lewis, Aleksandra Piktus, Tim Rocktäschel, Yuxiang Wu, Alexander H. Miller, and Sebastian Riedel. 2020. How context affects language models' factual predictions. In *Automated Knowledge Base Construction*.

Alec Radford, Karthik Narasimhan, Tim Salimans, and Ilya Sutskever. 2018. Improving language understanding by generative pre-training.

Mohammad Shoeybi, Mostofa Patwary, Raul Puri, Patrick LeGresley, Jared Casper, and Bryan Catanzaro. 2019. Megatron-lm: Training multi-billion parameter language models using model parallelism.

Thomas Wolf, Lysandre Debut, Victor Sanh, Julien Chaumond, Clement Delangue, Anthony Moi, Pierric Cistac, Tim Rault, Rémi Louf, Morgan Funtowicz, Joe Davison, Sam Shleifer, Patrick von Platen, Clara Ma, Yacine Jernite, Julien Plu, Canwen Xu, Teven Le Scao, Sylvain Gugger, Mariama Drame, Quentin Lhoest, and Alexander M. Rush. 2020. Transformers: State-of-the-art natural language processing. In *Proceedings of the 2020 Conference on Empirical Methods in Natural Language Processing: System Demonstrations*, pages 38–45, Online. Association for Computational Linguistics.

Rowan Zellers, Ari Holtzman, Yonatan Bisk, Ali Farhadi, and Yejin Choi. 2019. Hellaswag: Can a machine really finish your sentence?

Wei Zeng, Xiaozhe Ren, Teng Su, Hui Wang, Yi Liao, Zhiwei Wang, Xin Jiang, ZhenZhang Yang, Kaisheng Wang, Xiaoda Zhang, Chen Li, Ziyan Gong, Yifan Yao, Xinjing Huang, Jun Wang, Jianfeng Yu, Qi Guo, Yue Yu, Yan Zhang, Jin Wang, Hengtao Tao, Dasen Yan, Zexuan Yi, Fang Peng, Fangqing Jiang, Han Zhang, Lingfeng Deng, Yehong Zhang, Zhe Lin, Chao Zhang, Shaojie Zhang, Mingyue Guo, Shanzhi Gu, Gaojun Fan, Yaowei Wang, Xuefeng Jin, Qun Liu, and Yonghong Tian. 2021. Pangu-α: Large-scale autoregressive pretrained chinese language models with auto-parallel computation.

Yizhe Zhang, Siqi Sun, Michel Galley, Yen-Chun Chen, Chris Brockett, Xiang Gao, Jianfeng Gao, Jingjing Liu, and Bill Dolan. 2020a. Dialogpt: Large-scale generative pre-training for conversational response generation. In *ACL, system demonstration*.

Zhengyan Zhang, Xu Han, Hao Zhou, Pei Ke, Yuxian Gu, Deming Ye, Yujia Qin, Yusheng Su, Haozhe Ji, Jian Guan, Fanchao Qi, Xiaozhi Wang, Yanan Zheng, Guoyang Zeng, Huanqi Cao, Shengqi Chen, Daixuan Li, Zhenbo Sun, Zhiyuan Liu, Minlie Huang, Wentao Han, Jie Tang, Juanzi Li, Xiaoyan Zhu, and Maosong Sun. 2020b. Cpm: A large-scale generative chinese pre-trained language model.

Fuzhen Zhuang, Zhiyuan Qi, Keyu Duan, Dongbo Xi, Yongchun Zhu, Hengshu Zhu, Hui Xiong, and Qing He. 2019. A comprehensive survey on transfer learning.

A Experimental Details

In the distillation-based method, we used the Adam optimizer, the learning rate was set as 1E-4, batch size as 8, and the sequence length as 512. Other model configurations are shown in Table 3. We used the KVRET corpus to train the LayerNorm parameters in GPT-2 for 20k steps (about 3 hours on NVIDIA-V100) and discovered that using pseudo inputs constructed by randomly choosing word indices produced better results than those from the real corpus when transferring BERT's LayerNorm parameters.

In the continuing pre-training experiments, we used the Adam optimizer and linear warm-up at the first 100 steps, the learning rate was 1.5E-4, and the batch size was 32. As shown in Figure 4, we compared two padding strategies, padding zeros and padding random values $\theta \sim N(\mu, \sigma^2), \mu = 0, \sigma = 0.02$. When padding zeros, the testing loss starts from that of before-transferring, and it proved that our transferring method is feasible. However, the test loss converged slowly since padding zeros disturbed the initialization distribution. To speed up the incremental training process, we padded random values that follow a normal distribution with small variance instead of zeros. Although padding random values breaks the mathematical equivalence of transferring a bit and the loss value is higher at the beginning, the acceleration for the convergence is remarkable.

Table 3: Model configurations for inference

Model	Heads	Layers	Dim	Total
Source BERT	12	12	768	119.5M
Source GPT	12	12	768	124.4M
Target(LN) BERT	16	12	1024	184.0M
Target(LN) GPT	16	12	1024	203.7M

Table 4: Model configurations for pre-training

Model	Heads	Layers	Dim	Total
Model-Small	6	6	384	15.8M
Model-Medium	8	8	512	32.2M
Model-Large	12	12	768	95.5M

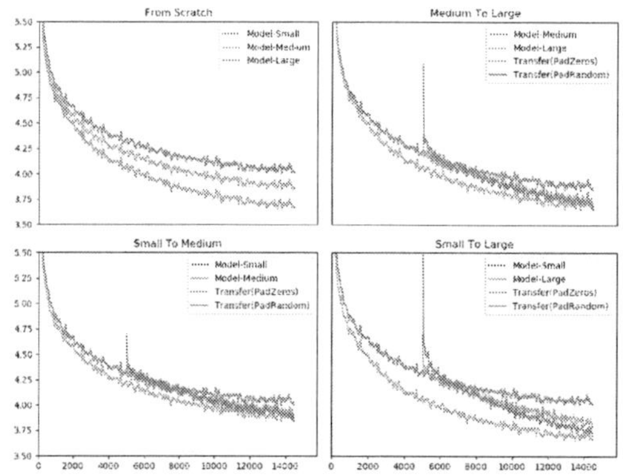

Figure 4: Comparison on the testing loss

B Proof-1

We prove that if we pad random values $\theta \sim N(0, \sigma^2)$ to the parameters of the dense layer, the changes of output can be controlled in $O(\sigma^2)$.

For simplicity of proof, we consider a fully connected layer with a mapping function $F : \mathbb{R}^H \to \mathbb{R}^H$, $F(x) = \mathbf{A}\mathbf{x} + \mathbf{b}$, where $\mathbf{A} \in \mathbb{R}^{H \times H}$, $\mathbf{b} \in \mathbb{R}^H$, and $\mathbf{x}$ is a input column vector such as word embeddings. The padded layer can be expressed alike, i.e. $\hat{F} : \mathbb{R}^D \to \mathbb{R}^D$, $\hat{F}(\hat{\mathbf{x}}) = \hat{\mathbf{A}}\hat{\mathbf{x}} + \hat{\mathbf{b}}$, $\hat{\mathbf{A}} \in \mathbb{R}^{D \times D}$, $\hat{\mathbf{b}} \in \mathbb{R}^D$, where

$$\hat{A} = \begin{pmatrix} \mathbf{A}, & \Lambda_1 \\ \Lambda_2, & \Lambda_3 \end{pmatrix}, \hat{b} = \begin{pmatrix} \mathbf{b} \\ \beta \end{pmatrix}, \hat{\mathbf{x}} = \begin{pmatrix} x \\ \chi \end{pmatrix},$$

All of the $\Lambda_i (i = 1, 2, 3)$, β, and χ are independent and identically distributed to the Gaussian distribution $N(0, \sigma^2)$, while A and x are constants.

$$\hat{F}(\hat{x}) = \begin{pmatrix} \mathbf{A}x + \Lambda_1 \chi + \mathbf{b} \\ \Lambda_2 x + \Lambda_3 \chi + \beta \end{pmatrix}$$

So the mathematical expectation is

$$\begin{aligned} \mathbb{E}(\hat{F}(\hat{\mathbf{x}})) &= \begin{pmatrix} \mathbb{E}(\mathbf{Ax}) + \mathbb{E}(\Lambda_1 \chi) + \mathbb{E}(\mathbf{b}) \\ \mathbb{E}(\Lambda_2 \mathbf{x}) + \mathbb{E}(\Lambda_3 \chi) + \mathbb{E}(\beta) \end{pmatrix} \\ &= \begin{pmatrix} \mathbb{E}(\mathbf{Ax}) + \mathbb{E}(\Lambda_1)\mathbb{E}(\chi) + \mathbb{E}(\mathbf{b}) \\ \mathbb{E}(\Lambda_2)\mathbf{x} + \mathbb{E}(\Lambda_3)\mathbb{E}(\chi) + \mathbb{E}(\beta) \end{pmatrix} \\ &= \begin{pmatrix} \mathbf{Ax} + \mathbf{b} \\ 0 \end{pmatrix} \end{aligned}$$

The variance is

$$\begin{aligned} \mathbb{D}(\hat{F}(\hat{\mathbf{x}})) &= \begin{pmatrix} \mathbb{D}(\mathbf{Ax}) + \mathbb{D}(\Lambda_1 \chi) + \mathbb{D}(\mathbf{b}) \\ \mathbb{D}(\Lambda_2 \mathbf{x}) + \mathbb{D}(\Lambda_3 \chi) + \mathbb{D}(\beta) \end{pmatrix} \\ &= \sigma^2 \begin{pmatrix} (D-H)\sigma^2 E_1 \\ (1 + |\mathbf{x}|^2 + (D-H)\sigma^2) E_2 \end{pmatrix} \end{aligned}$$

where $\mathbf{1}_{(*)}$ is all-one tensor with the same shape of tensor (*) ,$E_1 \in \mathbb{R}^H and E_2 \in \mathbb{R}^{D-H}$ are all-one column vectors, $\mathbf{x}_e^2$ is elements squared of $\mathbf{x}$, and $|\mathbf{x}|^2$ is the square of the norm of $\mathbf{x}$.

Above all, we proved that the padded dense layer maintains the same mathematical expectation with that of before-padding, and the variance is $O(\sigma^2)$. Therefore, if we pad random values with small variances, the output of the model will not change much. Especially, if the variance reduces to zero, the output will be unchanged.

When applying the method to the multi-head attention layer, we can pad random values $\theta \sim N(0, \sigma^2)$ to the parameters of queries, keys, and values. The output of the attention layer is $SoftMax((Q^T + O(\sigma^2)) \times (K + O(\sigma^2))) \times (V + O(\sigma^2))$, so if the variance σ^2 is zero, the output of attention layer remain unchanged after padding.

C Proof-2

We prove that Eq. 2 has no solution. According to the laws of linear equations, we only need to prove that the rank of the coefficient matrix is not equal to that of the augmented matrix. The augmented matrix $\hat{A}_0$ of Eq. 2 is

$$\hat{A}_0 = \begin{pmatrix} \hat{N}^1, & \mathbf{E}, & \mathbf{h}^1 \\ \hat{N}^2, & \mathbf{E}, & \mathbf{h}^2 \\ \vdots & \vdots & \vdots \\ \hat{N}^{|Vocab|}, & \mathbf{E}, & \mathbf{h}^{|Vocab|} \end{pmatrix}$$

Let the last $|Vocab| - 1$ row blocks subtract the first row block, the augmented matrix $\hat{A}_0$ changes to

$$\hat{A}_1 = \begin{pmatrix} \hat{N}^1, & \mathbf{E}, & \mathbf{h}^1 \\ \hat{N}^2 - \hat{N}^1, & \mathbf{0}, & \mathbf{h}^2 - \mathbf{h}^1 \\ \vdots & \vdots & \vdots \\ \hat{N}^{|Vocab|} - \hat{N}^1, & \mathbf{0}, & \mathbf{h}^{|Vocab|} - \mathbf{h}^1 \end{pmatrix}$$

Let the first column block subtract the product of $\hat{N}^1$ and the second column block, and the third column block subtract the product of $\mathbf{h}^1$ and the second column block, the augmented matrix $\hat{A}_1$ changes to

$$\hat{A}_2 = \begin{pmatrix} \mathbf{0}, & \mathbf{E}, & \mathbf{0} \\ \hat{N}^2 - \hat{N}^1, & \mathbf{0}, & \mathbf{h}^2 - \mathbf{h}^1 \\ \vdots & \vdots & \vdots \\ \hat{N}^{|Vocab|} - \hat{N}^1, & \mathbf{0}, & \mathbf{h}^{|Vocab|} - \mathbf{h}^1 \end{pmatrix}$$

After going through a similar matrix transformation, the coefficient matrix A_0 changes to

$$A_2 = \begin{pmatrix} \mathbf{0}, & \mathbf{E} \\ \hat{N}^2 - \hat{N}^1, & \mathbf{0} \\ \vdots & \vdots \\ \hat{N}^{|Vocab|} - \hat{N}^1, & \mathbf{0} \end{pmatrix}$$

We define $\hat{N}^*$ and h^* as follows:

$$\hat{N}^* = \begin{pmatrix} \hat{N}^2 - \hat{N}^1 \\ \hat{N}^3 - \hat{N}^1 \\ \vdots \\ \hat{N}^{|V|} - \hat{N}^1 \end{pmatrix}, h^* = \begin{pmatrix} \mathbf{h}^2 - \mathbf{h}^1 \\ \mathbf{h}^3 - \mathbf{h}^1 \\ \vdots \\ \mathbf{h}^{|V|} - \mathbf{h}^1 \end{pmatrix}$$

According to the calculation of $\hat{N}^*$ and h^*, they are not linearly dependent. Obviously, it is equivalent to that the matrices $\hat{A}_2$ and A_2 have different ranks. So Eq. 2 has no solution.

D Figures

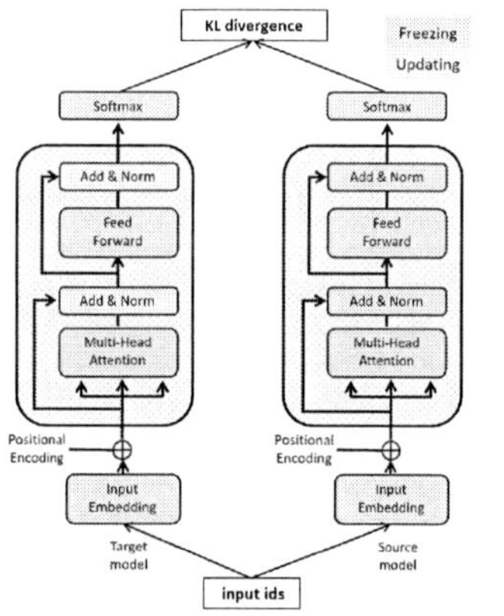

Figure 5: Overview of the distillation-based method

Holistic Exploration on Universal Decompositional Semantic Parsing: Architecture, Data Augmentation, and LLM Paradigm

Hexuan Deng, Xin Zhang, Meishan Zhang*, **Xuebo Liu, Min Zhang**
Institute of Computing and Intelligence, Harbin Institute of Technology, Shenzhen, China
hxuandeng@gmail.com, zhangxin2023@stu.hit.edu.cn
{zhangmeishan, liuxuebo, zhangmin2021}@hit.edu.cn

Abstract

In this paper, we conduct a holistic exploration of Universal Decompositional Semantic (UDS) parsing, aiming to provide a more efficient and effective solution for semantic parsing and to envision the development prospects after the emergence of large language models (LLMs). To achieve this, we first introduce a cascade model for UDS parsing that decomposes the complex task into semantically appropriate subtasks. Our approach outperforms prior models while significantly reducing inference time. Furthermore, to further exploit the hierarchical and automated annotation process of UDS, we explore the use of syntactic information and pseudo-labels, both of which enhance UDS parsing. Lastly, we investigate ChatGPT's efficacy in handling the UDS task, highlighting its proficiency in attribute parsing but struggles in relation parsing, revealing that small parsing models still hold research significance. Our code is available at https://github.com/hexuandeng/HExp4UDS.

1 Introduction

A long-standing objective in natural language understanding is to create a structured graph of linguistic meaning. Various efforts have been made to encode semantic relations and attributes into a semantic graph, such as Abstract Meaning Representation (AMR; Banarescu et al., 2013), Universal Conceptual Cognitive Annotation (UCCA; Abend and Rappoport, 2013), and Semantic Dependency Parsing formalisms (SDP; Oepen et al., 2014, 2016). Recently, Universal Decompositional Semantics (UDS; White et al., 2020) introduced a more advanced hierarchical approach, as shown in Figure 1. It can automatically construct semantic relations from syntactic annotations (Zhang et al., 2017) and annotates semantic attributes following decompositional semantics (Reisinger et al., 2015),

*Corresponding author: Meishan Zhang.

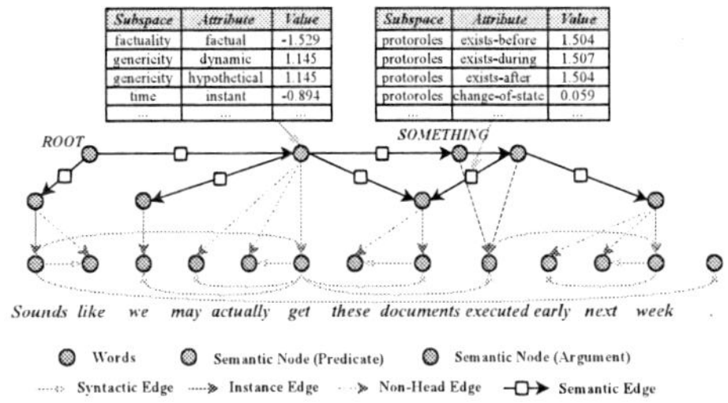

Figure 1: An example of UDS datasets with syntactic tree and semantic graph. Syntactic tree corresponds to the gray nodes and purple edges, semantic relations correspond to the red and blue nodes as well as the yellow edges, and semantic attributes are in the tables.

using only simple questions about words or phrases, significantly lowering the annotation cost.

However, existing solutions on UDS parsing remain suboptimal. Previous parsing approaches mainly rely on the Seq2Seq transduction framework (Stengel-Eskin et al., 2020), suffering from poor parallelism and long inference times that increase with sentence length. In this paper, we propose a cascade architecture that decomposes the complex parsing task into multiple semantically appropriate subtasks. Within each subtask, our model predicts all corresponding sentence elements simultaneously, enhancing parallelism and substantially reducing inference time. Experimental results show that our approach outperforms previous models while maintaining high efficacy during inference.

Furthermore, the structured data and highly automated annotation procedure of the UDS dataset enable low-cost data augmentation schemes. To take full advantage of this, we design two approaches. Firstly, we incorporate syntactic information, proven beneficial to various tasks (Zaremoodi et al., 2018; Zhang et al., 2020; Stengel-Eskin et al., 2021; Deng et al., 2023). We use multi-task training (Caruana, 1997) to incorporate syntactic information, and propose several approaches for further improvement. Secondly, to utilize the automated

Proceedings of the 10th SIGHAN Workshop on Chinese Language Processing (SIGHAN-10), pages 45–57

tool in UDS that derives semantic relation from syntax, PredPatt (Zhang et al., 2017), Stengel-Eskin et al. (2020) attempted to introduce this tool during inference but do not achieve improvements. In contrast, we propose a data augmentation method that effectively exploits PredPatt's capabilities, leading to significant performance gains in relation parsing. Detailed analysis is also provided to guide the design of parsing systems.

Lastly, we reveal the strengths and weaknesses of large language models (LLMs), such as ChatGPT (Bubeck et al., 2023), in semantic parsing tasks, providing guidance for future developments in this field. LLMs have shown considerable performance in various tasks (Jiao et al., 2023; Wu et al., 2023; Li et al., 2023). For semantic parsing tasks, we conduct preliminary experiments on ChatGPT for the UDS task, directly applying it for parsing, as well as using it for data augmentation. Due to poor performance when directly answering by ChatGPT, we carefully design prompts, breaking down questions into small steps. Results show that ChatGPT excels in attribute parsing but struggles in relation parsing, revealing that small, specialized models still hold research significance.

2 Background and Related Work

UDS Datasets Silveira et al. (2014) create a standard set of Stanford dependency annotations for the English Web Treebank (EWT, Silveira et al., 2014) corpus. Subsequently, White et al. (2016) proposed a framework aimed at constructing and deploying cross-linguistically robust semantic annotation protocols and proposed annotations on top of the EWT corpus using PredPatt (White et al., 2016; Zhang et al., 2017). Several works have then been proposed to provide semantic annotations within this framework, including annotations for semantic roles (Reisinger et al., 2015), entity types (White et al., 2016), event factuality (Rudinger et al., 2018), linguistic expressions of generalizations about entities and events (Govindarajan et al., 2019), and temporal properties of relations between events (Vashishtha et al., 2019). All of these efforts culminated in White et al. (2020), which presents the first unified decompositional semantics-aligned dataset, namely, Universal Decompositional Semantics (UDS).

UDS Parser UDS parsing has been conducted using transition-based parser (Chen and Manning, 2014), deep biaffine attention parser (Dozat and Manning, 2017), and sequence-to-graph transductive parser (Stengel-Eskin et al., 2020). The latter significantly outperforms the others by employing an efficient Seq2Seq transduction framework (Sutskever et al., 2014; Bahdanau et al., 2015). This approach is initially used in AMR parsing (Zhang et al., 2019a) and later extended to cover other semantic frameworks, such as UCCA and SDP, by Zhang et al. (2019b) in a unified transduction framework, which predicts nodes and corresponding edges simultaneously in a Seq2Seq manner. For UDS, an attribute module is added by Stengel-Eskin et al. (2020). Syntactic information is incorporated by Stengel-Eskin et al. (2021), yielding further improvements. Despite these attempts, cascade models with better parallelism and shorter inference time have not yet been explored.

Incorporating Syntactic Information Syntactic information has been shown to improve the performance of downstream tasks. Multi-task learning is widely used to incorporate syntactic information. Hershcovich et al. (2018) improve the performance of semantic parsing by using multi-task learning, with syntactic and other semantic parsing tasks serving as auxiliary tasks. Zaremoodi et al. (2018) use syntactic and semantic information to improve the efficacy of two low-resource translation tasks. Stengel-Eskin et al. (2021) employ a single model to parse syntactic and semantic information simultaneously to improve semantic parsing. Graph convolutional networks (GCN, Kipf and Welling, 2017) are also widely used. Marcheggiani and Titov (2017) use GCNs to incorporate syntactic information in neural models and construct a syntax-aware semantic role labeling model. Zhang et al. (2018) propose an extension of GCNs to help relation extraction models capture long-range relations between words. Zhang et al. (2020) presents a syntax-aware approach based on dependency GCNs to improve opinion role labeling tasks.

3 Preliminaries

The UDS dataset comprises three layers of annotations: syntactic annotations, semantic relation annotations, and decompositional semantic attribute annotations at the edge and node levels.

Syntactic Annotation is derived from the EWT dataset, which provides consistent annotation of grammar, including part-of-speech (*POS*) tag, morphological features, and syntactic dependencies, for human languages. These annotations are used to construct the *syntactic tree*, where each word is tied to a node. As shown in Figure 1, the headword of "we" is "get", and the headword of the root "Sounds" is defined as itself.

Semantic Relations consist of predicates, arguments, and edges between them, which forms the *semantic relations*. It is generated by Predpatt tool (Zhang et al., 2017) automatically, using the POS tag and the syntactic tree as input. Each semantic node explicitly corresponds to one word in the sentence called the center word, demonstrated by the instance edge. Additionally, each semantic node is also tied with several non-repetitive words with the non-head edge, which forms a multi-word span. As shown in Figure 1, the leftmost predict node has a span "Sounds like" with the center word "Sounds". Note that two semantic nodes may correspond to the same word in the case of clausal embedding. Then, an extra argument node "SOMETHING" is introduced as the root of the clause, e.g., "executed" corresponds to an extra argument node.

Semantic Attributes consist of crowdsourced decompositional annotations tied to the semantic relations, detailed in §2. These annotations can be further categorized into node-level and edge-level attributes, corresponding to the table on the left and right in Figure 1, respectively. For each node or edge, all attributes have a value in range $[-3, 3]$. Besides, each attribute also has a confidence in range $[0, 1]$, which shows how likely it is to have the property. Following Stengel-Eskin et al. (2020), we discretized it into $\{0, 1\}$ by setting every non-zero confidence to one.

4 Methodology

In this section, we introduce our cascade model and methods to improve its performance.

4.1 Efficient Cascade Model

As discussed in §3, our goal is to predict syntactic information (POS tags and syntactic tree), semantic relations (semantic nodes, edges, and spans), and semantic attributes (node- and edge-level) using a single model. To this end, we propose a cascade model to predict all of these information step by step, as illustrated in Figure 2. In the following paragraphs, we discuss each component of our model in detail. The sentence is represented as $x_1, x_2, \ldots, x_K$, where x_i represents the i-th word. The properties of the node are represented as t, the properties of the edge as e, the $\mathrm{softmax}$ function as σ, and the ReLU function as R.

Encoder Module embeds each word x_i into a corresponding context-aware representation h_i. We utilize three types of encoders: multi-layer BiLSTM, transformer encoder, and Pre-trained Language Model (BERT, Devlin et al., 2019). For BiLSTM and transformer encoder, we employ a similar embedding layer with Stengel-Eskin et al. (2021) to ensure comparability, concatenating GloVe word embeddings (Pennington et al., 2014), character CNN embeddings, and BERT contextual embeddings. For BERT encoder, we use the default subword embeddings layer and mean-pool over all subwords to obtain the word-level representations.

Syntactic Module predicts the part-of-speech (POS) tag and the syntactic tree. For POS, we use a simple multi-layer perceptron (MLP) over each word representation h_i. For the syntactic tree, each word has exactly one syntactic head, so we predict the headword x_i^y and the corresponding edge type t_i^y for each word x_i. We follow the approach of Dozat and Manning (2017) and Zhang et al. (2019b) to use a biaffine parser, formally:

$$\begin{aligned}\hat{x}_i^y &= p(x|x_i)\\ &= \sigma(\mathrm{Biaffine}(R(w_l^y h_i), R(w_r^y h_{1:K})))\\ \hat{t}_i^y &= p(t_y|x_i, \hat{x}_i^h)\\ &= \sigma(\mathrm{Bilinear}(R(w_l^t h_i), R(w_r^t \hat{h}_i^y)))\end{aligned} \tag{1}$$

where $x \in \{x_1, x_2, \ldots, x_K\}$, and $\hat{h}_i^y$ is the representation of the predicted head $\hat{x}_i^y$.

Word Classification Module predicts the semantic edge directly connected to each word (instance, non-head) and the type of the parent node. We simplify this edge prediction problem into a classification problem. We define:

- Type "Φ": Words with no connecting edge;
- Type "Syn": Words connect with a non-head edge;
- Type "Pre": Words connect with an instance edge, and its parent is a predicate node;
- Type "Arg": Words connect with an instance edge, and its parent is an argument node;
- Type "Pre + Arg": Words connect with two instance edges, and their parents are a predicate node and an argument node;

We use a simple MLP for classification, formally:

$$\hat{t}_i^m = p(t_m|x_i) = \sigma(\mathrm{MLP}(h_i)) \tag{2}$$

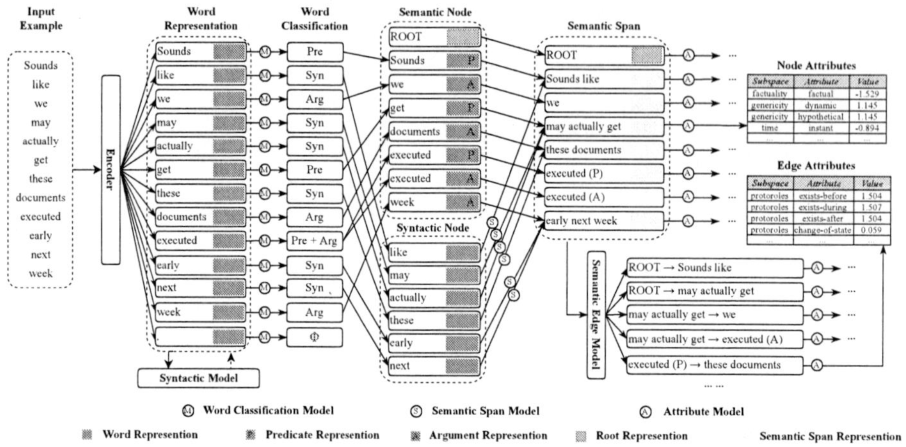

Figure 2: The data flow of our cascade model. The detailed definition of every block is shown in §4.1.

Node Generation predicts the syntactic nodes, semantic nodes, and their corresponding node embeddings. Syntactic nodes $n_1, n_2, \ldots, n_N$ have the label "Syn", and we define the embedding g_i^n of the syntactic node n_i the same as its word embeddings. semantic nodes $m_1, m_2, \ldots, m_M$ have label "Pre", "Arg", or "Pre + Arg". We generate two nodes for "Pre + Arg". So for node embeddings, we first concatenate a node type embedding with its word embedding to distinguish whether it is an argument or predicate node. Then we project it back to the previous dimension with a linear layer to generate the embedding g_i^m of the semantic node m_i. Furthermore, we generate a virtual root node for every sentence with the same trainable embeddings.

Semantic Span Module predicts the semantic span by separating each syntactic node from the semantic nodes. Each syntactic node belongs to exactly one semantic node. So we use the same model as Eq. 1 to predicted which semantic node m_i^h is the syntactic node n_i belongs to, formally:

$$\begin{aligned}\hat{m}_i^h =& p(m|n_i)\\ =&\sigma(\text{Biaffine}(R(w_l^m g_i^n), R(w_r^m g_{1:M}^m)))\end{aligned} \tag{3}$$

where $m \in \{m_1, m_2, \ldots, m_M\}$. The new span level embedding g_i^s for the semantic node m_i is the same as g_i^m by default. Besides, we have also tried to refine g_i^s with the syntactic node embedding, which does not achieve obvious effects.

Semantic Edge Module predicts the edge and the corresponding type $e_{i,j}^m$ between any two semantic nodes. We consider the case where there is no edge between two semantic nodes as a special type Φ. For prediction, we consider the span level embedding for each pair of nodes, formalized as:

$$\begin{aligned}\hat{e}_{i,j}^m =& p(e_m|m_i, m_j)\\ =&\sigma(\text{Biaffine}(R(w_l^e g_i^s), R(w_r^e g_j^s)))\end{aligned} \tag{4}$$

Attribute Module predicts the node-level attributes $\hat{t}_i^a$ for node m_i, and edge-level attributes $\hat{e}_{i,j}^a$ for edge between m_i and m_j. We use the MLP model as the main part, formalized as follows:

$$\begin{aligned}\hat{t}_i^a =& \text{MLP}(g_i^s)\\ v_i =& R(w_l^v g_i^s),\ v_j = R(w_r^v g_j^s)\\ \hat{e}_{i,j}^a =& \text{MLP}([v_i^T W v_j, v_i, v_j])\end{aligned} \tag{5}$$

Here, $W \in \mathbb{R}^{d_v \times d_v \times d_o}$, where d_v is the dimension of v_i and v_j, and d_o is the output dimension. i, j must satisfy $\hat{e}_{i,j}^m \neq \phi$ for $\hat{e}_{i,j}^a$ (edge exists). Note that attributes may not exist, and we use the same model as above to predict the mask of attributes.

Loss To train our models, we use different loss functions depending on the task. For word classification, semantic span, and semantic edge modules, we use cross-entropy loss. For the attribute module, when predicting the mask, we use binary cross-entropy loss. When predicting the attribute, we follow Stengel-Eskin et al. (2020) to use a composite loss function $\mathcal{L}$ for the values, formally:

$$\mathcal{L}_{attr}^{value}\left(\hat{t}, t\right) = \frac{2 \cdot \mathcal{L}_{\text{MSE}}\left(\hat{t}, t\right) \cdot \mathcal{L}_{\text{BCE}}\left(\hat{t}, t\right)}{\mathcal{L}_{\text{MSE}}\left(\hat{t}, t\right) + \mathcal{L}_{\text{BCE}}\left(\hat{t}, t\right)} \tag{6}$$

where $\mathcal{L}_{\text{MSE}}$ is the mean squared loss, $\mathcal{L}_{\text{BCE}}$ is the binary cross-entropy loss, t is the gold attribute, and $\hat{t}$ is our prediction. $\mathcal{L}_{\text{MSE}}$ encourages the predicted attribute value to be close to the true value, while $\mathcal{L}_{\text{BCE}}$ encourages the predicted and reference values to share the same sign.

Finally, to handle this multi-task problem, we use a weighted sum of all the loss functions mentioned above for our model:

$$\begin{aligned}\mathcal{L} =& a_1\mathcal{L}_{cls} + a_2\mathcal{L}_{span} + a_3\mathcal{L}_{edge} + \\ & a_4\mathcal{L}_{attr}^{mask} + a_5\mathcal{L}_{attr}^{value}\end{aligned} \quad (7)$$

where $a_i = 1$ for $i \in [1, .., 5]$, except $a_2 = 2$.

4.2 Incorporating Syntactic Information

By default, we incorporate syntactic information by *multi-task training*. Additionally, we propose *GCN* and *attention* approaches for a more profound incorporation of syntactic information. Specifically, we utilize the syntactic information to update the word embeddings generated by the encoder. The strategies are as follows:

Multi-task Training We add the loss of the syntactic module to term $\mathcal{L}$, which incorporates syntactic information into the shared encoder through back-propagation. We use cross-entropy loss for POS and syntactic tree parsing, formally:

$$\mathcal{L}_{syn} = \mathcal{L} + a_6\mathcal{L}_{pos} + a_7\mathcal{L}_{tree} \quad (8)$$

where $a_6 = a_7 = 1$ during our experiments.

GCN Inspired by the idea of GCN (Kipf and Welling, 2017), we try to encode the predicted adjacency matrix information into the embedding. In the syntactic tree, we consider two types of edges: directed edges from parent nodes (top) to child nodes (bottom), and those with reverse directions. Then we employ a bidirectional GCN consisting of 1) top-down GCN to convey sentence-level information to local words, and 2) bottom-up GCN to convey phrase-level information to the center word. Additionally, to further convey the edge type information corresponding to the current word, we 3) consider the probability distribution of its edge type, and use a GCN-like method to convey this information. With the word embedding matrix $\mathbf{H}$ being the input $\mathbf{H}^{(0)}$, we use a l layer model (with $l = 2$ in practice), formally:

$$\begin{aligned}\mathbf{V}^{(i)} =& [\mathbf{A}_h\mathbf{H}^{(i)}\mathbf{W}_1^{(i)}, \mathbf{A}_h^T\mathbf{H}^{(i)}\mathbf{W}_2^{(i)}, \mathbf{A}_t\mathbf{T}_e\mathbf{W}_3^{(i)}] \\ \mathbf{H}^{(i+1)} =& R(\mathbf{W}_4^{(i)}R(\mathbf{V}^{(i)})) \\ \mathbf{H}_o =& \mathbf{W}_o[\mathbf{H}^{(0)}, \mathbf{H}^{(l)}]\end{aligned} \quad (9)$$

where $\mathbf{A}_h$ is the top-down adjency matrix prediction, $\mathbf{A}_h^T$ is the bottom-up ones, $\mathbf{A}_t$ is the edge type probability distribution, and $\mathbf{T}_e$ is the trainable edge type embedding matrix. Note that the adjacency matrix does not self-loop, so GCN does not convey information about the words themselves. We then combine the original word embeddings $\mathbf{H}^{(0)}$ with the output $\mathbf{H}^{(l)}$ to get the new word embeddings $\mathbf{H}_o$. Under such a design, good results can be achieved with a relatively shallow network.

Attention Word representation after dimension reduction used in syntactic edge and type prediction contains basic information of the syntactic tree (Stengel-Eskin et al., 2021). So we directly use the representations in Eq. 1, which are used in the Biaffine and Bilinear model. Formally:

$$\begin{aligned}\mathbf{V} =& R([w_l^w\mathbf{H}, w_r^w\mathbf{H}, w_l^t\mathbf{H}, w_r^t\mathbf{H}]) \\ \mathbf{H}_o =& \mathbf{W}_o[\mathbf{H}, \mathbf{A}_h\mathbf{V}]\end{aligned} \quad (10)$$

where all the $w_*^*\mathbf{H}$ come from Eq. 1 without recalculation. Compared to the GCN approach, this method uses fewer new parameters and requires less additional calculation, while still preserving the performance improvements achieved by the GCN approach to some extent.

4.3 Data Augmentation with PredPatt

One of the features of the UDS dataset is the strong correlation with external tools PredPatt. Stengel-Eskin et al. (2020) attempt to use an external model to predict the POS tags and syntactic tree on the test dataset, which are then fed directly to PredPatt to obtain the semantic relations. However, the effectiveness of this method is relatively poor, likely due to two issues: 1) the error transmission problem comes from the prediction of the syntactic model, and 2) the rule-based tools are not as robust as neural networks towards noisy inputs.

To address these issues, we propose a data augmentation method. Instead of using it during inference, we use it to augment the data, with only the help of external unlabeled data. Specifically, we first train a model to predict the syntactic tree and POS tag, using the above syntactic model. Next, we use PredPatt to generate pseudo labels (i.e., semantic relations) for the unlabeled data. Finally, we use these data to pre-train our model, and then fine-tune it with a smaller learning rate using the labeled UDS dataset, which achieves significant improvements in relation parsing.

	Strategy	S-P	S-R	S-F1	Attr. ρ	Attr. F1	UAS	LAS	POS
Baseline	LSTM	89.90	85.85	87.83	0.46	60.41	-	-	-
	+ SYN	88.58	87.67	88.12	0.46	61.28	91.44	88.80	-
	TFMR	90.04	87.98	89.19	0.56	67.89	-	-	-
	+ SYN	**91.09**	89.01	90.04	0.56	66.85	92.40	89.96	-
Ours	LSTM	87.75	91.12†	89.79†	0.47†	57.93	-	-	-
	+ SYN	88.82†	92.50†	90.62†	0.46	57.34	91.71	89.10	96.29
	+ SYN + DA	90.00	93.37	91.65	0.33	49.66	92.65	90.51	96.67
	TFMR	88.34	92.90†	90.56†	0.49	59.68	-	-	-
	+ SYN	89.28	93.56†	91.37†	0.49	58.45	92.07	89.65	96.85
	+ SYN + DA	90.15	93.49	91.79	0.42	54.27	**93.03**	90.91	97.10
	BERT	88.90	92.77†	90.79†	**0.60**†	67.02	-	-	-
	+ SYN	89.51	94.18†	91.79†	0.59†	65.78	92.81†	90.73†	**97.18**
	+ SYN + DA	90.27	**94.23**	**92.20**	0.54	63.91	92.98	**90.93**	97.08
LLM	PRED	35.50	51.28	41.96	-	-	-	-	-
	CASC	38.13	53.26	44.44	-	-	-	-	-
	ATTR	-	-	-	-	**80.69**	-	-	-

Table 1: Main results. "LSTM", "TFMR"(Transformer), "BERT" stands for different encoder. We run t-test against the corresponding baseline, and † means significantly higher with > 95% confidence. "+SYN" means GCN approach in §4.2, and "+DA" means the data augmentation method in §4.3. Other abbreviations are detailed in §5.1.

5 Experiment and Analysis

5.1 Experimental Setup

Datasets We conduct experiments on the UDS dataset (White et al., 2020), with 10k valid training sentences. For English monolingual data, we use publicly available News Crawl 2021 corpus (Zhang and Zong, 2016; Wu et al., 2019). In the experiment of the data augmentation method, we first generate the pseudo-targets for all the monolingual data, then filter out the ones that have invalid syntactic and semantic graphs. Finally, we randomly select a 100k corpus subset.

LLMs We explore the direct use of LLMs for parsing tasks. First, for semantic relation parsing, we try two types of prompts: 1) The Predpatt prompt guides the LLM to first generate the syntactic parsing, then follow the instructions of the PredPatt tool step by step to generate the semantic relations (PRED). 2) The cascade approach follows the idea of our model to decompose the UDS parsing (CASC), which first selects the center phrase of the semantic node, and then expands every phrase into a span. To make sure that the center word has only one word, we select it at the last step. Second, for semantic attribute parsing, we provide the sentence and the corresponding node/edge as input, definitions of attribute types as instruction, and conduct experiments under the oracle setting defined in §A.2 (ATTR). As the scale of attribute scoring may vary across conversation rounds, we only let it predict positive or negative.

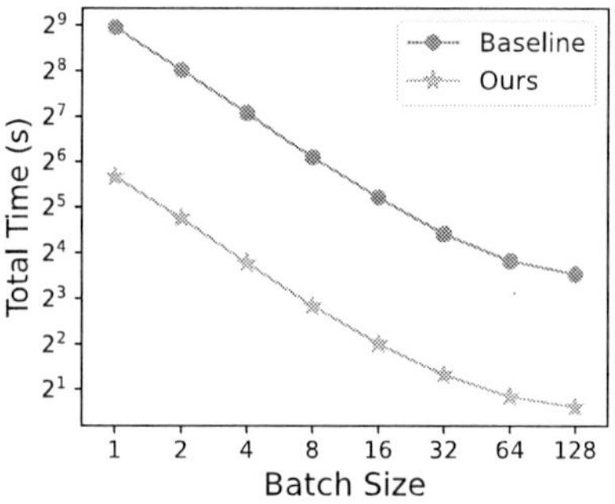

Figure 3: Total inference time for forward propagation of the two models, varying with the batch size. We use logarithmic coordinates for better comparison.

Metrics We follow the setting given by Stengel-Eskin et al. (2021), using S-score for semantic relation prediction, Attribute ρ and F1 for UDS attributes, UAS and LAS for heads and edge types, and POS for part-of-speech.

We use Stengel-Eskin et al. (2021) as the baseline. Details regarding the baseline for comparison, prompts and settings used for ChatGPT, the introduction of metrics, and model training configurations are provided in Appendix A.

5.2 Main Results

We conduct experiments on three types of encoders, as demonstrated in Table 1.

Our cascade model outperforms the baseline model. Under basic settings, our best setting (BERT) significantly improves the baseline (TFMR) in S-F1 (+1.60) and Attr. ρ (+0.04), and

	Strategy	S-P	S-R	S-F1	Attr. ρ	Attr. F1	UAS	LAS	POS
LSTM	Naive	87.75	91.12	89.79	0.47	57.93	-	-	-
	+ Joint	88.21	92.51	90.31	0.45	55.42	91.51	89.07	96.23
	+ Attn.	88.62	92.55	90.54	0.45	57.65	91.95	89.41	96.26
	+ GCN	88.82	92.50	90.62	0.46	57.34	91.71	89.10	96.29
	+ Span	88.45	92.31	90.34	0.47	57.85	91.58	89.08	96.37
TFMR	Naive	88.34	92.90	90.56	0.49	59.68	-	-	-
	+ Joint	88.64	93.53	91.02	0.51	59.56	91.99	89.42	96.60
	+ Attn.	88.82	93.46	91.08	0.49	58.86	91.84	89.35	96.77
	+ GCN	89.28	93.56	91.37	0.49	58.45	92.07	89.65	96.85
	+ Span	88.85	93.19	90.97	0.50	59.46	91.60	89.29	96.71
BERT	Naive	88.90	92.77	90.79	0.60	67.02	-	-	-
	+ Joint	88.87	93.75	91.25	0.60	67.63	92.95	90.79	97.12
	+ Attn.	89.25	94.05	91.59	0.58	66.60	92.94	90.77	97.02
	+ GCN	89.51	94.18	91.79	0.59	65.78	92.81	90.73	97.18
	+ Span	88.95	93.64	91.23	0.59	65.97	92.92	90.74	97.23

Table 2: The effect of different strategies to incorporate syntactic information. "Naive" means no additional syntactic information. "+Joint", "+Attn", and "+GCN" mean incorporating syntactic information using joint training, GCN, and attention in §4.2, separately. "+Span" means refine span embeddings using syntactic nodes.

slightly worse in Attr. F1. The above results are also preserved under +SYN settings (+1.75 and +0.03, respectively). Furthermore, we calculated the total inference time for forward propagation of the two models, averaging on validation and test datasets (about 1.3k sentences). The results are shown in Figure 3 under logarithmic coordinates. Our model significantly reduces the inference time for all batch sizes (9.56 times faster on average). Finally, using additional data augmentation methods, the S-F1 can be further improved (+2.16), which is also held in LSTM and Transformer (+3.53 and +1.75, respectively). The above results show that our model significantly outperforms the baseline.

Syntactic information and data augmentation methods enhance semantic relation parsing. Our model primarily focuses on improving semantic relation parsing, which LLMs are not good at. We summarize the corresponding result in Figure 4. We can see that both the two approaches can significantly improve relation parsing, with +0.88 for syntactic information and +0.62 for the data augmentation method on average. Besides, the improvements are orthogonal to each other and can be used simultaneously, pushing the results of different models towards a similar limit, since lower-performing models experience greater improvements.

The same methods do not benefit attribute prediction. However, our proposed methods for further improvements do not consistently improve the attribute parsing. Attributes derive from crowd-sourced annotation, which is not closely related to

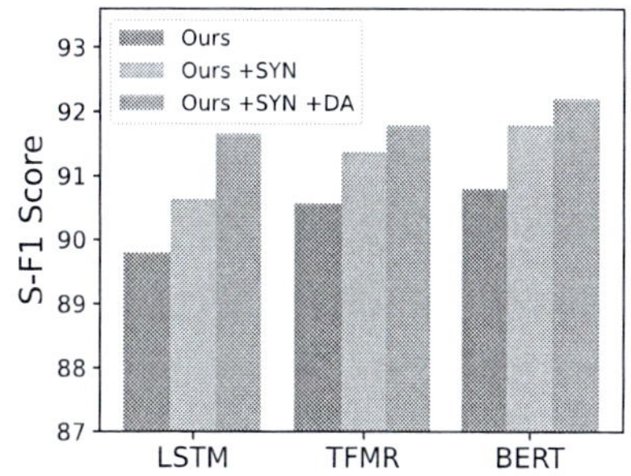

Figure 4: S-F1 score of different encoders. Abbreviations are defined in Table 1.

the syntactic or semantic information. Thus, syntactic information cannot provide useful information for attribute prediction, and using more data to pre-train a better model for semantic relation parsing is harmful to the performance of attribute parsing.

ChatGPT performs poorly on relation parsing but well on attribute parsing. The generated relations of ChatGPT are typically semantically compliant. However, they struggle to follow instructions step by step, resulting in poor performance on relation parsing. Additionally, data augmentation does not work well for the UDS task with ChatGPT, revealing significant distribution shifts for the data generated by ChatGPT. Despite these shortcomings, its high performance on attribute parsing demonstrates promising syntactic understanding. Detailed analysis can be found in Appendix B.

5.3 Exploration on Syntactic Information

We conduct experiments on different ways to join syntactic information into the model, and the re-

Model	In domain	Predpatt	S-P	S-R	S-F1	Δ	UAS	LAS	POS
Ours	×	×	89.34	94.05	91.63	+0.38	93.05	91.01	97.10
Ours	×	✓	90.15	94.28	92.17	+0.92	93.26	91.28	97.17
Ours	✓	×	89.08	94.03	91.49	+0.24	92.62	90.52	97.19
Ours	✓	✓	89.56	94.37	91.90	+0.65	92.88	90.91	97.22
Stanza	×	✓	89.24	94.12	91.62	+0.37	92.96	90.86	97.27
Stanza	✓	✓	89.69	94.24	91.90	+0.65	92.76	90.74	97.10
ChatGPT	×	✓	88.25	93.28	90.70	-0.55	92.38	90.28	96.99
Syntactic Teacher			-	-	-		93.24	91.14	97.54
Semantic Relation Teacher			88.87	93.75	91.25	-	92.95	90.79	97.12

Table 3: The effect of different data augmentation approaches. "Model" means which teacher model to use, "In domain" means whether to select data with closer domain, and "Predpatt" means whether to use an external tool or simply use the distillation method. "Syntactic Teacher" is trained only on syntactic targets, while "Semantic Relation Teacher" on syntactic and semantic relation targets. Both only use multi-task learning methods.

sults are shown in Table 2.

Syntactic information enhances semantic relation parsing. Our experiments show consistent improvements in S-F1 scores across different methods of integrating syntactic information, with +0.48 for SYN, +0.69 for Contact, and +0.88 for GCN, which is also used as our default settings. However, because of the different syntactic foundations arising from different annotation methods, we do not observe a consistent trend of attribute parsing, aligned with findings in Stengel-Eskin et al. (2021).

Incorporating child syntactic information has less impact on the results. We tried to use a better span representation, which uses a self-attention over all words in the span, instead of using only the representation of the center word. However, the attribute prediction does not achieve consistent improvements. This shows that the center word can well represent the semantics of the whole span, and is the default setting in our experiments.

5.4 Exploration on Data Augmentation

We conduct experiments using the data augmentation method under the basic multi-task training method to incorporate syntactic information, and the results are shown in Table 3.

Data augmentation significantly improves the semantic parsing. Under different ways to incorporate syntactic information, the S-F1 consistently improves, with +0.54 on average and +0.92 for best settings (ours without in-domain and with PredPatt), which is used as the default data augmentation method. Besides, our proposed ways to better utilize the external tool also significantly outperform the basic distillation settings, i.e., +0.48 on average, which shows the efficacy of our methods.

How does the in-domain unlabeled data act? We are also curious about how the domain of the datasets influences the results. We follow the idea of Moore and Lewis (2010) to score the unlabeled data by the difference between the score of the in-domain language model and the language model trained from which the unlabeled data is drawn. We refer the reader to the original paper for further details. Results have shown that for our larger models with better generalization, the in-domain data hurt the performance (-0.27). For the smaller model given in Stanza, the in-domain data performs better (+0.28), while both are worse than the results with our models. This shows that the performance of the teacher model is important, and for models with good generalization, always using in-domain data is not a good choice.

6 Conclusion

In this paper, we conduct a holistic exploration of semantic parsing, focusing on Universal Decompositional Semantic (UDS) parsing. First, we develop an efficient cascade model that offers improved performance and reduced training and inference costs. Additionally, we examine data augmentation methods that incorporate syntactic information and employ the PredPatt tool to strengthen the model's syntactic and semantic comprehension. Lastly, we find that ChatGPT performs poorly in relation parsing and data augmentation but excels in attribute parsing. This reveals that small, specialized models still hold research significance in semantic parsing.

Acknowledgements

This work is supported by the National Natural Science Foundation of China (No. 62176180).

Limitations

This study has several limitations. Firstly, due to computational constraints, the research is confined to using small models for solving semantic parsing problems, resulting in a lack of exploration in fine-tuning with LLMs. Better performance may be achieved with LLMs, given their stronger semantic understanding capabilities. Secondly, although the approach proposed in this study can be applied to various semantic parsing tasks, time constraints led to the selection of only one representative dataset for testing. This restricts a more comprehensive analysis of the proposed approach and LLMs' performance. Furthermore, due to cost constraints and regional lockouts, we were unable to include more LLMs, such as GPT-4, GPT-4o, and Claude, in our analysis. Lastly, before the era of LLMs, semantic parsing was able to enhance the performance of various downstream tasks. However, for LLMs, whether fine-tuning LLMs with semantic parsing datasets or providing semantic trees in the context can improve downstream tasks remains to be explored in future work.

References

Omri Abend and Ari Rappoport. 2013. Universal conceptual cognitive annotation (ucca). In *ACL*.

Dzmitry Bahdanau, Kyunghyun Cho, and Yoshua Bengio. 2015. Neural machine translation by jointly learning to align and translate. In *ICLR*.

Laura Banarescu, Claire Bonial, Shu Cai, Madalina Georgescu, Kira Griffitt, Ulf Hermjakob, Kevin Knight, Philipp Koehn, Martha Palmer, and Nathan Schneider. 2013. Abstract meaning representation for sembanking. In *LAW@ACL*.

Sébastien Bubeck, Varun Chandrasekaran, Ronen Eldan, Johannes Gehrke, Eric Horvitz, Ece Kamar, Peter Lee, Yin Tat Lee, Yuanzhi Li, Scott Lundberg, Harsha Nori, Hamid Palangi, Marco Tulio Ribeiro, and Yi Zhang. 2023. Sparks of artificial general intelligence: early experiments with gpt-4. *ArXiv*.

Shu Cai and Kevin Knight. 2013. Smatch: an evaluation metric for semantic feature structures. In *ACL*.

Rich Caruana. 1997. Multitask Learning. *Mach. Learn.*, 28(1):41–75.

Danqi Chen and Christopher D. Manning. 2014. A fast and accurate dependency parser using neural networks. In *EMNLP*.

Hexuan Deng, Liang Ding, Xuebo Liu, Meishan Zhang, Dacheng Tao, and Min Zhang. 2023. Improving simultaneous machine translation with monolingual data. *AAAI*.

Jacob Devlin, Ming-Wei Chang, Kenton Lee, and Kristina Toutanova. 2019. Bert: pre-training of deep bidirectional transformers for language understanding. In *NAACL-HLT*.

Timothy Dozat and Christopher D. Manning. 2017. Deep biaffine attention for neural dependency parsing. In *ICLR*.

Venkata Subrahmanyan Govindarajan, Benjamin Van Durme, and Aaron Steven White. 2019. Decomposing generalization: models of generic, habitual and episodic statements. *Trans. Assoc. Comput. Linguistics*.

Daniel Hershcovich, Omri Abend, and Ari Rappoport. 2018. Multitask parsing across semantic representations. In *ACL*.

Wenxiang Jiao, Wenxuan Wang, Jen-tse Huang, Xing Wang, and Zhaopeng Tu. 2023. Is chatgpt a good translator? a preliminary study. *ArXiv*.

Thomas N. Kipf and Max Welling. 2017. Semi-Supervised Classification with Graph Convolutional Networks. In *ICLR (Poster)*.

Bo Li, Gexiang Fang, Yang Yang, Quansen Wang, Wei Ye, Wen Zhao, and Shikun Zhang. 2023. Evaluating chatgpt's information extraction capabilities: an assessment of performance, explainability, calibration, and faithfulness. *ArXiv*.

Diego Marcheggiani and Ivan Titov. 2017. Encoding sentences with graph convolutional networks for semantic role labeling. In *EMNLP*.

Robert C. Moore and William D. Lewis. 2010. Intelligent selection of language model training data. In *ACL*.

Stephan Oepen, Marco Kuhlmann, Yusuke Miyao, Daniel Zeman, Silvie Cinková, Dan Flickinger, Jan Hajic, Angelina Ivanova, and Zdenka Uresová. 2016. Towards comparability of linguistic graph banks for semantic parsing. In *LREC*.

Stephan Oepen, Marco Kuhlmann, Yusuke Miyao, Daniel Zeman, Dan Flickinger, Jan Hajic, Angelina Ivanova, and Yi Zhang. 2014. Semeval 2014 task 8: broad-coverage semantic dependency parsing. In *SemEval@COLING*.

Jeffrey Pennington, Richard Socher, and Christopher D. Manning. 2014. Glove: global vectors for word representation. In *EMNLP*.

Barbara Plank, Héctor Martínez Alonso, Zeljko Agic, Danijela Merkler, and Anders Søgaard. 2015. Do dependency parsing metrics correlate with human judgments? In *CoNLL*.

Dee Ann Reisinger, Rachel Rudinger, Francis Ferraro, Craig Harman, Kyle Rawlins, and Benjamin Van Durme. 2015. Semantic proto-roles. *Trans. Assoc. Comput. Linguistics*.

Rachel Rudinger, Aaron Steven White, and Benjamin Van Durme. 2018. Neural models of factuality. In *NAACL-HLT*.

Abigail See, Peter J. Liu, and Christopher D. Manning. 2017. Get to the point: summarization with pointer-generator networks. In *ACL*.

Natalia Silveira, Timothy Dozat, Marie-Catherine de Marneffe, Samuel R. Bowman, Miriam Connor, John Bauer, and Christopher D. Manning. 2014. A gold standard dependency corpus for english. In *LREC*.

Elias Stengel-Eskin, Kenton W. Murray, Sheng Zhang, Aaron Steven White, and Benjamin Van Durme. 2021. Joint universal syntactic and semantic parsing. *Trans. Assoc. Comput. Linguistics*.

Elias Stengel-Eskin, Aaron Steven White, Sheng Zhang, and Benjamin Van Durme. 2020. Universal decompositional semantic parsing. In *ACL*.

Ilya Sutskever, Oriol Vinyals, and Quoc V. Le. 2014. Sequence to sequence learning with neural networks. In *NIPS*.

Siddharth Vashishtha, Benjamin Van Durme, and Aaron Steven White. 2019. Fine-grained temporal relation extraction. In *ACL*.

Aaron Steven White, Dee Ann Reisinger, Keisuke Sakaguchi, Tim Vieira, Sheng Zhang, Rachel Rudinger, Kyle Rawlins, and Benjamin Van Durme. 2016. Universal decompositional semantics on universal dependencies. In *EMNLP*.

Aaron Steven White, Elias Stengel-Eskin, Siddharth Vashishtha, Venkata Subrahmanyan Govindarajan, Dee Ann Reisinger, Tim Vieira, Keisuke Sakaguchi, Sheng Zhang, Francis Ferraro, Rachel Rudinger, Kyle Rawlins, and Benjamin Van Durme. 2020. The universal decompositional semantics dataset and decomp toolkit. In *LREC*.

Haoran Wu, Wenxuan Wang, Yuxuan Wan, Wenxiang Jiao, and Michael Lyu. 2023. Chatgpt or grammarly? evaluating chatgpt on grammatical error correction benchmark. *ArXiv*.

Lijun Wu, Yiren Wang, Yingce Xia, Tao Qin, Jianhuang Lai, and Tie-Yan Liu. 2019. Exploiting monolingual data at scale for neural machine translation. In *EMNLP/IJCNLP*.

Poorya Zaremoodi, Wray L. Buntine, and Gholamreza Haffari. 2018. Adaptive knowledge sharing in multi-task learning: improving low-resource neural machine translation. In *ACL*.

Bo Zhang, Yue Zhang, Rui Wang, Zhenghua Li, and Min Zhang. 2020. Syntax-aware opinion role labeling with dependency graph convolutional networks. In *ACL*.

Jiajun Zhang and Chengqing Zong. 2016. Exploiting source-side monolingual data in neural machine translation. In *EMNLP*.

Sheng Zhang, Xutai Ma, Kevin Duh, and Benjamin Van Durme. 2019a. Amr parsing as sequence-to-graph transduction. In *ACL*.

Sheng Zhang, Xutai Ma, Kevin Duh, and Benjamin Van Durme. 2019b. Broad-coverage semantic parsing as transduction. In *EMNLP/IJCNLP*.

Sheng Zhang, Rachel Rudinger, and Benjamin Van Durme. 2017. An evaluation of predpatt and open ie via stage 1 semantic role labeling. In *IWCS*.

Yuhao Zhang, Peng Qi, and Christopher D. Manning. 2018. Graph convolution over pruned dependency trees improves relation extraction. In *EMNLP*.

A Supplementary Experimental Setup

A.1 Experimental Configurations

Model Training Our model is trained on one NVIDIA A30 Tensor Core GPU with a batch size of 16 and a dropout rate of 0.3. We fix BERT parameters for LSTM and transformer encoders and keep them trainable when BERT itself is the encoder. For the majority of the training process, we set the learning rate to 2e-4, while for BERT encoder, we set it to 1e-5. For a fair comparison, we use a linear projection of the output of all the encoders to unify the output dimension to 1024. We run each model five times under different seeds in the main table and show the average score.

Baseline We use Stengel-Eskin et al. (2021) as the baseline. It first employs GloVe word embeddings (Pennington et al., 2014), character CNN embeddings, and BERT (Devlin et al., 2019) to generate the context-aware representations of the input sentence. Then, it generates each edge with a decoder in an autoregressive way, following the idea of a pointer-generator network (See et al., 2017). After that, it uses a deep biaffine (Dozat and Manning, 2017) graph-based parser to create edges. Node- and edge-level attributes are then predicted after every step, with a multi-layer perception for node attributes and a deep biaffine for edge attributes. Besides, the introduction of syntactic information is preliminarily tried, and we only report their optimal results for each metric.

LLMs For ChatGPT, we conduct experiments in the dialog box, using the ChatGPT Mar 23 Version in 2023. We provide details on the prompts used for evaluating ChatGPT under UDS tasks in Figure 5.

A.2 Metrics

We follow the setting given by Stengel-Eskin et al. (2021), detailed as follows.

S-score This metric measures performance on the semantic relation prediction task. Following the Smatch metric (Cai and Knight, 2013), which uses a hill-climbing approach to find an approximate graph matching between a reference and predicted graph, S-score (Zhang et al., 2017) provides precision (S-P), recall (S-R), and F1 score (S-F1) for nodes, edges, and attributes. We follow Stengel-Eskin et al. (2021) and evaluate the S-score for nodes and edges only, which evaluates against full UDS arborescences with linearized syntactic subtrees included as children of semantic heads.

Attribute ρ & F1 For UDS attributes, we use the pearson correlation ρ (Attr. ρ) between the predicted attributes at each node and the gold annotations in the UDS corpus. We also use F1-score (Attr. F1) to measure whether the direction of the attributes matches that of the gold annotations. We binarized the attribute with threshold value $\theta = 0$ for gold attributes, and tune θ for predicted ones per attribute type on validation data. Both of them are obtained under an "oracle" setting, where the gold graph structure is provided.

Syntactic Metric We follow Plank et al. (2015) to use Unlabeled Attachment Score (UAS) to compute the fraction of words with correctly assigned heads, and Labeled Attachment Score (LAS) to compute the fraction with correct heads and edge types. While for part-of-speech (POS), we simply use the accuracy of prediction.

B Exploration on LLM Paradigm

ChatGPT performs poorly on relation parsing. For semantic relation parsing, we use the prompt given in §A.1 3 times, which generates 9 different results. We filter out invalid output (no table or table with incorrect headers) and select the best result for each sentence. There are still 11.04% and 0.37% of the sentences that do not have correct results for PRED and CASC, respectively, which are filtered out. Despite this favorable setting, it still achieved poor results. Under our observation, the generated relations of LLMs are typically semantically compliant. However, they struggle to follow the instructions step by step, leading to outputs that often do not meet our requirements, and repetitions and incorrect summarizations in the table also commonly occur. As a result, LLMs perform poorly on relation parsing, especially in precision, and complex post-processing constructed by professionals is highly required.

ChatGPT performs perfectly on attribute parsing. For semantic attribute parsing, we only run ChatGPT once. 3.03% of the sentences do not have correct results and are filtered out. Results show that ChatGPT significantly outperforms the small models, achieving a +12.80 increase in Attribute F1 scores compared to the best model. We think that for ChatGPT, which is well-aligned with humans, it is easier to predict the attributes given by

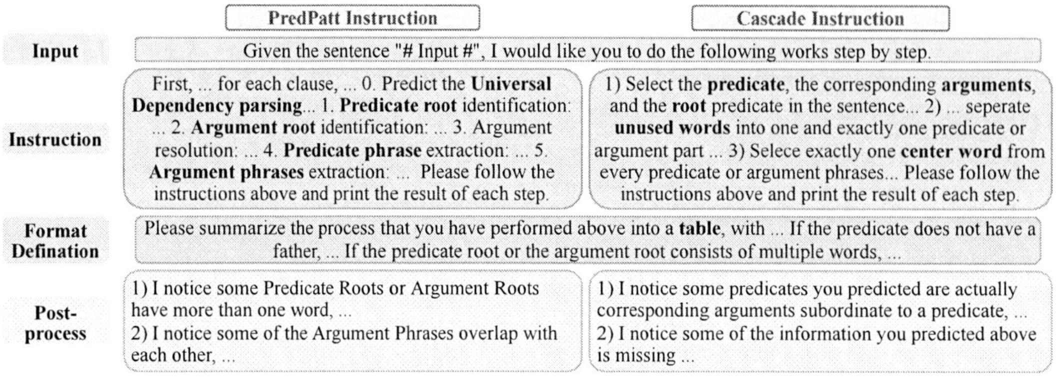

Figure 5: The prompt for semantic relation parsing for ChatGPT. For each generation, we first input the input and instruction, then input the format definition to get the prediction. Finally, we input the post-process part one by one to generate better predictions, i.e., three predictions for a sentence in a single conversation.

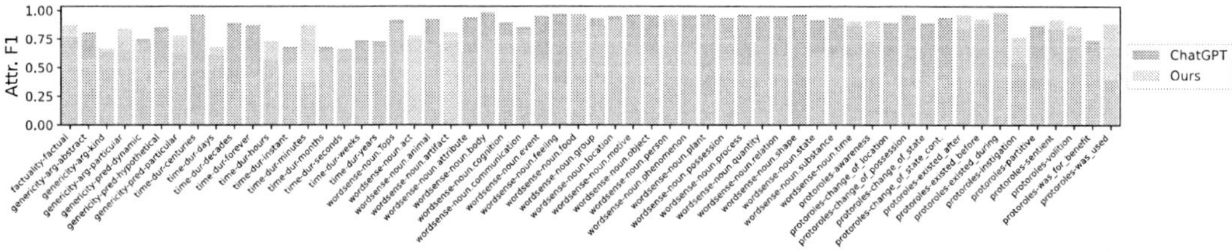

Figure 6: Attribute F1 score for each UDS attribute using ChatGPT (80.69 on average) or using our basic BERT model (67.02 on average). The x-axis is the UDS attribute name, with the ones beginning with "protoroles" being the edge-level attributes (the rightmost 14 attributes), and other attributes are at the node level.

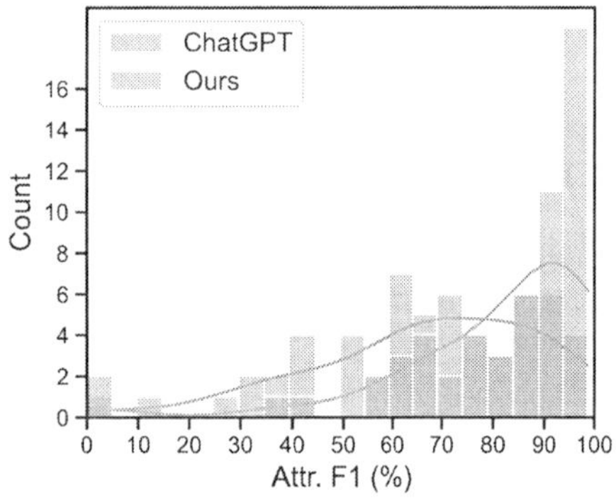

Figure 7: The Attribute F1 score distribution across each UDS attribute. "ChatGPT" stands for prompted with ATTR settings, and "Ours" represents our best strategy under attribute prediction.

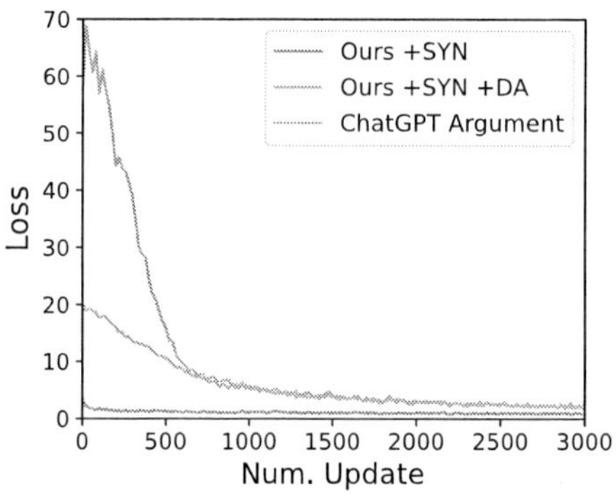

Figure 8: Loss function curve over the first 3k steps. The defination of "+SYN" and "+DA" are align with ones in Table 1.

human annotators rather than the long logical chain reasoning task. In addition, only need to predict positive and negative without considering the pearson correlation is also one of its advantages.

For further verification, we calculate the Attribute F1 scores for all attributes in Figure 6. We can observe that ChatGPT performs well on most of the attributes when compared to our model, with 60.34% and 25.86% of the attributes respectively having F1 scores above 85%. Furthermore, ChatGPT performs perfectly on word-sense attributes, achieving an F1 score of 86.99. In contrast, our models do not display significantly superior results, with an F1 score of 68.49. For a clearer comparison, we have compiled the distribution of Attribute F1 values for different attributes for our best-trained small model and ChatGPT, as shown in Figure 7.

We can see that ChatGPT scores higher on a greater number of attributes. We believe that with more detailed guidance and rigorous post-processing, LLMs have the potential to replace humans in annotation tasks.

How does data augmentation with ChatGPT act? We investigate the generation of new data for downstream model training, which is widely used. We use the random token lists as input rather than the unlabeled data, and let LLM generate the POS tag and syntax tree, which are further used to generate pseudo-labels, following §4.3. Since Universal Dependencies is a widely used dataset and contains both of the required information, a simple prompt can be used. For ChatGPT generation, we select a 10k corpus subset.

LLMs do not perform well in semantic relation generation, and directly using external tools to assist the test set is not effective (Stengel-Eskin et al., 2020), so it is natural to think of using LLM to augment the data in a similar way. We used the zero-shot settings, detailed in §A.1. However, the performance has declined. For further analysis, we propose the training loss for the first 3k updates for different models in Figure 8. We can see that our data augmentation method can significantly lower the initial training loss, which shows that similar data distribution is shared between our proposed pseudo-labeled data and the training data. However, the initial loss of ChatGPT argumentation is even higher than random initializing (Ours +SYN). This shows significant distribution shifts for the data generated by ChatGPT, which shows the need for more detailed prompts and ways to select properly generated data.

Who Responded to Whom: The Joint Effects of Latent Topics and Discourse in Conversation Structure

Lu Ji[1*], Lei Chen[2*], Jing Li[3†], Zhongyu Wei[2,4], Qi Zhang[1], Xuanjing Huang[1]
[1] School of Computer Science, Fudan University, China
[2] School of Data Science, Fudan University, China
[3] Department of Computing, The Hong Kong Polytechnic University, Hong Kong, China
[4] Research Institute of Intelligent and Complex Systems, Fudan University, China
[1,2,4]{17210240034, chenl18, zywei, qi_zhang, xjhuang}@fudan.edu.cn
[3]jing-amelia.li@polyu.edu.hk;

Abstract

Vast amount of online conversations are produced on a daily basis, resulting in a pressing need to automatic conversation understanding. As a basis to structure a discussion, we identify the responding relations in the conversation discourse, which link response utterances to their initiations. To figure out who responded to whom, here we explore how the consistency of topic contents and dependency of discourse roles indicate such interactions, whereas most prior work ignore the effects of latent factors underlying word occurrences. We propose a neural model to learn latent topics and discourse in word distributions, and predict pairwise initiation-response links via exploiting topic consistency and discourse dependency. Experimental results on both English and Chinese conversations show that our model significantly outperforms the previous state of the arts.

[C_1] I am aware that you can **thank** them in **private argument** but what does *that* matter? [C_2] The most important part of my argument is that it **hurts** literally nobody. [C_3] All they are doing is trying to be **polite**. [C_4] Some people gild comments anonymously and do not respond to the **private messages**, so the gildee never knows who gave them gold. [C_5] Note: for the purposes of my argument, assume I am talking about comments edited in such a way as to say **thanks** for the gold!
[R] We are all aware that you can do *that*, but sometimes people like to **express gratitude publicly**.

Figure 1: A Reddit conversation snippet. C_1 and R is an initiation-response pair while C_2 to C_5 are the other four candidates. **Topic words** reflecting the discussion points "public gratitude expression" are in bold. The blue and italic "*that*" occurring in both C_1 and R imply R's possible intention to answer C_1's question.

1 Introduction

The growing popularity of online platforms have resulted in the revolution of interpersonal communications. Individuals now engage in diverse forms of online conversations to exchange viewpoints and share ideas. It allows users to access an abundance of fresh materials, whereas the explosive growth of online texts — essentially conversational and usually in multiple threads (Wang and Rosé, 2010) — has also hindered human capability to find the information needed. There consequently presents a pressing need to develop conversation understanding methods to automatically digest massive texts and complex interactions therein. To that end, it is crucial to capture the interactions of who responded to whom — the base to build and understand the conversation structure, as pointed out in many previous studies (Wang and Rosé, 2010; Zeng et al., 2019b). By reflecting how participants interact with each other, such structure has shown useful to predict users' online social activities (Zeng et al., 2019b), summarize key discussion topics (Qin et al., 2017; Li et al., 2018a), measure argument persuasiveness (Ji et al., 2018a), and so forth.

To date, despite of the extensive efforts on user interaction modeling, many of them employ user-annotated in-reply-to signals, such as *@-mention* on Twitter (Li et al., 2018a; Zeng et al., 2019b). Nonetheless, such labels are usually unavailable or unreliable (Du et al., 2017; He et al., 2019), especially for online conversations in informal styles. Other studies assume utterances only respond to their chronological neighbors (Jiao et al., 2018; Zhao et al., 2018), largely ignoring the long-distance interactions prominent in online conversations (Wang and Rosé, 2010). All these concerns lay down our objective to investigate who responded to whom in conversation contexts.

Following previous practice (Schegloff, 2007), we define our task to predict pairwise initiation utterances and their responses in an online con-

[*]Lu Ji and Lei Chen have equal contribution.
[†]Corresponding author.

Proceedings of the 10th SIGHAN Workshop on Chinese Language Processing (SIGHAN-10), pages 58–68
August 16, 2024 ©2024 Association for Computational Linguistics

versation (henceforth **initiation-response pairs**), where an initiation sets up an expectation earlier and its response later react to it in process of a discussion. To illustrate our task, Figure 1 shows an example response R and the other five utterances C_1 to C_5 from R's previous post in a Reddit conversation. Our goal is to identify which utterance from C_1 to C_5 is R's initiation. As can be seen, R is most likely to respond to C_1 for two possible reasons: First, they both focus on the topic of *public gratitude expression* (as topic words "*thank*", "*public*", "*gratitude*" are mentioned); Second, C_1 raises a question (signaled by "*what*" and the question mark "*?*") that can be well answered by R (via echoing the pronoun "*that*").

Here, we examine two latent factors that implicitly link an initiation and its response — the consistency of the topics they center around (henceforth **topic consistency**) and the dependency of their discourse roles (henceforth **discourse dependency**). Our intuition is that responses tend to follow the points pushed forward in their initiations (such as *public gratitude expression* in Figure 1) and their discourse roles are likely to exhibit some dependency in interactions, such as an answer responding to an initiated question (like R answering C_1 in Figure 1) and an argument followed by another argument in a back-and-forth debate. To the best of our knowledge, *we are the first to analyze the effects of topics and discourse in conversational responding behavior*, while previous work predict initiation-response pairs without modeling such latent factors embedded in the relations (Du et al., 2017; He et al., 2019).

To learn topics and discourse, we separate two word distributions for representing each of them. The latent variables are inferred with a neural architecture in an unsupervised manner (Zeng et al., 2019a), which enables topic and discourse inference without either manually annotated data (Zhao et al., 2017) or expertise involvements to customize model inference (Li et al., 2018b). Afterwards, two neural modules are employed, one to capture topic consistency and the other discourse dependency, both aim to explore the implicit links of a response and a candidate initiation. The learned representations are hence coupled to predict how likely the two utterances form an initiation-response pair.

In an empirical study, we carry out extensive experiments on two conversation datasets, one contains English argumentative discussions on Reddit (from the ChangeMyView subreddit), and the other Chinese customer service dialogues from e-commerce platform *Wangwang*. Both of them will be released upon publication as part of our work. The experimental results show that our model significantly outperforms state-of-the-art methods from previous work. For example, we achieve 79.02 MRR on the Wangwang dialogues compared with 72.69 produced by He et al. (2019). In extensive analyses on latent topics and discourse, we find that meaningful representations can be learned by our model and both topics and discourse may contribute to indicate initiation-response pairs. Lastly, we show that our learned representation to indicate initiation-response relations can further benefit to identify persuasive arguments in social media debates.

2 Study Design

2.1 Task Formulation

We define initiation-response pairs following Schegloff (2007) and refer both initiations and responses to conversation utterances from different participants. In a discussion flow, responses appear and react to the points raised earlier in their initiations and hence hold responding relations with them.

In previous practice, an initiation-response pair is defined to cover a wide range of user interactions, such as questions and answers, quotations and replies, blames and denials, all existing in diverse genres of conversations (Wang and Rosé, 2010). In empirical study, we will experiment on quotation-reply pairs in forum discussions (Wang and Rosé, 2010) and question-answer pairs in customer service dialogues (He et al., 2019). We thus describe these two types of initiation-response relations in the following.

Quotations and Replies. Many popular online forums, such as Reddit and Usenet, allow users to quote utterances from previous messages to indicate what they are commenting on. Such quoting behaviors provide us with abundant user-annotated data to extensively study initiation-response relations in forum conversations.

Here we are interested in a specific type of online conversations — argumentative dialogues from the *ChangeMyView* subreddit (henceforth *CMV*) (Tan et al., 2016), exhibiting rich user interactions in back-and-forth social media debates. In *CMV*, an opinion holder (*OH*) first initiates a debate with their viewpoints and challengers then engage in, raising their arguments in comments and attempting to change *OH*'s mind. As challengers carry on the persuasion process, they usually quote *OH*'s utterances to explicitly point out what they are arguing against, followed by their own responsive arguments (replies). An example quotation in a *CMV* comment is shown in Figure 2, where the reply utterance questions the *positive aspects of early Americans* — a point initialized by *OH*.

Original Post from an Opinion Holder:
... Strong family values in society lead to great results. *I want society to take positive aspects of the early Americans and implement that into society.* This would be a huge improvement than what we have now. ...
Comment from a Challenger:
> I want society to take positive aspects of the early Americans and implement that into society. What do you believe those aspects to be? ...

Figure 2: An original post and its comment from the *CMV* subreddit. The comment quotes an utterance from the original post (in italic), followed by its reply utterance.

Questions and Answers. We also examine questions and answers in customer service dialogues on Chinese e-commerce platform *Wangwang* (henceforth *CS*) (He et al., 2019). In a dialogue thread, customers may raise multiple questions in a sequence of utterances and the seller's answers may appear in the following turns. Our goal is to pair a question from the customer's utterances and an answer from the seller's. Figure 3 shows a customer service dialogue excerpt centered around *a dress in winter style*. We observe two question-answer pairs therein focusing on the *product quality* and *dress style*, respectively.

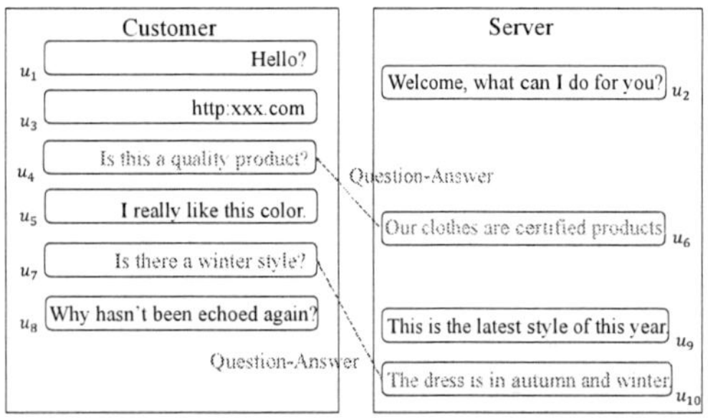

Figure 3: A Wangwang dialogue between a customer (on the left) and a seller (from the server team on the right) from He et al. (2019). Pairwise questions and answers are linked and displayed with the same color.

Pairwise Ranking. To explore how responses and initiations interact with each other, here we follow previous settings to formulate our task into a pairwise ranking problem (Wang and Rosé, 2010). It is shown that the determination of who responds to whom largely relies on subjective judgements (without explicit indicators); thus we view the pairing of responses to their initiations from a comparison perspective (instead of answering "yes or no" in binary classification fashion).

Specifically, given a response utterance r, we rank a set of candidate utterances with one positive initiation q^+ and u negative ones $q_1^- \sim q_u^-$. In practice, we measure a matching score $S(q, r)$ to indicate the likelihood of q as r's initiation and the one with the highest score will be considered as r's predicted initiation. In Section 2.2, we will describe how we form the candidate initiations.

2.2 Data Collection and Analysis

Data Collection. The *CMV* dataset gathers social media arguments, whose raw data is released by Tan et al. (2016). For each discussion, we only examine the context of an *OH*'s post and a challenger's comment to focus on the quotation-reply relations therein. In challenger's comments, we form a quotation and the utterance right after it to be an initiation-response pair. The rest utterances in the quoted post (from *OH*) are used as the negative instances, and the samples are randomly selected with a cap at 4 to avoid unbalanced labels. In addition, the quotation of the *OH*'s post is removed from the challenger's comment when forming an instance.

The *CS* dataset is annotated and released with He et al. (2019). The newest 4 consecutive customer's utterances (skipping the positive initiation) before a seller's response serve as the negative instances. Here the candidate number is also capped at 4 for comparable results with *CMV*.

	CMV Dataset	CS Dataset
# of utt. per conv	21.2±15.6	9.6±2.8
# of words per conv	403.1±292.5	130.8±73.1
# of convs	7,937	4,277
# of words per r	19.7±6.0	15.0±20.8
# of words per q^+	20.6±6.2	6.5±4.3
# of words per q^-	16.5±5.0	11.2±18.7
max # of pairs	14	7
avg. # of pairs	1.1±0.3	1.7±1.1

Table 1: Data statistics. Means and standard deviations appear before and after ±. utt. and r refers to utterance and response, while q^+ and q^- for positive and negative initiation. # of pairs represents the number of initiation-response pairs per conversation.

Data Analysis. Table 1 shows the data statistics, where the two datasets exhibit different characteristics. *CMV* arguments contain more utterances and richer contexts (with more words) compared with *CS*. For initiation-response pairs, *CMV* challengers only quote once on average while the maximum number is 14 (to extensively criticize *OH*'s weak points); whereas the number of question-answer pairs are diverse in *CS* dataset, ranging from 1 to 7 with 1.1 standard deviation.

3 Learning Topics and Discourse Effects for Initiation-Response Prediction

The overall architecture of our model is shown in Figure 4 (a). It takes an initiation candidate q, a response r, and their corresponding contexts c_q and c_r as inputs. The outputs are matching scores indicating how likely r responds to q.

3.1 Latent Topics and Discourse Modeling

Inspired by previous efforts in neural topic models (Miao et al., 2017; Zeng et al., 2019a), we adopt variational autoencoder (VAE) (Kingma and Welling, 2013; Rezende et al., 2014) to learn latent topics and discourse. It allows their associated word distributions to be learned in neural architecture and end-to-end training with other components in a deep learning framework. The corresponding networks are illustrated in Figure 4 (b). In below, we first describe how we model the topics, followed by the process to learn discourse.

Latent Topics. We first assume there are K latent topics in the corpus, each represented by a word distribution $\Phi^T_k (k = 1, 2, ..., K)$ over the vocabulary V. The latent topics of each utterance is defined as z and generated from the topic composition of its context c. Here we learn utterance-level topics in its conversation context assuming that utterances in a discussion excerpt tend to focus on similar topics. It allows the modeling of rich patterns of word statistics for topic inference.

The following process presents how to generate an utterance x in context of c. Here, we adopt the bag-of-words assumption of most latent topic models (Blei et al., 2002; Miao et al., 2017) and generate x in its bag of words (BoW) form x^{BoW}.

- Draw the latent topic $z \sim N(\mu, \sigma^2)$
- c's topic mixture $\theta = softmax(f_\theta(z))$
- For the n-th word in x:
  - $\beta_n = softmax(f_{\Phi^T}(\theta))$
  - Draw the word $w_n \sim Multi(\beta_n)$

where $f_*(\cdot)$ is a neural perceptron (fully connected layer). The weight matrix of $f_{\Phi^T}(\cdot)$ (after the softmax normalization) is viewed as the topic-word distributions Φ^T.

The prior parameters μ and σ are estimated from conversation c's bag of words c^{BoW}:

$$\mu = f_\mu(f_e(c^{BoW})), \log\sigma = f_\sigma(f_e(c^{BoW})) \quad (1)$$

f_μ, f_e and f_σ are neural perceptron defined above.

As can be seen, the entire topic modeling process follows a VAE fashion — for each utterance x, we first encode its latent topic z from the conversation context c (in BoW form c^{BoW}) and then reconstruct its BoW (x^{BoW}) via decoding.

Latent Discourse. Similar to latent topics, we represent latent discourse with word distributions Φ^D_d $(d = 1, 2, ..., D)$ and D denotes the number of discourse roles observed from the corpus.

Following Ritter et al. (2010), we assume each utterance x reflects only one discourse role d (to signal its dialogue act). It is hence represented by a D-dimensional one-hot vector over the discourse inventory (the high bit indicates x's discourse role). To learn latent discourse, we adopt the similar VAE-based process as topic modeling with both the input and output as utterance x's BoW (x^{BoW}). First, x^{BoW} is encoded into its latent discourse role d with the following formula:

$$\pi = gs(f_\pi(x^{BoW})), \ d = Multi(\pi) \quad (2)$$

where gs refers to Gumbel softmax function (Lu et al., 2017) to encode the discrete nature of latent discourse d and f_π is another neural perceptron. Afterwards, the decoding process reconstructs x^{BoW} conditioned on d with another fully connected layer:

$$x^{BoW} = f_{\Phi^D}(d) \quad (3)$$

Here similar to latent topics, we utilize f_{Φ^D}'s weights to compute discourse-word distributions.

3.2 Initiation-Response Pair Prediction

Given topic and discourse representations of a response r (z_r and d_r) and those of its candidate initiation q (z_q and d_q), we further predict how likely they form an initiation-response pair with an utterance matching process. Here we measure the effects of topic consistency and discourse dependency to indicate initiation-response relations.

For topic consistency, we capture how similar the topics of q and r is with the following score:

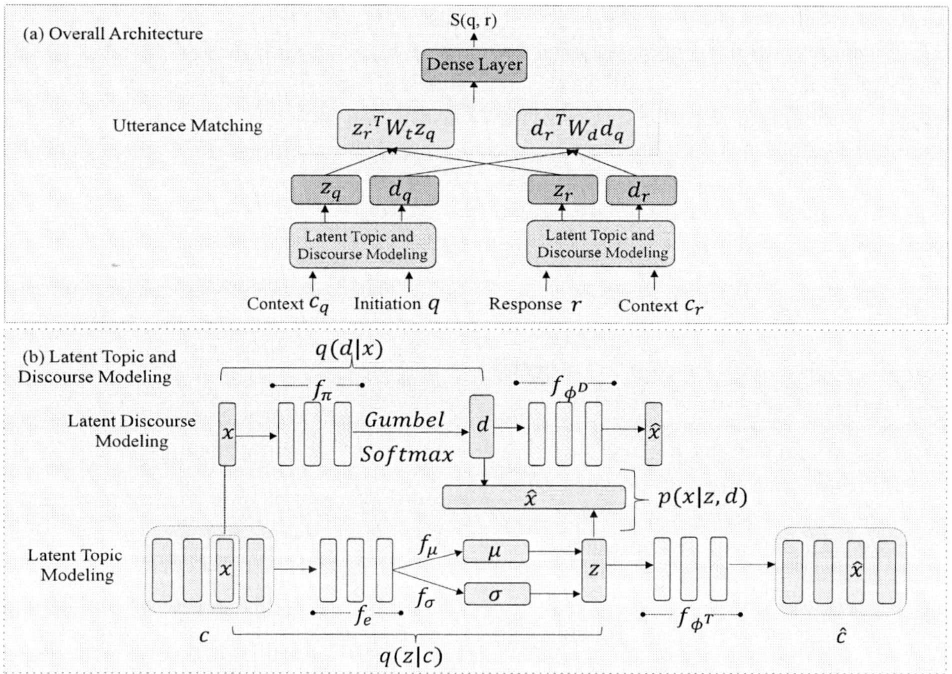

Figure 4: (a) Our model architecture to predict initiation-response pairs. We first learn latent topics and discourse factors for both response r and the candidate initiation q in award of their contexts c_r and c_q and show the detailed learning process in (b) (x denotes q or r.) Then, utterance matching is conducted to measure topic consistency and discourse dependency. Lastly, we predict $S(q, r)$ — the likelihood of r responding to q.

$$S_{topic}(q, r) = z_r^T W_t z_q \tag{4}$$

where W_t is a weight matrix learned to indicate the importance of each topic factor.

Likewise, q and r's discourse-level matching score is denoted as $S_{discourse}$ and defined below:

$$S_{discourse}(q, r) = d_r^T W_d d_q \tag{5}$$

where the trainable weight matrix W_d is employed to capture the transition probabilities from q's discourse role to r's ($Pr(d_r \mid d_q)$).

Further, to yield the final matching score $S(q, r)$ to estimate how likely r responding to q, we leverage $S_{topic}(q, r)$ and $S_{discourse}(q, r)$ to couple both topic and discourse effects with the weighted sum:

$$S(q, r) = \gamma S_{topic}(q, r) + (1 - \gamma) S_{discourse}(q, r) \tag{6}$$

where $\gamma \in [0, 1]$ is the parameter balancing the relative contributions of topic and discourse.

3.3 Learning Objectives

Latent Topics and Discourse Modeling Loss. We employ neural variational inference to approximate the posterior distributions over the latent topic z and the latent discourse d.

Encoding Topics and Discourse. To examine how to learn topics and discourse, the cross entropy loss is used to reflect the estimation of z and d from encoding process:

$$L_t = E_{q(z \mid c)}[\log p(c \mid z)] - KL(q(z \mid c) \,||\, p(z)) \tag{7}$$

$$L_d = E_{q(d \mid x)}[\log p(x \mid d)] - KL(q(d \mid x) \,||\, p(d)) \tag{8}$$

KL cost term is added to avoid posterior collapse. For space limitation, we leave out the derivation details and refer the readers to Zhao et al. (2018).

Reconstructing Utterances. For the reconstruction loss to reflect how an utterance can be inferred from z and d, we define the loss L_x as:

$$L_x = E_{q(z \mid x)q(d \mid c)}[\log p(x \mid z, d)] \tag{9}$$

Distinguishing Topics and Discourse. As discussed above, topics and discourse are modeled in different granularity (discourse in utterance only while topics in richer contexts). To further distinguish their respective word distributions, we follow Zeng et al. (2019a) to employ the mutual information to define the mutual dependency of latent topics and discourse:

$$E_{q(z)q(d)}[\log \frac{p(z, d)}{p(z)p(d)}] \tag{10}$$

Further, the mutual information loss (shown in below) is adopted to separate the semantic space of topics and discourse:

$$L_{MI} = E_{q(z)q(d)}[KL(p(d \mid z) \mid\mid p(d))] \quad (11)$$

Initiation-Response Pair Prediction Loss. To allow positive pairs to obtain higher matching scores than negative, we use hinge loss in training:

$$L_m = \sum_{i=1}^{u} max(0, \lambda - S(q^+, r) + S(q_i^-, r)) \quad (12)$$

where u is the number of negative initiations for each response. λ is a margin parameter and $S(q^+, r)$ and $S(q_i^-, r)$ are the matching scores of a response and its positive and negative initiations.

The Final Objective. Finally, we combine all the effects above and define the overall objective of the entire model as:

$$L = L_t + L_d + L_x + L_m - L_{MI} \quad (13)$$

In the training process, the optimization of final objective L enables the end-to-end exploration of topic and discourse representation and their joint effects to signal pairwise initiation-response relations in conversation structure.

4 Experimental Setup

Data Preprocessing. For *CMV* dataset, the raw data was preprocessed by Tan et al. (2016). We first filter out tokens occurring less than 15 to alleviate sparsity and maintain a vocabulary with 15, 182 tokens. Then, we remove too short (with less than 7 words) and too long utterances (with over 45 words) to better explore utterance-level word statistics for topic and discourse modeling. Next, to form context for quotations and replies (c_q and c_r), we consider all utterances in the original post (from *OH*) as c_q and those in the challenger's comment as c_r. Lastly, the training and test data is separated following Tan et al. (2016), where 6, 839 pairs are used for training and and 1, 098 for test.

For *CS* dataset, we don't remove words and the vocabulary size is 15, 407, with the scale similar to *CMV*. Short utterances with less than 5 words are removed. The Chinese word segmentation and the separation of training and test set has been done by He et al. (2019), with 3, 701 and 576 instances for training and test. Here all utterances in the dialogue thread are used to form both c_q and c_r due to the synchronous nature of *CS* conversations.

For both datasets, 10% data is further sampled from the training set for validation.

Model Settings. The hyperparameters are tuned on validation set. For the number of topics (K) and discourse roles (D), we set $K = 50, D = 5$ for *CMV* dataset and $K = 10, D = 3$ for *CS*. Max margin weight λ is set to 10 (Eq. 12) and $\gamma = 0.5$ for balancing topic consistency and discourse dependency (Eq. 6). In model training, we set the batch size to 32, dropout probability to 0.5, and the maximum epoch number to 200 (with early stop). The trainable parameters are optimized via stochastic gradient descent with learning rate decay, whose initial learning rate is set to 0.1.

Evaluation Metrics. In evaluation, we examine whether the positive initiations can be ranked higher than negative for each response. Two widely-used information retrieval metrics *Hits@N* and Mean Reciprocal Rank (*MRR*) are adopted. For *Hits@N* we only measure the hits at the top two retrieved initiations, i.e., $N = 1, 2$.

Comparison Models. We first consider three non-neural baselines that rank initiations based on: 1) POSITION, where earlier utterances are ranked higher for *CMV* while later is higher for *CS*; 2) EMBEDDING_SIM — the cosine similarity between a response and an initiation utterance measured by the average word embeddings from Glove (Pennington et al., 2014); 3) LDA_DISC — using cross entropy to discriminate initiation's and response's topic distributions inferred by latent Dirichlet allocation (LDA) (Du et al., 2017).

We also compare with the following neural models proposed by previous work: 1) MALSTM (Mueller and Thyagarajan, 2016) designed for sentence-level semantic matching (LSTM for utterance encoding and Manhattan distance for matching); 2) COATTENTION (Ji et al., 2018b) proposed for pairwise argument quality evaluation, where a co-attention network learns alignment representations and a BiGRU layer computes similarity for matching. 3) RPN (He et al., 2019), the state-of-the-art model for question-answer pairing in dialogues that ranks initiations by recurrent pointer networks (RPN).

In addition, we consider the following neural matching models with a fully connected layer to score initiation-response pairs and the following encoders for utterance-level representation learning: RNN (henceforth MATCH_RNN), autoencoder (henceforth MATCH_AE), variational autoencoder (henceforth MATCH_VAE), and discrete variational autoencoder (Zhao et al., 2018) (henceforth MATCH_DVAE).

Further, to study the relative contributions of topic consistency and discourse dependency, we compare with our two ablations, one only explores the topic effects (henceforth TOPIC_ONLY) and the other discourse (henceforth DISCOURSE_ONLY).

5 Results and Discussions

5.1 Main Comparison Results

The overall results are shown in Table 2. Several interesting observations can be drawn.

• *All models yield generally better performance on CS than CMV.* It shows that initiation-response links are more difficult to be identified on dialogues in argumentative than everyday styles.

• *Neural networks perform better than non-neural baselines.* Initiation-response pair prediction is challenging, where shallow features from position, word embeddings, and LDA-based latent topics cannot guarantee good performance. Neural models explore deeper semantic features and hence provide better results.

• *Autoencoders can learn useful representations.* It is observed that models based on autoencoders perform generally better than other neural models. This shows that autoencoders are effective in encoding utterances compared with other alternatives, such as RNN.

• *Topics contribute more on CMV while discourse is more useful in CS.* TOPIC_ONLY performs much better than DISCOURSE_ONLY on *CMV*, while the opposite is observed on *CS*. It is probably because of the richer context in *CMV* to learn latent topics (with more words per conversation as shown in Table 1), while the synchronous *CS* dialogues exhibits richer discourse word patterns from back and forth interactions between participants and hence allow better discourse modeling.

• *Our model significantly outperforms all comparisons.* This shows that the joint effects of topics and discourse can usefully indicate the relations of initiations and responses in conversation context.

5.2 Effects of Topics and Discourse

We have shown the joint effects of topics and discourse to signal initiation-response relations. Here we further analyze what we learn for topic and discourse representations.

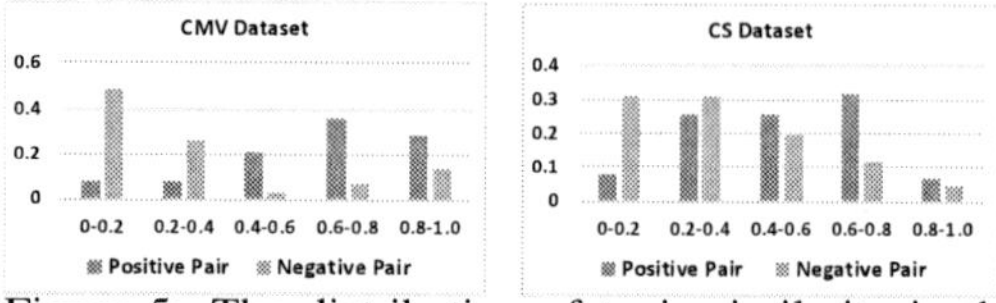

Figure 5: The distribution of topic similarity in the CMV dataset (a) and CS (b). X-axis shows similarity intervals and y-axis indicates proportions. For each interval, positive pair results are displayed on the left (in blue) and negative on the right (in orange).

Topic Effects. We first analyze the effects of topic consistency and compute the cosine similarity of the latent topics we learn for responses (z_r) and candidate initiations (z_q). The distributions over positive and negative pairs are shown in Figure 5. For both datasets, our model generally assigns higher topic similarity for positive pairs than negative, probably because responses tend to follow the concern of initiations and are hence likely to contain similar topic words. We also observe a proportion drop in very similar positive pairs ($sim > 0.8$), indicating that most responses do not echo what were said in initiations, though their topics might be similar. Nevertheless, negative pairs exhibit different distributions compared with the positive ones. Our model is able to capture such features in topic consistency modeling (Eq. 4), which might help in distinguishing positive and negative initiations for a response.

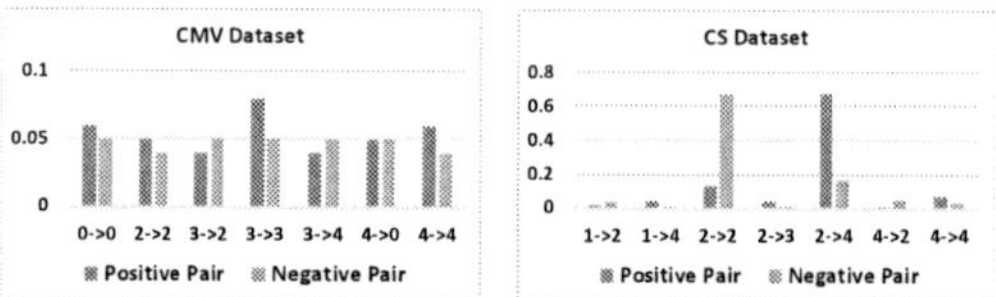

Figure 6: The transition distributions of discourse roles from initiations to responses, *CMV* in (a) and *CS* in (b). Only the top 5 transitions observed in positive (on the left in blue) and negative pairs (on the right in orange) are displayed. X-axis: initiation-response discourse roles ($d_q \rightarrow d_r$); Y-axis: proportions.

Discourse Effects. We then discuss how discourse dependency affects the prediction of initiation-response pairs. The transition distributions of discourse roles from initiations to responses ($d_q \rightarrow d_r$) are shown in Figure 6. As can

2*Models	CMV Dataset			CS Dataset		
	Hits@1	Hits@2	MRR	Hits@1	Hits@2	MRR
Non-Neural Models						
POSITION	24.68*	24.68*	24.68*	49.13*	49.13*	49.13*
EMBEDDING_SIM	22.77*	45.00*	48.66*	17.01*	39.06*	44.04*
LDA_DISC	24.68*	42.99*	47.77*	26.39*	49.65*	52.40*
Neural Models						
MALSTM (Mueller and Thyagarajan, 2016)	29.87*	42.99*	50.91*	43.58*	72.40*	65.80*
COATTENTION (Ji et al., 2018b)	47.72*	68.31*	67.26*	51.56*	79.17*	71.77*
RPN (He et al., 2019)	46.45*	67.21*	66.22*	52.95*	80.21*	72.69*
MATCH_RNN	49.45*	71.58*	68.79*	50.00*	80.38*	71.13*
MATCH_AE	51.82*	74.77‡	70.50*	52.78*	82.12‡	72.88*
MATCH_VAE	53.19*	73.95‡	71.11‡	52.60*	81.42*	72.70*
MATCH_DVAE	47.45*	69.95*	67.34*	53.82*	82.81‡	73.65*
Ablations						
TOPIC_ONLY	58.20	76.14	73.78	42.53*	69.10*	64.11*
DISCOURSE_ONLY	41.44*	63.02*	62.20*	48.96*	76.04*	69.76*
Our model	**59.74**	**76.23**	**74.41**	**64.93**	**84.20**	**79.23**

Table 2: Comparison results on two datasets and our model achieves the best results under all settings. * and ‡ indicates that our model significantly outperforms the comparison model (* for $p<0.01$ and ‡ for $p<0.05$, both measured with Wilcoxon signed rank test).

be seen, the discourse transition distributions in *CS* dataset are diverse for positive and negative pairs. It may help explain why discourse can better signal initiation-response pairs on *CS* compared with *CMV* (observed from DISCOURSE_ONLY's performance in Table 2). For *CMV*, there are slightly different distributions for positive and negative pairs. For this reason, topic factors may contribute more than discourse (seen via comparing DISCOURSE_ONLY and TOPIC_ONLY on *CMV*). This also indicates that discourse modeling for argumentative dialogues is challenging, which may require the learning of more complex features other than word statistics and is beyond the capacity of our model.

6 Related Work

Our work is in the line with prior efforts to detect initiation-response pairs. Wang and Rosé (2010) explore how topic features discovered via latent semantic analysis (LSA) work in this task, largely ignoring the effects of discourse roles. On the contrary, our study shows that both topics and discourse are helpful to identify who respond to whom in conversation structure. Other related work (Jamison and Gurevych, 2014; Du et al., 2017; Chen et al., 2017) focus on the design of hand-crafted features. Recently, there exists a growing attention over how neural framework perform to identify replying relations in conversation discourse (Guo et al., 2018; He et al., 2019). However, they ignore the effects of latent topics and discourse to structure a conversation, which are extensively studied here and shown useful to indicate initiation-response relations in experiments.

We are also inspired by the previous approaches to discover latent topics and discourse in conversations contexts. Many of them employ probabilistic graphical models in LDA-fashion to explore word statistics (Ritter et al., 2010; Li et al., 2018a; Zeng et al., 2018). We take the advantage of the recent progress to explore conversation representations via variational autoencoders (VAE) (Miao et al., 2017; Zhao et al., 2018; Zeng et al., 2019a), allowing to capture topic and discourse factors in an unsupervised manner. However, their effects to signal user interactions in conversation structure have never been studied before, which is a gap our work fills in.

7 Conclusion

This work explores the effects of latent topics and discourse roles to signal initiation-response relations that structure a conversation. We first employ a VAE-based neural model to capture topic and discourse representations in an unsupervised manner. Then, topic consistency and discourse dependency are further exploited to predict how likely an utterance responds to an initiation. Extensive experiments on large-scale datasets containing asynchronous English argumentative conversations (from the *CMV* subreddit) and synchronous Chinese customer service dialogues (from *Wangwang* platform) show that our model significantly outperform the previous state-of-the-art models.

Limitations

The model's performance relies on preprocessing steps, such as token filtering and utterance length restrictions, which could potentially introduce bias or eliminate valuable information. To address this issue, the use of modern tokenizers and large language models may be beneficial. Additionaly, in terms of multi-lingual generalizability, the model's ability to identify initiation-response pairs in asynchronous English argumentative conversations and synchronous Chinese customer service dialogues may not readily transfer to other languages.

Acknowledgments

This work is supported by National Natural Science Foundation of China (No. 62176058) and National Key RD Program of China (2023YFF1204800). The project's computational resources are supported by CFFF platform of Fudan University.

References

David M Blei, Andrew Y Ng, and Michael I Jordan. 2002. Latent dirichlet allocation. In *Advances in neural information processing systems*, pages 601–608.

Jun Chen, Chaokun Wang, Heran Lin, Weiping Wang, Zhipeng Cai, and Jianmin Wang. 2017. Learning the structures of online asynchronous conversations. In *International Conference on Database Systems for Advanced Applications*, pages 19–34. Springer.

Wenchao Du, Pascal Poupart, and Wei Xu. 2017. Discovering conversational dependencies between messages in dialogs. In *Thirty-First AAAI Conference on Artificial Intelligence*.

Gaoyang Guo, Chaokun Wang, Jun Chen, and Pengcheng Ge. 2018. Who is answering to whom? finding "reply-to" relations in group chats with long short-term memory networks. In *Proceedings of the 7th International Conference on Emerging Databases*, pages 161–171. Springer.

Shizhu He, Kang Liu, and Weiting An. 2019. Learning to align question and answer utterances in customer service conversation with recurrent pointer networks. In *Thirty-Third AAAI Conference on Artificial Intelligence*.

Emily Jamison and Iryna Gurevych. 2014. Adjacency pair recognition in wikipedia discussions using lexical pairs. In *Proceedings of the 28th Pacific Asia Conference on Language, Information and Computing*.

Lu Ji, Zhongyu Wei, Xiangkun Hu, Yang Liu, Qi Zhang, and Xuanjing Huang. 2018a. Incorporating argument-level interactions for persuasion comments evaluation using co-attention model. In *Proceedings of the 27th International Conference on Computational Linguistics, COLING 2018, Santa Fe, New Mexico, USA, August 20-26, 2018*, pages 3703–3714.

Lu Ji, Zhongyu Wei, Xiangkun Hu, Yang Liu, Qi Zhang, and Xuanjing Huang. 2018b. Incorporating argument-level interactions for persuasion comments evaluation using co-attention model. In *Proceedings of the 27th International Conference on Computational Linguistics*, pages 3703–3714.

Yunhao Jiao, Cheng Li, Fei Wu, and Qiaozhu Mei. 2018. Find the conversation killers: A predictive study of thread-ending posts. In *Proceedings of the 2018 World Wide Web Conference on World Wide Web, WWW 2018, Lyon, France, April 23-27, 2018*, pages 1145–1154.

Diederik P Kingma and Max Welling. 2013. Auto-encoding variational bayes. *arXiv preprint arXiv:1312.6114*.

Jing Li, Yan Song, Zhongyu Wei, and Kam-Fai Wong. 2018a. A joint model of conversational discourse and latent topics on microblogs. *Computational Linguistics*, 44(4).

Jing Li, Yan Song, Zhongyu Wei, and Kam-Fai Wong. 2018b. A joint model of conversational discourse and latent topics on microblogs. *Computational Linguistics*, 44(4):719–754.

Jiasen Lu, Anitha Kannan, Jianwei Yang, Devi Parikh, and Dhruv Batra. 2017. Best of both worlds: Transferring knowledge from discriminative learning to a generative visual dialog model. In *Advances in Neural Information Processing Systems*, pages 314–324.

Yishu Miao, Edward Grefenstette, and Phil Blunsom. 2017. Discovering discrete latent topics with neural variational inference. In *Proceedings of the 34th International Conference on Machine Learning-Volume 70*, pages 2410–2419. JMLR. org.

Jonas Mueller and Aditya Thyagarajan. 2016. Siamese recurrent architectures for learning sentence similarity. In *Thirtieth AAAI Conference on Artificial Intelligence*.

Jeffrey Pennington, Richard Socher, and Christopher Manning. 2014. Glove: Global vectors for word representation. In *Proceedings of the 2014 conference on empirical methods in natural language processing (EMNLP)*, pages 1532–1543.

Kechen Qin, Lu Wang, and Joseph Kim. 2017. Joint modeling of content and discourse relations in dialogues. In *Proceedings of the 55th Annual Meeting of the Association for Computational Linguistics, ACL 2017, Vancouver, Canada, July 30 - August 4, Volume 1: Long Papers*, pages 974–984.

Danilo Jimenez Rezende, Shakir Mohamed, and Daan Wierstra. 2014. Stochastic backpropagation and approximate inference in deep generative models. *arXiv preprint arXiv:1401.4082*.

Alan Ritter, Colin Cherry, and Bill Dolan. 2010. Unsupervised modeling of twitter conversations. In *Human Language Technologies: The 2010 Annual Conference of the North American Chapter of the Association for Computational Linguistics*, pages 172–180. Association for Computational Linguistics.

Emanuel A Schegloff. 2007. *Sequence organization in interaction: A primer in conversation analysis I*, volume 1. Cambridge University Press.

Chenhao Tan, Vlad Niculae, Cristian Danescu-Niculescu-Mizil, and Lillian Lee. 2016. Winning arguments: Interaction dynamics and persuasion strategies in good-faith online discussions. In *Proceedings of the 25th international conference on world wide web*, pages 613–624. International World Wide Web Conferences Steering Committee.

Yi-Chia Wang and Carolyn P Rosé. 2010. Making conversational structure explicit: identification of initiation-response pairs within online discussions. In *Human Language Technologies: The 2010 Annual Conference of the North American Chapter of the Association for Computational Linguistics*, pages 673–676. Association for Computational Linguistics.

Jichuan Zeng, Jing Li, Yulan He, Cuiyun Gao, Michael R Lyu, and Irwin King. 2019a. What you say and how you say it: Joint modeling of topics and discourse in microblog conversations. *Transactions of the Association for Computational Linguistics*, 7:267–281.

Xingshan Zeng, Jing Li, Lu Wang, Nicholas Beauchamp, Sarah Shugars, and Kam-Fai Wong. 2018. Microblog conversation recommendation via joint modeling of topics and discourse. In *Proceedings of the 2018 Conference of the North American Chapter of the Association for Computational Linguistics: Human Language Technologies, Volume 1 (Long Papers)*, pages 375–385.

Xingshan Zeng, Jing Li, Lu Wang, and Kam-Fai Wong. 2019b. Neural conversation recommendation with online interaction modeling. In *Proceedings of the 2019 Conference on Empirical Methods in Natural Language Processing and the 9th International Joint Conference on Natural Language Processing, EMNLP-IJCNLP 2019, Hong Kong, China, November 3-7, 2019*, pages 4632–4642.

Tiancheng Zhao, Kyusong Lee, and Maxine Eskenazi. 2018. Unsupervised discrete sentence representation learning for interpretable neural dialog generation. *arXiv preprint arXiv:1804.08069*.

Tiancheng Zhao, Ran Zhao, and Maxine Eskenazi. 2017. Learning discourse-level diversity for neural dialog models using conditional variational autoencoders. *arXiv preprint arXiv:1703.10960*.

A Position Distribution of Datasets

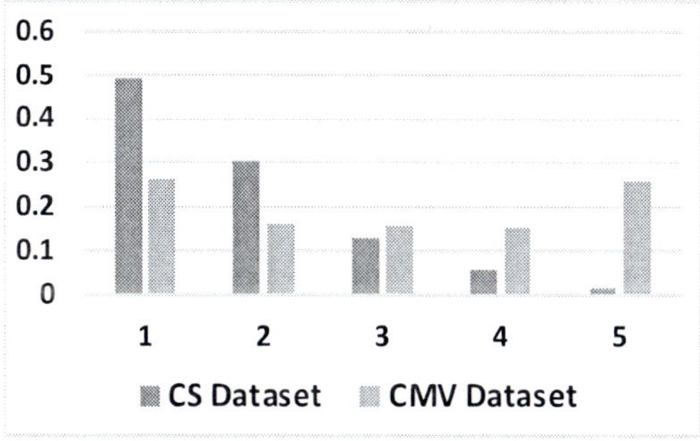

Figure 7: The distribution over relative positions of initiations and responses. X-axis: initiations' utterance order counted from responses (only considering customer's or *OH*'s turns). Y-axis: proportions.

We analyze the relative positions of initiations and responses and show the distribution of their intermediate utterance number in Figure 7. As can be seen, large proportion of responses do not interact with the closest utterance, though *CS* sellers do respond more to newer questions, probably because of recency effects in in synchronous dialogues — people's attention tends to be drawn by new information. However, in asynchronous forum discussions, *CMV* challengers are more likely to quote the opening points in *OH*'s post. Another possible reason is that most key arguments are located at the beginning of a post.

B Further Discussions

B.1 Parameter Analysis.

Here we present in-depth analyses of our model and start with the discussion of two important parameters — the number of topics (K) and discourse (D).

Varying Topic Number. Figure 8 (a) shows how Hits@1 scores change over varying number of topics (K). For comparison, we also display MATCH_DVAE's results, the best comparison model in Table 2. For relatively large K, our model performs consistently better than MATCH_DVAE. We also find that the our trend on both datasets are not monologues, where the best performance is attained at $K = 50$ for *CMV* and $K = 10$ for *CS*. This implies that the topics in customer service dialogues are limited (focusing on products) while participants may discuss wide range of topics in social media debates.

Varying Discourse Number. The results for varying discourse number (D) are displayed in Figure 8 (b). Similar to K, our model exhibits consistently better results than MATCH_DVAE for $D > 1$. It is also observed that *CS* is more sensitive to D compared with *CMV*, indicating that discourse factors largely affect the initiation-response prediction results on CS.

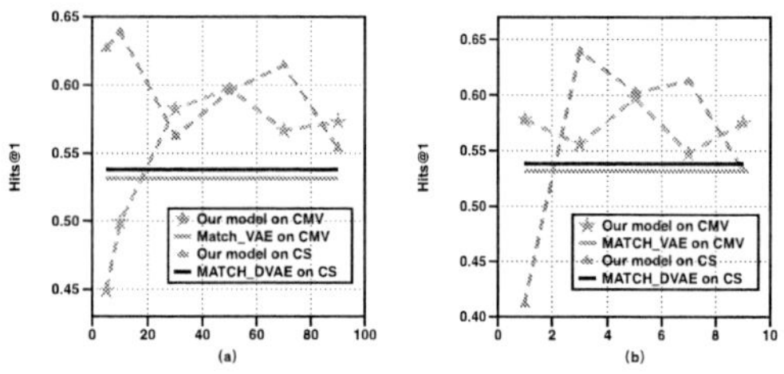

Figure 8: Hits@1 over varying number of topics and discourse X-axis: topic number (K in (a)) and discourse number (D in (b)). Y-axis: Hits@1 score. Blue and red curves: our model on *CMV* and *CS*. Purple and black lines: MATCH_DVAE on *CMV* and *CS*.

B.2 Case Study.

To further examine what we learn to represent topics and discourse, we take the *CMV* conversation snippet in Figure 1 as an example to analyze the topic and discourse words assigned by our model. Recall that R answers C_1's question suggested by the shared pronoun "that" and the similar topics they concern. Figure 9 shows the visualization results and displays topic words in red and discourse in blue. It is observed that our model is able to separate topic words (e.g., "thank", "private", and "public) from discourse (e.g., "that", "what", and "?"), which may resulting in coherent topic and discourse distributions and indicative representations to signal initiations-response relations. Interestingly, discourse words are mostly stop words and punctuation. Their meaningful clusters exhibiting different statistic patterns might usefully indicate varying discourse behaviors in conversations, which is consistent with the findings from previous studies (Li et al., 2018b; Zeng et al., 2019a).

B.3 Downstream Task.

In Introduction, we mentioned that the detection of initiation-response pairs may contribute to a better understanding of conversation structure and hence benefit downstream applications. Here we take the prediction of argument persuasiveness as an example to discuss whether the representations learned

[C_1] I am aware of the you can thank them in private argument but what does that matter ?
[C_2] The most important part of my argument is that it hurts literally nobody
[C_3] All they are doing is trying to be polite
[C_4] Some people comments anonymously and do not respond to the private messages so the never knows who gave them gold
[C_5] Note: for the purposes of my argument assume I am talking specifically about comments edited in such a way as to say thanks for the gold !
[R] We are all aware that you can do that, but sometimes people like to express publicly

Figure 9: Visualization of the topic and discourse word assignment for the *CMV* conversation snippet in Figure 1. The blue words are prone to indicate discourse ($p(w \mid d) > p(w \mid z)$) while red topic. Darker colors indicate higher confidence.

by our model can advance the state-of-the-art performance on this task. Table 3 shows the performance of the non-neural baseline (Tan et al., 2016), the state-of-the-art model (Ji et al., 2018b), and Ji et al. (2018b) incorporating the topic and discourse representations we learn (z and d). The dataset is also collected from *CMV* and argument quality is labeled by Δ (given by *OH* to indicate the successful persuasion). It is seen that the latent topics and discourse learned to signal initiation-response relations can indeed help to predict argument quality, suggesting that the persuasiveness of arguments are closely related to the structure of who respond to whom in argumentation processes.

Models	Pairwise accuracy
Tan et al. (2016) (*baseline*)	65.70
Ji et al. (2018b) (*SOTA*)	70.45
Ji et al. (2018b)+Our model	74.12

Table 3: The pairwise accuracy to predict argument persuasiveness. The results in the first two rows were reported in their original paper. Our representations help advance the state of the art (SOTA).

Cantonese Natural Language Processing in the Transformers Era

Rong Xiang **Ming Liao** **Jing Li**
Department of Computing, Hong Kong Polytechnic University, HKSAR, China
{rongxiang, mliao, jing-amelia.li}@polyu.edu.hk

Abstract

Despite being spoken by a large population of speakers worldwide, Cantonese is under-resourced in terms of the data scale and diversity compared to other major languages. This limitation has excluded it from the current "pre-training and fine-tuning" paradigm that is dominated by Transformer architectures. In this paper, we provide a comprehensive review on the existing resources and methodologies for Cantonese Natural Language Processing, covering the recent progress in language understanding, text generation and development of language models. We finally discuss two aspects of the Cantonese language that could make it potentially challenging even for state-of-the-art architectures: *colloquialism* and *multilinguality*.

1 Introduction

Cantonese, or Yue Chinese, is a diaspora language with over 85 million speakers all over the world (Lai, 2004; García and Fishman, 2011; Yu, 2013; Eberhard et al., 2022). [1] It is commonly used in colloquial scenarios (e.g., daily conversation and social media) but also in formal and written contexts, such as in the Legislative Council of the Hong Kong Special Administrative Region, or in sections of special local interests in the newspapers, such social and entertainment, or in horse racing and betting information. Otherwise Standard Chinese (SCN) [2], sometimes called Putonghua (普通话) or Guoyu (國語), is generally favored in formal and written contexts (Luke, 1995; Lee, 2016; Li, 2017; Wong and Lee, 2018).

In terms of digital language support, Mandarin Chinese thrives with a mature Natural Language Processing (NLP) environment. Chinese NLP has a versatile and growing literature from major conferences, such as ACL and COLING. In contrast, as for digital language support Cantonese is at the vital level, one level lower than thriving (cf. Ethnologue) (Zhao et al., 2024b; Zhu et al., 2024). In fact, Cantonese is an rare exception as a main diaspora language, as most diaspora languages -including but not limited to Arabic, Chinese, English, French, Hindi, Japanese, Korean, Portuguese, Spanish, etc.- have both a thriving digital language support and a strong NLP community, while Cantonese does not (Li et al., 2023; Zhao et al., 2024a).

More specifically, while current NLP paradigms have been deeply changed by large-scale pre-training models based on Transformer architectures, such as BERT (Devlin et al., 2019), RoBERTa (Liu et al., 2019), XLNet (Yang et al., 2019), ELECTRA (Clark et al., 2020), GPT-3 (Brown et al., 2020) and GPT-4 (Achiam et al., 2023), which have achieved state-of-the-art (SOTA) level of performance on several tasks. Compared to the previous generation systems, the progress was particularly remarkable in task requiring fine-grained semantic understanding, such as textual entailment, question answering and causal reasoning (Wang et al., 2018, 2019; Zhao et al., 2023). On the other hand, language technologies for Cantonese have not yet benefited from this revolution (Xiang et al., 2022). From this point of view, the number of publications in the ACL Anthology is emblematic (see Figure 1): only 61 papers are related to "Cantonese", compared to 9,756 papers for English, and 5,312 (4,919 + 393) for SCN/Mandarin.

The history of publications in Cantonese NLP, as in Figure 1, shows that the numbers of papers published yearly remains in single digit, although there is a moderate increasing trend (cf. Figure 2). However, as an emergent language in NLP, it is surprising that only a small portion (17/61, 27.9%) introduces language resources, as shown by Table

[1] https://www.ethnologue.com/language/yue.

[2] Notice that the written form of SCN includes both simplified and traditional orthographies for writing in a specific Chinese dialect or topolect.

Proceedings of the 10th SIGHAN Workshop on Chinese Language Processing (SIGHAN-10), pages 69–79
August 16, 2024 ©2024 Association for Computational Linguistics

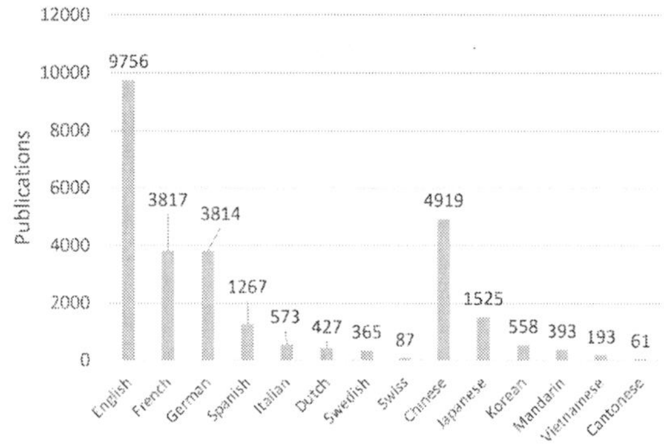

Figure 1: Number of publications in the ACL Anthology indexed by languages as of Mar 2024. The publications were retrieved via searching the language name in either the title or the abstract.

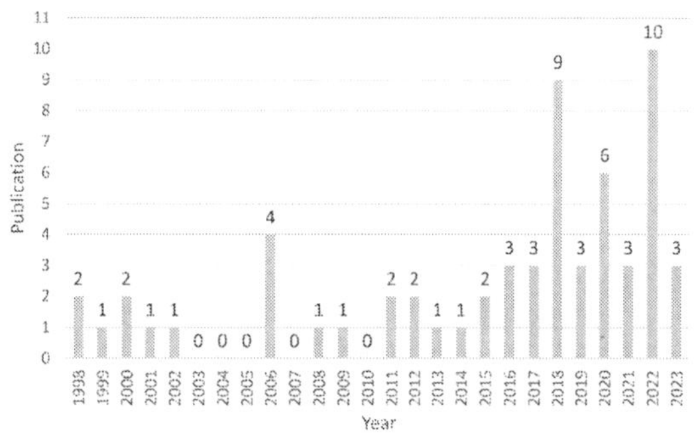

Figure 2: Yearly publications of the 61 papers for Cantonese NLP in the ACL Anthology from 1998 to 2024.

Research Topics	# of Papers
Phonetics&Phonology& Speech Recognition	22
Lexicography&Syntax& Semantics&Morphology	10
NLP Resources	17
NLP Tasks	12
Total	61

Table 1: Papers on Cantonese by research topic (statistics checked on Mar 2024).

1. This explains why Cantonese NLP has a problem in terms of scarcity of resources and lack of alignment to state-of-the-art practices.

In light of these concerns, this paper presents a first overview of Cantonese NLP, going through essential issues regarding this language's uniqueness, data scarcity, research progress, and major challenges. As a pilot study, we also present some preliminary analysis on Cantonese data from social media and discuss the possible challenges. We found that, given the prominence of *colloquial language* and *code-switching* in the data, it is desirable that future models will be developed to properly deal with such phenomena. Finally, we conclude our contribution by indicating some possible directions for future research.

2 Cantonese NLP Resources

2.1 Corpora

Cantonese was perhaps the most documented Sinitic languages in early bilingual dictionaries compiled by western missionaries (Huang et al., 2016). Some Cantonese words were included in the first 'modern' bilingual Chinese dictionary compiled by Matteo Ricci at the end of the 16th century. The majority of the bilingual dictionaries published throughout the 19th century were, indeed, dedicated to Cantonese. Given the important role of Cantonese in the context of the encounter between China and the West, it is perhaps no surprising that the first Cantonese corpus was a bilingual one. Wu (1994) introduced the work on the HKUST Chinese-English Bilingual Parallel Corpus, based on the transcriptions from the Hong Kong legislative Council. The first monolingual Cantonese corpus was most likely the CANCORP (Lee and Wong, 1998), consisting of one million characters from Cantonese-speaking children in Hong Kong. Another important corpus for child language acquisition is the CHILDES Cantonese-English Corpus by Yip and Matthews (2007), containing both audio and visual data of children conversation and the related transcripts.

The Hong Kong Cantonese Adult Language Corpus (HKCAC) focuses instead on adult language and contributes speech recorded from phone-in programs and forums (Leung and Law, 2001). This corpus also presents speech transcriptions for a total of 170k characters. Another resource, the Hong Kong University Cantonese Corpus (HKUCC) (Wong, 2006) was collected from transcribed spontaneous speech in conversations and radio programs and its annotation include word segmentation, Cantonese pronunciation and parts-of-speech, covering approximately 230,000 words.

Lee (2011) introduced a parallel corpus that aligns Cantonese and SCN at the sentence level for machine translation. The annotation materials are the transcriptions of Cantonese speeches from television shows in Hong Kong, and their correspond-

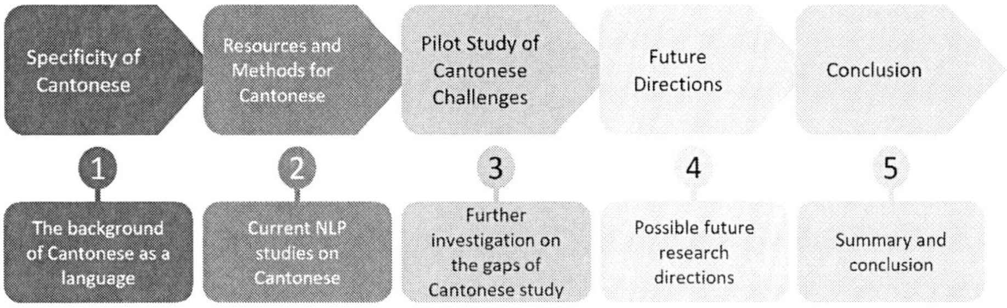

Figure 3: Outline of the survey.

ing Mandarin subtitles. The corpus contains 4,135 pairs of aligned sentences, with a total of 36,775 characters in Mandarin, and 39,192 in Cantonese. Wong et al. (2017) later published a small parallel dependency treebank for Cantonese and Mandarin, based on the same textual materials. The corpus consists, in total, of 569 aligned sentences and it is annotated with the Universal Dependencies scheme (De Marneffe et al., 2014; Nivre et al., 2016). Another corpus based on the transcripts of Hong Kong Cantonese movies has been presented by Chin (2015), and made accessible to the users via an online interface. [3]

Spoken Cantonese data from television and radio programmes broadcasted in Hong Kong are the source material also for the corpus introduced by Kwong (2015). The corpus covers different topics, such as politics, affairs, economics/finance, and food/entertainment, and a variety of textual typologies (interviews, phone call transcriptions, reviews etc.). The Hong Kong Cantonese Corpus by Luke and Wong (2015) includes 150,000 words, and it also consists of transcribed Cantonese speech recordings that are annotated with both segmentation and part-of-speech tags. Ng et al. (2017) proposed the first bilingual speech corpus of Cantonese and English, built with the goal of the assessment of correct Cantonese pronunciation. Finally, the most recent introduction is the MYCanCor corpus (Liesenfeld, 2018), which has been built with 20 hours of Cantonese speech recorded in Malaysia (plus the videos and the related transcriptions) to support studies on multimodal communication.

Concerning domain-specific resources, the parallel corpus by Ahrens (2015) includes 6 million words from political speeches from China, Hong Kong, Taiwan and USA, and it contains more than one million words of transcribed speeches of Hong Kong' leaders before and after the handover. It consist of more than 400k words in English, and more than 600k words in Chinese/Cantonese. Pan (2019) introduced a Chinese/English Political Corpus for translation and interpretation studies. With over 6 million word tokens, the corpus consists of transcripts of both Cantonese and Mandarin and their English translations. Lee et al. (2020) introduced a Counselling Corpus in Cantonese to research domain-specific dialogues: 436 input questions were solicited from native Cantonese speakers and 150 chatbot replies were harvested from mental health websites. The authors later extended their work by collecting another dataset used for text summarization and question generation (Lee et al., 2021), containing 12,634 post-restatement pairs and 9,036 post-question pairs, all with manual annotations. It also includes 89,000 unlabeled post-reply pairs collected from the online discussion forums in Hong Kong. Finally, the `SpiCE` corpus by Johnson et al. (2020) is an open-access corpus created specifically for translation tasks and contains bilingual speech conversations in Cantonese and English, for a total of 19 hours of conversation. The transcripts have been produced with the Google Cloud Speech-to-Text application, followed by manual corrections, orthographic alignment and phonetic transcriptions.

For corpus reading and preprocessing, Lee et al. (2022) recently introduced the PyCantonese package, which includes reader modules for some of the most popular Cantonese corpora (e.g. the CHILDES Cantonese-English Bilingual Corpus, the Hong Kong Cantonese Corpus etc.), stopword lists, modules for carrying out word segmentation and part-of-speech tagging, parsing and common computational tasks involving Jyutping (e.g. romanization of the characters).

[3] `https://hkcc.eduhk.hk/`.

2.2 NLP Benchmarks

The gap between Cantonese and other diaspora languages in NLP research and digital support is underlined by the scarcity of benchmark datasets specifically targeting Cantonese. A first example was the shared task for Chinese Spelling Check, which was conducted in co-location with the workshop on NLP for Educational Applications in 2017. The organizers published a benchmark dataset with 6,890 sentences for normalizing Cantonese, mapping from the spoken to the written form (Fung et al., 2017).

Xiang et al. (2019) provided a sentiment analysis benchmark collected `OpenRice`, a Hong Kong catering website, where over 60k comments are labeled with 5-level ratings indicating sentiment scores. The authors anonymized the data, filtered out comments written in other languages (e.g. SCN, English) and limited the length of the examples to 250 words. [4]

Chen et al. (2020) published a rumor detection benchmark collected from Twitter, including 27,328 web-crawled tweets (13,883 rumors and 13,445 non-rumors) written in Traditional Chinese characters, in part in Taiwanese Mandarin and in part in Cantonese [5]. However, the dataset does not provide the information about the language in which a tweet has been written.

For text genre categorization, a benchmark has been collected by the ToastyNews project [6]. The dataset consists of more than 11000 texts, divided into 20 different categories. The texts have been extracted from `LIHKG`, a popular Hong Kong forum with a structure similar to Reddit, and the category labels have been generated from the discussion threads they belong to.

Finally, for the development of dialogue systems, Wang et al. (2020) presented a food-ordering dialogue dataset for Cantonese called KddRES, including dialogues extracted from Facebook and OpenRice for 10 different Hong Kong restaurants. Using this dataset, it is possible to evaluate systems either on the classification of the intention of customer statements, or on sequence labeling tasks to identify the slot of interests of a conversation (e.g. the selected food, the number of people for a reservation, the time for take-out etc.).

[4] `https://github.com/Christainx/Dataset_Cantonese_Openrice`.

[5] `https://github.com/cxyccc/CR-Dataset`.

[6] `https://github.com/toastynews/lihkg-cat-v2`

3 Pilot Study for Cantonese

In the previous sections, we have illustrated the general scarcity of resources in NLP for Cantonese. We also mentioned that Cantonese has a numerous and active social media community, and Cantonese social media language provides an interesting example for analysis, as it can show the main challenges related to the automatic processing of this language.

As we anticipated, *colloquialism* and *multilinguality* are primary obstacles to robust and effective processing. In the next sections, we present an analysis of the two phenomena in Cantonese social media.

3.1 Colloquialism and Lexical Differences

In the introductory sections, we already discussed how the Cantonese vocabulary deeply diverges from SCN (Ouyang, 1993; Snow, 2004), and mentioned the fact that, due to the long tradition of all Sinitic languages sharing a written/formal strata (i.e. written Chinese), the divergence and challenges of Cantonese are in the spoken or informal strata. This include transcriptions of speech, as well as the habit in writing to adopt a colloquial style when dealing with topics of local interest, hence we refer to it as "colloquialism").

Data Source	Token Count	Text Size
DISCUSS	118.7 M	258.8 MB
LIHKG	632.7 M	651.9 MB
OpenRice	172.1 M	226.1 MB

Table 2: Scales of textual data from 3 different Cantonese forums (0.924 billion tokens and 1.1 Gigabytes size in total).

In this section, we analyze the colloquial features of Cantonese, with some examples, and present some data from a small-scale study on word surprisal (Hale, 2001, 2016). To start with, we examined the data from three popular Cantonese online forums: DISCUSS, LIHKG, and OpenRice (Hong Kong).[7] The first two are general forums with diverse topics, while OpenRice is s the most popular forum for sharing restaurant and food reviews. Table 2 shows the statistics of the forums, where the three sources altogether contribute 1.1 Gigabytes (G) texts and 0.924 billion

[7] DISCUSS: `discuss.com.hk`; LIHKG: `lihkg.com`; OpenRice:`https://www.openrice.com/zh/hongkong`.

(B) tokens. Just to give some figures for comparison, 80G texts and 16B tokens have been used for pre-training English models on tweets (BERTweet, Nguyen et al. (2020)), and 5.4B tokens have been used for a relatively small size model for SCN (MacBERT, Cui et al. (2021)). This would be, to the best of our knowledge, the largest social media text collection for pre-training a Cantonese model from scratch, although the data size is certainly smaller compared to other languages.

One reason why it is challenging to directly apply or adapt SCN NLP models for Cantonese is the large number of Cantonese specific vocabulary and expressions, including words with unknown forms and words with known forms but with novel meanings. These discrepancies made the pre-trained models based on Mandarin ineffective for Cantonese NLP. In addition, due to the low degree of conventionalizing, *spelling mistakes* are prominent in the data, such as the mis-replacement of *fan3 gaau3* 訓覺 instead of *fan3 gaau3* 瞓覺 (*sleep*), together with intentional misspellings in jokes and punning, which are commonly found also in newspapers headlines (Li and Costa, 2009).

As in all social media texts, *slang expressions and idioms* are also frequently found, requiring external knowledge and background for the correct understanding, and most of such expressions are unknown in standard Chinese. Consider the following example: *gam1 ci3 jin2 coeng3 wui2 hou2 naan4 maai5 dou3 fei1 , keoi5 dou1 hai6 zap1 sei2 gai1 sin1 zi3 jau5 dak1 tai2 zaa3* 。今次演唱會好難買到飛，佢都係執死雞先至有得睇咋。(*It's extremely hard to buy tickets for the concert. He would not have a chance to go to the concert if he did not collect a lucky coin*). There are at least two expressions that would be challenging to a SCN trained model. The first is the word 飛 'fare, ticket', which is a phonetic borrowing as discussed above. A Mandarin trained model would treat it as the verb 'to fly', with a different PoS and totally different behavior. The second is the expression *zap1 sei2 gai1* 執死雞 is a Cantonese idiom originated from football terminology, literally meaning 'to hold (a) dead chicken', which is shared by Mandarin and Cantonese. However, in Cantonese, it also has the idiomatic meaning that was originally used in soccer 'scoring a goal with pure luck.' These two meanings in Cantonese cannot be obtained without either a comprehensive Cantonese lexicon of colloquial usages or a large training corpus. Without the prior knowledge of its extended meaning of "to get a great deal", even for humans it would be challenging to make sense of the sentence, not to mention NLP models.

We studied the bigram distributions of DISCUSS, containing forum threads in 20 different topics, and compare it with the Gigaword corpus, which is composed of text from news outlets in Chinese (Huang, 2009; Parker et al., 2011). Both datasets concern contemporary and widely-discussed events in diverse news topics and are written in traditional Chinese. For both datasets, we sampled 260 megabytes of textual data and computed the average frequency of the union of the top 1000 most frequent bigrams in the two datasets. The relative frequencies of the bigrams are shown in Figure 4. We can observe, at a glance, that the distribution of DISCUSS exhibits a high spike on the left, and then it has a long tail of low-frequency bigrams. Notice that, given the bigger size and the more standardized nature of GigaWord, the relative frequencies of many of the shared bigrams in the long tail are comparably higher.

To explore the predictability of Cantonese text by SCN models, we utilized two representative models to extract and compare surprisal scores for Cantonese sentences and the corresponding translations in Simplified and Traditional Chinese. We chose to use the *BERT-CKIP* model [8], which was trained on Traditional Chinese on a concatenation of a 2020 dump of the Chinese Wikipedia and the Chinese Gigaword Corpus (Huang, 2009; Parker et al., 2011); and the *RoBERTa-HFL* model [9], an implementation of RoBERTa by Cui et al. (2021). It has been trained on both Simplified and Traditional characters on a 2019 dump of the Chinese Wikipedia and various news and question answering websites.

The surprisal of a word w (Hale, 2001; Levy, 2008) is generally defined as the negative log probability of the word conditioned on the sentence context, according to the following:

$$Surprisal(w) = -logP(w|context) \quad (1)$$

The higher the surprisal for a given linguistic expression, the more unpredictable that expression is for a given computational model. If a model instead is able to provide confident estimates of

[8] https://github.com/ckiplab/ckip-transformers

[9] https://huggingface.co/hfl/chinese-roberta-wwm-ext

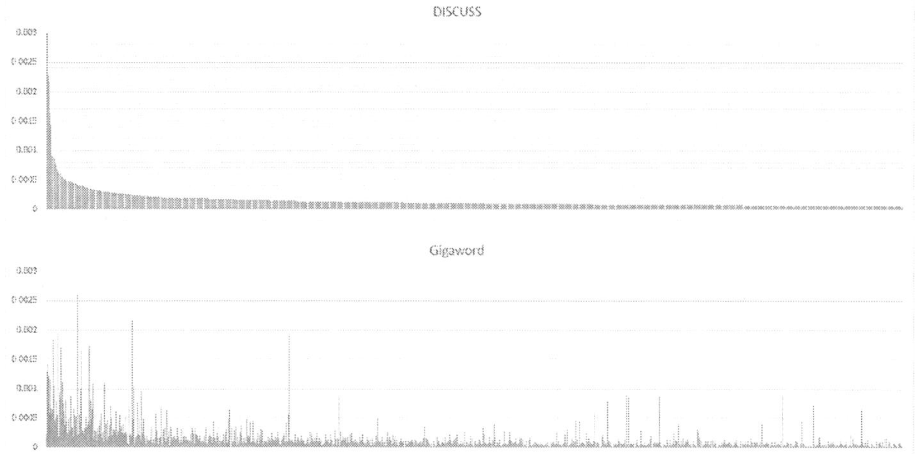

Figure 4: Distribution of bigrams from DISCUSS and Gigaword datasets. The x-axis shows the union dataset of the top 1,000 bigrams from each dataset ordered by the average relative frequency in the two datasets. The top curve refers to DISCUSS, the bottom one to Gigaword.

words occurring in a corpus, the surprisal will be low.

To run our small experiment, we adopted the implementation of the minicons library (Misra, 2022), which provides handy functions to estimate probability and surprisal scores of a sentence. We randomly sampled 50 sentences from the Cantonese forums in Section 4.1, and for each of them we generate the translation in both Traditional and Simplified Chinese using the Baidu translation interface [10]. Then we computed the surprisal score for each sentence using the two SCN models, and took the average across sentences. The sampling was repeated 10 times (Table 3 reports the average across different samples). Notice that, since both BERT-CKIP and RoBERTa-HFL are bidirectional models trained, the surprisal scores for each word are computed by masking the words in the sentence one-by-one, computing their probabilities in context and then applying the formula in (1). Once the scores for single words are obtained, the minicons library outputs their average as the surprisal score for the sentence. [11]

We tested both Cantonese sentences and Taiwan Mandarin sentences from the Academia Sinica Corpus (Huang and Chen, 1992). Note that both Hong Kong and Taiwan use traditional characters with variations in lexical choices. Thus, our study was carried out in three different writing systems to ensure that the differences in writing systems do not contribute to the surprisal scores. Thus each set of data are tested in 1) original writing forms, 2) converted writing forms with each other (i.e. Hong Kong vs. Taiwan), and 3) converted to simplified Chinese. The results in Table 3 show that for both models and for three possible writing system settings (i.e. original, switched, simplified), the Cantonese sentences tend to have higher surprisal scores. The experiment establishes that it is more difficult for SCN trained models to predict Cantonese sentences. One of the reasons of the additional difficulties may be the usage of different words in Cantonese: we computed that, compared to the translated sentences, there is an overlap of characters of 69.1% for the Traditional Chinese translation and 65.5% for the Simplified Chinese one (i.e. more than 30% of the Cantonese characters do not appear in the translations). Still, given the relatively high overlap degree, it is likely that Cantonese-specific words play a role together with other factors, such as regional usages of the same words/characters and differences in grammar.

The two models behave very differently when the Cantonese text is translated into Simplified Chinese: RoBERTa-HFL, which is trained on both Traditional and Simplified characters, reports lower surprisal scores than on the original Cantonese sentences, and has a slightly higher score for the translation from Traditional to Simplified

[10] `https://fanyi.baidu.com/`

[11] This method for estimating probabilities/surprisals for sentences with bidirectional language models is known as *pseudo log-likelihood*, and it has been introduced by Salazar et al. (2020). This method has a standard implementation in the minicons library.

	BERT-CKIP	RoBERTa-HFL
Can_Orig	4.30	4.39
Trad_Translated	3.17	2.89
Simp_Translated_Can	5.84	2.79
Trad_Orig	0.61	1.09
Can_Translated	1.71	2.20
Simp_Translated_Trad	5.38	1.15

Table 3: Surprisal analysis on 50 Cantonese and Traditional Chinese sentences. The average surprisal scores are shown in the table. Can_Orig: 50 Cantonese sentences. Trad_Translated: 50 Traditional Chinese sentences translated from Can_Orig. Simp_Translated_Can: 50 Simplified sentences translated from Can_Orig.

(which might be due to the ambiguity of the conversion, as for a traditional character there might be multiple corresponding characters in Simplified Chinese); BERT-CKIP has instead extremely high surprisal scores when either Cantonese or Traditional Chinese are translated into Simplified Chinese, as it was not exposed to Simplified characters during pretraining. In any case, we can notice that predicting words in Cantonese is much more challenging for SCN models, and that extra difficulties may come in when there is a conversion from Traditional to Simplified characters.

3.2 Multilinguality

language	Cantonese	SCN	English	Others
DISCUSS	31.49%	52.00%	9.19%	7.32%
LIHKG	40.57%	33.40%	11.85%	14.18%
OpenRice	73.65%	18.91%	4.93%	2.55%

Table 4: Ratio of language usage. Cantonese and Standard Chinese are dominant in all the datasets under consideration.

To better understand the nature of multilingualism, we examine the contribution of different languages to Hong Kong social media data. The open-source toolkit *fastlangid* is employed to analyze the language usage ratio of the datasets [12]. More specifically, we used *fastlangid* with the default settings and the parameter $k = 1$, meaning that only the most likely language shall be detected. The percentages are shown in Table 4, where the statistics have been computed as an aggregation of sentence-level results. As it can be seen, the code-switching behavior across Cantonese and SCN is frequent; English is also very often attested in our data [13], and we can even observe code-mixing with other languages. This is because Cantonese-speaking areas happen to integrate speakers of multiple nationalities (Yue-Hashimoto, 1991; Li, 2006).

To exemplify the multilingualism phenomenon in Cantonese, we present some typical code-switching cases of Cantonese and English. The original texts are followed by the English translations in brackets. The switched scripts are underlined in both the original texts and the translations.

- E1: *sau1 dou3 offer, gam1 nin4 gau2 jyut6 zung6 heoi3 m4 heoi3 dou3 ngoi6 gwok3 duk6 syu1 hou2?* 收到offer, 今年 9 月仲去唔去到外國讀書好? (*Got the offer. Will it be better or not to go for overseas study in September this year?*)

- E2: *hai6 ge3 zau6 wai4 jau5 hai2 hoeng1 gong2 maai5 liu5, tung4 maai4 dim2 gaai2 hoeng1 gong2 di1 din6 hei3 dim3 m4 gaau2 haa6 di1 si3 sik6 wut6 dung6*。係嘅就唯有喺香港買了, 同埋點解香港啲電器店唔搞下啲試食活動。(*I can only buy it in Hong Kong. And why don't the electrical appliance stores of Hong Kong do some trial promotion campaigns.*)

- E3: *zaa3 zoeng3 bei2 gaau3 taam5, bat1 gwo3 min6 hou2 Q, zan1 hai6 hou2 zeng3*。炸醬比較淡, 不過麵好Q, 真係好正。(*The fried sauce is bland, but the noodles are very chewy. it's really tasty.*)

The code-switching phenomenon in E1 is commonly observed in the data: the English nouns "offer" is directly taken and inserted in a Cantonese context. E2 uses "D" in the alphabet as an alternative to Cantonese tokens *di1* "啲" (*of*) and

[12]https://github.com/currentsapi/fastlangid

[13]It should be kept in mind that English is still one of the primary languages in Hong Kong education.

dim2 "點" (*some*) because of their similar pronunciations. For E3, "Q" is borrowed from Hokkien, another Chinese variety of the Southern Min group that is widely used in Fujian and Taiwan, and it means "chewy". The borrowing can be explained by the geographical proximity of the Cantonese and Hokkien speaking areas and by the constant migratory flows between the two regions.

In sum, our analysis shows how colloquialism and code-switching with multiple languages are pervasive in Cantonese social media data, and thus models for Cantonese NLP will have to be robust to such phenomena. For example, future Cantonese language understanding systems could be integrated with spelling correction and dialect identification components, in order to mitigate the irregularity of the input data.

4 Conclusions

In this paper, our goal is to present the status of the research on Cantonese NLP, to describe the uniqueness of this language and to suggest possible solutions for addressing the current shortcoming, due to the lack of resources. Indeed, most research on Cantonese NLP has not translated into the release of useful models, corpora and benchmark datasets, which are often not publicly available or not up to date. A possible reason of this difficulty is the limited number of online sources of Cantonese text with non-restrictive licenses (Eckart de Castilho et al., 2018), which does not leave too many options to researchers for putting together new benchmarks and for training large-scale models that are Cantonese-specific.

After reviewing the existing resources and methods, we analyzed the two main challenges that such data pose to automatic systems: the pervasive colloquialism and the multilinguality of Cantonese text, which often leads to the simultaneous presence of multiple languages in the same message or post. As strategies to tackle the challenges of Cantonese NLP, we could safely indicate data augmentation and crosslingual learning as two possible ways to go, in case the collection and balancing of large-scale Cantonese corpora turn out to be too problematic.

Cantonese is one of the most pervasive diaspora languages with native speaking communities spread around the world and has a vibrant and multicultural online community, and unique features that deserve a special attention for computational modeling. With our contribution, we hope we will manage to stimulate a new interest around this language in the NLP community, and to encourage future studies that will be devoted to resource sharing and to the reproducibility of the research results on public benchmarks.

Limitations

The main limitation of this work is that we only conduct our pilot study on limited number of domains since the textual data demands more efforts to clean. In future work, we plan to extend our study in more domains and more specifically focus on multi/cross lingual scenarios.

References

Josh Achiam, Steven Adler, Sandhini Agarwal, Lama Ahmad, Ilge Akkaya, Florencia Leoni Aleman, Diogo Almeida, Janko Altenschmidt, Sam Altman, Shyamal Anadkat, et al. 2023. GPT-4 Technical Report. *arXiv preprint arXiv:2303.08774*.

Kathleen Ahrens. 2015. Corpus of Political Speeches. Hong Kong Baptist University Library, URL `https://digital.lib.hkbu.edu.hk/corpus/`.

Tom B. Brown, Benjamin Mann, Nick Ryder, Melanie Subbiah, Jared Kaplan, Prafulla Dhariwal, Arvind Neelakantan, Pranav Shyam, Girish Sastry, Amanda Askell, Sandhini Agarwal, Ariel Herbert-Voss, Gretchen Krueger, Tom Henighan, Rewon Child, Aditya Ramesh, Daniel M. Ziegler, Jeffrey Wu, Clemens Winter, Christopher Hesse, Mark Chen, Eric Sigler, Mateusz Litwin, Scott Gray, Benjamin Chess, Jack Clark, Christopher Berner, Sam McCandlish, Alec Radford, Ilya Sutskever, and Dario Amodei. 2020. Language Models are Few-Shot Learners. In *Advances in Neural Information Processing Systems*.

Xinyu Chen, Liang Ke, Zhipeng Lu, Hanjian Su, and Haizhou Wang. 2020. A Novel Hybrid Model for Cantonese Rumor Detection on Twitter. *Applied Sciences*, 10(20):7093.

Andy Chin. 2015. A Linguistics Corpus of Mid-20th Century Hong Kong Cantonese. *Department of Linguistics and Modern Language Studies, The Hong Kong Institute of Education, Retrieved*, 23(3):2015.

Kevin Clark, Minh-Thang Luong, Quoc V. Le, and Christopher D. Manning. 2020. ELECTRA: Pre-training Text Encoders as Discriminators Rather Than Generators. In *Proceedings of the International Conference on Learning Representations*.

Yiming Cui, Wanxiang Che, Ting Liu, Bing Qin, and Ziqing Yang. 2021. Pre-training with Whole Word

Masking for Chinese BERT. *IEEE/ACM Transactions on Audio, Speech and Language Processing*, 29:3504–3514.

Marie-Catherine De Marneffe, Timothy Dozat, Natalia Silveira, Katri Haverinen, Filip Ginter, Joakim Nivre, and Christopher D Manning. 2014. Universal Stanford Dependencies: A Cross-linguistic Typology. In *Proceedings of LREC*.

Jacob Devlin, Ming-Wei Chang, Kenton Lee, and Kristina Toutanova. 2019. Bert: Pre-training of Deep Bidirectional Transformers for Language Understanding. In *Proceedings of NAACL*.

David M Eberhard, Gary F Simons, and Charles D Fennig. 2022. *Ethnologue: Languages of the World*. Dallas: SIL International.

Richard Eckart de Castilho, Giulia Dore, Thomas Margoni, Penny Labropoulou, and Iryna Gurevych. 2018. A Legal Perspective on Training Models for Natural Language Processing. In *Proceedings of LREC*.

Gabriel Fung, Maxime Debosschere, Dingmin Wang, Bo Li, Jia Zhu, and Kam-Fai Wong. 2017. NLPTEA 2017 Shared Task–Chinese Spelling Check. In *Proceedings of the IJCNLP Workshop on Natural Language Processing Techniques for Educational Applications*.

Ofelia García and Joshua A Fishman. 2011. *The Multilingual Apple: Languages in New York City*. Walter de Gruyter.

John Hale. 2001. A Probabilistic Earley Parser as a Psycholinguistic Model. In *Proceedings of NAACL-HLT*.

John Hale. 2016. Information-Theoretical Complexity Metrics. *Language and Linguistics Compass*, 10(9):397–412.

Chu-Ren Huang. 2009. Tagged Chinese Gigaword Version 2.0. *Linguistic Data Consortium*.

Chu-Ren Huang and Keh-jiann Chen. 1992. A Chinese Corpus for Linguistic Research. In *Proceedings of COLING*.

Guangpu Huang, Arseniy Gorin, Jean-Luc Gauvain, and Lori Lamel. 2016. Machine Translation Based Data Augmentation for Cantonese Keyword Spotting. In *IEEE International Conference on Acoustics, Speech and Signal Processing*, pages 6020–6024. IEEE.

Khia A Johnson, Molly Babel, Ivan Fong, and Nancy Yiu. 2020. SpiCE: A New Open-access Corpus of Conversational Bilingual Speech in Cantonese and English. In *Proceedings of LREC*.

Olivia OY Kwong. 2015. Toward a Corpus of Cantonese Verbal Comments and their Classification by Multi-dimensional Analysis. In *Proceedings of PACLIC*.

Him Mark Lai. 2004. *Becoming Chinese American: A History of Communities and Institutions*, volume 13. Rowman Altamira.

Carmen Lee. 2016. *Multilingualism Online*. Routledge.

Jackson Lee, Litong Chen, Charles Lam, Chaak Ming Lau, and Tsz-Him Tsui. 2022. PyCantonese: Cantonese Linguistics and NLP in Python. In *Proceedings of LREC*.

John Lee, Tianyuan Cai, Wenxiu Xie, and Lam Xing. 2020. A Counselling Corpus in Cantonese. In *Proceedings of the LREC Joint Workshop on Spoken Language Technologies for Under-resourced languages and Collaboration and Computing for Under-Resourced Languages*.

John SY Lee. 2011. Toward a Parallel Corpus of Spoken Cantonese and Written Chinese. In *Proceedings of IJCNLP*.

John SY Lee, Baikun Liang, and Haley Fong. 2021. Restatement and Question Generation for Counsellor Chatbot. In *Proceedings of the Workshop on NLP for Positive Impact*.

Thomas Lee and Colleen Wong. 1998. CANCORP: The Hong Kong Cantonese Child Language Corpus. *Cahiers de Linguistique Asie Orientale*, 27(2):211–228.

Man-Tak Leung and Sam-Po Law. 2001. HKCAC: The Hong Kong Cantonese Adult Language Corpus. *International Journal of Corpus Linguistics*, 6(2):305–325.

Roger Levy. 2008. Expectation-Based Syntactic Comprehension. *Cognition*, 106(3):1126–1177.

David CS Li. 2017. *Multilingual Hong Kong: Languages, Literacies and Identities*. Springer.

David CS Li and Virginia Costa. 2009. Punning in Hong Kong Chinese Media: Forms and Functions. *Journal of Chinese Linguistics*, 37(1):77–107.

Jiazheng Li, Runcong Zhao, Yongxin Yang, Yulan He, and Lin Gui. 2023. Overprompt: Enhancing chatgpt through efficient in-context learning. *arXiv preprint arXiv:2305.14973*.

Qingxin Li. 2006. *Maritime Silk Road*. China Intercontinental Press.

Andreas Maria Liesenfeld. 2018. MYCanCor: A Video Corpus of Spoken Malaysian Cantonese. In *Proceedings of LREC*.

Yinhan Liu, Myle Ott, Naman Goyal, Jingfei Du, Mandar Joshi, Danqi Chen, Omer Levy, Mike Lewis, Luke Zettlemoyer, and Veselin Stoyanov. 2019. Roberta: A Robustly Optimized BERT Pretraining Approach. *arXiv preprint arXiv:1907.11692*.

Kang Kwong Luke and May LY Wong. 2015. The Hong Kong Cantonese Corpus: Design and Uses. *Journal of Chinese Linguistics*, 25(2015):309–330.

KK Luke. 1995. Between Big Words and Small Talk: The Writing System in Cantonese Paperbacks in Hong Kong. 香港文化與社會.

Kanishka Misra. 2022. minicons: Enabling Flexible Behavioral and Representational Analyses of Transformer Language Models. *arXiv preprint arXiv:2203.13112*.

Raymond WM Ng, Alvin CM Kwan, Tan Lee, and Thomas Hain. 2017. Shefce: A Cantonese-English Bilingual Speech Corpus for Pronunciation Assessment. In *IEEE International Conference on Acoustics, Speech and Signal Processing (ICASSP)*, pages 5825–5829. IEEE.

Dat Quoc Nguyen, Thanh Vu, and Anh Tuan Nguyen. 2020. BERTweet: A Pre-trained Language Model for English Tweets. *arXiv preprint arXiv:2005.10200*.

Joakim Nivre, Marie-Catherine De Marneffe, Filip Ginter, Yoav Goldberg, Jan Hajic, Christopher D Manning, Ryan McDonald, Slav Petrov, Sampo Pyysalo, and Natalia Silveira. 2016. Universal Dependencies v1: A Multilingual Treebank Collection. In *Proceedings of LREC*.

Jueya Ouyang. 1993. Putonghua Guangzhouhua De Bijiao Yu Xuexi (The Comparison and Learning of Mandarin and Cantonese).

Jun Pan. 2019. The Chinese/English Political Interpreting Corpus (CEPIC): A New Electronic Resource for Translators and Interpreters. In *Proceedings of the Human-Informed Translation and Interpreting Technology Workshop*, pages 82–88.

Robert Parker, David Graff, Ke Chen, Junbo Kong, and Maeda Kazuaki. 2011. Chinese Gigaword. In *Web Download. Philadelphia: Linguistic Data Consortium*.

Julian Salazar, Davis Liang, Toan Q Nguyen, and Katrin Kirchhoff. 2020. Masked Language Model Scoring. In *Proceedings of ACL*.

Don Snow. 2004. *Cantonese as Written Language: The Growth of a Written Chinese Vernacular*, volume 1. Hong Kong University Press.

Alex Wang, Yada Pruksachatkun, Nikita Nangia, Amanpreet Singh, Julian Michael, Felix Hill, Omer Levy, and Samuel Bowman. 2019. SuperGLUE: A Stickier Benchmark for General-purpose Language Understanding Systems. *Advances in Neural Information Processing Systems*, 32.

Alex Wang, Amanpreet Singh, Julian Michael, Felix Hill, Omer Levy, and Samuel R Bowman. 2018. GLUE: A Multi-task Benchmark and Analysis Platform for Natural Language Understanding. *arXiv preprint arXiv:1804.07461*.

Hongru Wang, Min Li, Zimo Zhou, Gabriel Pui Cheong Fung, and Kam-Fai Wong. 2020. KddRES: A Multi-level Knowledge-driven Dialogue Dataset for Restaurant Towards Customized Dialogue System. *arXiv preprint arXiv:2011.08772*.

Ping-Wai Wong. 2006. The Specification of POS Tagging of the Hong Kong University Cantonese Corpus. *International Journal of Technology and Human Interaction*, 2(1):21–38.

Tak-sum Wong, Kim Gerdes, Herman Leung, and John SY Lee. 2017. Quantitative Comparative Syntax on the Cantonese-Mandarin Parallel Dependency Treebank. In *Proceedings of Depling*.

Tak-sum Wong and John SY Lee. 2018. Register-Sensitive Translation: A Case Study of Mandarin and Cantonese. In *Proceedings of the Conference of the Association for Machine Translation in the Americas*, pages 89–96.

Dekai Wu. 1994. Aligning a Parallel English-Chinese Corpus Statistically with Lexical Criteria. *arXiv preprint cmp-lg/9406007*.

Rong Xiang, Ying Jiao, and Qin Lu. 2019. Sentiment-augmented Attention Network for Cantonese Restaurant Review Analysis. In *Proceedings of KDD Workshop on Issues of Sentiment Discovery and Opinion Mining (WISDOM)*.

Rong Xiang, Hanzhuo Tan, Jing Li, Mingyu Wan, and Kam-Fai Wong. 2022. When Cantonese NLP Meets Pre-training: Progress and Challenges. In *Proceedings of AACL-IJCNLP: Tutorials*.

Zhilin Yang, Zihang Dai, Yiming Yang, Jaime Carbonell, Ruslan Salakhutdinov, and Quoc V Le. 2019. XLNet: Generalized Autoregressive Pretraining for Language Understanding. *arXiv preprint arXiv:1906.08237*.

Virginia Yip and Stephen Matthews. 2007. *The Bilingual Child. Early Development and Language Contact*. Cambridge University Press.

Henry Yu. 2013. Mountains of Gold: Canada, North America, and the Cantonese Pacific. In *Routledge Handbook of the Chinese Diaspora*, pages 124–137. Routledge.

Anne Yue-Hashimoto. 1991. The Yue Dialect. *Journal of Chinese Linguistics Monograph Series*, 1(3):292–322.

Runcong Zhao, Lin Gui, and Yulan He. 2023. Cone: Unsupervised contrastive opinion extraction. In *Proceedings of the 46th International ACM SIGIR Conference on Research and Development in Information Retrieval*, pages 1066–1075.

Runcong Zhao, Wenjia Zhang, Jiazheng Li, Lixing Zhu, Yanran Li, Yulan He, and Lin Gui. 2024a. Narrativeplay: An automated system for crafting visual worlds in novels for role-playing. In *Proceedings of the AAAI Conference on Artificial Intelligence*, volume 38, pages 23859–23861.

Runcong Zhao, Qinglin Zhu, Hainiu Xu, Jiazheng Li, Yuxiang Zhou, Yulan He, and Lin Gui. 2024b. Large language models fall short: Understanding complex relationships in detective narratives. *arXiv preprint arXiv:2402.11051*.

Qinglin Zhu, Runcong Zhao, Jinhua Du, Lin Gui, and Yulan He. 2024. Player*: Enhancing llm-based multi-agent communication and interaction in murder mystery games. *arXiv preprint arXiv:2404.17662*.

Auto-ACE: An Automatic Answer Correctness Evaluation Method for Conversational Question Answering

Zhixin Bai[1*], Bingbing Wang[2*], Bin Liang[3†], Ruifeng Xu[2,4†]

[1] Harbin Institute of Technology, Harbin, China

[2] Harbin Institute of Technology, Shenzhen, China

[3] The Chinese University of Hong Kong, Hong Kong, China

[4] Guangdong Provincial Key Laboratory of Novel Security Intelligence Technologies

{baizhixin,bingbing.wang}@stu.hit.edu.cn,
bin.liang@cuhk.edu.hk, xuruifeng@hit.edu.cn

Abstract

Conversational question answering aims to respond to questions based on relevant contexts and previous question-answer history. Existing studies typically use ground-truth answers in history, leading to the inconsistency between the training and inference phases. However, in real-world scenarios, progress in question answering can only be made using predicted answers. Since not all predicted answers are correct, indiscriminately using all predicted answers for training introduces noise into the model. To tackle these challenges, we propose an automatic answer correctness evaluation method named **Auto-ACE**. Specifically, we first construct an Att-BERT model which employs attention weight to the BERT model, so as to bridge the relation between the current question and the question-answer pair in history. Furthermore, to reduce the interference of the irrelevant information in the predicted answer, A-Scorer, an answer scorer is designed to evaluate the confidence of the predicted answer. We conduct a series of experiments on QuAC and CoQA datasets, and the results demonstrate the effectiveness and practicality of our proposed Auto-ACE framework.

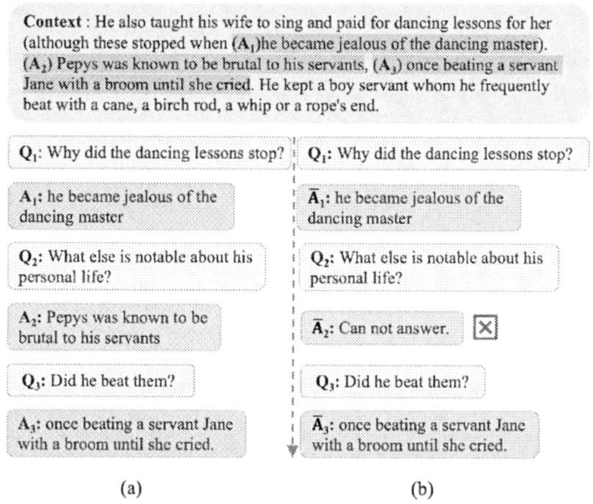

Figure 1: Examples of using (a) ground-truth answers and (b) predicted answers.

1 Introduction

Conversational Question Answering (ConvQA) involves responding to a sequence of questions within a conversation, while considering the relevant context provided (Qu et al., 2020; Pearce et al., 2023; Reddy et al., 2019). Different from the traditional extractive question-answering tasks which conduct one-turn dialog, as shown in Figure 1, ConvQA is expected to resolve such implicit information from the conversational history in a multi-turn way.

With the rise of virtual assistants and chatbots, ConvQA has recently garnered increased interest. Hence, numerous works have been conducted for further study. Raposo et al. (2022) proposed a conversational question answering system specifically designed for the Search-Oriented Conversational AI (SCAI) shared task, and provided a detailed analysis of its question rewriting module. Qu et al. (2019b) introduced a positional history answer embedding method to encode conversation history with positional information using BERT (Devlin et al., 2018). They also designed a history attention mechanism (HAM) for each question-answer pair and utilized multi-task learning to predict the final answer. Nevertheless, despite their successes, these works on ConvQA rely on the ground-truth answer, overlooking the fact that real-world progress can only be achieved using predicted answers.

Existing researchers found a way to tackle this limitation by using the predicted label (Mandya et al., 2020; Christmann et al., 2022). This method can partially trade off the balance between training and inference. However, if the predicted answer is incorrect, it will introduce noisy samples into the model, thereby affecting performance. For example, as shown in Figure 1, $\{Q_2, A_2, Q_1, A_1\}$ are

*These authors contributed equally to this work.

†Corresponding author.

Proceedings of the 10th SIGHAN Workshop on Chinese Language Processing (SIGHAN-10), pages 80–87
August 16, 2024

input as the conversation history of Q_3 into the Question Answering (QA) model to perform inference for A_3. Figure 1(a) indicates that ground-truth answers are used for inference, which significantly differs from the real-world inference scenarios. Figure 1(b) indicates the use of all predicted answers for inference. Although this way is more practical, it introduces noise into the model to some extent when the predicted answers are incorrect. Therefore, we propose an answer scorer model that can automatically assign attention weights to predicted answers and incorporate them into the QA model's inference phase. The most similar work to ours is the work of Jeong et al. (2023), which requires an initial round of training and prediction to obtain the predicted answers along with their confidences and uncertainties before the official training. This additional training and prediction step increases the overall training time and computational resource consumption.

In this paper, we propose an automatic answer correctness evaluation method named Auto-ACE, which comprises an Att-BERT and an A-Scorer method to maximize the use of effective information from the predicted answers. To be more specific, we first construct an Att-BERT model which employs attention weight to the BERT model, so as to bridge the relation between the current question and the question-answer pair in history. Furthermore, to reduce the disturbance of the irrelevant content in the predicted answer, A-Scorer, an answer scorer is designed to evaluate the confidence of the predicted answer. During the training phase, Att-BERT and A-Scorer are trained, while in the inference period, A-Scorer evaluates each question-answering pair in the history to obtain the correctness of the predicted answer. Numerous experiments on QuAC and CoQA datasets demonstrate the effectiveness and practicality of our proposed Auto-ACE framework[1].

The main contributions of our work can be summarized as follows:

- We propose an Auto-ACE framework to establish the connection between the current question and historical question-answer pairs, balancing the process between training and inference phases.

- To bridge the relation between the current question and the historical question-answer pair, Att-BERT is designed. Moreover, we devised the A-Scorer, which is trained with Att-BERT during the training phase and evaluates the correctness of the predicted answer during the inference phase to mitigate the impact of erroneous predicted answers and maximize the utilization of historical conversation information.

- Our Auto-ACE framework achieves excellent performances on QuAC and CoQA datasets, which shows our approach is effective.

[1] https://github.com/baibaizhixin/Auto-ACE

2 Related Works

2.1 Conversational Question Answering

ConvQA is an extension of the QA task which aims to train a model that can answer the question by means of understanding the context of the given context and the previous conversational questions and answers. In the work by Nishida and Tomita (2019), BERT is utilized to encode contexts independently conditioned with each question and answer within a multi-turn context. This process enables the method to predict answers based on the context representations encoded with BERT. Qu et al. (2019a) presented a distinct method termed history answer embedding, which incorporates conversation history into a ConvQA model built on BERT. Query rewriting became a popular technique for ConvQA. Vakulenko et al. (2021) addressed question ambiguity by rewriting them, ensuring they can be effectively processed by existing QA models as standalone questions, independent of the conversation context. Wu et al. (2022) introduced a query rewriting model tailored for converting conversational questions within a context into standalone queries. This model is trained using a novel reward function, optimized directly for retrieval via reinforcement learning. Although the above studies attain excellent performance in ConvQA, they ignore the unbalance between training and inference phases due to the utilization of ground truth or predicted answers.

2.2 Score-based Methods

Score-based methods have gained significant attention in various Natural Language Processing (NLP) tasks due to their capability to enable models to selectively focus on relevant parts of the input sequence. For example, Osama et al. (2020) introduced the Score-Based Ambiguity Detector and Resolver method. This system uses Stanford

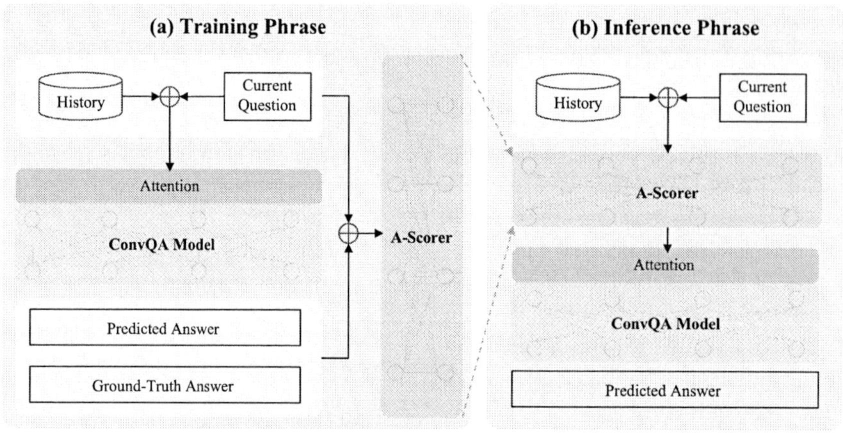

Figure 2: A figure

CoreNLP to generate possible parse trees for each sentence in a given textual requirement. It then analyzes these parse trees through four filtering pipelines to detect syntactic ambiguities and suggest multiple possible interpretations, effectively resolving the ambiguities. Several attempts have been made to enable self-attention to learn dependencies between words in a sentence and capture the sentence's inner structure (Tan et al., 2018; Cao et al., 2018). Liu et al. (2021) devised an attention score-based word rank approach, incorporating a word sequence encoder and a word-level attention layer. Despite the extensive work on score-based methods in various natural language tasks, their application in ConvQA remains under-explored. This is particularly important when historical questions and answers contain implicit information, making the predicted answer unusable directly.

3 Methodology

This section begins with a concise introduction to the ConvQA task, then we describe how the proposed Auto-ACE framework can bridge the gap between training and real-world inference scenarios by incorporating predicted answers into model training, as demonstrated in Figure 2. In addition, we discuss the calculation of attention weights and the overall training pipeline.

3.1 Conversational Question Answering

We first provide a general description of the ConvQA task. For the i-th turn of the conversation, a question Q_i and its corresponding context C are given, as well as a conversation history H_i composed of previous questions and answers: $H_i = \{Q_{i-1}, A_{i-1}, ..., Q_1, A_1\}$. Then, the goal of ConvQA is to correctly extract the answer A_i from C, along with Q_i and H_i, as shown below:

$$\begin{aligned} P(A_i) &= P(A_i \mid C, Q_i, \mathcal{H}_i) \\ &= M_\theta (C, Q_i, Q_{i-1}, A_{i-1}, \ldots, Q_1, A_1) \end{aligned} \tag{1}$$

where M_θ is the ConvQA model.

In previous work, some of them assumed that the ground-truth answers $\{A_{i-1}, A_{i-2}, ..., A_1\}$ are available in the inference phase, as shown in Equation 1. However, this setup is far from reality because progress in the real world can only be made using the predicted answer. If the training process always uses ground-truth answers, it will lead to the model not performing well in real-world inference scenarios. Another part of them recognized this and tried to select whether to include the predicted answer of a certain historical turn in the conversation history by setting a threshold. However, it often requires an additional step of training to calculate the confidence of all predicted answers and determine the value of the threshold, which increases the overall training time and computational resource consumption. Therefore, we modify the formulation in Equation 1 to bridge the gap between the training and the inference phase, which we will describe in the following section.

3.2 Training with Predicted Answers

As delineated in Section 3.1, employing ground-truth answers during model training and predicted answers during inference is inadvisable. To align the model's training phase more closely with real-world inference scenario, a rational strategy entails utilizing the model's prior predictions as inputs to the conversation history for subsequent turns of prediction, as follows:

$$P(A_i) = M_\theta(C, Q_i, Q_{i-1}, \overline{A}_{i-1}, \ldots, Q_1, \overline{A}_1) \quad (2)$$

where $\{\overline{A}_{i-1}, \overline{A}_{i-2}, ..., \overline{A}_1\}$ are the predicted answers.

Given that the accuracy of the model's predictive answers is not infallible, incorporating erroneous predictions into the conversation history may introduce superfluous noise, thereby potentially degrading the efficacy of the predictions. Therefore, we propose an Att-BERT model that applies attention weights to the BERT model, giving higher weights to answers with high confidence and lower weights to answers with low confidence, which allows for the use of predicted answers during training while minimizing the noise caused by incorrect predicted answers.

To be more specific, we assign attention weights to each turn's question Q_j and predicted answer $\overline{A}_j$ in the conversation history. The weight of the Q_j represents the degree of relevance to the current question, and on this basis, the weight of the $\overline{A}_j$ also represents the confidence of the predicted answer, as shown in the following.

$$P(A_i) = M_\theta(C, Q_i, W^q_{i-1}Q_{i-1}, W^a_{i-1}\overline{A}_{i-1}, \ldots, W^q_1 Q_1, W^a_1 \overline{A}_1) \quad (3)$$

Considering the real-world inference scenario, we assign attention weights to the questions and answers at each turn of the conversation history. The attention weight W^q_j of the question Q_j represents the degree of relevance to the current question Q_i, that is, the more similar Q_j is to the Q_i, the more attention the model will give to this sequence. Notably, the attention weight is complemented by the cosine similarity between Q_j and Q_i, as shown in Equation 4. Since all questions in the conversation history are provided in the inference scenario, the whole attention weights can be directly calculated.

$$W^q_j = \text{Similarity}(Q_j, Q_i) \quad (4)$$

where W^q_j represents the attention weight of the question in the j-th turn of the conversation history, Similarity is used to compute the cosine similarity.

3.3 Confidence-based Attention Calculation

In this section, we aim to enhance the model's focus on the most relevant content of the predicted answers. However, it is impractical to calculate weights for all predicted answers, as some of them may be incorrect. To address this challenge, an A-Scorer is devised to automatically evaluate the confidence of predicted answers and is trained in conjunction with the Att-BERT model. In specific, after the Att-BERT model generates a predicted answer each turn, we input the question Q_j, the predicted answer $\overline{A}_j$, and the corresponding context C into the A-Scorer model to evaluate the confidence of the $\overline{A}_j$, and use the cosine similarity between the predicted answer and the actual answer as the ground truth for the confidence.

$$W^a_j = W^q_j \times \text{A-Scorer}(Q_j, \overline{A}_j) \quad (5)$$

where W^q_j and W^a_j represent the attention weights of the question and the predicted answer in the j-th turn of the conversation history, A-Scorer is the model we proposed for automatic confidence evaluation.

Following the joint training of the Att-BERT model and the A-Scorer model, these two models become capable of operating in concert with real-world inference scenarios. The answer predicted by the Att-BERT model is evaluated for confidence by the A-Scorer model. Furthermore, during the prediction of an answer, the attention weight of each question or answer within the conversation history is ascertained contingent upon the predicted answer's confidence, as well as the degree of correspondence to the current question.

3.4 Overall Pipeline

In this subsection, we describe the training pipeline for the Att-BERT model and the A-Scorer model, which are trained together in a single step and are also applied together in the inference phase.

We divide the training data into batches, ensuring that (1) the same batch does not contain examples from the same conversation, and (2) for any two examples from the same conversation, the batch of the example that appears later in the conversation is also later. We do this to ensure that when an example is input into the model, all predicted answers for the questions in its conversation history have already been obtained, thus ensuring that only predicted answers are used during the training phase, not the ground-truth answers. Then, we train the Att-BERT model and the A-Scorer model together following the training protocol in Equation 3. The Att-BERT model assigns different attention weights to the questions and predicted answers in the conversation, while the A-Scorer model evaluates the confidence of the answers predicted by the Att-BERT model.

For evaluation, we still use Equation 3 as the actual evaluation protocol. Instead of using ground-truth answers or sampling predicted answers based on the confidence obtained during training, we directly apply the predictions of the A-Scorer model to the attention weights of the Att-BERT model. Doing so not only bridges the gap between training and real-world inference scenarios but also avoids the need for additional training steps and reduces the demand for excessive computational resources.

4 Experiments

4.1 Datasets and metrics

QuAC (Choi et al., 2018) is a benchmark ConvQA dataset, which comprises 14K conversations and 100K question-context pairs and is designed to simulate realistic information-seeking conversations. In QuAC, questioners did not have access to the contexts during data collection. Since the test set is not publicly available, we use the development set for evaluation.

CoQA (Reddy et al., 2019) is another ConvQA dataset, containing 127K question-context pairs. Similar to QuAC, we use the development set for CoQA as the test set is not publicly accessible.

F1-score: To assess the performance of our models, we use the F1-score as the evaluation metric. This follows the standard evaluation protocol established by (Kim et al., 2021). The F1-score is a widely recognized metric that balances precision and recall, making it particularly suitable for evaluating the quality of predictions in natural language tasks.

Baselines: We compare Auto-ACE with several relevant baselines. Except for the gold and No Pred models, all other models used predicted answers as the conversation history in the inference phase.

- **Gold**: which uses an unrealistic setting in both training and inference phases, using ground-truth answers as conversation history.
- **No Pred**: which does not use predicted answers during training and inference.
- **All Pred**: which retains all predicted answers as conversation history during both training and inference.

Method	QuAC		CoQA	
	BERT	RoBERTa	BERT	RoBERTa
Gold†	59.86	65.08	72.79	77.62
No Pred†	55.44	61.24	70.83	75.56
All Pred†	55.76	61.53	71.28	75.42
CoQAM†	55.83	61.55	71.27	74.29
AS-ConvQA†	57.06	62.18	71.99	76.76
Auto-ACE (ours)	**58.38**	**63.04**	**72.56**	**77.29**

Table 1: Performance(%) on QuAC and CoQA. **Bold** indicates the model with the best performance. Results with † comes from Jeong et al. (2023).

- **CoQAM**: which dynamically adjusts the sampling rate to alternately select ground truth answers or predicted answers during training, and uses predicted answers during inference phase.
- **AS-ConvQA**: This method decides whether to include the predicted answer in the conversation history during the training and inference phases based on the confidence and uncertainty of the predicted answer.

4.2 Main Results

As shown in Table 1, the Auto-ACE framework, which includes an Att-BERT and an A-Scorer model, demonstrates significant performance improvements across all baselines. The evaluation results show that, our method outperforms the strongest baseline that does not use ground-truth answers by 1.32%. In addition, our model can be trained in one step, unlike AS-ConvQA, which requires additional training and prediction steps. It should be noted that since the Gold model uses an unrealistic evaluation setting where ground-truth answers are used as conversation history, it is not fair when compared with other methods.

It is worth mentioning that the No Pred methods outperform those using predicted answers or heuristic sampling of conversation history, which demonstrates incorrect predicted answers can introduce noise to the QA model. Moreover, our method shows a significant advantage, it might attribute to the A-Scorer can automatically evaluate the confidence of predicted answers, allowing the QA model to truly focus on relevant and correct answers, and minimize the impact of noise at the same time.

4.3 Ablation Study

We also conducted an ablation study on the use of the attention mechanism. Specifically, we di-

Method	QuAC		CoQA	
	BERT	RoBERTa	BERT	RoBERTa
Auto-ACE	**58.38**	**63.04**	**72.56**	**77.29**
w/o attention(Q&Q)	57.32	62.08	70.95	75.29
w/o attention(Q&A)	57.88	62.25	71.19	76.68
w/o attention(both)	56.46	60.98	69.23	74.57

Table 2: Performance (%) of ablation study on QuAC and CoQA datasets. **Bold** indicates the model with the best performance.

vided it into three scenarios: not considering the attention between the current question and the historical question-answer pairs, not considering the attention to the predicted answers in the history, and not using the attention mechanism at all. The evaluation results are shown in Table 2. The performances of all ablation models are worse than the complete model, which demonstrates the necessity of the attention mechanism.

The most significant performance drop occurs when neither of the two attention mechanisms is considered, so using either one of them alone can improve the performance, indicating that both of them are effective. An interesting finding is that disregarding the attention between the current and previous questions (Q&Q) often results in worse performance than disregarding the attention to the predicted answer (Q&A), indicating that the similarity between the current question and the historical question-answer pairs seems to have a greater impact on the model's performance.

4.4 Difference of Evaluator

To demonstrate that our proposed Auto-ACE framework can deliver robust performance across different QA models, we also evaluated it by replacing the evaluator with Roberta, with the results shown in Table 1. It can be seen that our model has performed well in both configurations using BERT and Roberta as evaluators. In the configuration using RoBERTa as an evaluator, Auto-ACE improved the F1 scores on the quac and coqa datasets by % and % compared to the best-performing baseline, respectively.

4.5 Effect of the Contextual Number

To examine and analyze the impact of the max length of utterances over the performance of our proposed Auto-ACE framework, we conduct experiments by varying the max length from 1 to 12. Since the maximum number of conversation turns in all sessions of the QuAC dataset is 12, setting

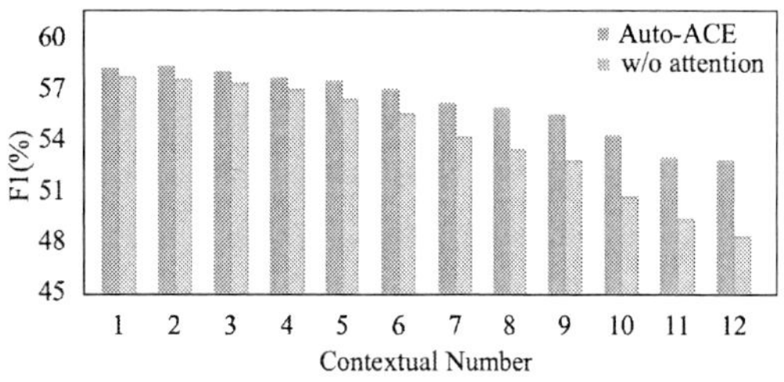

Figure 3: Results(%) of the effect of the different contextual number.

the contextual number to 12 means that all samples retain the complete conversation history. In other cases, samples retain the most recent contextual number of conversation turns' history.

We plotted the experimental results in a bar chart and demonstrate them in Figure 3. It should be noted that, to consider the relationship between the attention in our proposed Att-BERT model and the contextual number, we also evaluated the model without applying the attention under different contextual number settings. From Figure 1, it can be seen that as the contextual number increases, the model's performance gradually decreases, with the best results for the model being achieved when the contextual number is set to 1-3. This also conforms to our intuition: the more recent Q&A turns in the conversation history tend to be more relevant to the current question.

Another point worth noting is: with the increase of contextual number, although the model's performance declines, the model without attention to the conversation history declines more significantly than our model. This is because, even though there are many irrelevant Q&A pairs in the long conversation history, the proposed Auto-ACE model can allocate attention to the conversation history based on relevance and predicted answer's confidence, thus allowing the model to focus on the information that is relevant and reliable to the current question in a long sequence.

4.6 Case Study

Two representative conversation scenarios are provided in Figure 4. These two examples demonstrate that our method of weighting the conversation history in the form of attention is highly practical and meaningful. From example (a), we can observe that the current question Q_3 has a strong correlation with the historical question Q_1, because "first film" in the current question refers to the answer

Context : Gerard Soeteman also wrote the script for Verhoeven's first American film, (A_1) Flesh and Blood ((A_3) 1985), which starred Rutger Hauer and Jennifer Jason Leigh. Verhoeven moved to Hollywood for a wider range of opportunities in filmmaking. Working in the U.S. he made a serious change in style, directing big-budget, very violent, (A_2)special-effects-heavy smashes RoboCop and Total Recall.

Q_1: What was the first film he did in the US? *0.82*

$\overline{A}_1$: Flesh and Blood *0.80*

Q_2: What genre of films did he make? *0.29*

$\overline{A}_2$: big-budget, very violent, special-effects-heavy smashes *0.21*

Q_3: What year did his first film debut? *1.00*

$\overline{A}_3$: 1985

(a)

Context : (A_1) His lawsuit was unsuccessful, partly because he had been using steroids for a decade preceding his WWF debut. ... (A_2)Graham went on a public awareness campaign regarding the dangers of steroids during this time, including an appearance with McMahon on The Phil Donahue Show in 1992. (A_3) During the Donahue taping Graham claimed to have witnessed WWF officials sexually abuse children.

Q_1: did he win the lawsuit? *0.23*

$\overline{A}_1$: His lawsuit was unsuccessful, *0.20*

Q_2: what happened after the suit failed? *0.16*

$\overline{A}_2$: Can not answer. *0.00*

Q_3: how did the campaign do? *1.00*

$\overline{A}_3$: During the Donahue taping Graham claimed to have witnessed WWF officials sexually abuse children.

(b)

Figure 4: Examples of applying the attention weight to the history.

of question Q_1:"Flesh and Blood". In our method, due to the high similarity to Q_3, Q_1 is assigned a high attention weight. $\overline{A}_1$, as the predicted answer for Q_1, also receives a high final attention weight because the A-Scorer deems it to have a high degree of confidence. When these weights are applied in the form of attention to Att-BERT, the model can focus more on the useful information in the history: Q_1 and $\overline{A}_1$, and thus it is easier to predict the correct answer.

The opposite scenario is depicted in Figure 4(b). Although the predicted answer $\overline{A}_2$ is crucial for the current question as it includes the keyword "campaign" from Q_3, the model's prediction for question Q_2 is "Can not answer" at this point, which could introduce noise into the model when being used as part of the conversation history. In our method, "Can not answer" is assigned an attention weight of 0 by the A-Scorer, hence its final attention weight is 0. The Att-BERT does not pay attention to this incorrect answer, thus not affecting the prediction of the answer for the current turn.

5 Conclusion

In this paper, we introduce an automatic answer correctness evaluation method named Auto-ACE for ConvQA task, which can balance the inconsistency between training and inference. The proposed Auto-ACE method consists of two primary components including Att-BERT and A-Scorer. The Att-BERT effectively bridges the current question with historical Q&A pairs using attention mechanisms, enabling the model to focus on more relevant content. Furthermore, the A-Scorer is designed to evaluate the confidence of predicted answers and is applied to the Att-BERT as the confidence-based attention. Experiments conducted on QuAC and CoQA datasets demonstrate that our proposed Auto-ACE method significantly improves the performance and reliability of other baseline models.

Limitations

Although the Auto-ACE framework demonstrates promising results in the Conversational Question Answering task, there are still some limitations that require further attention: 1) The model's capability to process lengthy conversational histories needs enhancement to ensure consistent performance. In the future, we will consider the richness of real-world conversations to improve the model's performance. 2) The A-Scorer may still introduce noise due to inappropriate evaluation of predicted answers, future work could consider employing large language models to further enhance the accuracy of answer evaluation.

Acknowledgements

This work was partially supported by the National Natural Science Foundation of China (62176076), the Natural Science Foundation of Guangdong (2023A1515012922), the Shenzhen Foundational Research Funding (JCYJ20220818102415032), and the Guangdong Provincial Key Laboratory of Novel Security Intelligence Technologies (2022B1212010005).

References

Pengfei Cao, Yubo Chen, Kang Liu, Jun Zhao, and Shengping Liu. 2018. Adversarial transfer learning for chinese named entity recognition with self-attention mechanism. In *Proceedings of the 2018 conference on empirical methods in natural language processing*, pages 182–192.

Eunsol Choi, He He, Mohit Iyyer, Mark Yatskar, Wen-tau Yih, Yejin Choi, Percy Liang, and Luke Zettlemoyer. 2018. Quac: Question answering in context. In *Proceedings of the 2018 Conference on Empirical Methods in Natural Language Processing*, pages 2174–2184.

Philipp Christmann, Rishiraj Saha Roy, and Gerhard Weikum. 2022. Conversational question answering on heterogeneous sources. In *Proceedings of the 45th International ACM SIGIR Conference on Research and Development in Information Retrieval*, pages 144–154.

Jacob Devlin, Ming-Wei Chang, Kenton Lee, and Kristina Toutanova. 2018. Bert: Pre-training of deep bidirectional transformers for language understanding. *arXiv preprint arXiv:1810.04805*.

Soyeong Jeong, Jinheon Baek, Sung Ju Hwang, and Jong C Park. 2023. Realistic conversational question answering with answer selection based on calibrated confidence and uncertainty measurement. *arXiv preprint arXiv:2302.05137*.

Gangwoo Kim, Hyunjae Kim, Jungsoo Park, and Jaewoo Kang. 2021. Learn to resolve conversational dependency: A consistency training framework for conversational question answering. In *Proceedings of the 59th Annual Meeting of the Association for Computational Linguistics and the 11th International Joint Conference on Natural Language Processing (Volume 1: Long Papers)*, pages 6130–6141.

Yueyang Liu, Hunmin Lee, and Zhipeng Cai. 2021. An attention score based attacker for black-box nlp classifier. *arXiv preprint arXiv:2112.11660*.

Angrosh Mandya, James O'Neill, Danushka Bollegala, and Frans Coenen. 2020. Do not let the history haunt you: Mitigating compounding errors in conversational question answering. In *Proceedings of the Twelfth Language Resources and Evaluation Conference*, pages 2017–2025.

Yasuhito Ohsugi Itsumi Saito Kyosuke Nishida and Hisako Asano Junji Tomita. 2019. A simple but effective method to incorporate multi-turn context with bert for conversational machine comprehension. *ACL 2019*, page 11.

Mohamed Osama, Aya Zaki-Ismail, Mohamed Abdelrazek, John Grundy, and Amani Ibrahim. 2020. Score-based automatic detection and resolution of syntactic ambiguity in natural language requirements. In *2020 IEEE International Conference on Software Maintenance and Evolution (ICSME)*, pages 651–661. IEEE.

Kate Pearce, Sharifa Alghowinem, and Cynthia Breazeal. 2023. Build-a-bot: teaching conversational ai using a transformer-based intent recognition and question answering architecture. In *Proceedings of the AAAI Conference on Artificial Intelligence*, volume 37, pages 16025–16032.

Chen Qu, Liu Yang, Cen Chen, Minghui Qiu, W Bruce Croft, and Mohit Iyyer. 2020. Open-retrieval conversational question answering. In *Proceedings of the 43rd International ACM SIGIR conference on research and development in Information Retrieval*, pages 539–548.

Chen Qu, Liu Yang, Minghui Qiu, W Bruce Croft, Yongfeng Zhang, and Mohit Iyyer. 2019a. Bert with history answer embedding for conversational question answering. In *Proceedings of the 42nd international ACM SIGIR conference on research and development in information retrieval*, pages 1133–1136.

Chen Qu, Liu Yang, Minghui Qiu, Yongfeng Zhang, Cen Chen, W Bruce Croft, and Mohit Iyyer. 2019b. Attentive history selection for conversational question answering. In *Proceedings of the 28th ACM International Conference on Information and Knowledge Management*, pages 1391–1400.

Gonçalo Raposo, Rui Ribeiro, Bruno Martins, and Luísa Coheur. 2022. Question rewriting? assessing its importance for conversational question answering. In *European Conference on Information Retrieval*, pages 199–206. Springer.

Siva Reddy, Danqi Chen, and Christopher D Manning. 2019. Coqa: A conversational question answering challenge. *Transactions of the Association for Computational Linguistics*, 7:249–266.

Zhixing Tan, Mingxuan Wang, Jun Xie, Yidong Chen, and Xiaodong Shi. 2018. Deep semantic role labeling with self-attention. In *Proceedings of the AAAI conference on artificial intelligence*, volume 32.

Svitlana Vakulenko, Shayne Longpre, Zhucheng Tu, and Raviteja Anantha. 2021. Question rewriting for conversational question answering. In *Proceedings of the 14th ACM international conference on web search and data mining*, pages 355–363.

Zeqiu Wu, Yi Luan, Hannah Rashkin, David Reitter, Hannaneh Hajishirzi, Mari Ostendorf, and Gaurav Singh Tomar. 2022. Conqrr: Conversational query rewriting for retrieval with reinforcement learning. In *Proceedings of the 2022 Conference on Empirical Methods in Natural Language Processing*, pages 10000–10014.

TMAK-Plus at SIGHAN-2024 dimABSA Task: Multi-Agent Collaboration for Transparent and Rational Sentiment Analysis

Xin Kang[1], Zhifei Zhang[2], Jiazheng Zhou[1], Yunong Wu[3], Xuefeng Shi[4], Kazuyuki Matsumoto[1],

[1]Department of Computer Science, Tokushima University, Tokushima, Japan.
[2]Department of Computer Science and Technology, Tongji University, Shanghai, China.
[3]NLP Department, Dataa Robotics (Chengdu Branch), Chengdu, China.
[4]School of Artificial Intelligence and Computer Science, Nantong University, Nantong, China.

Correspondence: kang-xin@is.tokushima-u.ac.jp

Abstract

The TMAK-Plus team proposes a Multi-Agent Collaboration (MAC) model for the dimensional Aspect-Based Sentiment Analysis (dimABSA) task at SIGHAN-2024. The MAC model leverages Neuro-Symbolic AI to solve dimABSA transparently and rationally through symbolic message exchanges among generative AI agents. These agents collaborate on aspect detection, opinion detection, aspect classification, and intensity estimation. We created 8 sentiment intensity agents with distinct character traits to mimic diverse sentiment perceptions and average their outputs. The AI agents received clear instructions and 20 training examples to ensure task understanding. Our results suggest that the MAC model is effective in solving the dimABSA task and offers a transparent and rational approach to understanding the solution process.

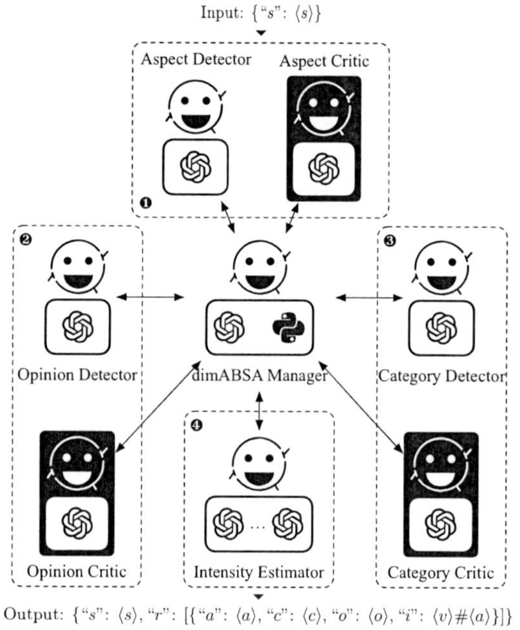

Figure 1: MAC model in the dimABSA Task. The central dimABSA Manager (DM) agent manages the overall collaboration, reading the input sentence, generating the dimABSA result, and coordinating other agents. These agents include the Aspect Detector (AD) and Opinion Detector (OD) for sentiment term extraction, the Category Detector (CD) for aspect classification, the Aspect Critic (AC), Opinion Critic (OC), and Category Critic (CC) for critical evaluation, and the Intensity Estimator (IE) for averaging sentiment intensities from 8 distinct estimators. All messages, including the input sentence, output quadruples, and intermediate results, are exchanged in JSON format.

1 Introduction

We consider the dimABSA task a challenging sentiment analysis problem (Cai et al., 2021; Pontiki et al., 2016) that requires a deep understanding of natural language and the ability to sense sentiments with distinct character traits. Specifically, aspect detection, opinion detection, and aspect classification account for distinct sentiment analysis abilities, while intensity estimation requires a comprehensive understanding of valence and arousal intensities corresponding to the empathetic sentiment sensitivity of different individuals.

To address the dimABSA task, we propose a MAC model that sequentially solves the aforementioned challenges, as shown in Figure 1. The model consists of GPT-4o (`gpt-4o-2024-05-13`) powered generative neural AI agents, including AD, OD, CD, AC, OC, CC, and IE. We pair AD and AC for collaborative aspect detection, OD and OC for collaborative opinion detection, and CD and CC for collaborative aspect classification. IE averages the sentiment intensities from 8 estimators with distinct character traits. All agents exchange messages in JSON format, including the detected results or critical feedback, in a symbolic manner to ensure transparency and rationality.

Unlike previous approaches that focus on the end-to-end training of a single neural network with a particular training set (Chen et al., 2021; Mao

Proceedings of the 10th SIGHAN Workshop on Chinese Language Processing (SIGHAN-10), pages 88–95
August 16, 2024

et al., 2021, 2022; Peng et al., 2020; Xu et al., 2020; Peper and Wang, 2022; Zhang et al., 2021), the MAC model is powered by multiple generative AI agents. These agents require only a few training examples and clear instructions to perform their tasks in a more robust manner and generalize easily to out-of-domain data. Our results demonstrate that MAC provides a generalizable and transparent Neuro-Symbolic AI framework for solving key phrase detection, multi-class classification, and regression tasks that require a deep understanding of natural language.

The main contributions are as follows:

- We propose a transparent and rational MAC model for the dimABSA task.
- We provide a new paradigm of Neuro-Symbolic AI powered by generative AI with symbolic collaboration.
- We demonstrate the effectiveness and generalizability of MAC in solving a challenging sentiment analysis task.

2 MAC Model for dimABSA

2.1 Formal Definition of dimABSA

The dimABSA task consists of 3 subtasks:

Subtask 1: Intensity Prediction involves predicting sentiment intensities (i) in the valence and arousal (v#a) dimensions for given aspect terms in a sentence.

Subtask 2: Triplet Extraction requires extracting sentiment triplets composed of an aspect term (a), an opinion term (o), and their corresponding intensity (i).

Subtask 3: Quadruple Extraction focuses on extracting sentiment quadruples that include an aspect term (a), an aspect category (c), an opinion term (o), and their intensity (i).

We use the following running example throughout this paper. The example is presented in traditional Chinese with an English translation for clarity and analysis purposes.

```
{
  "k": "R0645:S125",
  "s": "這牛排外面裹著一層麵包粉看起來蠻粉嫩的，吃下去外皮
       酥脆卡滋卡滋真的好吃。",
  e_s: "This steak is coated with a layer of
       breadcrumbs on the outside, making it
       look quite tender. When you bite into
       it, the crust is crispy and crunchy
       and really delicious.",
  "a": ["牛排", "外皮", "牛排"],
  e_a: ["steak", "crust", "steak"],
  "c": ["食物#品質", "食物#品質", "食物#品質"],
  e_c: ["food#quality", "food#quality",
       "food#quality"],
  "o": ["蠻粉嫩的", "酥脆", "真的好吃"],
  e_o: ["quite tender", "crispy",
       "really delicious"],
  "i": ["6.25#5.75", "6.62#6.0", "6.88#6.62"]
}
```

In this example, the aspect terms (a) are 牛排 (steak) and 外皮 (crust), the opinion terms (o) are 蠻粉嫩的 (quite tender), 酥脆 (crispy), and 真的好吃 (really delicious), and the sentiment intensities (i) are expressed as valence and arousal scores (v#a) with $v, a \in [1, 9]$.

2.2 MAC Model Architecture

Figure 2 illustrates the MAC model architecture for the dimABSA task. This model integrates multiple generative AI agents that collaborate to perform the subtasks required for dimABSA. The agents involved in this process include DM, AD, AC, OD, OC, CD, CC, and various IE agents.

The DM agent manages the overall collaboration, reading input sentences, generating results, and coordinating the other agents. The AD agent detects all sentiment aspects in a given sentence, while the AC agent evaluates the performance of AD and provides constructive feedback. The OD agent detects sentiment opinions associated with each aspect, and the OC agent evaluates the performance of OD, offering feedback. The CD agent classifies each aspect into predefined categories, and the CC agent evaluates the performance of CD, ensuring accuracy and consistency.

The 8 sentiment intensity estimators in the MAC model reflect distinct human characters, grounded in psychological and linguistic theories. According to the Big Five personality traits model (John et al., 1999), human personalities can be categorized into dimensions such as openness, conscientiousness, extraversion, agreeableness, and neuroticism, each influencing how individuals perceive and react to emotional stimuli. Additionally, the circumplex model of affect (Russell, 1980) provides a framework for understanding emotions in a valence-arousal space. Integrating these perspectives ensures the model captures a broad range of human emotional responses, enhancing its robustness and generalizability. Specifically, the IE agents estimate sentiment intensities analytically (IE^A), empathetically (IE^E), critically (IE^C), optimistically (IE^O), realistically (IE^R), pessimistically (IE^P), balanced (IE^B), and intuitively (IE^I).

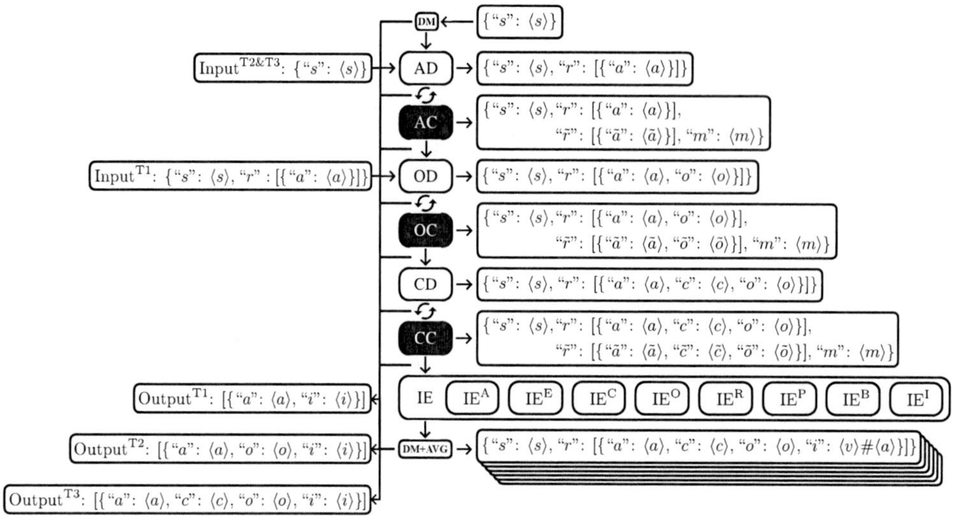

Figure 2: MAC Model Architecture. This diagram illustrates the MAC prediction process, involving agents DM, AD, AC, OD, OC, CD, CC, and intensity estimators (IE^A, IE^E, IE^C, IE^O, IE^R, IE^P, IE^B, IE^I). Inputs and outputs of subtasks T1, T2, and T3 are depicted, with T1 connecting to OD and T2&T3 connecting to AD. Outputs are generated by DM + AVG, showing the entire prediction process. JSON-formatted messages flow between agents, managed by DM.

The input for subtask T1 is processed by the OD agent, as it already contains the aspect (a). In contrast, the input for subtasks T2 and T3, which only contain the sentence (s), is processed by the AD agent. Outputs of T1, T2, and T3 are generated by the bottom agent DM + AVG, showing that all final outputs are predicted through the entire process, with variations only in their format.

Symbolic messages in JSON format are exchanged among these neural generative AI agents, as depicted in Figure 2, ensuring a transparent and rational approach to solving the dimABSA task. Critic agents provide feedback messages (m) indicating suggested results for aspects (ã), categories (c̃), and opinions (õ), while the original results from detector agents do not include these symbols. This new paradigm of Neuro-Symbolic AI not only addresses the dimABSA problem but also provides a general framework for solving key phrase detection, multi-class classification, and regression tasks.

3 Experimental Results

3.1 Experimental Setup

The dimABSA task provides a dataset with 3,000 training examples, each manually annotated with aspect terms, aspect categories, opinion terms, and sentiment intensities. There are also two test sets, each containing 2,000 examples for subtask T1 and subtasks T2&T3. The detailed annotation guidelines and data splits are described in the official summary paper of the dimABSA task (Lee et al., 2024).

For T1, the evaluation metrics include Mean Absolute Error (MAE) to measure the accuracy of predicted v and a scores, and Pearson Correlation Coefficient (PCC) to assess the correlation between predicted and actual values. For T2&T3, Precision, Recall, and F1-score assess the accuracy of the extracted triplets (a, o, i) and quadruples (a, c, o, i). Detailed experimental setup can be found in Appendix A.

3.2 Experimental Results

We report our experimental results in Tables 1 and 2, where V, A, and VA represent results related to Valence, Arousal, and both Valence and Arousal, respectively. Due to format issues, only the results of T2 are officially ranked, while the results of T1 and T3 were post-processed and evaluated through the post-evaluation process and are provided for reference. Detailed result comparisons with other participating teams are available in the summary paper (Lee et al., 2024).

3.3 Result Analysis

We demonstrate the transparency and rationality of the MAC model through the analysis of agent col-

Subtask	V-MAE	V-PCC	A-MAE	A-PCCA
$T1^{post}$	0.4706	0.9266	0.4618	0.6745

Table 1: Experimental Results for dimABSA subtask 1.

Subtask	V-P	V-R	V-F1	A-P	A-R	A-F1	VA-P	VA-R	VA-F1
T2	25.64	28.24	26.88	29.31	32.28	30.72	14.97	16.49	15.69
$T3^{post}$	23.85	26.19	24.97	27.68	30.40	28.98	14.15	15.54	14.81

Table 2: Experimental Results for dimABSA subtasks 2 and 3, in percentage.

laborations based on the running example provided in Section 2.1. For a detailed analysis, please refer to Appendix B.

Given the input restaurant review sentence, the AD agent detects aspect terms (a) 牛排 (steak) and 外皮 (crust), consistent with the ground truth. The AC agent evaluates AD's performance, provides critical feedback, and suggests results ($\tilde{r}$) with feedback messages (m).

Once AD and AC reach a consensus, DM forwards it to the OD agent to detect opinion terms (o). The OC agent then evaluates OD's performance, pointing out that 好吃 (delicious) should be 真的好吃 (really delicious), aligning with the ground truth. DM forwards the consensus to the CD agent to classify aspect terms into predefined categories (c), and the CC agent evaluates CD's performance and concurs with its output.

Finally, DM forwards the consensus to 8 IE agents, each with distinct character traits, to estimate sentiment intensities and average their outputs as the consensus intensity (i). The final prediction, shown below, correctly identifies aspects, categories, and opinions, and provides intensity values close to the ground truth.

```
{
  "s": same_as_above,
  "r": [
    {"a": "牛排", "c": "食物#品質",
     "o": "蠻粉嫩", "i": "6.06#5.56"},
    {"a": "外皮", "c": "食物#品質",
     "o": "酥脆卡滋卡滋", "i": "6.71#6.22"},
    {"a": "牛排", "c": "食物#品質",
     "o": "真的好吃", "i": "7.19#6.72"},
  ]
}
```

4 Conclusion

In this paper, we proposed a MAC model for the dimABSA task, representing a new paradigm of Neuro-Symbolic AI. Our approach employs multiple generative AI agents, each specializing in different subtasks, ensuring a robust and transparent workflow. The MAC model operates in a transparent and rational manner, demonstrated by its accurate identification of aspects, categories, opinions, and sentiment intensities. By incorporating agents with distinct character traits, we mimic the sentiment receptions of different individuals, enhancing the model's effectiveness. Additionally, the use of generative AI agents with few-shot learning enables MAC to easily generalize to out-of-domain data.

Future work will focus on addressing the hallucination problem within the Neuro-Symbolic AI framework, improving reliability and consistency of outputs, and extending the model's applicability to other domains.

Limitations

This study presents several limitations that should be considered. Firstly, few-shot learning with only 20 examples may not capture the full variability and nuances of the data, potentially leading to less robust models compared to those fine-tuned with the entire dataset. While fine-tuning with the entire dataset could improve task-specific performance, it may reduce the generalization ability of the agents, making them less adaptable to unseen data or different domains. Future research could investigate hybrid learning approaches that integrate the strengths of both few-shot and full dataset methods to enhance model robustness and generalizability.

Although the critic multi-agent collaboration (MAC) framework effectively mitigates error propagation, the sequential nature of the model could still lead to cumulative errors if initial detections are flawed. Future efforts could focus on developing more sophisticated error correction mechanisms and exploring alternative architectures that reduce the dependency on initial accuracy, thereby further minimizing the risk of error propagation.

Utilizing advanced models like GPT-4o requires

substantial computational resources, which might not be accessible to all researchers or practitioners. Additionally, the cost of calling the GPT-4o API may be a limitation for refining the agents or the MAC framework. Future research could explore fine-tuning more recent open-source large language models, such as LLaMA-3 (Meta, 2024) and Phi-3 (Abdin et al., 2024), as cost-effective alternatives. Fine-tuning these models could mitigate the financial and computational constraints while maintaining high performance and accessibility.

Despite efforts to ensure transparency, the complexity of the multi-agent system might make it challenging to interpret individual agent decisions and their contributions to the overall output. Enhancing model interpretability remains a crucial area for future work, potentially through improved visualization techniques and the development of methods to clearly attribute specific decisions to individual agents within the system.

Furthermore, the scalability of the proposed method to other languages, domains, or larger datasets has not been fully explored and might present additional challenges. Future research could test the scalability and adaptability of the MAC framework across various languages, domains, and dataset sizes to evaluate its broader applicability and performance.

Acknowledgments

This work was supported by JKA and its promotion funds from KEIRIN RACE and National Natural Science Foundation of China (Grant Number 61906137).

References

Marah Abdin, Sam Ade Jacobs, Ammar Ahmad Awan, Jyoti Aneja, Ahmed Awadallah, Hany Awadalla, Nguyen Bach, Amit Bahree, Arash Bakhtiari, Harkirat Behl, et al. 2024. Phi-3 technical report: A highly capable language model locally on your phone. *arXiv preprint arXiv:2404.14219*.

Hongjie Cai, Rui Xia, and Jianfei Yu. 2021. Aspect-category-opinion-sentiment quadruple extraction with implicit aspects and opinions. In *Proceedings of the 59th Annual Meeting of the Association for Computational Linguistics and the 11th International Joint Conference on Natural Language Processing (Volume 1: Long Papers)*, pages 340–350.

Shaowei Chen, Yu Wang, Jie Liu, and Yuelin Wang. 2021. Bidirectional machine reading comprehension for aspect sentiment triplet extraction. In *Proceedings of the AAAI conference on artificial intelligence*, volume 35, pages 12666–12674.

Oliver P John, Sanjay Srivastava, et al. 1999. The big-five trait taxonomy: History, measurement, and theoretical perspectives.

Lung-Hao Lee, Liang-Chih Yu, Suge Wang, and Jian Liao. 2024. Overview of the sighan 2024 shared task for chinese dimensional aspect-based sentiment analysis. In *Proceedings of the 10th SIGHAN Workshop on Chinese Language Processing*, pages 1–10. Association for Computational Linguistics.

Yue Mao, Yi Shen, Jingchao Yang, Xiaoying Zhu, and Longjun Cai. 2022. Seq2Path: Generating sentiment tuples as paths of a tree. In *Findings of the Association for Computational Linguistics: ACL 2022*, pages 2215–2225, Dublin, Ireland. Association for Computational Linguistics.

Yue Mao, Yi Shen, Chao Yu, and Longjun Cai. 2021. A joint training dual-mrc framework for aspect based sentiment analysis. In *Proceedings of the AAAI conference on artificial intelligence*, volume 35, pages 13543–13551.

AI Meta. 2024. Introducing meta llama 3: The most capable openly available llm to date. *Meta AI*.

Haiyun Peng, Lu Xu, Lidong Bing, Fei Huang, Wei Lu, and Luo Si. 2020. Knowing what, how and why: A near complete solution for aspect-based sentiment analysis. In *Proceedings of the AAAI conference on artificial intelligence*, volume 34, pages 8600–8607.

Joseph Peper and Lu Wang. 2022. Generative aspect-based sentiment analysis with contrastive learning and expressive structure. In *Findings of the Association for Computational Linguistics: EMNLP 2022*, pages 6089–6095, Abu Dhabi, United Arab Emirates. Association for Computational Linguistics.

Maria Pontiki, Dimitris Galanis, Haris Papageorgiou, Ion Androutsopoulos, Suresh Manandhar, Mohammad AL-Smadi, Mahmoud Al-Ayyoub, Yanyan Zhao, Bing Qin, Orphée De Clercq, Véronique Hoste, Marianna Apidianaki, Xavier Tannier, Natalia Loukachevitch, Evgeniy Kotelnikov, Nuria Bel, Salud María Jiménez-Zafra, and Gülşen Eryiğit. 2016. SemEval-2016 task 5: Aspect based sentiment analysis. pages 19–30, San Diego, California.

James A Russell. 1980. A circumplex model of affect. *Journal of personality and social psychology*, 39(6):1161.

Lu Xu, Hao Li, Wei Lu, and Lidong Bing. 2020. Position-aware tagging for aspect sentiment triplet extraction. In *Proceedings of the 2020 Conference on Empirical Methods in Natural Language Processing (EMNLP)*, pages 2339–2349, Online. Association for Computational Linguistics.

Wenxuan Zhang, Xin Li, Yang Deng, Lidong Bing, and Wai Lam. 2021. Towards generative aspect-based sentiment analysis. In *Proceedings of the 59th Annual Meeting of the Association for Computational Linguistics and the 11th International Joint Conference on Natural Language Processing (Volume 2: Short Papers)*, pages 504–510, Online. Association for Computational Linguistics.

A Detailed Experimental Setup

This section details the comprehensive templates utilized for various agents in our study, along with methods for hyper-parameter configuration and sample selection strategies. The templates standardize procedures and outputs, ensuring consistency and reproducibility across different experiments.

Below are the templates for different agents, including detection agents and critic agents. Each template specifies the agent's name, task description, input and output formats, and examples. The JSON formats ensure structured input data and output results. For critic agents, additional instructions on identifying potential errors and providing feedback are included.

```
Agent Name: {AgentName}
Task Description: {TaskDescription}
1. Read the input in the following JSON
   format: {JSONInput}
2. Assess and identify {AgentTargets}.
3. Output the results strictly in the
   following JSON format: {JSONOutput}
Examples:
[{Example}]
```

```
Agent Name: {CriticAgentName}
Task Description: {CriticTaskDescription}
1. Read the input in the following JSON
   format:{CriticJSONInput}
2. Identify potential {ErrorTypes}.
3. Provide feedback and suggestions in the
   following JSON format: {CriticJSONOutput}
Examples:
[{CriticExample}]
```

The JSON formats for inputs and outputs can be found in Appendix B, with sample strings replaced by symbols: ⟨s⟩ for sentence, ⟨a⟩ for aspect, ⟨c⟩ for category, ⟨o⟩ for opinion, and ⟨i⟩ for intensity. For critic JSON, critic strings are represented as ⟨ã⟩, ⟨c̃⟩, ⟨õ⟩, and ⟨ĩ⟩. The message from the critic agent is denoted as ⟨m⟩.

Samples for few-shot learning are selected randomly from the training dataset and fixed using a seed value of 41. This modified stratified sampling method respects the original distribution of different aspect categories and ensures the inclusion of all aspect categories. Additionally, the "NULL" aspect is included, which is unique to the dimABSA task. All agents share this common set of samples. The GPT-4o (`gpt-4o-2024-05-13`) model with the above system messages is used with the default temperature and top-p values as hyper-parameters.

B Detailed Result Analysis

This section analyzes the results from the MAC model, focusing on transparency, rationality, and error analysis.

We demonstrate the transparency and rationality of the MAC model by analyzing the collaborations among the agents based on the running example provided in Section 2.1. The collaborative messages are JSON-formatted as shown in Figure 2, and we use the same format with English translations for clarity and analysis purposes.

```
{
  "s": "這牛排外面裹著一層麵包粉看起來蠻粉嫩的，吃下去外皮
     酥脆卡滋卡滋真的好吃。",
  e_s: "This steak is coated with a layer of
        breadcrumbs on the outside, making it
        look quite tender. When you bite into
        it, the crust is crispy and crunchy
        and really delicious.",
  "r": [
    {"a": "牛排"},
    {e_a: "steak"},
    {"a": "外皮"},
    {e_a: "crust"}
  ]
}
```

The AC agent evaluates the performance of AD and provides critical feedback, with suggested results (r̃) and feedback message (m), as follows.

```
{
  "s": same_as_above,
  "r": same_as_above,
  "r̃": [
    {"ã": "牛排"},
    {e_ã: "steak"},
    {"ã": "外皮"},
    {c_ã: "crust"}
  ],
  "m": "Correctly identified aspects."
}
```

Since AD and AC have reached a consensus, DM forwards this consensus to the OD agent to detect opinion terms (o), as follows.

```
{
  "s": same_as_above,
  "r": [
    {"a": "牛排", "o": "蠻粉嫩"},
    {e_a: "steak", e_o: "quite tender"},
    {"a": "外皮", "o": "酥脆卡滋卡滋"},
    {e_a: "crust", e_o: "crispy and crunchy"},
    {"a": "牛排", "o": "好吃"},
    {e_a: "steak", e_o: "delicious"}
```

```
  ]
}
```

The OC agent evaluates the performance of OD and critically points out that the opinion term 好吃 (delicious) should be 真的好吃 (really delicious), which aligns with the ground truth.

```
{
  "s": same_as_above,
  "r": same_as_above,
  "r̃": [
    {"ã": "牛排", "õ": "蠻粉嫩"},
    {e_ã: "steak", e_õ: "quite tender"},
    {"ã": "外皮", "o": "酥脆卡滋卡滋"},
    {e_ã: "crust", e_õ: "crispy and crunchy"},
    {"ã": "牛排", "õ": "真的好吃"},
    {e_ã: "steak", e_õ: "really delicious"}
  ],
  "m": "Incomplete opinion: '好吃' should be '
     真的好吃'."
  m_e: "Incomplete opinion: 'delicious' should
     be 'really delicious'."
}
```

DM then forwards the consensus to the CD agent to classify the aspect terms into predefined categories (c), as follows.

```
{
  "s": same_as_above,
  "r": [
    {"a": "牛排", "c": "食物#品質",
     "o": "蠻粉嫩"},
    {e_a: "steak", e_c: "food#quality",
     e_o: "quite tender"},
    {"a": "外皮", "c": "食物#品質",
     "o": "酥脆卡滋卡滋"},
    {e_a: "crust", e_c: "food#quality",
     e_o: "crispy and crunchy"},
    {"a": "牛排", "c": "食物#品質",
     "o": "真的好吃"},
    {e_a: "steak", e_c: "food#quality",
     e_o: "really delicious"}
  ]
}
```

The CC agent evaluates the performance of CD and concurs with its output, as follows.

```
{
  "s": same_as_above,
  "r": same_as_above,
  "r̃": [
    {"ã": "牛排", "c̃": "食物#品質",
     "õ": "蠻粉嫩"},
    {e_ã: "steak", e_c̃: "food#quality",
     e_õ: "quite tender"},
    {"ã": "外皮", "c": "食物#品質",
     "õ": "酥脆卡滋卡滋"},
    {e_ã: "crust", e_c̃: "food#quality",
     e_õ: "crispy and crunchy"},
    {"ã": "牛排", "c̃": "食物#品質",
     "õ": "真的好吃"},
    {e_ã: "steak", e_c̃: "food#quality",
     e_õ: "really delicious"}
  ],
  "m": "Correctly classified categories."
}
```

Finally, DM forwards the consensus to 8 IE agents, each with distinct character traits, to estimate sentiment intensities and average their outputs as the consensus intensity (i). We use superscripts to denote intensity predictions given by the IE agents with distinct character traits, as follows.

```
{
  "s": same_as_above,
  "r": [
    {"a": "牛排", "c": "食物#品質",
     "o": "蠻粉嫩", "i": "6.06#5.56",
     "i^A": "6.00#5.50", "i^E": "6.00#5.00",
     "i^C": "6.00#5.75", "i^O": "6.00#6.00",
     "i^R": "6.50#5.75", "i^P": "5.50#5.00",
     "i^B": "6.00#5.50", "i^I": "6.50#6.00"},
    {"a": "外皮", "c": "食物#品質",
     "o": "酥脆卡滋卡滋", "i": "6.71#6.22",
     "i^A": "6.75#6.00", "i^E": "6.50#6.00",
     "i^C": "6.75#6.25", "i^O": "7.00#7.00",
     "i^R": "7.20#6.50", "i^P": "5.75#5.50",
     "i^B": "6.75#6.00", "i^I": "7.00#6.50"},
    {"a": "牛排", "c": "食物#品質",
     "o": "真的好吃", "i": "7.19#6.72",
     "i^A": "7.00#6.50", "i^E": "7.00#6.50",
     "i^C": "7.00#6.50", "i^O": "8.00#8.00",
     "i^R": "8.00#7.00", "i^P": "6.00#5.75",
     "i^B": "7.00#6.50", "i^I": "7.50#7.00"},
  ]
}
```

Analyzing the final predictions reveals a notable discrepancy in the opinion term 酥脆卡滋卡滋 (crispy and crunchy) predicted by the OD agent compared to the ground truth 酥脆 (crispy). This term was justified as reasonable by the OC agent, highlighting the variability in sentiment perception among humans, which AI agents reflect. Conversely, the OC agent correctly criticized another OD prediction, where 好吃 (delicious) was adjusted to 真的好吃 (really delicious), aligning with the ground truth. These observations suggest that critic multi-agent collaboration effectively mitigates the error propagation problem, which is more prevalent in sequential models. However, accurately mimicking the sentiment perception of a group of human beings, as reflected in the dimABSA data annotations, remains challenging. This issue could be mitigated by further fine-tuning the agents with the entire training dataset, although this approach is costly and may reduce the generalization capability of the agents.

The valence and arousal intensities predicted by the IE agents with distinct character traits also exhibit variability. These differences underscore the subjective nature of sentiment analysis, influenced by individual perspectives. The deviations between the IE agents' predictions and the ground truth values illustrate the difficulty in accurately mimicking the diversity of sentiment perception in human beings.

YNU-HPCC at SIGHAN-2024 dimABSA Task: Using PLMs with a Joint Learning Strategy for Dimensional Intensity Prediction

Zehui Wang, You Zhang*, Jin Wang, Dan Xu, and Xuejie Zhang
School of Information Science and Engineering
Yunnan University
Kunming, China
Contact: wangzehui@stu.ynu.edu.cn, yzhang0202@ynu.edu.cn

Abstract

The dimensional approach can represent more fine-grained emotional information than discrete affective states. In this paper, a pre-trained language model (PLM) with a joint learning strategy is proposed for the SIGHAN-2024 shared task on Chinese dimensional aspect-based sentiment analysis (dimABSA), which requires submitted models to provide fine-grained multi-dimensional (Valence and Arousal) intensity predictions for given aspects of a review. The proposed model consists of three parts: an input layer that concatenates both given aspect terms and input sentences; a Chinese PLM encoder that generates aspect-specific review representation; and separate linear predictors that jointly predict Valence and Arousal sentiment intensities. Moreover, we merge simplified and traditional Chinese training data for data augmentation. Our system ranked 2nd place out of 5 participants in subtask 1-intensity prediction. The code is publicly available at https://github.com/WZH5127/2024_subtask1_intensity_prediction.

1 Introduction

Aspect-based sentiment analysis (ABSA) (Pontiki et al., 2014, 2015, 2016) is used to identify the sentiment polarity regarding specific aspects within a sentence. In recent years, ABSA tasks have gradually extended into diverse subtasks, including aspect sentiment triplet extraction (ASTE) (Chen et al., 2022; Xu et al., 2021; Zhao et al., 2022; Zhang et al., 2023) and aspect sentiment quadruple prediction (ASQP) (Hu et al., 2022a; Wang et al., 2023; Zhou et al., 2023; Zhang et al., 2021). In contrast to these tasks, which consider affective states as discrete classes (positive, neutral, and negative), the dimensional approach provides more fine-grained emotional information (Lee et al., 2022).

Dimensional sentiment analysis represents affective states as continuous numerical values in multiple dimensions, such as Valence and Arousal space (Yu et al., 2016), as illustrated in Figure 1(a). The Valence dimension indicates the degree of positive or negative sentiments, while the Arousal dimension refers to the degree of calmness or excitement. Valence and Arousal are represented by continuous real-valued scores ranging from 1 to 9, with lower scores indicating stronger negative or calm sentiments, higher scores indicating stronger positive or excited sentiments, and mid-range scores, such as 5, indicating neutral states. Combining aspect-based and multi-dimensional sentiment analysis, a shared task of Chinese dimensional ABSA shared task (dimABSA) (Lee et al., 2024) is proposed in SIGHAN-2024, which primarily includes

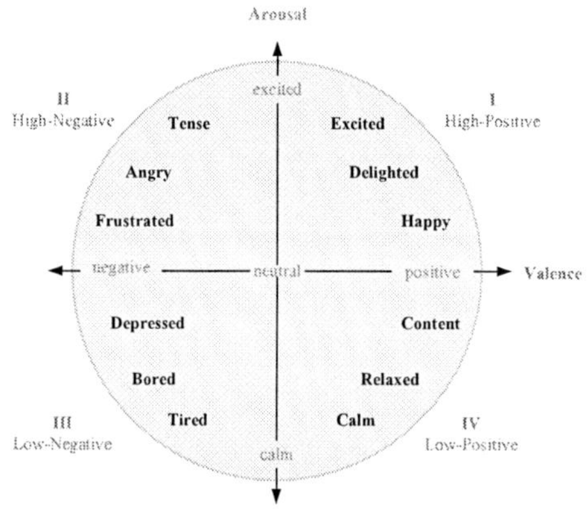

(a) Valence and Arousal Spaces

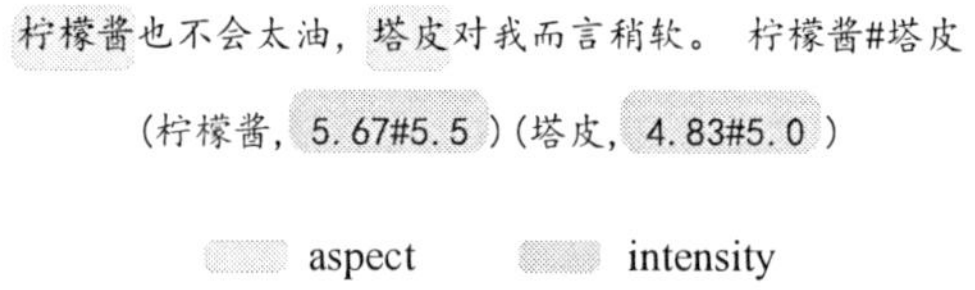

(b) An example of intensity prediction

Figure 1: The diagram of Valence and Arousal space and dimABSA.

*Corresponding author.

Proceedings of the 10th SIGHAN Workshop on Chinese Language Processing (SIGHAN-10), pages 96–101
August 16, 2024

intensity prediction, triplet extraction, and quadruple extraction. In subtask 1 intensity prediction, given a sentence and an aspect, the system is required to predict the Valence and Arousal intensities of the sentence regarding the aspect. For instance, in the sentence shown in Figure 1(b), there are two aspects, "柠檬酱"(lemon sauce) and "塔皮"(tart crust), with required two-dimensional (Valence#Arousal) intensity predictions of 5.67#5.5 and 4.83#5.0, respective.

Recently, pre-trained language models (PLMs) (Devlin et al., 2018; Li et al., 2020; Hu et al., 2022b) have achieved significant success in various natural language processing (NLP) tasks, including sentiment analysis. For instance, using Chinese-based PLMs such as BERT-base-Chinese and BERT-wwm-ext (Cui et al., 2021) for intensity prediction on Chinese EmoBank (Lee et al., 2022) has yielded superior results compared to traditional methods. However, when these methods tackle dimABSA tasks, they continue to encounter challenges in (1) integrating traditional and simplified Chinese for robust review representation and (2) capturing internal relatedness across multiple dimensions for a comprehensive understanding of semantics.

To address these issues, we utilized whole-word masking (wwm) (Cui et al., 2021; Pandey et al., 2022) PLM of BERT-wwm-ext with a joint learning strategy for dimensional intensity prediction in ABSA. The model consists of the input layer, PLM encoder, and dimensional linear layer (dimLinear). Initially, we concatenate one aspect term and the review sentence as model sequence input. Then, we utilize BERT-wwm-ext as the PLM encoder to generate robust text representation. Finally, the dimLinear layer contains separate linear predictors that jointly predict Valence and Arousal sentiment intensities. Moreover, we merge traditional and simplified Chinese training samples into an augmented training set for generalized optimization. In experiments, we found that the integrations between two types of Chinese corpora and the joint optimization of multiple dimensions resulted in better performance. Consequently, our team ranked 2nd out of 5 participants in subtask 1 of the shared dimABSA task.

The remainder of this paper is structured as follows: Section 2 describes the architecture of our model in detail. Section 3 presents extensive experiments, analysis, and results. Finally, conclusions and future work are discussed in Section 4.

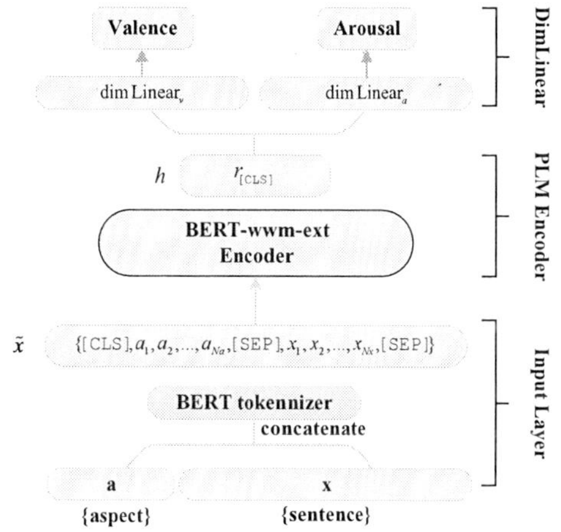

Figure 2: The overview of model architecture.

2 System Description

In this section, we primarily describe the architecture of our model. As depicted in Figure 2, the model comprises three main components: input layer, PLM encoder, and dimLinear layer.

2.1 Input Layer

Both an aspect $\mathbf{a}$ and a review text $\mathbf{x}$ are first tokenized into discrete tokens, denoted by $\mathbf{a} = \{a_1, a_2, ..., a_{Na}\}$ and $\mathbf{x} = \{x_1, x_2, ..., x_{Nx}\}$, respectively, where Na and Nx represent the length of the aspect and the review. To feed both the aspect and the review into models, we concatenate the aspect and the review tokens, denoted as $\tilde{\mathbf{x}} = \{\texttt{[CLS]}, \mathbf{a}, \texttt{[SEP]}, \mathbf{x}, \texttt{[SEP]}\}$, where [CLS] and [SEP] are special tokens for syntactic separation.

2.2 Chinese PLM Encoder

To learn the hidden aspect-specific review representation h, we use the Chinese PLM of BERT-wwm-ext to encode the concatenated input sequence formally:

$$\mathbf{r} = f(\tilde{\mathbf{x}}; \theta_{\text{BERT-wwm-ext}}) \in \mathbb{R}^{N \times d} \quad (1)$$

where $f(\cdot)$ represents the encoder propagation; $\theta_{\text{BERT-wwm-ext}}$ is the trainable parameters initialized from a pre-trained checkpoint and fine-tuned for the specific task; and $N = (Na + Nx + 3)$ and d indicates the input length and hidden dimensionality, respectively.

Similar to BERT families, we take as the final review representation the first token representation, i.e., $h = r_{\texttt{[CLS]}} \in \mathbb{R}^d$.

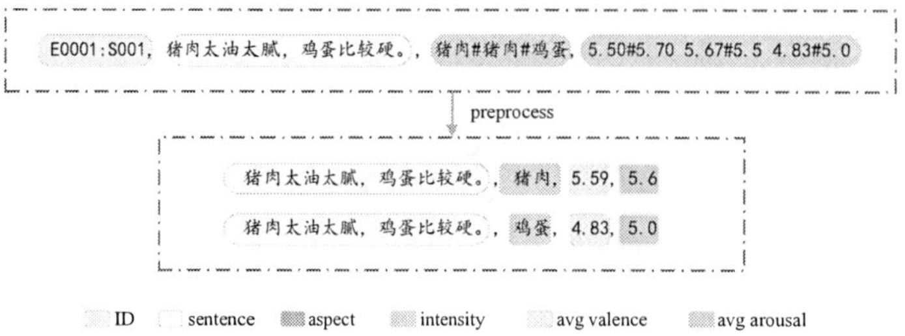

Figure 3: An example of data preprocessing.

2.3 Dimensional Intensity Prediction

To predict the intensities of Valence $v \in \mathbb{R}^1$ and Arousal $a \in \mathbb{R}^1$, we use the dimLinear that contains two linear projections to estimate $p(v|h)$ and $p(a|h)$ simultaneously. This multi-task learning strategy could facilitate the model in learning robust review representation. The prediction is as follows:

$$\begin{aligned} v &= \dim \text{Linear}_v(h) \\ a &= \dim \text{Linear}_a(h) \end{aligned} \tag{2}$$

where each $\text{dimLinear\_}(\cdot)$ is implemented via two stacked fully connected layers.

During model optimization, we employ mean absolute error (MAE) as the cost function to maximize the likelihood of model performance $p_\theta(v, a|\mathbf{a}, \mathbf{x})$ in an end-to-end manner.

3 Experimental Results

In this section, we present the comparative results of the proposed methods.

3.1 Datasets

Throughout the competition, we utilized datasets exclusively provided by the organizers of the shared dimABSA task. These datasets were formally partitioned into Train, Dev, and Test sets. Since golden labels were not provided for participants, an additional Dev* set was created by randomly sampling 10% of the Train sample to aid in model selections.

Furthermore, the dataset encompassed traditional and simplified Chinese versions, the only difference being the language. To enhance the generalization performance of our models, we augmented the Train set by integrating both versions. For more detailed statistics on the datasets, please refer to Table 1.

Dataset	# samples	Max length
Train	6050	56
Merged-Train	12100	56
Dev	100	40
Dev*	1210	46
Test	2000	59

Table 1: Detailed statistics of the datasets.

3.2 Evaluation Metrics

To evaluate the performance of participant systems for Subtask 1, the organizers furnished MAE and the Pearson Correlation Coefficient (PCC) as evaluation metrics.

- MAE

$$\text{MAE} = \frac{1}{n}\sum_{i=1}^{n} |\hat{p}_i - p_i| \tag{3}$$

where $\hat{p}_i$ and p_i respectively denoted the ith actual value and predicted value, n is the number of test samples.

- PCC

$$\text{PCC} = \frac{1}{n-1}\sum_{i=1}^{n}(\frac{\hat{p}_i - \hat{\mu}}{\hat{\sigma}})(\frac{p_i - \mu_p}{\sigma_p}) \tag{4}$$

where $\hat{\mu}$ and $\hat{\sigma}$ respectively represent the mean value and the standard deviation of all predictions, while μ_p and σ_p respectively represent that of golden labels. A lower MAE and a higher PCC indicate more accurate prediction performance.

3.3 Implementation Details

Data preprocessing. We observed that certain samples in the Train set contained multiple intensity values for a single aspect, reflecting different opinions, as illustrated in Figure 3. As Subtask 1 only concerns the overall sentiment towards an aspect in a review, we computed the average intensity across various opinions to derive an overall sentiment score.

Model	Dev*				Test			
	Valence		Arousal		Valence		Arousal	
	MAE↓	PCC↑	MAE↓	PCC↑	MAE↓	PCC↑	MAE↓	PCC↑
BERT-base-chinese	0.222	0.951	0.280	0.817	0.299	0.911	**0.318**	0.767
BERT-wwm	**0.221**	**0.956**	**0.277**	**0.822**	0.298	0.912	0.319	0.766
RoBERTa-wwm-ext	0.241	0.954	0.294	0.808	0.306	0.913	0.327	0.766
MacBERT-wwm-ext	0.253	0.936	0.296	0.803	0.312	0.905	0.327	0.761
BERT-wwm-ext (Ranked 2nd)	0.227	0.952	0.284	0.814	**0.294**	**0.917**	**0.318**	**0.771**
BERT-wwm-ext†	0.247	0.948	0.283	0.803	0.311	0.910	0.323	0.748
BERT-wwm-ext‡	0.249	0.934	0.300	0.787	0.311	0.904	**0.318**	0.760

Table 2: Comparative Dev* and Test results for subtask 1. **Bold figures** meant the best performance regarding various metrics.

Hyperparameters. The maximum length of the longest sentence in a batch sample was the maximum. We employed the base version of BERT-wwm-ext as the backbone model. Specifically, the model consisted of 12 transformer layers with a hidden representation dimensionality (d) of 768 (Vaswani et al., 2017). For optimization, we utilized the Adam optimizer with a linear warmup schedule. The base learning rate was set to 3e-5, with a batch size of 32.

Baselines. We implemented several baseline models to evaluate the performance of BERT-wwm-ext in dimensional prediction. Initially, we employed various PLMs as our backbones, including BERT-base-chinese, BERT-wwm, RoBERTa-wwm-ext, and MacBERT-wwm-ext (Cui et al., 2021). Subsequently, we introduce two variants of models: (1) BERT-wwm-ext†, which independently predicted Valence and Arousal intensities, and (2) BERT-wwm-ext‡, trained solely on the traditional Chinese-based Train set.

3.4 Result and Analysis

As depicted in Table 2, our proposed system's comparable Dev* and Test results against several baselines in terms of MAE and PCC were reported. With different PLMs as backbones, models achieved varying performances. In contrast to RoBERTa and MacBERT, Chinese-based BERT families achieved relatively lower MAE and higher PCC. This performance discrepancy could be attributed to the utilization of a next-sentence prediction task during the pretraining phase of BERT PLMs. This task's alignment with our input structure, which combines aspect and review texts, likely facilitated the model in better understanding the relationship between aspects and sentences during the fine-tuning phase.

In our settings, BERT-wwm performed relatively better than BERT-Chinese in Dev* and on par in Test. This is because the adopted wwm strategy could enhance Chinese sentence modeling. In contrast to BERT-wwm, BERT-wwm-ext leveraged a larger pretraining corpus to acquire more comprehensive language knowledge, demonstrating better generalization in the Test set.

Furthermore, we conducted ablation studies to examine the effect of our joint learning strategy. Without the joint optimization of Valence and Arousal dimensions, the performance of BERT-wwm-ext† degraded, and so did BERT-wwm-ext‡ when only the traditional Chinese version was utilized as the Train set. These phenomena underscored the effectiveness of our joint learning strategy in facilitating robust aspect-specific review representation.

In conclusion, our proposed methods attained the best Test scores in both MAE and PCC metrics, which ranked 2nd place out of 5 participants. This result highlights the competitiveness and effectiveness of our system in the shared subtask 1.

4 Conclusions

This paper presented our system developed for the SIGHAN-2024 shared Task dimABSA. Our experimental results in subtask 1 demonstrated that our proposed model achieved significant performance in the dimensional intensity prediction of ABSA. As a result, our team ranked 2nd place in subtask 1.

Future works will explore incorporating our model with the existing dimensional sentiment analysis corpus and investigating a unified model handling multiple targets in dimABSA.

Limitations

Although our proposed system enhances the quality of dimensional intensity prediction, there are still several limitations. First, we have only validated the effectiveness of the joint learning strategy for intensity prediction and have not tested it for fine-grained aspect extraction. Second, our current approach uses traditional PLMs as backbones. In the future, we plan to explore the use of large-scale PLMs, such as ChatGPT and LLaMA, for dimABSA tasks.

Acknowledgments

This work was supported by the National Natural Science Foundation of China (NSFC) under Grant Nos. 61966038 and 62266051, and Caiyun Postdoctoral Foundation under Grant No. C615300504090.

References

Yuqi Chen, Chen Keming, Xian Sun, and Zequn Zhang. 2022. A Span-level Bidirectional Network for Aspect Sentiment Triplet Extraction. In *Proceedings of the 2022 Conference on Empirical Methods in Natural Language Processing*, pages 4300–4309, Abu Dhabi, United Arab Emirates. Association for Computational Linguistics.

Yiming Cui, Wanxiang Che, Ting Liu, Bing Qin, and Ziqing Yang. 2021. Pre-Training with Whole Word Masking for Chinese BERT. *IEEE/ACM Transactions on Audio, Speech, and Language Processing*, 29:3504–3514.

Jacob Devlin, Ming-Wei Chang, Kenton Lee, and Kristina Toutanova. 2018. Bert: Pre-training of Deep Bidirectional Transformers for Language Understanding. *arXiv preprint arXiv:1810.04805*.

Mengting Hu, Yike Wu, Hang Gao, Yinhao Bai, and Shiwan Zhao. 2022a. Improving Aspect Sentiment Quad Prediction via Template-Order Data Augmentation. In *Proceedings of the 2022 Conference on Empirical Methods in Natural Language Processing*, pages 7889–7900, Abu Dhabi, United Arab Emirates. Association for Computational Linguistics.

Yibo Hu, MohammadSaleh Hosseini, Erick Skorupa Parolin, Javier Osorio, Latifur Khan, Patrick Brandt, and Vito D'Orazio. 2022b. ConfliBERT: A Pre-trained Language Model for Political Conflict and Violence. In *Proceedings of the 2022 Conference of the North American Chapter of the Association for Computational Linguistics: Human Language Technologies*, pages 5469–5482, Seattle, United States. Association for Computational Linguistics.

Lung-Hao Lee, Jian-Hong Li, and Liang-Chih Yu. 2022. Chinese EmoBank: Building Valence-Arousal Resources for Dimensional Sentiment Analysis. *Transactions on Asian and Low-Resource Language Information Processing*, 21(4):1–18.

Lung-Hao Lee, Liang-Chih Yu, Suge Wang, and Jian Liao. 2024. Overview of the SIGHAN 2024 shared task for Chinese dimensional aspect-based sentiment analysis. In *Proceedings of the 10th SIGHAN Workshop on Chinese Language Processing*. Association for Computational Linguistics.

Bohan Li, Hao Zhou, Junxian He, Mingxuan Wang, Yiming Yang, and Lei Li. 2020. On the Sentence Embeddings from Pre-trained Language Models. In *Proceedings of the 2020 Conference on Empirical Methods in Natural Language Processing (EMNLP)*, pages 9119–9130, Online. Association for Computational Linguistics.

Amit Pandey, Swayatta Daw, Narendra Unnam, and Vikram Pudi. 2022. Multilinguals at SemEval-2022 Task 11: Complex NER in Semantically Ambiguous Settings for Low Resource Languages. In *Proceedings of the 16th International Workshop on Semantic Evaluation (SemEval-2022)*, pages 1469–1476, Seattle, United States. Association for Computational Linguistics.

Maria Pontiki, Dimitris Galanis, Haris Papageorgiou, Ion Androutsopoulos, Suresh Manandhar, Mohammad AL-Smadi, Mahmoud Al-Ayyoub, Yanyan Zhao, Bing Qin, Orphée De Clercq, Véronique Hoste, Marianna Apidianaki, Xavier Tannier, Natalia Loukachevitch, Evgeniy Kotelnikov, Nuria Bel, Salud María Jiménez-Zafra, and Gülşen Eryiğit. 2016. SemEval-2016 Task 5: Aspect Based Sentiment Analysis. In *Proceedings of the 10th International Workshop on Semantic Evaluation (SemEval-2016)*, pages 19–30, San Diego, California. Association for Computational Linguistics.

Maria Pontiki, Dimitris Galanis, Haris Papageorgiou, Suresh Manandhar, and Ion Androutsopoulos. 2015. SemEval-2015 Task 12: Aspect Based Sentiment Analysis. In *Proceedings of the 9th International Workshop on Semantic Evaluation (SemEval 2015)*, pages 486–495, Denver, Colorado. Association for Computational Linguistics.

Maria Pontiki, Dimitris Galanis, John Pavlopoulos, Harris Papageorgiou, Ion Androutsopoulos, and Suresh Manandhar. 2014. SemEval-2014 Task 4: Aspect Based Sentiment Analysis. In *Proceedings of the 8th International Workshop on Semantic Evaluation (SemEval 2014)*, pages 27–35, Dublin, Ireland. Association for Computational Linguistics.

Ashish Vaswani, Noam Shazeer, Niki Parmar, Jakob Uszkoreit, Llion Jones, Aidan N Gomez, Łukasz Kaiser, and Illia Polosukhin. 2017. Attention Is All You Need. *Advances in neural information processing systems*, 30.

An Wang, Junfeng Jiang, Youmi Ma, Ao Liu, and Naoaki Okazaki. 2023. Generative Data Augmentation for Aspect Sentiment Quad Prediction. In *Proceedings of the 12th Joint Conference on Lexical and Computational Semantics (*SEM 2023)*, pages 128–140, Toronto, Canada. Association for Computational Linguistics.

Lu Xu, Yew Ken Chia, and Lidong Bing. 2021. Learning Span-Level Interactions for Aspect Sentiment Triplet Extraction. In *Proceedings of the 59th Annual Meeting of the Association for Computational Linguistics and the 11th International Joint Conference on Natural Language Processing (Volume 1: Long Papers)*, pages 4755–4766, Online. Association for Computational Linguistics.

Liang-Chih Yu, Lung-Hao Lee, Shuai Hao, Jin Wang, Yunchao He, Jun Hu, K. Robert Lai, and Xuejie Zhang. 2016. Building Chinese Affective Resources in Valence-Arousal Dimensions. In *Proceedings of the 2016 Conference of the North American Chapter of the Association for Computational Linguistics: Human Language Technologies*, pages 540–545, San Diego, California. Association for Computational Linguistics.

Wenxuan Zhang, Yang Deng, Xin Li, Yifei Yuan, Lidong Bing, and Wai Lam. 2021. Aspect Sentiment Quad Prediction as Paraphrase Generation. In *Proceedings of the 2021 Conference on Empirical Methods in Natural Language Processing*, pages 9209–9219, Online and Punta Cana, Dominican Republic. Association for Computational Linguistics.

Yice Zhang, Yifan Yang, Meng Li, Bin Liang, Shiwei Chen, and Ruifeng Xu. 2023. Target-to-Source Augmentation for Aspect Sentiment Triplet Extraction. In *Proceedings of the 2023 Conference on Empirical Methods in Natural Language Processing*, pages 12165–12177, Singapore. Association for Computational Linguistics.

Yichun Zhao, Kui Meng, Gongshen Liu, Jintao Du, and Huijia Zhu. 2022. A Multi-Task Dual-Tree Network for Aspect Sentiment Triplet Extraction. In *Proceedings of the 29th International Conference on Computational Linguistics*, pages 7065–7074, Gyeongju, Republic of Korea. International Committee on Computational Linguistics.

Junxian Zhou, Haiqin Yang, Yuxuan He, Hao Mou, and Junbo Yang. 2023. A Unified One-Step Solution for Aspect Sentiment Quad Prediction. *arXiv preprint arXiv:2306.04152*.

CCIIPLab at SIGHAN-2024 dimABSA Task: Contrastive Learning-Enhanced Span-based Framework for Chinese Dimensional Aspect-Based Sentiment Analysis

Zeliang Tong, Wei Wei ✉
Cognitive Computing and Intelligent Information Processing (CCIIP) Laboratory,
School of Computer Science and Technology, Huazhong University of Science and Technology
{tongzeliang, weiw}@hust.edu.cn

Abstract

This paper describes our system and findings for SIGHAN-2024 Shared Task Chinese Dimensional Aspect-Based Sentiment Analysis (dimABSA). Our team **CCIIPLab** proposes an Contrastive Learning-Enhanced Span-based (**CL-Span**) framework to boost the performance of extracting triplets/quadruples and predicting sentiment intensity. We first employ a span-based framework that integrates contextual representations and incorporates rotary position embedding. This approach fully considers the relational information of entire aspect and opinion terms, and enhancing the model's understanding of the associations between tokens. Additionally, we utilize contrastive learning to predict sentiment intensities in the valence-arousal dimensions with greater precision. To improve the generalization ability of the model, additional datasets are used to assist training. Experiments have validated the effectiveness of our approach. In the official test results, our system ranked **2nd** among the three subtasks. Our code is publicly available at https://github.com/tongzeliang/SIGHAN2024.

1 Introduction

Aspect-Based Sentiment Analysis (ABSA) is an important task in Natural Language Processing (NLP), and is beneficial for many downstream tasks, such as emotional conversation generation (Wei et al., 2019; Liu et al., 2022) and recommendation system (Zhao et al., 2023; Wang et al., 2023). However, previous work has focused primarily on discrete sentiment polarity, with little attention given to the Valence-Arousal (VA) space. This dimensional approach represents affective states as continuous numerical values across multiple dimensions, providing more fine-grained sentiment information.

To address this issue, the SIGHAN-2024 shared task formulates three subtasks that challenge participants to develop ABSA systems based on dimensional sentiment information (Lee et al., 2024). As Figure 1 shows, the three subtask can be illustrated as follows:

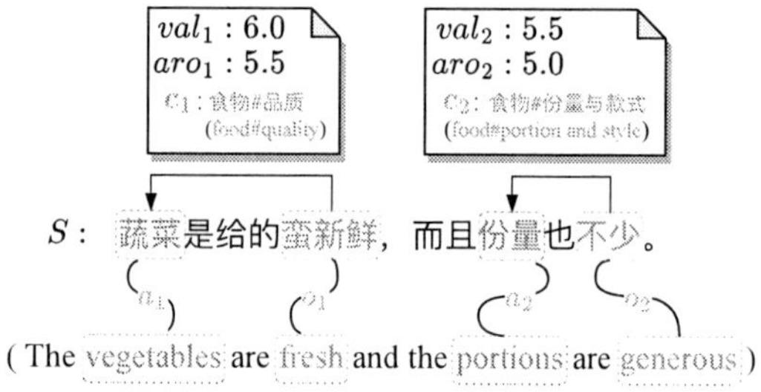

Subtask	Input	Output
Intensity Prediction	$S + a_1$	(a_1, val_1, aro_1)
	$S + a_2$	(a_2, val_2, aro_2)
Triplet Extraction	S	(a_1, o_1, val_1, aro_1)
	S	(a_2, o_2, val_2, aro_2)
Quadruple Extraction	S	$(a_1, o_1, c_1, val_1, aro_1)$
	S	$(a_2, o_2, c_2, val_2, aro_2)$

Figure 1: Illustration of three dimABSA subtasks. Aspect terms, opinion terms and categories are highlighted in red, blue and green, respectively. The terms "val" and "aro" represent the valence and arousal intensity of affective states, respectively, both ranging from 1 to 9.

- **Subtask 1: Intensity Prediction.** Predict the *valence-arousal ratings* for a given sentence and its specific aspect.
- **Subtask 2: Triplet Extraction.** Extract all sentiment triplets (*aspect*, *opinion*, *intensity*) from a given sentence.
- **Subtask 3: Quadruple Extraction.** Extract all sentiment quadruples (*aspect*, *category*, *opinion*, *intensity*) from a given sentence.

As an extension of the ABSA task, dimABSA becomes notably challenging due to the following two difficulties: 1) **Multiple Aspect-Opinion Pairing**. In sentences with multiple aspects and opinions, determining which opinion corresponds

✉ Corresponding Author

Proceedings of the 10th SIGHAN Workshop on Chinese Language Processing (SIGHAN-10), pages 102–111
August 16, 2024

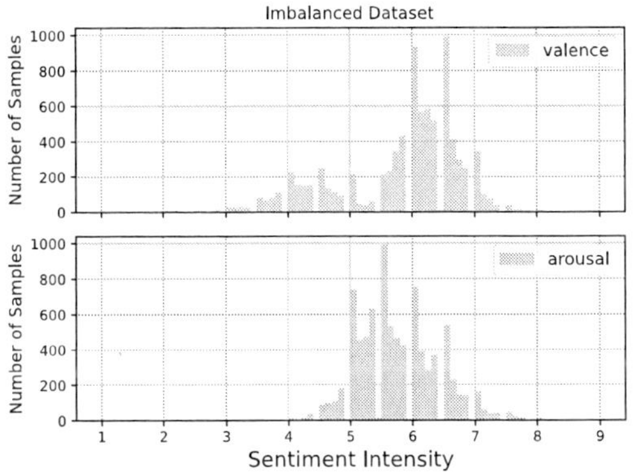

Figure 2: The distribution of valence-arousal ratings, where intensity ratings ranging from 1 to 9 are segmented into equal interval groups.

to which aspect becomes particularly challenging. To mitigate this problem, several efforts (Wu et al., 2020; Chen et al., 2022b; Liang et al., 2023) have been made, but they are not comprehensive for modeling the relationship between tokens, which is significant in the aspect-opinion pairing process (Chen et al., 2022a). 2) **Imbalanced Dataset**. As illustrated by Figure 2, the number of samples with neutral sentiment intensity is much greater than those with extreme sentiment intensity for both the valence and arousal dimensions, which leads to biased predictions from the model. Although there are some methods for addressing data imbalance like Re-Sampling (RS) (Zhou et al., 2020; Zhang and Pfister, 2021), most of them improve the performance of sparsely labeled samples at the expense of densely labeled samples (Zhang et al., 2023), leading to suboptimal results and and cannot be seamlessly migrated to dimABSA tasks.

In this paper, we develop a Contrastive Learning-Enhanced Span-based Framework for the dimABSA task to address the aforementioned challenges. **Firstly**, given the excellent performance of span-based methods in various NLP tasks (Xu et al., 2021), we explicitly generate span representations for all possible aspect and opinion spans. To comprehensively capture the relational information between spans, we integrate the contextual representations and incorporate Rotary Position Embedding (RoPE) (Su et al., 2024), which facilitates improved semantic understanding. **Secondly**, as self-supervised learning can improve robustness to data imbalance (Li et al., 2022), we employ contrastive learning to optimize feature representations in regression tasks. This approach adjusts the distance between samples in the embedding space according to their target values and subsequently leverages this feature to predict sentiment intensity.

Extensive experiments show that our method performs well across all three subtasks. On the official leaderboard, the Mean Absolute Error (MAE) for valence and arousal in subtask 1 ranks **2nd** and **1st**, respectively. The Pearson Correlation Coefficient (PCC) for valence and arousal in subtask 1 both rank **3rd**. The F1 scores for triplet and quadruple extraction in Subtasks 2 and 3 both rank **2nd**.

The paper is structured as follows: Section 2 provides a concise review of related work. In Section 3, we outline our proposed system. Section 4 covers the experimental details, including the dataset, setup, results, and discussions. Section 5 analyzes the effectiveness of contrastive learning and further examines the performance of our methods in low-resource settings. Finally, Section 6 presents a brief conclusion.

2 Related Work

2.1 ABSA Tasks

ABSA tasks, which aim to analyze sentiment from a fine-grained perspective, include three fundamental subtasks: Aspect Term Extraction (ATE) (Xu et al., 2018; Ma et al., 2019; Yang et al., 2020), Opinion Term Extraction (OTE) (Wan et al., 2020; Veyseh et al., 2020), and Aspect Sentiment Classification (ASC) (Tian et al., 2021; Wang et al., 2021a; Zhou et al., 2021). In recent years, research has increasingly focused on composite ABSA tasks, which integrate multiple basic tasks. Peng et al. (2020) introduced the Aspect Sentiment Triplet Extraction (ASTE) task, and they proposed a two-stage pipeline model to independently extract aspect-opinion-sentiment triplets. Subsequently, some end-to-end methods (Fei et al., 2021; Liang et al., 2023) were also applied to this task. Following this advancement, Zhang et al. (2021) introduced the Aspect-Sentiment Quad Prediction (ASQP) task, addressing it through the Seq2Seq generative modeling paradigm. However, these works primarily focus on discrete sentiment polarity, making it challenging to perceive subtle sentiment differences when predicting continuous sentiment intensity.

2.2 Contrastive Learning

Contrastive Learning methods learn feature representations by contrasting positive pairs against negative pairs, and have widely used in many downstream tasks, such as recommendation systems (Zou et al., 2022; Wang et al., 2022), knowledge graphs (Fang et al., 2022; Xu et al., 2023), etc.. Recent research has started to utilize contrastive learning to address the long-tail distribution problem in image classification (Wang et al., 2021b; Xuan and Zhang, 2024), aiming to obtain improved feature representations. This prompts us to utilize contrastive learning in the dimABSA task to tackle the challenge of imbalanced datasets.

3 Methodology

3.1 Overview

Problem Statement. Let $s = \{w_i\}_n$ and $\mathbf{A} = \{a_j\}_m$ be a sentence and a predefined set of aspects, where n and m represents the length of s and the number of aspects contained in s ($\mathbf{A}$ is only provided in subtask 1). The goal of subtask 1 is to predict the sentiment intensity $val_j, aro_j \in [1, 9]$ for each aspect $a_j \in \mathbf{A}$. The object of subtask 2 and 3 is to extract a set of sentiment triplets $\mathcal{T} = \{(a, o, val\text{-}aro)_m\}_{m=1}^{|\mathcal{T}|}$ and quadruples $\mathcal{Q} = \{(a, o, c, val\text{-}aro)_m\}_{m=1}^{|\mathcal{Q}|}$, where a, o and c represent aspect term, opinion term and category.

Architecture. As Figure 3 demonstrates, our system contains three components: 1) the **Aspect-Opinion Pairing Module** identifies aspect terms and opinion terms from the original sentence, and establishes their relationships to form valid aspect-opinion pairs, 2) the **Sentiment Scoring Module** assesses the sentiment intensity based on the original sentence and the extracted aspect-opinion pairs, 3) the **Category Prediction Module** conducts category classification utilizing the original sentence and the extracted aspect-opinion pairs. Each module is trained independently, and each subtask is accomplished through the collaboration of different modules. This pipeline structure enhances the flexibility and scalability of the system, allowing different processing steps to be optimized and adjusted independently.

3.2 Aspect-Opinion Pairing Module

This module identifies relevant aspects and their corresponding opinions within the sentence and accurately pairs them. As Figure 4 shows, this foundational step is crucial for subsequent analysis and prediction, ensuring that each aspect is matched with its opinion, forming the basis for further inference.

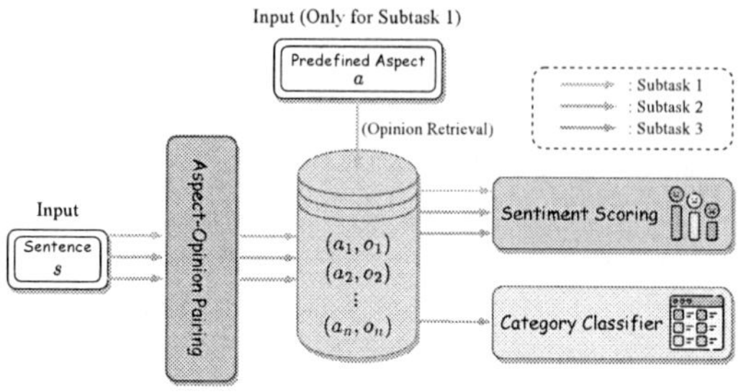

Figure 3: Architecture of our system. Arrows of different colors indicate the computational processes specific to each corresponding subtask.

Sentence Encoder. We use MacBERT (Cui et al., 2021) to generate contextual word representations by,

$$\hat{\mathbf{H}} = \hat{\mathbf{h}}_{cls}, \{\hat{\mathbf{h}}_j\}_n, \hat{\mathbf{h}}_{sep} = \text{MacBERT}(\{w_i\}_n) \tag{1}$$

where $\hat{\mathbf{h}}_j$ is the contextual embedding of word w_j. We then integrate RoPE into the token representation via an additional multi-head attention layer,

$$\mathbf{H} = \text{MultiHead}(\mathbf{Q}, \mathbf{K}, \mathbf{V}) \tag{2}$$

$$= ||_{z=1}^{Z} \text{Attention}\left(R_\theta^i \mathbf{W}_q^z \hat{\mathbf{H}}, R_\theta^j \mathbf{W}_k^z \hat{\mathbf{H}}, \mathbf{W}_v^z \hat{\mathbf{H}}\right) \tag{3}$$

Z is the number of attention heads, W_q^z, W_k^z and W_v^z are trainable parameter of the zth head of attention. Note that the rotational position encoding matrix should vary for different positions in the sequence, here we use R_θ^i and R_θ^j for simplicity.

Aspect and Opinion Extraction. We use $SP = \{\mathbf{sp}_{i,j} \mid 0 \leq j - i \leq l\}$ to represent all possible spans in s, where i and j represent the start and end positions in s respectively, and the maximum length of span $\mathbf{sp}_{i,j}$ is l. We define the representation of span $\mathbf{sp}_{i,j}$ as,

$$\mathbf{sp}_{i,j} = [\mathbf{h}_i; \mathbf{h}_j] \tag{4}$$

where the semicolon represents concatenation.

Next, we employ a fully connected layer to evaluate the validity of each span $\mathbf{sp}_{i,j}$, assigning a label distribution $y_e \in \{Aspect, Opinion, Invalid\}$,

$$p_{i,j}^{A}, p_{i,j}^{O}, p_{i,j}^{IV} = \text{softmax}\left(\mathbf{W}_e \mathbf{sp}_{i,j} + \mathbf{b}_e\right) \tag{5}$$

where W_e, b_e are trainable parameters.

Inspred by Xu et al. (2021), to mitigate the complexity inherent in the subsequent calculation process, we retain a specified proportion of spans for

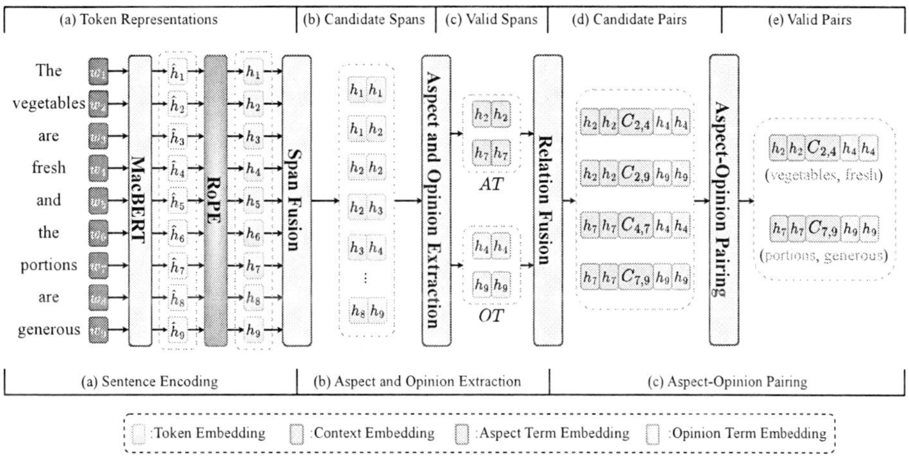

Figure 4: The overall framework of our Aspect-Opinion Pairing Module. Initially, the encoder derives base contextual representations for the input sentence. Subsequently, we integrate Rotary Position Embedding (RoPE) into the token representations to facilitate enhanced discourse comprehension. Following this, aspect terms and opinion terms are extracted based on the RoPE-enhanced representations. Finally, we identify valid aspect-opinion pairs from the extracted aspect and opinion terms.

both the aspect and the opinion candidate set, selecting those with the highest scores as determined by Equation 5. The refined sets of aspects and opinions can be denoted as $AT = \{\ldots, \mathbf{sp}^{A}_{i,j}, \ldots\}$ and $OT = \{\ldots, \mathbf{sp}^{O}_{i,j}, \ldots\}$, respectively, each comprising nr elements, where $r \in [0, 1]$ indicates the proportion of retained elements.

Aspect-Opinion Pairing. After acquiring the aspect and opinion candidate sets from the previous stage, we proceed by pairing them in all possible combinations, resulting in the following representation,

$$\mathbf{f}_{a,b,c,d} = \left[\mathbf{sp}^{A}_{a,b}; \mathbf{sp}^{O}_{c,d}; \mathbf{C}_{b,c}\right] \quad (6)$$

$$\mathbf{C}_{b,c} = \text{Max-Pooling}\left([\mathbf{h}_{b+1} : \mathbf{h}_{c-1}]\right) \quad (7)$$

$\mathbf{C}_{b,c}$ represents the contextual information of $\mathbf{sp}_{a,b}$ and $\mathbf{sp}_{c,d}$. Subsequently, we employ a fully connected layer to process the representation of each $\mathbf{f}_{a,b,c,d}$. This layer evaluates the validity of each aspect-opinion pair, assigning a label distribution $y_g \in \{Valid, Invalid\}$.

$$p^{V}_{a,b,c,d}, p^{IV}_{a,b,c,d} = \text{softmax}\left(\mathbf{W}_g \mathbf{f}_{a,b,c,d} + \mathbf{b}_g\right) \quad (8)$$

where W_g, b_g are trainable parameters.

Training. The training target is to minimize the cross-entropy loss of the extraction and pairing tasks.

$$\mathcal{L} = \alpha \mathcal{L}_e + \beta \mathcal{L}_g \quad (9)$$

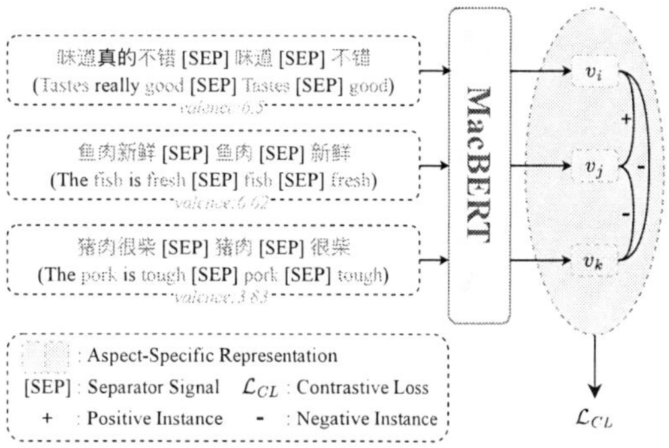

Figure 5: The overall framework of the Sentiment Scoring Module employs a contrastive loss, which ensures that samples with similar regression labels share similar features in the embedding space, while samples with differing labels are positioned further apar.

$$\mathcal{L}_e = -\sum_{sp_{i,j} \in SP} \log P\left(y^*_e \mid p^e_{i,j}\right) \quad (10)$$

$$\mathcal{L}_g = -\sum_{sp_{a,b} \in AT, sp_{c,d} \in OT} \log P\left(y^*_g \mid p^g_{a,b,c,d}\right) \quad (11)$$

Here, y^*_e and y^*_g represents the ground-truth label of the extraction and pairing tasks for $\mathbf{sp}_{i,j}$ and $\mathbf{f}_{a,b,c,d}$, respectively.

3.3 Sentiment Scoring Module

In this section, we employ contrastive learning to enhance aspect-specific representations and predict sentiment intensity for each aspect in the valence-arousal space, as illustrated in Figure 5.

Aspect Specific Representation. In this part, we first utilize MacBERT as encoder to generate aspect-specific representation for each aspect:

$$u_j = < \{w_i\}_n, \text{[SEP]}, \{a_j\}_{\hat{t}}, \text{[SEP]}, \{o_j\}_{\tilde{t}} > \tag{12}$$

$$\mathbf{H}_j = \text{MacBERT}(u_j) \tag{13}$$

where $\hat{t}$ and $\tilde{t}$ are lengths of the aspect a_j and its corresponding opinion o_j. Note that in the case of multi-aspect sentences, this module is employed multiple times, with each iteration focusing on one aspect. The aspect-specific feature representations is then obtained by max pooling,

$$\mathbf{v}_j = \text{Max-Pooling}(\mathbf{H}_j) \tag{14}$$

Contrastive Learning. After generating aspect-specific representations, most prior studies directly employ these representations for downstream tasks. Nonetheless, the performance is constrained by imbalanced datasets, resulting in suboptimal outcomes. To address this limitation, we incorporate contrastive learning to enhance feature optimization. Let $\{\mathbf{v}_i\}_G$ be defined as the set of all representations within a batch, and G denote the number of these representations, we first translate them for contrastive loss through a MLP combined with ℓ_2-normalization,

$$\mathbf{u}_i = \ell_2\text{-norm}(\text{MLP}(\mathbf{v}_i)) \tag{15}$$

In the absence of category labels, we establish two thresholds, δ_1 and δ_2, to facilitate the selection of positive and negative sample pairs respectively,

$$< i, j > = \begin{cases} + & \text{if } |y_i^* - y_j^*| \leq \delta_1 \\ - & \text{if } |y_i^* - y_j^*| \geq \delta_2 \end{cases} \tag{16}$$

where y_i^*, y_j^* represent the ground-truth of the sentiment intensity. Therefore, through the above rules, we can construct a positive set $\mathcal{P}_i$ and a negative set $\mathcal{N}_i$ for each representation u_i. The contrastive loss is calculated as follows,

$$\mathcal{L}_{CL} = -\frac{1}{G}\sum_{i=1}^{G}\sum_{\mathbf{u}_j \in \mathcal{P}_i} \log \frac{e^{\text{sim}(\mathbf{u}_i, \mathbf{u}_j^+)/\tau}}{\sum_{\mathbf{u}_k \in \mathcal{N}_i} e^{\text{sim}(\mathbf{u}_i, \mathbf{u}_k^-)/\tau}} \tag{17}$$

Training. The sentiment intensity was calculate by the aspect-specific representations $\{v_i\}_G$ through a single linear layer, and the total loss can be calculated as follow,

$$\mathcal{L} = \alpha\mathcal{L}_R + (1-\alpha)\mathcal{L}_{CL} \tag{18}$$

$$\mathcal{L}_R = \frac{1}{G}\sum_{i=1}^{G} ||y_i^* - f_\theta(v_i)|| \tag{19}$$

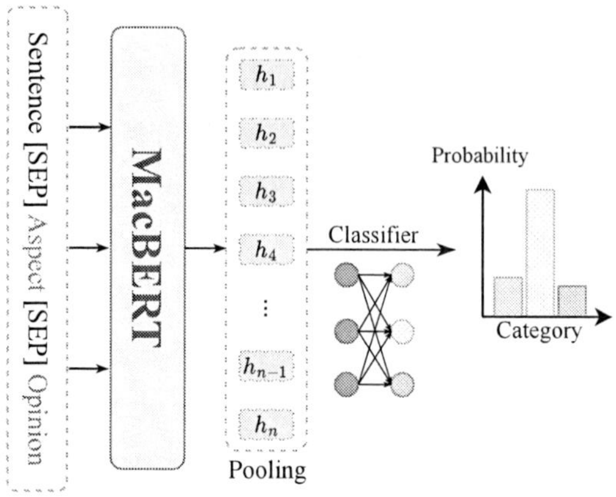

Figure 6: Architecture of the Category Prediction Module.

where f_θ denotes the linear projection. Note that the Sentiment Scoring Module is deployed twice within the system, with two identical components operating in parallel to independently extract valence and arousal features for regression prediction. This design allows each encoder to specialize in a specific emotional dimension, optimizing for the unique characteristics of each dimension and reducing feature interference during the contrastive learning process.

3.4 Category Prediction Module

This part employs the same method as the Sentiment Scoring Module to obtain aspect-specific representations v_i. As Figure 6 shows, these representations are subsequently passed through a fully connected layer with a softmax activation function, producing probability distributions across all categories,

$$p_i = \text{softmax}(\mathbf{W}_p\mathbf{v}_i + \mathbf{b}_p) \tag{20}$$

The training loss is formulated as the cross-entropy loss between the ground-truth and the predicted label distributions for all aspects,

$$\mathcal{L}_{CE} = -\frac{1}{N}\sum_{i=1}^{N} \log(y_i^* \mid p_i) \tag{21}$$

where y^* represent the ground-truth label.

3.5 Deployment Order

Table 1 illustrates the computational sequence of each component in the model across the three subtasks. All three subtasks necessitate an initial phase

	Task 1	Task 2	Task 3
Aspect-Opinion Pairing	✓	✓	✓
Opinion Retrieval	✓	✗	✗
Category Prediction	✗	✗	✓
Sentiment Scoring	✓	✓	✓

Table 1: The computational sequence of each component within the model across the three subtasks.

Dataset	Sentence-Level			Aspect-Level	
	Sgl-Senti	Mul-Senti	All	Null	All
train	4165	1885	6000	169	8354
$test_1$	1460	540	2000	-	2658
$test_{2,3}$	-	-	2000	-	-

Table 2: Dataset statistics. "Sgl-Senti" and "Mul-Senti" indicate the number of sentences expressing sentiment toward single or multiple aspects, respectively. "NULL" signifies that the aspect entity is omitted in sentence.

of aspect-opinion extraction and pairing. In Subtask 1, the Opinion Retrieval (OR) Module is employed, meaning that during sentiment intensity regression, we retrieve the corresponding opinion extracted in the aspect-opinion pair module for each predefined aspect, as this is a critical feature for both valence and arousal predictions. In cases where extraction or pairing fails, "NULL" is used to fill the missing opinion term.

4 Experiment

4.1 Dataset and Setup

We evaluate our model on the official dataset of the SIGHAN-2024 shared task (Lee et al., 2024), which uses Simplified Chinese characters. Dataset statistics are shown in Table 2. To enhance the model's ability to discern subtle sentiment nuances when predicting continuous sentiment intensity, we incorporated the Chinese EmoBank (EB) (Lee et al., 2022) as an auxiliary training resource. We fine-tuned the Sentiment Scoring Module on this supplementary dataset using the methodology outlined in Section 3.3, subsequently employing the fine-tuned parameters to initialize the model for the ensuing task training.

The Aspect-Opinion Pairing Module is trained for 30 epochs with a batch size of 16, and the other modules are trained for 10 epochs with a batch size of 128. AdamW optimizer (Loshchilov and Hutter, 2018) is adopted with a learning rate 2e-5 and weight decay 1e-2 for model training. The two thresholds δ_1 and δ_2 used in contrastive learning are set to 0.5 and 2 respectively. The maximum span length l is set as 10. We select the best model weights for testing based on performance on the validation set. MAE and PCC are evaluation metrics for subtask 1, while the F1 score is used as the evaluation metric for subtasks 2 and 3.

4.2 Baseline

Since no existing method is specifically designed for dimABSA, we re-implemented Span-ASTE (Xu et al., 2021) and STAGE (Liang et al., 2023), which are high-performing span-based systems closely related to the task, and used them as our baseline.

4.3 Main Results

Table 3 presents the results of out method in the final test set. Observations are: 1) Our purposed model outperforms the baseline, and achieves relatively good results in the final rankings, with one metric ranking **1st**, seven metrics ranking **2nd**, and two metrics ranking **3rd**. The performance improvement of our model primarily stems from a more powerful pre-training model, richer relational information for aspect-opinion pairing, and more robust feature representation for sentiment scoring. 2) Predicting sentiment intensities in the arousal dimension is significantly more challenging than in the valence dimension. In subtask 1, all models exhibit higher MAE in the arousal dimension compared to the valence dimension. In subtask 2 and 3, the F1 score based on arousal is about 5% lower than the F1 score based on valence. We infer that this complexity arises because predicting the level of arousal requires a comprehensive assessment of the overall context, tone, and other nuanced factors, which introduces corresponding challenges in the data annotation and training process.

4.4 Ablation Study

We also conduct an ablation study to verify the effectiveness of our proposed method. The results are shown in Table 3. Observations are: 1) For the Aspect-Opinion Pairing Module, **w/o CR** and **w/o RoPE** mean that we remove the contextual representation and rotational position embedding during the computation. Without the enhancement of relational features between spans and spans, the model's performance slightly degrades. 2) For the Sentiment Scoring Module, **w/o OR** indicates that the opinion term has been removed from the input, and **w/o CL** indicates that the contrastive loss has been omitted during the training process. As

Models	Subtask 1				Subtask 2			Subtask 3		
	V-MAE	V-PCC	A-MAE	A-PCC	V-F1	A-F1	VA-F1	V-F1	A-F1	VA-F1
Span-ASTE$^\natural$	-	-	-	-	0.473	0.458	0.310	-	-	-
STAGE$^\natural$	-	-	-	-	0.491	0.468	0.324	-	-	-
CL-Span$^\natural$	0.320	0.900	0.321	**0.767**	0.562	0.517	0.385	0.540	0.500	0.375
CL-Span†	0.302	0.910	0.314	**0.767**	0.565	0.519	0.391	0.547	0.505	0.379
CL-Span$^\circ$	**0.294**$_{(2)}$	**0.916**$_{(3)}$	**0.309**$_{(1)}$	0.766$_{(3)}$	**0.573**$_{(2)}$	**0.522**$_{(2)}$	**0.403**$_{(2)}$	**0.555**$_{(2)}$	**0.507**$_{(2)}$	**0.389**$_{(2)}$
CL-Span$^\circ_{\text{w/o-OR}}$	0.327	0.913	0.354	0.761	0.523	0.484	0.371	0.511	0.470	0.359
CL-Span$^\circ_{\text{w/o-CL}}$	0.311	0.912	0.331	0.764	0.548	0.511	0.380	0.542	0.503	0.377
CL-Span$^\circ_{\text{w/o-EB}}$	0.319	0.912	0.340	**0.767**	0.539	0.501	0.374	0.535	0.487	0.364
CL-Span$^\circ_{\text{w/o-RoPE}}$	-	-	-	-	0.565	0.514	0.391	0.547	0.510	0.379
CL-Span$^\circ_{\text{w/o-CR}}$	-	-	-	-	0.564	0.518	0.391	0.545	0.504	0.378

Table 3: Main results and ablation results on the test set. "○", "†" and "♮" indicates that the context encoder is MacBERT-base, RoBERTa-base (Cui et al., 2020) and BERT-base (Kenton and Toutanova, 2019) in Chinese version respectively. Note that "w/o" indicates the removal of the corresponding component from the model. The numbers in brackets represent the ranking of the metric in the official leaderboard.

a result, the model's performance drops dramatically, indicating that the opinion term is crucial for predicting sentiment intensity and that contrastive loss guides the model to obtain a more appropriate feature distribution when the dataset is imbalanced. 3) **w/o EB** indicates that the additional data from Chinese EmoBank was not used during training, resulting in deteriorated model performance. This verifies that Chinese EmoBank provides valuable supplementary information when the training data is insufficient. In summary, each module of our method significantly contributes to the overall performance on the dimABSA task.

5 Analysis

5.1 Effect of Contrastive Learning

To further verify the effectiveness of contrastive learning, we visualize the sample features with and without it, as shown in Figure 7. Models without contrastive loss struggle to capture the underlying continuous information in the data, resulting in fragmented and disordered representations. Conversely, features derived through contrastive learning preserve a coherent semantic structure, ensuring that semantically similar target values remain proximate in the feature space. Therefore, we infer that the improvement in effect comes from the neat and sequential feature representation brought by contrastive learning, which makes the feature space more discriminative and has stronger generalization ability in unknown data. At the same time, through contrastive learning, even if there are fewer samples with labels in certain intervals, the model will still learn the feature representation of these samples because they are frequently used for comparison during training. This method helps to balance the model's attention to different labels, thereby alleviating the problem of imbalanced datasets.

5.2 Low-Resource Scenario

As a challenging task, dimABSA faces significant issues related to data scarcity. To address this, we investigated the impact of contrastive learning under various training data conditions. As depicted in Figure 8, the model utilizing contrastive learning consistently achieves lower MAE values, especially as the dataset size diminishes. Furthermore, the slower increase in MAE for the contrastive learning model indicates that contrastive learning enhances the model's robustness and generalization capabilities, allowing it to maintain performance even under low-resource conditions.

5.3 Case Study

Figure 9 presents some case studies of this system, where aspect terms are highlighted in red and opinion terms in blue. Observations are: 1) In cases (a) and (b), the complete system achieved optimal results in the majority of sentiment intensity predictions. Notably, even for test data with sparse training data distribution, such as values like "7.62" and "2.17", CL-Span consistently outperformed other methods, underscoring its robustness in accurately predicting less frequent valence and arousal values. 2) In case (c), our proposed CL-Span successfully pairs all aspect terms with their corresponding opinion terms. In contrast, Span-ASTE fails to recognize the pair ("*onion*", "*caught*

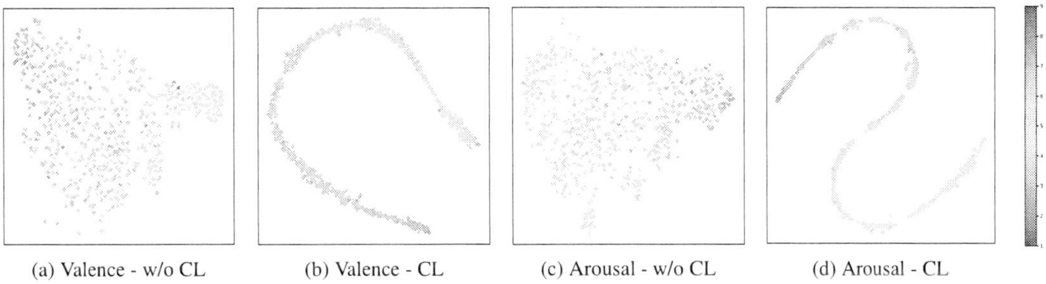

Figure 7: Visualization of learned aspect-specific representations of different methods on the validation set of dimABSA. The features are reduced to two dimensions using TSNE (Van der Maaten and Hinton, 2008), with the sentiment intensity ranging from 1 to 9. The color gradient from blue to red represents the increasing intensity of sentiment, where blue indicates the lowest intensity (1) and red indicates the highest intensity (9).

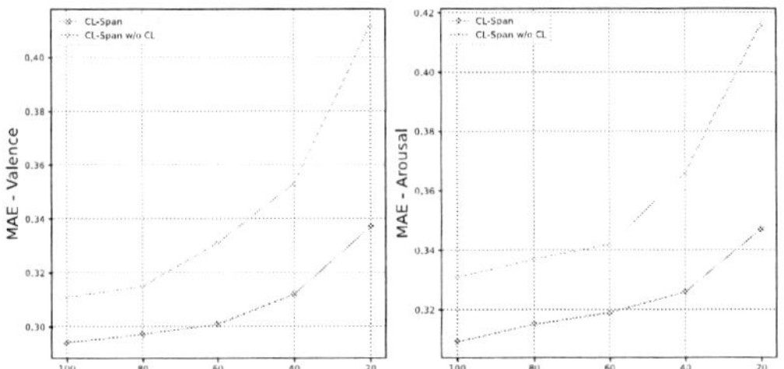

Figure 8: Comparison of the MAE for valence and arousal predictions by models with contrastive learning (red) and without contrastive learning (yellow) at different data usage ratios.

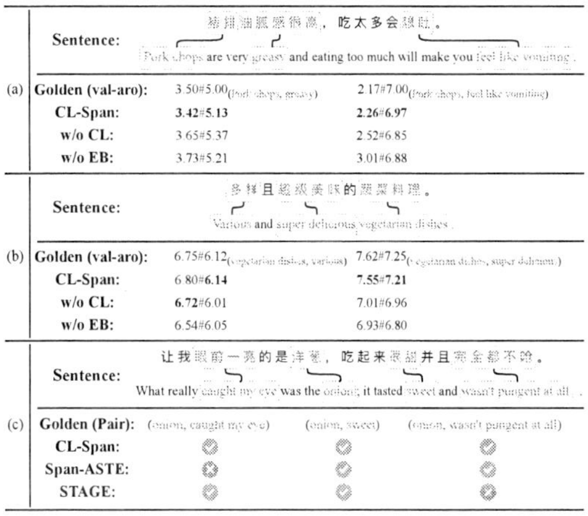

Figure 9: Example cases with golden standard labels alongside the predictions from our model compared with other baseline models. The bold numbers indicate the relatively optimal results.

my eye"), and the STAGE model overlooks the pair ("*onion*", "*wasn't pungent at all*"). We attribute the superior performance of our model to the integration of contextual representations and RoPE, which enhances the semantic understanding and connectivity between aspect and opinion terms.

6 Conclusion

This paper describes our system for the dimABSA task. We develop a Contrastive Learning-Enhanced Span-based Framework, which integrates contextual representations and RoPE into feature representation to enhance semantic understanding. Additionally, we employ contrastive learning to optimize feature representations. Our system demonstrates significant effectiveness, achieving a 2nd place ranking across three subtasks.

Limitations

This section discusses some improvements that can be made in future work. 1) The pipeline model structure used in this study divides the processing steps into independent modules, allowing each module to be developed, tested, and optimized separately. However, it also introduces the issue of error propagation, where errors in earlier stages can affect subsequent modules. In future work, we will focus on minimizing the impact of error propagation or consider testing an end-to-end model paradigm. 2) In the Sentiment Scoring Module, our system employs two MacBERT encoders to separately extract valence and arousal features for independent regression prediction. This approach reduces feature interference during the contrastive learning process and better captures the unique characteristics of each dimension. However, this results in the parameters of this module doubling to 204M. We will consider other encoding strategies instead of simply deploying two MacBERT separately.

Acknowledgments

This work was supported in part by the National Natural Science Foundation of China under Grant No. 62276110, No. 62172039 and in part by the fund of Joint Laboratory of HUST and Pingan Property Casualty Research (HPL). The authors would also like to thank the anonymous reviewers for their comments on improving the quality of this paper.

References

Hao Chen, Zepeng Zhai, Fangxiang Feng, Ruifan Li, and Xiaojie Wang. 2022a. Enhanced multi-channel graph convolutional network for aspect sentiment triplet extraction. In *Proceedings of the 60th Annual Meeting of the Association for Computational Linguistics (Volume 1: Long Papers)*, pages 2974–2985.

Yuqi Chen, Chen Keming, Xian Sun, and Zequn Zhang. 2022b. A span-level bidirectional network for aspect sentiment triplet extraction. In *Proceedings of the 2022 Conference on Empirical Methods in Natural Language Processing*, pages 4300–4309.

Yiming Cui, Wanxiang Che, Ting Liu, Bing Qin, Shijin Wang, and Guoping Hu. 2020. Revisiting pre-trained models for Chinese natural language processing. In *Proceedings of the 2020 Conference on Empirical Methods in Natural Language Processing: Findings*, pages 657–668, Online. Association for Computational Linguistics.

Yiming Cui, Wanxiang Che, Ting Liu, Bing Qin, and Ziqing Yang. 2021. Pre-training with whole word masking for chinese bert. *IEEE/ACM Transactions on Audio, Speech, and Language Processing*, 29:3504–3514.

Yin Fang, Qiang Zhang, Haihong Yang, Xiang Zhuang, Shumin Deng, Wen Zhang, Ming Qin, Zhuo Chen, Xiaohui Fan, and Huajun Chen. 2022. Molecular contrastive learning with chemical element knowledge graph. In *Proceedings of the AAAI conference on artificial intelligence*, volume 36, pages 3968–3976.

Hao Fei, Yafeng Ren, Yue Zhang, and Donghong Ji. 2021. Nonautoregressive encoder–decoder neural framework for end-to-end aspect-based sentiment triplet extraction. *IEEE Transactions on Neural Networks and Learning Systems*, 34(9):5544–5556.

Jacob Devlin Ming-Wei Chang Kenton and Lee Kristina Toutanova. 2019. Bert: Pre-training of deep bidirectional transformers for language understanding. In *Proceedings of NAACL-HLT*, pages 4171–4186.

Lung-Hao Lee, Jian-Hong Li, and Liang-Chih Yu. 2022. Chinese emobank: Building valence-arousal resources for dimensional sentiment analysis. *Transactions on Asian and Low-Resource Language Information Processing*, 21(4):1–18.

Lung-Hao Lee, Liang-Chih Yu, Suge Wang, and Jian Liao. 2024. Overview of the sighan 2024 shared task for chinese dimensional aspect-based sentiment analysis. In *Proceedings of the 10th SIGHAN Workshop on Chinese Language Processing. Association for Computational Linguistics.*

Tianhong Li, Peng Cao, Yuan Yuan, Lijie Fan, Yuzhe Yang, Rogerio S Feris, Piotr Indyk, and Dina Katabi. 2022. Targeted supervised contrastive learning for long-tailed recognition. In *Proceedings of the IEEE/CVF Conference on Computer Vision and Pattern Recognition*, pages 6918–6928.

Shuo Liang, Wei Wei, Xian-Ling Mao, Yuanyuan Fu, Rui Fang, and Dangyang Chen. 2023. Stage: span tagging and greedy inference scheme for aspect sentiment triplet extraction. In *Proceedings of the AAAI Conference on Artificial Intelligence*, volume 37, pages 13174–13182.

Yifan Liu, Wei Wei, Jiayi Liu, Xianling Mao, Rui Fang, and Dangyang Chen. 2022. Improving personality consistency in conversation by persona extending. In *Proceedings of the 31st ACM International Conference on Information & Knowledge Management*, pages 1350–1359.

Ilya Loshchilov and Frank Hutter. 2018. Decoupled weight decay regularization. In *International Conference on Learning Representations*.

Dehong Ma, Sujian Li, Fangzhao Wu, Xing Xie, and Houfeng Wang. 2019. Exploring sequence-to-sequence learning in aspect term extraction. In *Proceedings of the 57th annual meeting of the association for computational linguistics*, pages 3538–3547.

Haiyun Peng, Lu Xu, Lidong Bing, Fei Huang, Wei Lu, and Luo Si. 2020. Knowing what, how and why: A near complete solution for aspect-based sentiment analysis. In *Proceedings of the AAAI conference on artificial intelligence*, volume 34, pages 8600–8607.

Jianlin Su, Murtadha Ahmed, Yu Lu, Shengfeng Pan, Wen Bo, and Yunfeng Liu. 2024. Roformer: Enhanced transformer with rotary position embedding. *Neurocomputing*, 568:127063.

Yuanhe Tian, Guimin Chen, and Yan Song. 2021. Aspect-based sentiment analysis with type-aware graph convolutional networks and layer ensemble. In *Proceedings of the 2021 conference of the North American chapter of the association for computational linguistics: human language technologies*, pages 2910–2922.

Laurens Van der Maaten and Geoffrey Hinton. 2008. Visualizing data using t-sne. *Journal of machine learning research*, 9(11).

Amir Pouran Ben Veyseh, Nasim Nouri, Franck Dernoncourt, Dejing Dou, and Thien Huu Nguyen. 2020. Introducing syntactic structures into target opinion word extraction with deep learning. In *Proceedings of the 2020 Conference on Empirical Methods in*

Natural Language Processing (EMNLP), pages 8947–8956.

Hai Wan, Yufei Yang, Jianfeng Du, Yanan Liu, Kunxun Qi, and Jeff Z Pan. 2020. Target-aspect-sentiment joint detection for aspect-based sentiment analysis. In *Proceedings of the AAAI conference on artificial intelligence*, volume 34, pages 9122–9129.

Bo Wang, Tao Shen, Guodong Long, Tianyi Zhou, and Yi Chang. 2021a. Eliminating sentiment bias for aspect-level sentiment classification with unsupervised opinion extraction. In *Findings of the Association for Computational Linguistics: EMNLP 2021*, pages 3002–3012.

Peng Wang, Kai Han, Xiu-Shen Wei, Lei Zhang, and Lei Wang. 2021b. Contrastive learning based hybrid networks for long-tailed image classification. In *Proceedings of the IEEE/CVF conference on computer vision and pattern recognition*, pages 943–952.

Ziyang Wang, Huoyu Liu, Wei Wei, Yue Hu, Xian-Ling Mao, Shaojian He, Rui Fang, and Dangyang Chen. 2022. Multi-level contrastive learning framework for sequential recommendation. In *Proceedings of the 31st ACM International Conference on Information & Knowledge Management*, pages 2098–2107.

Ziyang Wang, Wei Wei, Shanshan Feng, Xian-Ling Mao, Minghui Qiu, Dangyang Chen, and Rui Fang. 2023. Exploiting group-level behavior pattern for session-based recommendation. *IEEE Transactions on Knowledge and Data Engineering*.

Wei Wei, Jiayi Liu, Xianling Mao, Guibing Guo, Feida Zhu, Pan Zhou, and Yuchong Hu. 2019. Emotion-aware chat machine: Automatic emotional response generation for human-like emotional interaction. In *Proceedings of the 28th ACM international conference on information and knowledge management*, pages 1401–1410.

Zhen Wu, Chengcan Ying, Fei Zhao, Zhifang Fan, Xinyu Dai, and Rui Xia. 2020. Grid tagging scheme for aspect-oriented fine-grained opinion extraction. In *Findings of the Association for Computational Linguistics: EMNLP 2020*, pages 2576–2585.

Hu Xu, Bing Liu, Lei Shu, and S Yu Philip. 2018. Double embeddings and cnn-based sequence labeling for aspect extraction. In *Proceedings of the 56th Annual Meeting of the Association for Computational Linguistics (Volume 2: Short Papers)*, pages 592–598.

Lu Xu, Yew Ken Chia, and Lidong Bing. 2021. Learning span-level interactions for aspect sentiment triplet extraction. In *Proceedings of the 59th Annual Meeting of the Association for Computational Linguistics and the 11th International Joint Conference on Natural Language Processing (Volume 1: Long Papers)*, pages 4755–4766.

Yi Xu, Junjie Ou, Hui Xu, and Luoyi Fu. 2023. Temporal knowledge graph reasoning with historical contrastive learning. In *Proceedings of the AAAI Conference on Artificial Intelligence*, volume 37, pages 4765–4773.

Shiyu Xuan and Shiliang Zhang. 2024. Decoupled contrastive learning for long-tailed recognition. In *Proceedings of the AAAI Conference on Artificial Intelligence*, volume 38, pages 6396–6403.

Yunyi Yang, Kun Li, Xiaojun Quan, Weizhou Shen, and Qinliang Su. 2020. Constituency lattice encoding for aspect term extraction. In *Proceedings of the 28th international conference on computational linguistics*, pages 844–855.

Wenxuan Zhang, Yang Deng, Xin Li, Yifei Yuan, Lidong Bing, and Wai Lam. 2021. Aspect sentiment quad prediction as paraphrase generation. In *Proceedings of the 2021 Conference on Empirical Methods in Natural Language Processing*, pages 9209–9219.

Yifan Zhang, Bingyi Kang, Bryan Hooi, Shuicheng Yan, and Jiashi Feng. 2023. Deep long-tailed learning: A survey. *IEEE Transactions on Pattern Analysis and Machine Intelligence*.

Zizhao Zhang and Tomas Pfister. 2021. Learning fast sample re-weighting without reward data. In *Proceedings of the IEEE/CVF International Conference on Computer Vision*, pages 725–734.

Sen Zhao, Wei Wei, Xian-Ling Mao, Shuai Zhu, Minghui Yang, Zujie Wen, Dangyang Chen, and Feida Zhu. 2023. Multi-view hypergraph contrastive policy learning for conversational recommendation. In *Proceedings of the 46th International ACM SIGIR Conference on Research and Development in Information Retrieval*, pages 654–664.

Boyan Zhou, Quan Cui, Xiu-Shen Wei, and Zhao-Min Chen. 2020. Bbn: Bilateral-branch network with cumulative learning for long-tailed visual recognition. In *Proceedings of the IEEE/CVF conference on computer vision and pattern recognition*, pages 9719–9728.

Yuxiang Zhou, Lejian Liao, Yang Gao, Zhanming Jie, and Wei Lu. 2021. To be closer: Learning to link up aspects with opinions. In *Proceedings of the 2021 Conference on Empirical Methods in Natural Language Processing*, pages 3899–3909.

Ding Zou, Wei Wei, Xian-Ling Mao, Ziyang Wang, Minghui Qiu, Feida Zhu, and Xin Cao. 2022. Multi-level cross-view contrastive learning for knowledge-aware recommender system. In *Proceedings of the 45th international ACM SIGIR conference on research and development in information retrieval*, pages 1358–1368.

ZZU-NLP at SIGHAN-2024 dimABSA Task: Aspect-Based Sentiment Analysis with Coarse-to-Fine In-context Learning

Senbin Zhu, Hanjie Zhao, Xingren Wang, Shanhong Liu, Yuxiang Jia*, **Hongying Zan**
School of Computer and Artificial Intelligence, Zhengzhou University, China
nlpbin@gs.zzu.edu.cn, {hjzhao_zzu,13257081272,18437919080}@163.com
ieyxjia@zzu.edu.cn

Abstract

The DimABSA task requires fine-grained sentiment intensity prediction for restaurant reviews, including scores for Valence and Arousal dimensions for each Aspect Term. In this study, we propose a Coarse-to-Fine In-context Learning(CFICL) method based on the Baichuan2-7B model for the DimABSA task in the SIGHAN 2024 workshop. Our method improves prediction accuracy through a two-stage optimization process. In the first stage, we use fixed in-context examples and prompt templates to enhance the model's sentiment recognition capability and provide initial predictions for the test data. In the second stage, we encode the Opinion field using BERT and select the most similar training data as new in-context examples based on similarity. These examples include the Opinion field and its scores, as well as related opinion words and their average scores. By filtering for sentiment polarity, we ensure that the examples are consistent with the test data. Our method significantly improves prediction accuracy and consistency by effectively utilizing training data and optimizing in-context examples, as validated by experimental results.

1 Introduction

Aspect-Based Sentiment Analysis (ABSA) (Pontiki et al., 2014; 2015; 2016) is a critical NLP research topic that aims to identify the aspects of a given entity and analyze the sentiment polarity associated with each aspect. ABSA involves predicting tuples of sentiment elements for a given text, with four main elements constituting the focus of ABSA research: aspect term (a), aspect category (c), opinion term (o), and sentiment polarity (s)(Zhang et al., 2022).

Early studies on ABSA primarily focused on single sentiment elements such as aspect term (Liu et al., 2015; Ma et al., 2019), aspect category (Zhou et al., 2015), or sentiment polarity (Wang et al., 2016; Chen et al., 2017). However, recent research has introduced compound ABSA tasks involving multiple associated elements. These include Aspect Sentiment Triplet Extraction (ASTE) (Peng et al., 2020; Yuan et al., 2023; Chen et al., 2021; Mao et al., 2021; Wu et al., 2020; Xu et al., 2020; Zhang et al., 2020), which extracts three elements in a triplet—aspect/target term, opinion term, and sentiment polarity.

Furthermore, Aspect Sentiment Quadruple Prediction (ASQP)(Zhang et al., 2021; Cai et al., 2021; Gao et al., 2022; Mao et al., 2022; Peper and Wang, 2022; Zhou et al., 2023) extends ASTE by including an additional aspect category, thus constructing a quadruple. In contrast to representing affective states as discrete classes (i.e., polarity), there is also a dimensional approach that represents affective states as continuous numerical values, such as in the valence-arousal (VA) space (Russell, 1980), providing more fine-grained emotional information (Lee et al., 2022). For example, in the sentence "独家的鲔鱼抹酱超好吃。", the corresponding elements are "鲔鱼抹酱" (aspect term), "食物#品质" (aspect category), "超好吃" (opinion term), and "7.5#7.25" (valence#arousa score).

Resently, large language models (LLMs)(Brown et al., 2020; Touvron et al., 2023) have shown an impressive few-shot ability on several NLP tasks. To expect LLMs to perform better on few-shot tasks, in-context learning (ICL)(Dong et al., 2022) paradigm is becoming a flourishing research direction. This paradigm can generate a prediction of the test input by conditioning on few-shot input-output examples (also known as in-context examples or demonstrations), without requiring any updates to parameters. Previous studies (Liu et al., 2022; Min et al., 2022) found that LLMs are highly sensitive to the choice of in-context examples. One typical strategy for retrieving helpful in-context examples is to leverage the overall semantic similar-

*Corresponding author

Proceedings of the 10th SIGHAN Workshop on Chinese Language Processing (SIGHAN-10), pages 112–120
August 16, 2024

ity between the candidate examples and test input. Further research has shown that retrieving highly relevant examples across multiple dimensions has achieved significant performance improvements in multi-domain ABSA tasks(Yang et al., 2024).

Supervised Fine-Tuning (SFT) is a method that involves further training a pre-trained model using a labeled dataset to achieve better performance on specific tasks. In-context learning helps the model understand the task by providing a few examples during inference, but its performance is often limited by the selection and number of examples. SFT, on the other hand, directly trains on a large amount of labeled data, allowing the model to deeply understand various aspects of the task, thereby exhibiting higher accuracy and consistency in practical applications and achieving good performance on specific tasks(Zhang et al., 2024).

Our study addresses the DimABSA task at the SIGHAN 2024 workshop by proposing a two-stage context learning method based on the Baichuan2-7B(Yang et al., 2023) model to improve the accuracy of fine-grained sentiment intensity prediction for restaurant reviews. Our work consists of two main stages: In the first stage, we use fixed context examples to train the model, enhancing its ability to recognize sentiment elements. In the second stage, we utilize the Chinese BERT(Devlin et al., 2018) to encode the Opinion field and select the most similar training data as new context examples based on similarity calculations, thereby further improving the model's prediction accuracy and granularity. Experimental results show that our method significantly enhances the model's performance in both valence and arousal dimensions and effectively reduces sentiment polarity bias. Overall, our approach provides an efficient solution for the DimABSA task and offers valuable insights for the optimization of future fine-grained sentiment analysis models.

2 Background

The Chinese Dimensional Aspect-Based Sentiment Analysis (dimABSA)(Lee et al., 2024) shared task is part of the SIGHAN 2024 workshop[1]. This task focuses on providing fine-grained sentiment intensity predictions for each extracted aspect of a restaurant review. The four sentiment elements are defined as follows:

Aspect Term (A): Denotes an entity indicating the opinion target. If the aspect is omitted and not mentioned clearly, "NULL" is used to represent the term. Aspect Category (C): Represents a predefined category for the explicit aspect within the restaurant domain. The categories are based on the SemEval-2016 Restaurant dataset (Pontiki et al., 2016) and include twelve categories, each split into an entity and attribute using the symbol "#". Opinion Term (O): Describes the sentiment words or phrases related to the aspects. Sentiment Intensity (I): Reflects the sentiments using continuous real-valued scores in the valence-arousal dimensions. Valence indicates the degree of pleasantness (positive or negative feelings), while arousal indicates the degree of excitement or calmness. Both dimensions use a nine-degree scale, where 1 denotes extremely high-negative or low-arousal sentiment, 9 denotes extremely high-positive or high-arousal sentiment, and 5 denotes neutral or medium-arousal sentiment. This task aims to evaluate the capability of automatic systems for Chinese dimensional ABSA and is divided into three subtasks:

Subtask 1: Intensity Prediction: Focuses on predicting sentiment intensities in the valence-arousal dimensions. Given a sentence and a specific aspect, the system should predict the valence-arousal ratings. Subtask 2: Triplet Extraction: Aims to extract sentiment triplets composed of three elements (aspect, opinion, intensity) from a given sentence. Subtask 3: Quadruple Extraction: Aims to extract sentiment quadruples composed of four elements (aspect, category, opinion, intensity) from a given sentence.

Our team chose to participate in the more challenging second and third subtasks, and we achieved third place in the evaluation task.

3 System Overview

We use Baichuan2-7B as the base model and propose a two-stage context learning method to improve prediction accuracy in the DimABSA task. This method incrementally optimizes the model output through preliminary and refined prediction stages, fully utilizing the information in the training data. Our framework is shown in Figure 1.

Baichuan2(Yang et al., 2023) is a Chinese and English bilingual language model. It achieved the best performance among models of the same size on standard benchmarks(C-Eval(Huang et al., 2024), MMLU(Hendrycks et al., 2020)).

[1]https://dimabsa2024.github.io

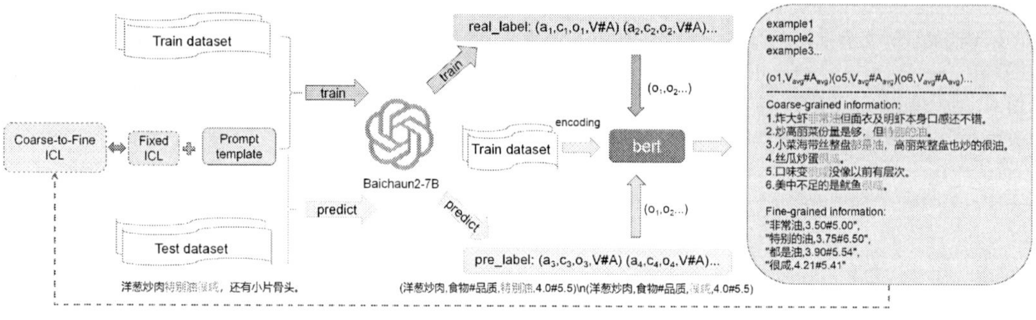

Figure 1: The architecture of our system. The figure illustrates a two-stage in-context learning method based on the Baichuan2-7B model to improve prediction accuracy in the DimABSA task. In the first stage, fixed in-context examples (Fixed ICL) are used to process training data. The model's sentiment recognition ability is enhanced through a prompt template, and initial predictions are made for the test data. In the second stage, the Opinion field is encoded using BERT, and the most similar training data is selected as new in-context examples based on similarity. These examples include the Opinion field and its scores, as well as related opinion words and average scores. Sentiment polarity filtering ensures that the in-context examples are consistent with the test data. Finally, these new in-context informations are input into the model along with the test data for re-prediction, yielding optimized quadruple results.

3.1 Fixed In-context Learning Stage

In the first stage, we utilize a few-shot learning method to process the training data. Specifically, we prepare three fixed context examples for each training sample and input these examples along with the training data into the model. This approach allows the model to learn task-related features from limited context information. After training, we use the trained model to predict the test data and obtain preliminary quadruplet results (aspect, category, opinion, intensity).

3.2 Example Retrieval Enhancement Stage

The objective of the second stage is to further enhance the model's prediction accuracy through similarity calculation and context example optimization. First, we use a BERT model to encode the Opinion field of each data label and calculate the cosine similarity between the Opinion encoding of each test data and that of each training data. The similarity calculation results are used to select the three most similar training data as new context examples. These examples include not only the Opinion fields and their scores but also related opinion words and their average scores, providing more detailed reference information.

To prevent significant bias in emotional polarity, we filter candidate examples based on the Valence scores predicted in the first stage, ensuring that the selected context examples are consistent with or similar to the current test data in terms of emotional polarity. Then, we input the new context examples along with the test data into the model for re-prediction, ultimately obtaining the optimized quadruplet prediction results.

This two-stage method significantly improves the model's prediction performance. The preliminary prediction in the first stage lays the foundation for the refined prediction in the second stage. The second stage, through similarity calculation and context example optimization, further enhances the accuracy and granularity of the prediction results. The overall method not only fully utilizes the information in the training data but also effectively reduces the impact of emotional polarity bias through careful filtering and context construction.

4 Experimental Setup

4.1 Dataset

The DimABSA dataset provided by the evaluation organizers includes 6000 training samples, 100 validation samples, and 2000 test samples of restaurant reviews. These data provide a substantial foundation for model training, validation, and final evaluation. The innovation of this evaluation task lies in the requirement to assign scores for valence and arousal dimensions to each aspect term, which is also the main challenge of the task.

We conduct a detailed examination of the sample distribution in these two dimensions and the correlation between the scores. Figure 2 shows the sample distribution for the valence and arousal

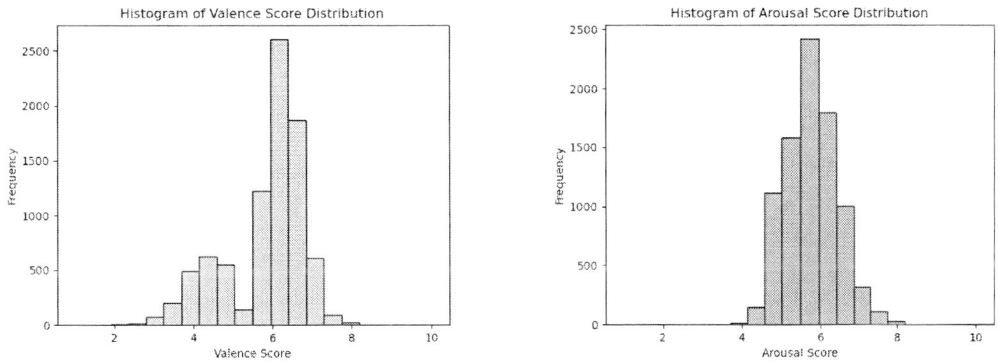

Figure 2: The distribution of valence and arousal scores of train dataset

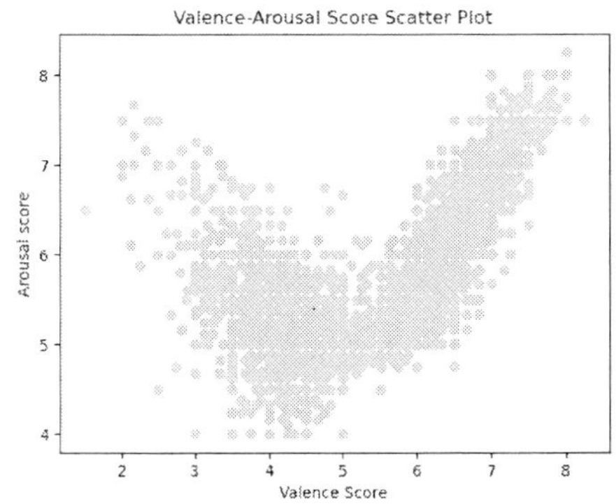

Figure 3: The distribution of continuous real-valued scores in the valence-arousal dimensions

dimensions, respectively. It can be seen that there are more samples with low valence scores (4-5) and more samples with high valence scores (6-7). The majority of arousal scores are concentrated between 5 and 7, with fewer samples at extreme values. Figure 3 shows the scatter plot of valence and arousal scores, illustrating the relationship between these two dimensions.

Through our analysis, we find that the distribution characteristics of this dataset align with those of The Chinese EmoBank (Lee et al., 2022), a dimensional sentiment resource. The reasonable distribution of valence and arousal dimensions provides authentic and effective data support for model training, helping the model to make accurate predictions under different levels of emotional intensity.

4.2 Implementation Details

We use Baichuan2-7B as our base model. During training, we use a batch size of 4 and a gradient accumulation step size of 4. We further employ the Adam optimizer with a learning rate of 8×10^{-5}. The training employs the LoRA efficient tuning method with precision set to fp16. We conduct the training on an NVIDIA V100 GPU.

4.3 Evaluation Metrics

First, the valence and arousal values are rounded to an integer. Next, a triplet/quadruple is regarded as correct if and only if the three/four elements and their combination match those in the gold triplet/quadruple. On this basis, we calculate the Precision, Recall, and F1-score as the evaluation metrics, defined as the following equations.

$$Precision = \frac{TP}{TP + FP} \tag{1}$$

$$Recall = \frac{TP}{TP + FN} \tag{2}$$

$$F1 = \frac{2 * Precision * Recall}{Precision + Recall} \tag{3}$$

where TP, FP, and FN denote true positives, false positives, and false negatives, respectively. Precision is defined as the percentage of triplets/quadruples extracted by the system that are correct. Recall is the percentage of triplets/quadruples present in the test set found by the system. The F1-score is the harmonic mean of precision and recall. All metrics range from 0 to 1. A higher Precision, Recall, and F1 score indicate more accurate performance. A system's overall ranking is based on the F1 score. The higher the F1 score, the better the system performance.

method	V-Quat-F1	A-Quat-F1	VA-Quat-F1
4 shot+Prompt1	0.53	0.38	0.27
4 shot+Prompt2	0.54	0.46	0.32
4 shot+Instruction Tuning	0.61	0.47	0.32
Coarse-to-Fine ICL+Instruction Tuning	0.62	0.51	0.38

Table 1: Evalution dataset results for quadruple extraction task

task	V-F1	A-F1	VA-F1
Triplet Extraction	0.542	0.507	0.389
Quadruple Extraction	0.522	0.489	0.376

Table 2: The result of test dataset for triplet and quadruple extraction

4.4 Evaluation Results

Each metric for the valence and arousal dimensions is calculated and ranked either independently or in combination. Precision is defined as the percentage of triplets/quadruples extracted by the system that are correct. Recall is the percentage of triplets/quadruples present in the test set found by the system. The F1-score is the harmonic mean of precision and recall. All metrics range from 0 to 1. A higher Precision, Recall, and F1 score indicate more accurate performance.

Previous research has shown that within certain limits, the performance of large language models improves with an increasing number of context examples. Considering computational constraints, we fine-tune Baichuan2-7B using four manually selected context examples. The selection criteria aim to ensure that examples are diverse and representative of the most common features in the dataset, thereby optimizing model performance to the greatest extent.

Additionally, adjustments to the prompt template significantly impact model performance. We use ChatGPT to optimize the logic and content quality of the prompt templates, emphasizing specific task characteristics and common pitfalls to further refine the templates. The initial template (prompt1) and the optimized template (prompt2) will be shown in the appendix. Experimental results indicate that the optimized prompt2 improves performance by five percentage points.

Instruction-tuning is a method to enhance the model's understanding of task instructions, thereby improving its generalization ability in specific tasks. Based on the above strategy for prompt adjustment, we design ten task templates for the model to randomly choose from, aiming to help the model comprehensively understand the task. After incorporating instruction-tuning, the V-Quat-F1 and A-Quat-F1 scores of the model's predictions improve, but the VA-Quat-F1 score shows no significant change. This suggests that while the model's understanding of valence and arousal dimensions improves individually, it does not adequately address the consistency between these two dimensions.

Given the challenge of this task, which requires scoring aspect sentiment in two dimensions—particularly the more difficult arousal dimension—we further optimize context examples using initially predicted test set label information and provide the model with more granular word-level standard score information. Specifically, in the second stage, we use an example retrieval method to find 3 to 5 context examples for each data sample and provide more than three word-level standard score examples. By providing dual-granularity information (sentence-level context examples and word-level standard scores), the prediction scores for both valence and arousal dimensions improve further. More importantly, the consistency between these two dimensions also significantly improves, with the VA-Quat-F1 score reaching 0.38. Detailed experimental results on the validation set are shown in Table 1.

Finally, the test results on the test set are shown in Table 2. For the triplet extraction task, we ignore the "category" aspect and adopt the same strategy, achieving good results as well. This further validates the effectiveness and broad applicability of our method.

4.5 Case Study

As shown in figure 4, after adopting the optimized examples, the reference for the term "my love" in the predictions becomes more precise. Initially,

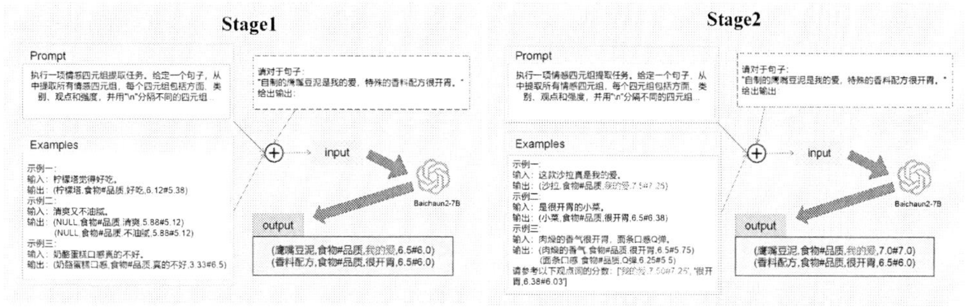

Figure 4: Case Study

when using fixed examples, the valence and arousal scores for "my love" are 6.5 and 6.0, respectively. Although these scores reflect a certain level of emotional intensity, they are not entirely accurate. By employing optimized examples in the second phase, we provide more relevant context. In the optimized example, the sentence "This salad is really my love." corresponds to valence and arousal scores of 7.50 and 7.25, respectively. These scores capture the emotional nuances more effectively. Considering this more fitting example, we re-predict the scores for "Homemade hummus is my love," resulting in adjusted valence and arousal scores of 7.0 and 7.0. These revised scores are more reasonable, demonstrating that using optimized context examples can significantly improve the accuracy and consistency of predictions, thereby better meeting the demands of fine-grained sentiment analysis.

5 Conclusion

This study proposes a two-stage context learning method based on the Baichuan2-7B model for the DimABSA task at the SIGHAN 2024 workshop. The task requires fine-grained sentiment intensity prediction for restaurant reviews.

In the first stage, we enhance the model's sentiment element recognition ability using fixed context examples. In the second stage, we utilize BERT to encode the Opinion field and select the most similar training data based on similarity calculation as new context examples. These relevant examples improve the accuracy of sentiment intensity prediction.

Experimental results show that our two-stage method significantly enhances the accuracy and granularity of predictions. The method effectively utilizes training data and reduces sentiment polarity bias.

Overall, our approach provides an efficient solution for the DimABSA task and offers valuable insights for optimizing future models for fine-grained sentiment analysis.

Limitations

Although our proposed method demonstrates significant performance improvements in the DimABSA task, there are still some limitations. First, our method focuses on enhancing the accuracy of sentiment intensity prediction, without further optimization for the Aspect field and its Category. Second, the success of the second stage is relatively dependent on the accuracy of the similarity measure between the Opinion field and the training data, and the issue of error propagation requires further analysis and discussion. Additionally, our method has high computational resource demands, especially when performing large-scale data training and optimization. This could limit its practicality and widespread adoption in real-world applications.

Acknowledgments

We express our gratitude to the organizers for providing such an inspiring competition and resolving our questions patiently. We would like to express our sincere gratitude to those who have provided detailed suggestions for our paper. Their diligent efforts are greatly appreciated.

References

Tom Brown, Benjamin Mann, Nick Ryder, Melanie Subbiah, Jared D Kaplan, Prafulla Dhariwal, Arvind Neelakantan, Pranav Shyam, Girish Sastry, Amanda Askell, et al. 2020. Language models are few-shot learners. *Advances in neural information processing systems*, 33:1877–1901.

Hongjie Cai, Rui Xia, and Jianfei Yu. 2021. Aspect-category-opinion-sentiment quadruple extraction with implicit aspects and opinions. In *Proceedings of the 59th Annual Meeting of the Association for Computational Linguistics and the 11th International Joint Conference on Natural Language Processing (Volume 1: Long Papers)*, pages 340–350.

Peng Chen, Zhongqian Sun, Lidong Bing, and Wei Yang. 2017. Recurrent attention network on memory for aspect sentiment analysis. In *Proceedings of the 2017 conference on empirical methods in natural language processing*, pages 452–461.

Shaowei Chen, Yu Wang, Jie Liu, and Yuelin Wang. 2021. Bidirectional machine reading comprehension for aspect sentiment triplet extraction. In *Proceedings of the AAAI conference on artificial intelligence*, volume 35, pages 12666–12674.

Jacob Devlin, Ming-Wei Chang, Kenton Lee, and Kristina Toutanova. 2018. Bert: Pre-training of deep bidirectional transformers for language understanding. *arXiv preprint arXiv:1810.04805*.

Qingxiu Dong, Lei Li, Damai Dai, Ce Zheng, Zhiyong Wu, Baobao Chang, Xu Sun, Jingjing Xu, and Zhifang Sui. 2022. A survey on in-context learning. *arXiv preprint arXiv:2301.00234*.

Tianhao Gao, Jun Fang, Hanyu Liu, Zhiyuan Liu, Chao Liu, Pengzhang Liu, Yongjun Bao, and Weipeng Yan. 2022. Lego-absa: A prompt-based task assemblable unified generative framework for multi-task aspect-based sentiment analysis. In *Proceedings of the 29th international conference on computational linguistics*, pages 7002–7012.

Dan Hendrycks, Collin Burns, Steven Basart, Andy Zou, Mantas Mazeika, Dawn Song, and Jacob Steinhardt. 2020. Measuring massive multitask language understanding. *arXiv preprint arXiv:2009.03300*.

Yuzhen Huang, Yuzhuo Bai, Zhihao Zhu, Junlei Zhang, Jinghan Zhang, Tangjun Su, Junteng Liu, Chuancheng Lv, Yikai Zhang, Yao Fu, et al. 2024. C-eval: A multi-level multi-discipline chinese evaluation suite for foundation models. *Advances in Neural Information Processing Systems*, 36.

Lung-Hao Lee, Jian-Hong Li, and Liang-Chih Yu. 2022. Chinese emobank: Building valence-arousal resources for dimensional sentiment analysis. *Transactions on Asian and Low-Resource Language Information Processing*, 21(4):1–18.

Lung-Hao Lee, Liang-Chih Yu, Suge Wang, and Jian Liao. 2024. Overview of the sighan 2024 shared task for chinese dimensional aspect-based sentiment analysis. *In Proceedings of the 10th SIGHAN Workshop on Chinese Language Processing*.

Jiachang Liu, Dinghan Shen, Yizhe Zhang, Bill Dolan, Lawrence Carin, and Weizhu Chen. 2022. What makes good in-context examples for gpt-3? *DeeLIO 2022*, page 100.

Pengfei Liu, Shafiq Joty, and Helen Meng. 2015. Fine-grained opinion mining with recurrent neural networks and word embeddings. In *Proceedings of the 2015 conference on empirical methods in natural language processing*, pages 1433–1443.

Dehong Ma, Sujian Li, Fangzhao Wu, Xing Xie, and Houfeng Wang. 2019. Exploring sequence-to-sequence learning in aspect term extraction. In *Proceedings of the 57th annual meeting of the association for computational linguistics*, pages 3538–3547.

Yue Mao, Yi Shen, Jingchao Yang, Xiaoying Zhu, and Longjun Cai. 2022. Seq2path: Generating sentiment tuples as paths of a tree. In *Findings of the Association for Computational Linguistics: ACL 2022*, pages 2215–2225.

Yue Mao, Yi Shen, Chao Yu, and Longjun Cai. 2021. A joint training dual-mrc framework for aspect based sentiment analysis. In *Proceedings of the AAAI conference on artificial intelligence*, volume 35, pages 13543–13551.

Sewon Min, Xinxi Lyu, Ari Holtzman, Mikel Artetxe, Mike Lewis, Hannaneh Hajishirzi, and Luke Zettlemoyer. 2022. Rethinking the role of demonstrations: What makes in-context learning work? In *EMNLP*.

Haiyun Peng, Lu Xu, Lidong Bing, Fei Huang, Wei Lu, and Luo Si. 2020. Knowing what, how and why: A near complete solution for aspect-based sentiment analysis. In *Proceedings of the AAAI conference on artificial intelligence*, volume 34, pages 8600–8607.

Joseph J Peper and Lu Wang. 2022. Generative aspect-based sentiment analysis with contrastive learning and expressive structure. *arXiv preprint arXiv:2211.07743*.

Maria Pontiki, Dimitris Galanis, Haris Papageorgiou, Ion Androutsopoulos, Suresh Manandhar, Mohammed AL-Smadi, Mahmoud Al-Ayyoub, Yanyan Zhao, Bing Qin, Orphée De Clercq, et al. 2016. Semeval-2016 task 5: Aspect based sentiment analysis. In *ProWorkshop on Semantic Evaluation (SemEval-2016)*, pages 19–30. Association for Computational Linguistics.

James A Russell. 1980. A circumplex model of affect. *Journal of personality and social psychology*, 39(6):1161.

Hugo Touvron, Louis Martin, Kevin Stone, Peter Albert, Amjad Almahairi, Yasmine Babaei, Nikolay Bashlykov, Soumya Batra, Prajjwal Bhargava, Shruti Bhosale, et al. 2023. Llama 2: Open foundation and fine-tuned chat models. *arXiv preprint arXiv:2307.09288*.

Yequan Wang, Minlie Huang, Xiaoyan Zhu, and Li Zhao. 2016. Attention-based lstm for aspect-level sentiment classification. In *Proceedings of the 2016 conference on empirical methods in natural language processing*, pages 606–615.

Zhen Wu, Chengcan Ying, Fei Zhao, Zhifang Fan, Xinyu Dai, and Rui Xia. 2020. Grid tagging scheme for aspect-oriented fine-grained opinion extraction. *arXiv preprint arXiv:2010.04640*.

Lu Xu, Hao Li, Wei Lu, and Lidong Bing. 2020. Position-aware tagging for aspect sentiment triplet extraction. *arXiv preprint arXiv:2010.02609*.

Aiyuan Yang, Bin Xiao, Bingning Wang, Borong Zhang, Ce Bian, Chao Yin, Chenxu Lv, Da Pan, Dian Wang, Dong Yan, et al. 2023. Baichuan 2: Open large-scale language models. *arXiv preprint arXiv:2309.10305*.

Songhua Yang, Xinke Jiang, Hanjie Zhao, Wenxuan Zeng, Hongde Liu, and Yuxiang Jia. 2024. FaiMA: Feature-aware in-context learning for multi-domain aspect-based sentiment analysis. In *Proceedings of the 2024 Joint International Conference on Computational Linguistics, Language Resources and Evaluation (LREC-COLING 2024)*, pages 7089–7100, Torino, Italia. ELRA and ICCL.

Li Yuan, Jin Wang, Liang-Chih Yu, and Xuejie Zhang. 2023. Encoding syntactic information into transformers for aspect-based sentiment triplet extraction. *IEEE Transactions on Affective Computing*.

Chen Zhang, Qiuchi Li, Dawei Song, and Benyou Wang. 2020. A multi-task learning framework for opinion triplet extraction. *arXiv preprint arXiv:2010.01512*.

Hao Zhang, Yu-N Cheah, Osamah Mohammed Alyasiri, and Jieyu An. 2024. Exploring aspect-based sentiment quadruple extraction with implicit aspects, opinions, and chatgpt: a comprehensive survey. *Artificial Intelligence Review*, 57(2):17.

Wenxuan Zhang, Yang Deng, Xin Li, Lidong Bing, and Wai Lam. 2021. Aspect-based sentiment analysis in question answering forums. In *Findings of the Association for Computational Linguistics: EMNLP 2021*, pages 4582–4591.

Wenxuan Zhang, Xin Li, Yang Deng, Lidong Bing, and Wai Lam. 2022. A survey on aspect-based sentiment analysis: Tasks, methods, and challenges. *IEEE Transactions on Knowledge and Data Engineering*.

Junxian Zhou, Haiqin Yang, Yuxuan He, Hao Mou, and Junbo Yang. 2023. A unified one-step solution for aspect sentiment quad prediction. *arXiv preprint arXiv:2306.04152*.

Xinjie Zhou, Xiaojun Wan, and Jianguo Xiao. 2015. Representation learning for aspect category detection in online reviews. In *Proceedings of the AAAI conference on artificial intelligence*, volume 29.

A Appendix

Prompt 1: 执行一项情感四元组提取任务。给定一个句子，提取句子中所有的情感四元组(方面、类别、观点、强度)，用"\n"分隔不同的四元组。

每个四元组中的"方面"是句子中被评价对象的特定方面或特征，如果省略了该方面而没有明确提及，使用"NULL"来表示该术语。"类别"是预定义的12种类别之一，根据常识判断。预定义类别：餐厅#概括、餐厅#价格、餐厅#杂项、食物#价格、食物#品质、食物#份量与款式、饮料#价格、饮料#品质、饮料#份量与款式、氛围#概括、服务#概括、地点#概括。"观点"是对方面的情感词或短语。"强度"指效价-唤醒的二维情绪强度，其中效价代表情绪体验的整体愉悦程度(高兴-不高兴)，唤醒代表情绪的强度水平(平静-兴奋)，每个指标的范围应为 1.0 到 9.0。在效价和唤醒维度上的值为 1 表示极度负面和低唤醒情感，相反，9 表示极度正面和高唤醒情感，5 表示中性和中等唤醒情感。精确到小数点后两位，效价-唤醒值以#分隔。

示例如下： examples

请对于句子：

给出输出：

Prompt 1 in English: Extract sentiment quads. Given a sentence, extract all sentiment quads (aspect, category, opinion, intensity) in the sentence, separated by "\n".

In each quad, the "aspect" is the specific aspect or feature of the object being evaluated in the sentence. If the aspect is omitted or not explicitly mentioned, use "NULL" to represent the term. The "category" is one of the predefined 12 categories, determined based on common sense. The predefined categories are: Restaurant#General, Restaurant#Price, Restaurant#Miscellaneous, Food#Price, Food#Quality, Food#Portion and Style, Drink#Price, Drink#Quality, Drink#Portion and Style, Ambience#General, Service#General, Location#General. The "opinion" is the sentiment word or phrase describing the aspect. The "intensity" refers to the two-dimensional emotion intensity of Valence-Arousal, where valence represents the overall pleasantness of the emotional experience (happy-unhappy), and arousal represents the intensity level of the emotion (calm-excited). Each indicator ranges from 1.0 to 9.0. A value of 1 on the valence and arousal dimensions indicates extremely negative and low arousal emotions, respectively, while 9 indicates extremely positive and high arousal emotions, and 5 indicates neutral and medium arousal emotions. Values should be precise to two decimal places, with valence and arousal values separated by #.

Example: examples

For the sentence:

Provide the output:

Prompt 2: 执行一个情感四元组提取任务。给定一个句子，从中提取所有情感四元组，其中包括方面、类别、观点和强度，并用"\n"分隔不同的四元组。

每个四元组包括以下要素："方面"指的是句子中被评价对象的具体方面或特征。如果没有明确提及方面，则使用"NULL"表示。"类别"是根据常识判断的预定义类别之一，共有12种。预定义类别包括：餐厅#概括、餐厅#价格、餐厅#杂项、食物#价格、食物#品质、食物#份量与款式、饮料#价格、饮料#品质、饮料#份量与款式、氛围#概括、服务#概括、地点#概括。"观点"是对被评价对象特定方面的情感词或短语。"强度"表示情感的效价和唤醒，分别代表情绪体验的整体愉悦程度（高兴-不高兴）和情绪的强度水平（平静-兴奋）。效价和唤醒的范围是1.0到9.0，其中1表示极度负面和低唤醒情感，9表示极度正面和高唤醒情感，5表示中性和中等唤醒情感。效价和唤醒值以#分隔，精确到小数点后两位。输出格式应严格按照以下示例的格式：(方面, 类别, 观点, 强度) 每个四元组在括号内，不要输出无关信息。观点是最细粒度的情感词，需要为每一个提取出的观点生成相应的四元组。

示例如下：examples

请对于句子：

给出输出：

Prompt 2 in English: Execute a task of extracting sentiment quadruples. Given a sentence, extract all sentiment quadruples from it, including aspect, category, opinion, and intensity, and separate different quadruples with "\n".

Each quadruple includes the following elements:

"Aspect" refers to the specific aspect or feature of the evaluated object in the sentence. If the aspect is not explicitly mentioned, use "NULL" to represent it. "Category" is one of the predefined categories judged based on common sense. There are 12 predefined categories: Restaurant#General, Restaurant#Prices, Restaurant#Miscellaneous, Food#Prices, Food#Quality, Food#Style and Options, Drinks#Prices, Drinks#Quality, Drinks#Style and Options, Ambience#General, Service#General, and Location#General. "Opinion" is the emotional word or phrase regarding the specific aspect of the evaluated object. "Intensity" represents the valence and arousal of the emotion, where valence indicates the overall pleasantness of the emotional experience (happy-unhappy) and arousal indicates the intensity level of the emotion (calm-excited). The range of valence and arousal is from 1.0 to 9.0, where 1 indicates extremely negative and low arousal emotion, 9 indicates extremely positive and high arousal emotion, and 5 indicates neutral and moderate arousal emotion. The valence and arousal values are separated by # and precise to two decimal places. The output format should strictly follow the format of the following example: (aspect, category, opinion, intensity). Each quadruple should be enclosed in parentheses, and do not output any irrelevant information. Each opinion is the most granular emotional word, and a corresponding quadruple should be generated for each extracted opinion.

Example: examples

Given the sentence:

Provide the output:

JN-NLP at SIGHAN-2024 dimABSA Task: Extraction of Sentiment Intensity Quadruples Based on Paraphrase Generation

Yunfan Jiang and **Tianci Liu** and **Hengyang Lu**
School of Artificial Intelligence and Computer Science, Jiangnan University, China
{1033200623,liutianci}@stu.jiangnan.edu.cn
luhengyang@jiangnan.edu.cn

Abstract

Aspect-based sentiment analysis (ABSA) is a fine-grained sentiment analysis task, which aims to extract multiple specific sentiment elements from text. The current aspect-based sentiment analysis task mainly involves four basic elements: aspect term, aspect category, opinion term, and sentiment polarity. With the development of ABSA, methods for predicting the four sentiment elements are gradually increasing. However, traditional ABSA usually only distinguishes between "positive", "negative", or "neutral" attitudes when judging sentiment polarity, and this simplified classification method makes it difficult to highlight the sentiment intensity of different reviews. SIGHAN 2024 provides a more challenging evaluation task, the Chinese dimensional ABSA shared task (dimABSA), which replaces the traditional sentiment polarity judgment task with a dataset in a multidimensional space with continuous sentiment intensity scores, including valence and arousal. Continuous sentiment intensity scores can obtain more detailed emotional information. In this task, we propose a new paraphrase generation paradigm that uses generative questioning in an end-to-end manner to predict sentiment intensity quadruples, which can fully utilize semantic information and reduce propagation errors in the pipeline approach.

1 Introduction

Traditional Aspect-based sentiment analysis (ABSA) can extract four specific emotional elements from the text: 1) *Aspect term*, which is a specific aspect in the sentence, generally a word or phrase expressed in the text, and may not exist; 2) *Aspect category*, the category involved by the aspect term, usually a predefined set of categories; 3) *Opinion term*, the expression of a specific emotional view on an aspect; 4) *Sentiment polarity*, the emotional tendency towards a certain aspect. For example, for the review "*The pizza at this restaurant is delicious, but the service is terrible.*", the ABSA task can extract two emotional quadruples: (*pizza, food type, delicious, positive*) and (*service, service attitude, terrible, negative*).

The Chinese dimensional ABSA shared task (dimABSA) (Lee et al., 2024) dataset is a collection of comments extracted by organizers from online catering industry social media platforms. After removing HTML tags and multimedia tags, the text was split into multiple sentences. A selection of these sentences was then manually annotated with aspect term, aspect category, opinion term, and sentiment intensity. For sentiment intensity, the organizers used the valence and arousal provided by the "Chinese EmoBank" (Lee et al., 2022;Yu et al., 2016) to represent emotional states as continuous numerical values in a multidimensional space. Using valence-arousal as sentiment intensity, this method provides more detailed emotional information. The "Chinese EmoBank" is a manually annotated Chinese emotional dictionary. In it, valence describes the positivity or negativity of emotions, ranging continuously from negative (such as *sadness*, *anger*) to positive (such as *happiness*, *excitement*). Valence is often seen as the "pleasantness" of an emotional experience and is a standard for assessing the quality of emotional experiences. Arousal, on the other hand, refers to the level of excitement of an emotion. It reflects the intensity of an individual's physiological and psychological response to an emotional stimulus. Arousal is also a continuous range, from very low (such as *boredom*, *tiredness*) to very high (such as *surprise*, *panic*). In the "Chinese EmoBank", both valence and arousal are measured on a scale from 1 to 9. In the sentiment intensity of the dimABSA dataset, valence and arousal are separated by a '#'.

The dimABSA task provides three subtasks: Subtask 1: For a given sentence and its aspect term, predict the sentiment intensity of the aspect term

Proceedings of the 10th SIGHAN Workshop on Chinese Language Processing (SIGHAN-10), pages 121–126
August 16, 2024

in the comment; Subtask 2: For a given sentence, extract the aspect term and opinion term from the comment and predict the sentiment intensity; Subtask 3: For a given sentence, extract the aspect term, aspect category, and opinion term from the comment and predict the sentiment intensity. In this task, we have implemented Subtask 3, where the system could extract all sentiment quadruples (aspect, category, opinion, intensity). For example, for the comment "*This bowl of ramen is super invincibly thunderously bad.*", the final extraction of the sentiment intensity quadruple would be: *(ramen, food#quality, super invincibly thunderously bad, 2.00#7.88)*.

This work processes the dataset provided by the dimABSA task and proposes a new paraphrase generation paradigm. It replaces the traditional sentiment polarity judgment task in ABSA with the judgment of sentiment intensity: valence#arousal, using the T5 pre-trained model (Raffel et al., 2020) that unifies natural language processing tasks into text-to-text tasks. Through fine-tuning training, it accomplishes the task of extracting sentiment intensity quadruples. Experiments demonstrate that our newly proposed paraphrase generation paradigm achieves good performance in predicting sentiment intensity quadruples. Our contributions are summarized as follows: 1) We propose transforming the dimABSA task into a paraphrase generation problem and introduce a new paraphrase generation paradigm, allowing us to fully utilize semantic information while predicting sentiment intensity quadruple in one shot; 2) Our model has been experimentally validated to perform excellently in extracting aspect term, aspect category, and opinion term.

2 Related Work

With the emergence of pre-trained language models like BERT, research in ABSA has made significant progress. Sun et al. (2019) proposed a method based on pre-trained language models, utilizing models like BERT to extract the subjects and aspects from online comments, and employing multi-task learning to determine their sentiment polarity. This was the first method for ABSA based on pre-trained language models and is representative of methods based on transfer learning. Li et al. (2019) were the first to apply BERT to end-to-end ABSA tasks, achieving the best results at the time with a simple linear classifier. Subsequently, composite ABSA tasks began to develop. Researchers proposed various end-to-end models for extracting multiple sentiment elements, capable of handling multiple subtasks in sentiment analysis tasks, such as Aspect Term Extraction (ATE) and Aspect Sentiment Classification (ASC). This integrated approach reduced error propagation and improved overall performance. Liu et al. (2021) adopted the Seq2Seq modeling paradigm to extract aspect category and sentiment polarity, based on pre-trained generative models, using natural language sentences to represent the desired output for Aspect Category Sentiment Analysis (ACSA) tasks. Peng et al. (2020) proposed a two-stage pipeline method for extracting aspect term, opinion term, and sentiment polarity to address the Aspect Sentiment Triplet Extraction (ASTE) task; Wan et al. (2020) introduced the Target-aspect-sentiment joint detection task for aspect-based sentiment analysis (TASD), aimed at simultaneously predicting aspect category, aspect term, and sentiment polarity.

The Aspect Sentiment Quad Prediction (ASQP) task aims to extract the four sentiment elements of a specific sentence at once, revealing a more comprehensive and complete aspect-level sentiment structure. Zhang et al.(2021) proposed a Paraphrase Generation paradigm to solve the ASQP task in English. This approach generates natural language sentences from sentiment quadruples using pre-established templates, making the generated natural language sequence the target sequence, which forms a mapping relationship with the original review sentence. Zhang et al. transformed the original quad element prediction task into a text generation problem, which was then solved using a sequence-to-sequence (Seq2Seq) approach. Compared to the pipeline method, the Seq2Seq approach can reduce the cumulative propagation error caused by accuracy errors at each step in the pipeline, and since the subtasks of ASQP are usually expressed as token-level or sequence-level classification problems, the Seq2Seq approach can make full use of semantic information.

3 Methodology

3.1 Problem Statement

Subtask 3 of the dimABSA task involves extracting a sentiment intensity quadruple (a, c, o, i) from a given sentence, which corresponds to aspect term, aspect category, opinion term, and sentiment intensity, respectively. The aspect term in the original comment sentence may not exist, and when it is absent, 'NULL' is used as the aspect term. The aspect category in the original comment are predefined, and the dimABSA task divides comments on different aspects of the catering industry into twelve categories, each with one entity and one attribute corresponding to the aspect term. The aspect term can be directly extracted from the comment. Sentiment intensity is divided into valence and arousal.

The dimABSA task dataset provides 6050 training entries, 2000 test entries, and 100 validation entries.

3.2 ASQP Task

To highlight the main content of the sentiment quadruple, Zhang et al.'s paraphrase generation task linearizes the sentiment quadruple $Q = (c, a, o, p)$ into a natural sentence as follows:

$$P_c(c)\, is\, P_p(p)\, because\, P_a(a)\, is\, P_o(o)$$

Herein,$P_z(\cdot)$ belongs to the mapping function of $z \in \{c, a, o, p\}$, which maps the sentiment element z from its original format into natural language form. In the sentiment quadruple, c and o are already in natural language form. As for the sentiment polarity, its mapping is as follows:

$$P_p(p) = \begin{cases} great & if\, p = positive \\ ok & if\, p = neutral \\ bad & if\, p = negative \end{cases} \quad (1)$$

Aspect term may not exist in the original sentence, in which case they are considered as an implicit aspect term 'NULL'; otherwise, they are in natural language form. Their mapping method is as follows:

$$P_a(a) = \begin{cases} it & if\, a = NULL \\ a & otherwise \end{cases} \quad (2)$$

When Zhang et al. handle Seq2Seq learning, for a given sentence x, the encoder first converts it into a contextualized encoded sequence e. Then, the decoder simulates the conditional probability distribution of the target sentence y given the encoded input representation: $P_\theta(y|e)$, which is parameterized by θ.

At the i-th time step, the output y_i of the decoder is based on the encoded input sequence e and the previous output $y_{<i}$, where $y_{<i} : y_i = f_{dec}(e, y_{<i})$, and $f_{dec}(\cdot)$ represents the computed value of the decoder. To obtain the probability distribution of the next token, the following softmax function is applied:

$$P_\theta(y_{i+1}|e, y_{<i+1}) = softmax(W^T y_i) \quad (3)$$

Here, W maps the predicted value y_i to a logit vector, which is defined as the logarithmic odds ratio of an event occurring versus not occurring. It can be used to calculate the probability distribution over the entire vocabulary set. The formula is as follows:

$$logit(P) = log(\frac{P}{1-P}) \quad (4)$$

Training with the T5 pre-trained model can achieve the initialization of pre-trained parameter weights θ, and further fine-tune the input-target pairs, thus maximizing the probability distribution $P_\theta(y|e)$:

$$\max_\theta log P_\theta(y|e) = \sum_{i=1}^{n} log P_\theta(y_i|e, y_{<i}) \quad (5)$$

where n is the length of the sequence target y.

3.3 DimABSA as Paraphrase Generation

Regarding the 'Sentence', 'Aspect', 'Category', 'Opinion', and 'Intensity' aspects in the dimABSA task dataset, the data format is processed into the following format:

$$Sentence[[A_1, C_1, O_1, I_1], ...[A_n, C_n, O_n, I_n]]$$

We propose a new paraphrase generation paradigm to handle the task of Chinese sentiment intensity quadruple extraction, for a given sentence tuple pair (x,Q), with the goal of generating a target pair of sentences in Chinese natural language (x,y), the sentiment intensity quadruple is linearized into a natural sentence as follows:

$$P_C(C)\, valence\, is\, P_I(I - v)\, arousal \\ is\, P_I(I - a)\, because\, P_A(A)\, is\, P_O(O)$$

Wherein,$P_z(\cdot)$ is the mapping function $z \in \{C, A, O, I\}$, which transforms sentiment elements from their original format into natural language form. In the sentiment intensity quadruple, the aspect category (C) and opinion term (O) are already in natural language form. The aspect term (A) may not exist in the original sentence, in which case it is considered an implicit aspect term

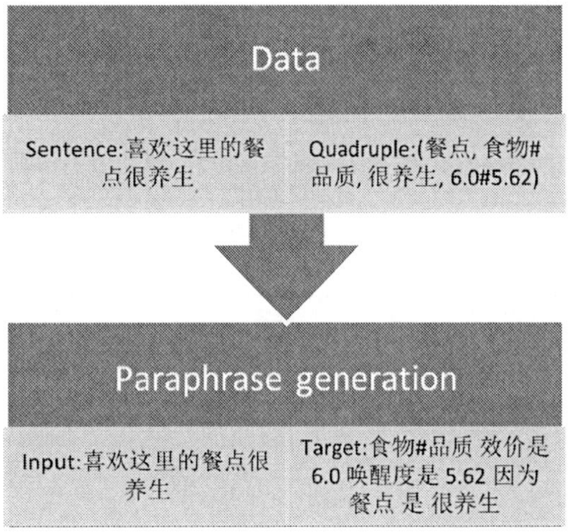

Figure 1: An example of sentence tuple pairs generating sentence target pairs.

'NULL', otherwise, it is directly regarded as natural language form. Its mapping method is as follows:

$$P_A(A) = \begin{cases} it & if\, a = NULL \\ a & otherwise \end{cases} \tag{6}$$

The sentiment intensity (I) will be directly retained as a scoring standard in the natural language generated after paraphrase generation, representing the valence and arousal ratings for the given aspect term. The final target sentence y generated can form a mapping relationship with the original comment sentence x, which is then directly fine-tuned using the T5 pre-trained language model. When there are multiple sentiment intensity quadruples Q in a sentence x, the separator [SSEP] is used to divide the multiple target sentences generated. Figure 1 shows an example of paraphrase generation.

4 Experiment

4.1 Experiment Details

The mt5-base (Xue et al., 2021) is a model proposed by Google, pre-trained on the mC4 corpus, and includes 101 languages, including Chinese. In this work, the t5-base-chinese pre-trained model is selected as the task model. The t5-base-chinese is based on mt5-base, retaining only Chinese and English for pre-training. Fine-tune training on T5-base-Chinese. Both training and evaluation batch sizes are set to 16; gradient_accumulate_steps is set to 1, the learning rate is set to 3e-4, and the number of training rounds is set to 10.

4.2 Main Results

Organizers use accuracy, recall, and F1-score to evaluate the model. The higher these three metrics, the better the model's performance. A quadruple is regarded as correct if and only if the four elements and their combination match those in the gold quadruple. Table 1 shows the scores of the three metrics: accuracy, recall, and F1-score, for valence and arousal in this work.

A total of 7 teams submitted, and the published F1-scores for valence, arousal, and valence-arousal are as shown in Table 2. Our work is ranked fifth.

At the same time, this work also trained a T5 pre-trained model without using the paraphrase generation paradigm, to comparatively evaluate the model's ability to extract aspect term, aspect category, and opinion term in sentiment triplets. The test model, which does not use paraphrase generation, directly maps the golden triplets containing aspect term, aspect category, and opinion term as the target sequence, forming a mapping with the original comment sentence. The final test model outputs predicted triplets for the input comments. After manually removing some problematic test data, the performance of this test model and the task model on 900 test data in terms of accuracy, recall rate, and F1-score for the aforementioned three types of sentiment elements is shown in Table 3.

4.3 Error Analysis

When the model processes some more complex natural language sentences, it outputs some problematic target sentences: 1) 'The watermelon and strawberries are very fresh and delicious.', this sentence in chinese contains two aspect terms and two opinion terms. Both opinion terms are expressions of sentiment for the two aspect terms, and there is no conjunction between the two opinion terms. The model has difficulty correctly matching aspect terms with opinion terms for comments that have multiple aspect terms and opinion terms without direct conjunctions, resulting in the repeated output of the same target sentence: 'Food#quality valence is 6.75 arousal is 6.25 because watermelon is delicious'. When a conjunction is added between the two opinion terms, the model's output is normal; 2) Due to the diversity of Chinese language forms, the model struggles to process some idioms or longer comments. In the output of target sentences, it will manifest as the target sentence not conforming to the rules of paraphrase generation paradigms, such

	Precision	Recall	F1-score
Valence	0.484	0.480	0.482
Arousal	0.441	0.437	0.439
V-A	0.333	0.330	0.331

Table 1: The scores of the model's valence, arousal, and valence-arousal on accuracy, recall, and F1-score.

Team	Valence-F1	Arousal-F1	V-A-F1
HITSZ-HLT	**0.567**	**0.526**	**0.417**
CCIIPLab	0.555	0.507	0.389
ZZU-NLP	0.522	0.489	0.376
SUDA-NLP	0.487	0.444	0.336
JN-NLP (ours)	0.482	0.439	0.331
BIT-NLP	0.470	0.434	0.329
USTC-NLP	0.438	0.437	0.312

Table 2: The F1-scores of the participating teams in valence, arousal, and valence-arousal.

as the absence of a certain sentiment element in the target sentence, or the appearance of multiple setting words from paraphrase generation paradigms in one target sentence, such as 'valence is', 'arousal is', etc. The model still has limitations in the above examples.

5 Conclusions

The goal of dimABSA subtask 3 is to extract sentiment intensity quadruples from online review sentences in the catering industry, including aspect term, aspect category, opinion term, and the valence-arousal representing sentiment intensity. This work proposes a new paraphrase generation paradigm, utilizing the dataset provided by the dimABSA task, and ultimately achieves a model based on the T5 pre-trained model fine-tuned for training. This model uses the new paraphrase generation paradigm to facilitate Seq2Seq learning, transforming sentiment intensity quadruples into natural language target sentences, forming a mapping relationship with the review sentences. The model can generate an output sentence according to the paraphrasing rules for the input sentence, and the sentiment intensity quadruples can be obtained by processing the output sentence. By comparing the performance of this work's model with the test model in extracting triples of aspect term, aspect category, and opinion term, it is evident that this work's model performs better.

Model	precision	recall	F1-score
test model	0.434	0.395	0.414
JN-NLP (ours)	**0.462**	**0.470**	**0.466**

Table 3: Comparison of the test model and our model in terms of accuracy, recall, and F1-score on predicting sentiment triplets.

Limitations

After training the model with the paraphrase generation paradigm we proposed, it can complete the task of extracting the sentiment intensity quadruples. However, the model still has limitations in predicting sentiment intensity. When a comment contains multiple aspect terms, the model may predict the same score for the sentiment intensity of multiple aspect terms. Moreover, due to the complexity of the Chinese language, the model may generate incorrect target sentences for some Chinese comments.

Acknowledgments

This research was funded by the China Postdoctoral Science Foundation (Grant No. 2022M711360) and the Laboratory for Advanced Computing and Intelligence Engineering.

References

[1] Lung-Hao Lee, Jian-Hong Li and Liang-Chih Yu, "Chinese EmoBank: Building Valence-Arousal Resources for Dimensional Sentiment Analysis," *ACM Trans. Asian and Low-Resource Language Information Processing*, vol. 21, no. 4, article 65, 2022.

[2] Liang-Chih Yu, Lung-Hao Lee, Shuai Hao, Jin Wang, Yunchao He, Jun Hu, K. Robert Lai, and Xuejie Zhang. 2016. "Building Chinese affective resources in valence-arousal dimensions. In *Proceedings of NAACL/HLT-16*, pages 540-545.

[3] Wenxuan Zhang, Yang Deng, Xin Li, Yifei Yuan, Lidong Bing, and Wai Lam. 2021. Aspect Sentiment Quad Prediction as Paraphrase Generation. In *Proceedings of the 2021 Conference on Empirical Methods in Natural Language Processing*, pages 9209–9219, Online and Punta Cana, Dominican Republic. Association for Computational Linguistics.

[4] Lung-Hao Lee, Liang-Chih Yu, Suge Wang, and Jian Liao. 2024. Overview of the SIGHAN 2024 shared task for Chinese dimensional aspect-based sentiment analysis. In *Proceedings of the 10th SIGHAN Workshop on Chinese Language Processing*. Association for Computational Linguistics.

[5] Colin Raffel, Noam Shazeer, Adam Roberts, Katherine Lee, Sharan Narang, Michael Matena, Yanqi Zhou,Wei Li, and Peter J. Liu. 2020. Exploring the limits of transfer learning with a unified text-to-text transformer. J. Mach. Learn. Res., 21:140:1–140:67.

[6] Linting Xue, Noah Constant, Adam Roberts, Mihir Kale, Rami Al-Rfou, Aditya Siddhant, Aditya Barua, and Colin Raffel. 2021. mT5: A Massively Multilingual Pre-trained Text-to-Text Transformer. In Proceedings of the 2021 Conference of the North American Chapter of the Association for Computational Linguistics: Human Language Technologies, pages 483–498, Online. Association for Computational Linguistics.

[7] Chi Sun, Luyao Huang, and Xipeng Qiu. 2019. Utilizing BERT for Aspect-Based Sentiment Analysis via Constructing Auxiliary Sentence. In *Proceedings of the 2019 Conference of the North American Chapter of the Association for Computational Linguistics: Human Language Technologies, Volume 1 (Long and Short Papers)*, pages 380–385, Minneapolis, Minnesota. Association for Computational Linguistics.

[8] X. Li, L. Bing, P. Li, and W. Lam, "A unified modelfor opinion target extraction and target sentiment prediction," in AAAI, 2019, pp. 6714–6721.

[9] Jian Liu, Zhiyang Teng, Leyang Cui, Hanmeng Liu, and Yue Zhang. 2021. Solving Aspect Category Sentiment Analysis as a Text Generation Task. In *Proceedings of the 2021 Conference on Empirical Methods in Natural Language Processing*, pages 4406–4416, Online and Punta Cana, Dominican Republic. Association for Computational Linguistics.

[10] H. Peng, L. Xu, L. Bing, F. Huang, W. Lu, and L. Si, "Knowing what, how and why: A near complete solution for aspect-based sentiment analysis," in AAAI, 2020, pp. 8600–8607.

[11] H. Wan, Y. Yang, J. Du, Y. Liu, K. Qi, and J. Z. Pan, "Target-aspect-sentiment joint detection for aspect-based sentiment analysis," in AAAI, 2020, pp. 9122–9129.

DS-Group at SIGHAN-2024 dimABSA Task: Constructing In-context Learning Structure for Dimensional Aspect-Based Sentiment Analysis

Ling-ang Meng, Tianyu Zhao and Dawei Song*
School of Computer Science & Technology,
Beijing Institute of Technology, China
{ling.ang.meng, tyzhao, dwsong}@bit.edu.cn

Abstract

Aspect-Based Sentiment Analysis (ABSA) is an important subtask in Natural Language Processing (NLP). More recent research within ABSA have consistently focused on conducting more precise sentiment analysis on aspects, i.e., dimensional Aspect-Based Sentiment Analysis (dimABSA). However, previous approaches have not systematically explored the use of Large Language Models (LLMs) in dimABSA. To fill the gap, we propose a novel In-Context Learning (ICL) structure with a novel aspect-aware ICL example selection method, to enhance the performance of LLMs in dimABSA. Experiments show that our proposed ICL structure significantly improves the fine-grained sentiment analysis abilities of LLMs. Our code is publicly available at: `https://github.com/Maydayflower/dimABSA-ICL`.

1 Introduction

Aspect-based Sentiment Analysis (ABSA) has been a significant research topic in Natural Language Processing (NLP). The goal of ABSA is to identify specific aspects within a sentence and determine the corresponding sentiment polarity (positive, neutral, or negative) for each aspect (Zhang et al., 2023b). This is different from traditional sentiment analysis (SA) that provides an overall sentiment prediction for the sentence. ABSA has been extensively studied, resulting in numerous effective algorithms.

However, human emotions are inherently continuous rather than discrete, involving two finer-grained dimensions of sentiment, including valence and arousal Russell (1980). As illustrated in Figure 1, the valence dimension represents the degree of pleasure or displeasure sentiment, while the arousal dimension indicates the intensity of the sentiment. In this two-dimensional space, all emotions can be precisely represented. For instance, an emotion with a valence of 7 and an arousal of 7 would be closer to delighted, whereas a valence of 1 and an arousal of 9 would signify a very intense negative sentiment. Extending the traditional SA and ABSA to the two-dimensional space of sentiment has led to Dimensional Sentiment Analysis (DSA) and Dimensional Aspect-Based Sentiment Analysis (dimABSA).

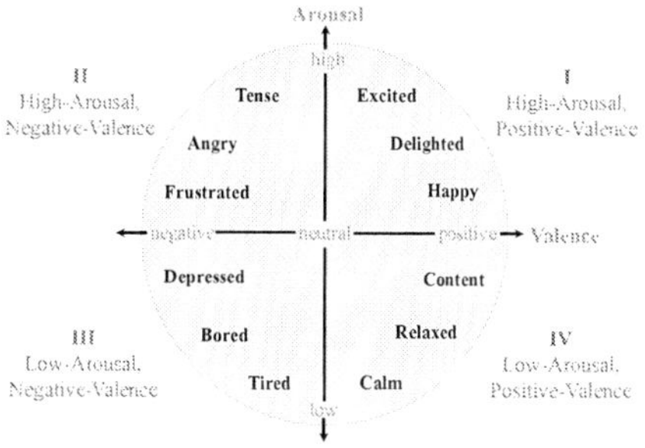

Figure 1: Valence-Arousal space. The picture is originally from (Yu et al., 2016).

As a recently emerging yet largely under-investigated task, dimABSA aims to conduct finer-grained sentiment analysis by assigning corresponding valence and arousal values to each aspect in a sentence, as illustrated in Figure 2. Despite various DSA methods have been developed, which are mainly based on lexicons at the word-level or phrase-level, there is a lack of extensive and systematic studies on the aspect-level dimABSA. This paper aims to fill the gap. Inspired by the success of Large Language Models (LLMs) on the aspect-level sentiment analysis tasks (Wang et al., 2023; Zhang et al., 2023a; Yang et al., 2024), we propose an in-context learning (ICL) framework for dimABSA and evaluates its effectiveness on three mainstream LLMs: qwen-plus (Bai et al., 2023), GPT-3.5 (OpenAI, 2023) and GPT-4 (Achiam et al., 2023). The main contributions of this paper are as follows:

*Corresponding author.

Proceedings of the 10th SIGHAN Workshop on Chinese Language Processing (SIGHAN-10), pages 127–132
August 16, 2024 ©2024 Association for Computational Linguistics

(1) This paper is the first to explore the performance of LLMs on the dimABSA task. (2) This paper proposes an ICL framework for the dimABSA task, which is facilitated by a novel sample selection method. Experimental results demonstrate that our method significantly improves the performance of LLMs on the dimABSA task.

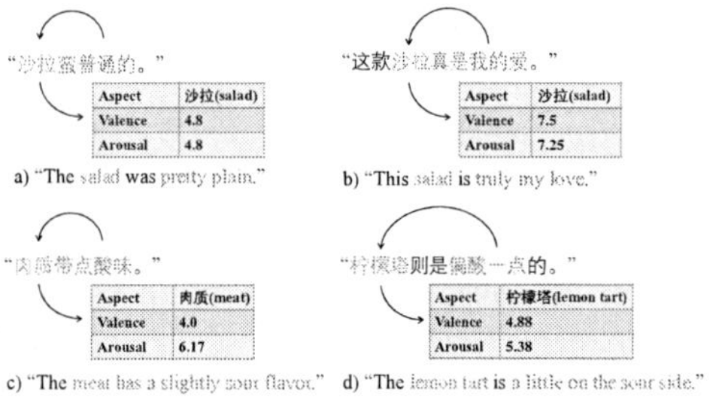

Figure 2: Some examples of dimABSA task demonstrate that when the same aspect is described differently, the aspect can have different valence and arousal. Similarly, when different aspects receive similar evaluations, they can also have different valence and arousal.

2 Related work

2.1 Aspect-based Sentiment Analysis

Early ABSA research is focused on the assessment of single sentiment elements. However, with advancements in the field, ABSA has evolved to include a growing number of sub-tasks, such as Aspect Sentiment Triplet Extraction (ASTE) (Zhang et al., 2020, 2022) and Aspect Sentiment Quad Prediction (ASQP) (Cai et al., 2021; Mao et al., 2022). A more recently emerged area is Dimensional Aspect-Based Sentiment Analysis (dimABSA), which introduces two scalar dimensions to more accurately describe sentiment.

2.2 Dimensional Aspect-Based Sentiment Analysis

Russell proposed a two-dimensional space for more precise emotion modeling, as illustrated in Figure 1. One dimension describes the intensity ranging from pleasant to unpleasant (i.e., Valence), while the other captures the intensity from calm to excited (i.e., Arousal). Based on this model, human emotional states can be represented in a more accurate manner (Bradley and Lang, 1999; Malandrakis et al., 2011). Researchers have incorporated this two-dimensional VA space into sentiment analysis, leading to the development of Dimensional Sentiment Analysis (DSA).

Existing research on DSA is heavily based on lexicons. In the field of Chinese research, the most commonly used lexicon is the Chinese EmoBank proposed by Lee et al., which includes 5,512 single words, 2,998 multi-word phrases, 2,582 single sentences, and 4,969 multi-sentence texts. Consequently, current DSA methods have primarily focused on the word-level (Wei et al., 2011) and phrase-level (Wu et al., 2017), neglecting high-level emotional features. Lee et al. proposed the task of dimensional aspect-based sentiment analysis (dimABSA), extending DSA to the aspect-level. Our work primarily focuses on this task.

2.3 In-Context Learning

In recent years, Large Language Models (LLMs) have demonstrated remarkable performance across various NLP downstream tasks, and have shown excellent In-Context Learning (ICL) capabilities. ICL refers to the ability of LLMs to be applied directly to downstream tasks by adding a few examples to the prompt, without the need for parameter updates (Dong et al., 2023). Demonstration designing is a crucial component in constructing an in-context learning structure. Although the capabilities of LLMs in sentiment analysis have been widely studied (Lian et al., 2023; Wang et al., 2023; Yang et al., 2024), there has been no research exploring the impact of ICL on the dimensional ABSA abilities of LLMs. In this paper, we propose an ICL framework, demonstrating through experiments that our ICL framework significantly enhances the sentiment analysis capabilities of LLMs.

3 Methodology

In this section, we introduce the task definition and the components of our proposed ICL structure.

3.1 Task definition

Given a n-word sentence $s = \{w_1, w_2, ..., w_n\}$, the output of dimABSA is $y = \{(A_1, v_1\#a_1), (A_2, v_2\#a_2), ..., (A_x, v_x\#a_x)\}$, where A_i denotes the representation of an aspect and x represents the number of aspects in the sentence. v_i denotes the valence value of the aspect A_i, ranging from 1 to 9, with 1 representing unpleasant and 9 representing pleasant. a_i denotes the arousal value of A_i, also ranging from 1 to 9, with 1 representing calm and 9 representing excited.

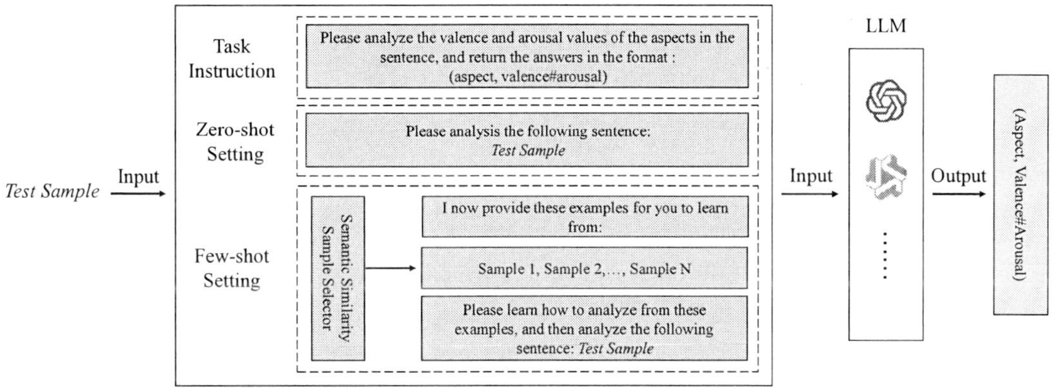

Figure 3: The framework of our proposed ICL method.

3.2 Semantic Similarity Sample Selector (S4)

To select the most helpful samples for the dimABSA task, inspired by (Liu et al., 2021), we choose samples from the training set that are semantically closest to the test samples and use them as examples in the prompt. Given the specific nature of the dimABSA task, we believe that directly computing the semantic similarity of two sentences is inadequate. Instead, the aspect present in the samples should also be considered. The same description can represent different sentiment orientations for different aspects. For instance, the word "sour" typically does not convey negative sentiment when describing a lemon, but when referring to spoiled meat, it strongly indicates a negative sentiment.

Therefore, in our approach, we consider the aspect's presence in the sentence when calculating similarity, leading to an aspect-aware semantic similarity measure.

First, we use BERT (Devlin et al., 2019) to obtain the representation $\mathcal{T}_i$ of the text for calculating semantic similarity. BERT is also used to obtain the representation $\mathcal{A}_i$ of the aspect. The process of obtaining $\mathcal{T}_i$ and $\mathcal{A}_i$ from a sentence S_i and an aspect a is as follows:

$$\mathcal{T}_i = BERT(S_i), \mathcal{A}_i = BERT(a) \quad (1)$$

Then we use Cosine similarity to calculate the semantic similarity between two sentences S_p and S_q. The formula is as follows:

$$sim_t = \text{cosine}(\mathcal{T}_p, \mathcal{T}_q) = \frac{\mathcal{T}_p \cdot \mathcal{T}_q}{||\mathcal{T}_p|| \cdot ||\mathcal{T}_q||} \quad (2)$$

Next, we take into consideration the aspects contained in the sentences. Assuming the test sample and the target sample in the training dataset contain m and n aspects respectively, we will calculate the similarity between each pair of aspects across the test sample and the target sample using Equation 3, and ultimately select the highest similarity value for the final computation.

$$sim_a = \max_{\substack{i \in \{1,2,\ldots,m\} \\ j \in \{1,2,\ldots,n\}}} \frac{\mathcal{A}_i \mathcal{A}_j}{||\mathcal{A}_i|| ||\mathcal{A}_j||} \quad (3)$$

We believe that the presence of semantically similar aspects in two samples indicates that these reviews were likely given in similar contexts to some extent.

The overall aspect-aware similarity between two samples is ultimately computed, as shown in Equation 4, where α_0 and α_1 are trade-off parameters[1].

$$sim(S_t, S_i) = \alpha_0 \cdot sim_t(\mathcal{T}_t, \mathcal{T}_i) + \alpha_1 \cdot sim_a(\mathcal{A}_t, \mathcal{A}_i) \quad (4)$$

We select N samples from the training set with the highest aspect-aware similarity scores to the test sample for use in subsequent prompt construction. Considering the impact of context length on the performance of LLMs, we set N to 10 in this paper.

3.3 In-context Learning Structure

The prompt we construct comprises a detailed description of the task, including the meanings of Valence, Arousal and Aspect, the input format, the required processing of the input, and the output format. Additionally, depending on various settings, the prompt may also include different sample examples for the LLMs to learn from. Figure 3 illustrates the prompt construction process of our proposed ICL framework.

[1] In our experiment, α_0 and α_1 are both set to 0.5.

Zero-shot setting. To demonstrate the effectiveness of our method, we first test the sentiment analysis capabilities of LLMs in a zero-shot setting. In the zero-shot setting, the prompt does not include additional examples for the LLMs to learn from. The prompt content is: [*Please analyze the following sentence: test sample*].

Few-shot setting with Random Selection. In NLP downstream tasks, the zero-shot setting often fails to achieve satisfactory results. Consequently, a common approach is to randomly select some examples for prompt construction. However, the samples chosen through this method often lack task representativeness, leading to limited improvements in the capabilities of LLMs.

Few-shot setting with S4. To address the lack of effective ICL frameworks in the dimABSA domain, we have proposed a Semantic Similarity Sample Selector (S4) for sample selection, detailed in Section 3.2. After obtaining samples through the S4, we construct the prompt in the following format: [*I now provide these examples for you to learn from: Sample 1, Label 1; Sample 2, Label 2;...; Sample N, Label N. Please learn how to analyze from these examples, and then analyze the following sentence: Test Sample*].

4 Experiments

4.1 Experimental Settings

4.1.1 Dataset

In this task we use the dataset provided by the organizer which contains 3000 sentences. Each sentence contains one or more aspects, and each of these aspects is annotated with corresponding valence and arousal values from 1-9.

4.1.2 Evaluation Metrics

To compare the sentiment analysis capabilities of different models, we use two metrics, Mean Absolute Error (MAE) and Pearson Correlation Coefficient (PCC), to indicate the performance of different models. The formulas for these two metrics are shown in Equation 5 and Equation 6, where $a_i \in A$ represents the ground truth value, and $p_i \in P$ represents the model prediction result. μ_A and μ_P denote the arithmetic mean of **A** and **P**, respectively. σ denotes the standard deviation.

$$MAE = \frac{1}{n}\sum_{i=1}^{n}|a_i - p_i| \quad (5)$$

The smaller MAE value, the better quality of the model's predictions.

$$PCC = \frac{1}{n-1}\sum_{i=1}^{n}(\frac{a_i - \mu_A}{\sigma_A})(\frac{p_i - \mu_P}{\sigma_P}) \quad (6)$$

A larger PCC value indicates a better quality of the model's predictions.

4.2 Main Results

The evaluation results of our proposed ICL structure are presented in Table 1. Among all the results, the GPT-4o model utilizing our proposed ICL framework achieved the best performance on the V-MAE, V-PCC, and A-PCC metrics. The qwen-plus model with our proposed ICL framework, slightly outperformed GPT-4o on the A-MAE metric. Experimental results show that our proposed method significantly improves the sentiment analysis capability of LLMs.

	V-MAE	V-PCC	A-MAE	A-PCC
qwen-plus†	0.697	0.713	0.911	0.300
qwen-plus w. RS	0.541	0.845	0.718	0.345
qwen-plus w. S4	0.542	0.891‡	**0.480‡**	0.495‡
GPT3.5†	0.600	0.882	0.524	0.515
GPT3.5 w. RS	0.460	0.858	0.501	0.490
GPT3.5 w. S4	0.392‡	0.890‡	0.500‡	0.528‡
GPT4o†	0.552	0.838	0.676	0.453
GPT4o w. RS	0.409	0.870	0.500	0.510
GPT4o w. S4	**0.391‡**	**0.900‡**	0.485‡	**0.606‡**

Table 1: Comparison between LLMs with different settings, where † indicates that the LLM is using a zero-shot setting, RS denotes Random Select and S4 denotes our proposed ICL Structure. ‡indicates that our method is significantly better than zero-shot setting and Random Select with p-value < 0.05 based on t-test.

5 Conclusions

This paper explores the enhancement of LLMs for the dimABSA task through ICL. We have designed a sample selection method called Semantic Similarity Sample Selector (S4) and used it to select samples for prompt construction. Experimental results indicate that our proposed ICL framework significantly improves the performance of LLMs for the dimABSA task.

Limitations

The primary limitation of our proposed approach lies in its reliance on proprietary LLMs, which may pose challenges for reproducibility. To achieve optimal results, we did not conduct experiments on mainstream open-source LLMs such as LLaMA2 and LLaMA3. However, the experimental results on proprietary LLMs demonstrate that our proposed method is significantly effective. In future work, we plan to extend our experiments to include a broader range of LLMs to develop a more performant and generalized approach.

Acknowledgements

This work is funded by the Natural Science Foundation of China (grant no: 62376027) and Beijing Municipal Natural Science Foundation (grant no: 4222036 and IS23061).

References

Josh Achiam, Steven Adler, Sandhini Agarwal, Lama Ahmad, Ilge Akkaya, Florencia Leoni Aleman, Diogo Almeida, Janko Altenschmidt, Sam Altman, Shyamal Anadkat, et al. 2023. Gpt-4 technical report. arXiv preprint arXiv:2303.08774.

Jinze Bai, Shuai Bai, Yunfei Chu, Zeyu Cui, Kai Dang, Xiaodong Deng, Yang Fan, Wenbin Ge, Yu Han, Fei Huang, et al. 2023. Qwen technical report. arXiv preprint arXiv:2309.16609.

Margaret M. Bradley and Peter J. Lang. 1999. Affective norms for english words (anew): Instruction manual and affective ratings.

Hongjie Cai, Rui Xia, and Jianfei Yu. 2021. Aspect-category-opinion-sentiment quadruple extraction with implicit aspects and opinions. In Proceedings of the 59th Annual Meeting of the Association for Computational Linguistics and the 11th International Joint Conference on Natural Language Processing (Volume 1: Long Papers), pages 340–350.

Jacob Devlin, Ming-Wei Chang, Kenton Lee, and Kristina Toutanova. 2019. Bert: Pre-training of deep bidirectional transformers for language understanding. Preprint, arXiv:1810.04805.

Qingxiu Dong, Lei Li, Damai Dai, Ce Zheng, Zhiyong Wu, Baobao Chang, Xu Sun, Jingjing Xu, Lei Li, and Zhifang Sui. 2023. A survey on in-context learning. Preprint, arXiv:2301.00234.

Lung-Hao Lee, Jian-Hong Li, and Liang-Chih Yu. 2022. Chinese emobank: Building valence-arousal resources for dimensional sentiment analysis. ACM Trans. Asian Low-Resour. Lang. Inf. Process., 21(4).

Lung-Hao Lee, Liang-Chih Yu, Suge Wang, and Jian Liao. 2024. Overview of the sighan 2024 shared task for chinese dimensional aspect-based sentiment analysis. In Proceedings of the 10th SIGHAN Workshop on Chinese Language Processing.

Zheng Lian, Licai Sun, Haiyang Sun, Kang Chen, Zhuofan Wen, Hao Gu, Shun Chen, Bin Liu, and Jianhua Tao. 2023. Gpt-4v with emotion: A zero-shot benchmark for multimodal emotion understanding. arXiv preprint arXiv:2312.04293.

Jiachang Liu, Dinghan Shen, Yizhe Zhang, Bill Dolan, Lawrence Carin, and Weizhu Chen. 2021. What makes good in-context examples for gpt-3? Preprint, arXiv:2101.06804.

Nikos Malandrakis, Alexandros Potamianos, Elias Iosif, and Shrikanth Narayanan. 2011. Kernel models for affective lexicon creation. In Twelfth annual conference of the international speech communication association.

Yue Mao, Yi Shen, Jingchao Yang, Xiaoying Zhu, and Longjun Cai. 2022. Seq2path: Generating sentiment tuples as paths of a tree. In Findings of the Association for Computational Linguistics: ACL 2022, pages 2215–2225.

OpenAI. 2023. Chatgpt.

James A Russell. 1980. A circumplex model of affect. Journal of personality and social psychology, 39(6):1161.

Zengzhi Wang, Qiming Xie, Yi Feng, Zixiang Ding, Zinong Yang, and Rui Xia. 2023. Is chatgpt a good sentiment analyzer? a preliminary study. arXiv preprint arXiv:2304.04339.

Wen-Li Wei, Chung-Hsien Wu, and Jen-Chun Lin. 2011. A regression approach to affective rating of chinese words from anew. In Affective Computing and Intelligent Interaction, pages 121–131, Berlin, Heidelberg. Springer Berlin Heidelberg.

Chuhan Wu, Fangzhao Wu, Yongfeng Huang, Sixing Wu, and Zhigang Yuan. 2017. Thu_ngn at ijcnlp-2017 task 2: Dimensional sentiment analysis for chinese phrases with deep lstm. In International Joint Conference on Natural Language Processing.

Li Yang, Zengzhi Wang, Ziyan Li, Jin-Cheon Na, and Jianfei Yu. 2024. An empirical study of multimodal entity-based sentiment analysis with chatgpt: Improving in-context learning via entity-aware contrastive learning. Information Processing & Management, 61(4):103724.

Liang-Chih Yu, Lung-Hao Lee, Shuai Hao, Jin Wang, Yunchao He, Jun Hu, K Robert Lai, and Xuejie Zhang. 2016. Building chinese affective resources in valence-arousal dimensions. In Proceedings of the 2016 Conference of the North American Chapter of the Association for Computational Linguistics: Human Language Technologies, pages 540–545.

Chen Zhang, Qiuchi Li, Dawei Song, and Benyou Wang. 2020. A multi-task learning framework for opinion triplet extraction. In Proceedings of the 2020 Conference on Empirical Methods in Natural Language Processing: Findings, pages 819–828, Online. Association for Computational Linguistics.

Chen Zhang, Lei Ren, Fang Ma, Jingang Wang, Wei Wu, and Dawei Song. 2022. Structural bias for aspect sentiment triplet extraction. In COLING.

Wenxuan Zhang, Yue Deng, Bing Liu, Sinno Jialin Pan, and Lidong Bing. 2023a. Sentiment analysis in the era of large language models: A reality check. arXiv preprint arXiv:2305.15005.

Wenxuan Zhang, Xin Li, Yang Deng, Lidong Bing, and Wai Lam. 2023b. A survey on aspect-based sentiment analysis: Tasks, methods, and challenges. IEEE Transactions on Knowledge and Data Engineering, 35(11):11019–11038.

Fine-tuning after Prompting: an Explainable Way for Classification

Zezhong Wang[1,2*] **, Luyao Ye**[3*] **, Hongru Wang**[1,2]**,**
Boyang Xue[1,2]**, Yiming Du**[1,2]**, Bin Liang**[1,2]**, Kam-Fai Wong**[1,2]
[1]The Chinese University of Hong Kong, Hong Kong, China
[2]MoE Key Laboratory of High Confidence Software Technologies, China
[3]Central China Normal University, Wuhan, China
zzwang@se.cuhk.edu.hk

Abstract

Prompting is an alternative approach for utilizing pre-trained language models (PLMs) in classification tasks. In contrast to fine-tuning, prompting is more understandable for humans because it utilizes natural language to interact with the PLM, but it often falls short in terms of accuracy. While current research primarily focuses on enhancing the performance of prompting methods to compete with fine-tuning, we believe that these two approaches are not mutually exclusive, each having its strengths and weaknesses. In our study, we depart from the competitive view of prompting versus fine-tuning and instead combine them, introducing a novel method called F&P. This approach enables us to harness the advantages of **F**ine-tuning for accuracy and the explainability of **P**rompting simultaneously. Specifically, we reformulate the sample into a prompt and subsequently fine-tune a linear classifier on top of the PLM. Following this, we extract verbalizers according to the weight of this classifier. During the inference phase, we reformulate the sample in the same way and query the PLM. The PLM generates a word, which is then subject to a dictionary lookup by the verbalizer to obtain the prediction. Experiments show that keeping only 30 keywords for each class can achieve comparable performance as fine-tuning. On the other hand, both the prompt and verbalizers are constructed in natural language, making them fully understandable to humans. Hence, the F&P method offers an effective and transparent way to employ a PLM for classification tasks.

1 Introduction

Prompting (Heinzerling and Inui, 2021) is a novel method for adapting pre-trained language models (PLMs) to downstream classification tasks (Brown et al., 2020; Zhao et al., 2024). Generally, a prompt typically consists of a sample, a task description, and a reserved blank. PLM is required to generate an appropriate word to fill in this blank based on the task description and the sample. A verbalizer then assigns a class to this word, finalizing the sample's classification. For example,

I like this movie. The sentiment is ____.

is a manual prompt designed for sentiment analysis. A typical verbalizer uses a lookup table to determine the class to which the predicted word should belong (Schick and Schütze, 2021; Hu et al., 2021; Webson and Pavlick, 2021; Ding et al., 2022). In this manner, a classification task is transformed into a language modeling task, aligning with the pre-training tasks of PLMs.

Compared with fine-tuning, prompting methods are more transparent to humans as the prompt consists of real words and is more explainable than a classifier with numerous parameters. However, prompting methods exhibit a lower performance than fine-tuning (Shin et al., 2020; Jiang et al., 2020). Because of the context sensitivity inherent to PLMs, their responses to identical queries exhibit inconsistencies when prompted in varying ways. Simply altering the wording of prompts, or even making minor lexical adjustments, can result in performance variations of up to 20% (Jiang et al., 2020). To this end, a series of studies (Liu et al., 2021; Zhong et al., 2021; Qin and Eisner, 2021; Wang et al., 2022; Li and Liang, 2021; Wang et al., 2023; Li et al., 2023) delved into methods for formulating effective prompts. They believed that prompts are not necessarily composed of real words and proposed a novel approach called "prompt tuning," wherein a set of k trainable vectors is employed as prompts, rather than conventional natural language, e.g.,

I like this movie. $v_1, \cdots, v_k$ ____.

These methods greatly enhance the capabilities of prompts, yielding performance comparable to or

[*] Equal contribution.

Proceedings of the 10th SIGHAN Workshop on Chinese Language Processing (SIGHAN-10), pages 133–142
August 16, 2024

even surpassing that of fine-tuning. However, it is noteworthy that prompts become less explainable for humans. Despite the absence of explicit research on the connection between explainability and performance, current efforts inadvertently prioritize performance over explainability when developing capable prompts. We believe that the relationship between explainability and performance is not mutually exclusive. It is feasible to enhance prompt performance while simultaneously taking into account their explainability. In this work, we depart from the competition paradigm between prompting and fine-tuning. Instead, we integrate both techniques and propose a novel method F&P that attains performance on par with **F**ine-tuning, while preserving the outstanding explainability inherent to **P**rompting methods.

Specifically, referring to the prompting method, we create a task description for each classification task and leave a blank space for the PLM to make predictions. We concatenate such a task description at the end of each sample, forming a prompt. Next, we refer to the fine-tuning, by adding a linear layer on top of the PLM to classify its output. It is worth mentioning that traditional fine-tuning methods often replace the Language Model Head with a linear layer, whereas we add an additional linear layer on top of the Language Model Head. Therefore, the linear layer classifies the word distribution predicted by the PLM rather than word embeddings. Furthermore, in contrast to classifying sentence representations, such as `[CLS]`, we classify the word distribution output from the blank space in the model. After the fine-tuning, the weights of the linear layer represent the significance of words for each class. To create a verbalizer, we sort all words in the vocabulary based on these weights and select the top-k words for each class. Then we remove the linear layer. During inference, given the new sample, we construct the prompt in the same way and input it into the PLM. The PLM's predicted word is then associated with a class based on the verbalizer. In this approach, we replace the classifier with a prompt and a verbalizer, yielding two key advantages. Firstly, both the prompt and verbalizer employ real, easily understandable words, making the classification process transparent to humans. This contrasts with the use of complex classifiers, which often obscure the classification process. Secondly, this approach avoids introducing additional parameters to the PLM, allowing us to maintain the original PLM size. Consequently, it can be applied to prob the linguistic knowledge embedded in the PLM, a crucial technique to explain the PLM (Tenney et al., 2019; Li et al., 2022).

2 Related Work

Fine-tuning represents the predominant method for customizing PLMs to specific downstream tasks. However, these tasks often diverge significantly from the cloze test used during the PLM's pre-training phase. For instance, RoBERTa (Liu et al., 2019) demonstrates proficiency across various tasks such as text classification, and sequence labeling. However, its pre-training task is a cloze test. The disparity between pre-training tasks and downstream applications is believed by researchers to hinder the optimal utilization of PLMs' knowledge (Han et al., 2021). This gap poses challenges, notably the propensity for PLMs to exhibit overfitting on limited training samples post fine-tuning, particularly when data availability is constrained. Therefore, addressing this gap is crucial to fully harnessing the potential of PLMs across diverse applications and ensuring robust performance in practical scenarios.

Prompt-based methods have been introduced as a strategic bridge between pre-training and fine-tuning stages in NLP. According to Petroni et al. (2019), these methods leverage the relational knowledge inherently encoded within PLMs, thereby demonstrating their efficacy in various tasks. Additionally, Brown et al. (2020) substantiated that the expansive knowledge encoded within large-scale PLMs is substantial enough to execute tasks effectively without necessitating parameter tuning. Furthermore, these methods enhance the usability of PLMs across different tasks by appending supplementary descriptions and examples in a cloze-style format, aligning each downstream task consistently with the structure of the pre-training tasks. This standardization not only facilitates smoother transitions between stages but also optimizes task performance. Recent studies have underscored the competitive advantages of prompt-based methods, showing that they can achieve comparable or superior performance compared to traditional fine-tuning approaches (Gao et al., 2021; Qin and Eisner, 2021; Zhong et al., 2021; Zhu et al., 2022; Li et al., 2021; Chen et al., 2022; Wang et al., 2023). Moreover, they have demonstrated remarkable efficacy in scenarios requiring minimal training data, such as few-shot or zero-shot settings. This adapt-

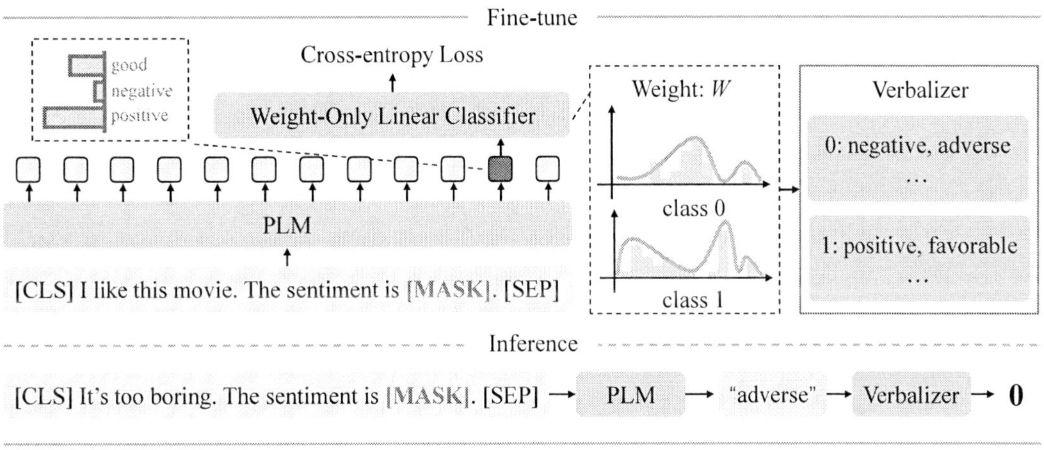

Figure 1: The upper part illustrates the process of fine-tuning the whole model and constructing the verbalizer from the classifier's weight. The lower part shows the inference process with a tuned PLM and the verbalizer.

ability underscores their potential to significantly advance the field of NLP by making efficient use of pre-existing model knowledge (Schick and Schütze, 2021; Puri and Catanzaro, 2019; Schick et al., 2020; Zhang et al., 2021; Ben-David et al., 2022).

3 Methodology

Figure 1 illustrates the overview of F&P. A prompt p is composed of three parts, including an input x, a task description with k tokens $t_1, \cdots, t_k$, and a symbol of mask, i.e., $p = [x, t_1, \cdots, t_k, \text{[MASK]}]$. Fed the prompt p, the PLM $\mathcal{F}(\cdot)$ predicts the word distribution for [MASK]:

$$\mathcal{F}(p) = P(\text{[MASK]} = t_i|p), t_i \in \mathcal{V} \quad (1)$$

where $\mathcal{V}$ is the vocabulary that contains n unique words t_i. In practice, the PLM's output is in the format of a vector, i.e., $\mathcal{F}(p) \in \mathbb{R}^n$. We add a weight-only linear classifier on top of the PLM to project $\mathcal{F}(p)$ into C classes, i.e.,

$$y = W^T \text{softmax}(\mathcal{F}(p)) \quad (2)$$

where $W \in \mathbb{R}^{n \times C}$. We use the cross-entropy loss as the objective and fine-tune the model until converge. After fine-tuning, each column of the classifier's weight, i.e., $W_i^T \in \mathbb{R}^n$, can represent how significant a word is to the class i. We rank and select top-k words from the vocabulary with the highest weight in W_i^T as the mapping to the class i, i.e.,

$$\mathcal{M}_i : i \leftarrow \{t_j | j \in \underset{j}{\text{top-k}}([W_{ij}^T]_{1 \leq j \leq n})\} \quad (3)$$

where t_j is the j-th token in the PLM's vocabulary. We gather all mappings of classes to construct a lookup table as the verbalizer $\mathcal{M} = \{\mathcal{M}_1, \cdots, \mathcal{M}_C\}$.

In the inference, the input is wrapped into a prompt $\hat{p}$ in the same way and processed by the PLM following the equation 1. The token in the verbalizer with the largest probability is the predicted word, i.e., $t^* = \arg\max P(\text{[MASK]} = t_i|\hat{p}), t_i \in \mathcal{M}$. The final prediction is made by looking up the verbalizer, $\mathcal{M}(t^*)$.

4 Experiments

4.1 Experiment Setting

4.1.1 Datasets

We conducted experiments on two benchmarks, GLUE(Wang et al., 2018) and CLUE (Xu et al., 2020).

- **General Language Understanding Evaluation (GLUE)** benchmark comprises nine natural language understanding tasks. These include single-sentence tasks like CoLA and SST-2, similarity and paraphrasing tasks such as MRPC, STS-B, and QQP, and natural language inference tasks including MNLI, QNLI, RTE, and WNLI.

- **Chinese Language Understanding Evaluation (CLUE)** is a community-driven, open-ended project that combines nine tasks, covering well-established single-sentence and sentence-pair classification tasks, as well as

LLM	Checkpoints
BERT-base	bert-base-cased
BERT-large	bert-large-cased
RoBERTa-base	roberta-base
OpenAI GPT	openai-gpt
BERT-wwm-ext-base	chinese-bert-wwm-ext
RoBERTa-wwm-ext-base	chinese-roberta-wwm-ext
RoBERTa-wwm-ext-large	chinese-roberta-wwm-ext-large

Table 1: PLMs involved in the experiments and the corresponding checkpoints.

machine reading comprehension, all based on original Chinese text.

The dataset split schema adheres to the same configuration as the benchmark.

4.1.2 PLMs

All experiments are conducted with four PLMs including BERT (Devlin et al., 2018), RoBERTa (Liu et al., 2019), OpenAI GPT (Radford et al., 2018), and the Chinese version of BERT and RoBERTa (Cui et al., 2020). We provide the detailed version of checkpoints in Table 1.

4.1.3 Baseline Methods

We compare three methods to tune PLMs:

- **Fine-tuning (FT)** refers to the process of replacing the Language Model Head of a the PLM with a linear classifier and subsequently updating the entire model. The input for this linear classifier is the sentence representation generated by the PLM.
- **Fine-tuning and Prompting (F&P)** is our method presented in the section 3.
- **Fine-tuning and AUTOPROMPT (F&AP).** AUTOPROMPT (Shin et al., 2020) is a method to search prompts automatically. We consider it an enhancement tool for identifying high-performing prompts. We employ it to discover six trigger words, denoted as $t_1, \cdots, t_6$, within the training dataset to replace the manual prompt. Subsequently, we repeat the same procedures as described in F&P.

4.1.4 Hyperparameter

For all of the experiment, We use Adam (Kingma and Ba, 2014) as the optimizer with the following parameters: $\beta_1 = 0.9$, $\beta_2 = 0.999$, $\epsilon = 1e-6$. Besides that, we consider a hyperparameter grid search for each task, with weight decay $\in \{1e-5, 1e-4, 1e-3\}$ and learning rates $\in \{1e-5, 2e-5, 3e-5\}$, with an exponential warmup for the first 8% of steps followed by a linear decay to 0.

4.2 Main Results

4.2.1 The verbalizer can be regarded as a classifier after denoising.

F&P does not introduce any extra parameters to the PLM. But from Table 2, it achieves performance that is comparable to, or even superior to, fine-tuning, which involves the incorporation of an extra linear classifier.

For example, when using BERT-base, employing just 5 words per class can effectively substitute a classifier that typically requires over 22 million parameters. Despite this reduction in complexity, the model experiences only a marginal decrease in performance, approximately 0.22%. Interestingly, in certain scenarios, there is even a noticeable improvement; for instance, the accuracy of BERT-large on MNLI-mm rises from 85.25% to 86.82%. This phenomenon can be explained from a denoising standpoint. In contrast to a conventional weight-only classifier, the verbalizer, by focusing on a select set of words, tends to omit information associated with words carrying lower weights. Moreover, it simplifies the prediction process by treating all selected words equally in determining the outcome, thereby potentially enhancing clarity and reducing noise in the decision-making process. This selective attention mechanism not only streamlines the model but also serves as an effective denoising filter, enhancing overall performance in certain tasks.

We fine-tune the BERT-base model on the SST-2 dataset using the F&P method. Through this process, we extracted the weights of the linear classifier and proceeded to visualize the difference between the weights assigned to the two classes, specifically denoted as $W_1 - W_0$. Moreover, to underscore the efficacy of our approach, we also visualized the verbalizer generated by F&P in a manner similar to the weight comparison, demonstrating its effectiveness in enhancing classification accuracy.

In Figure 2, the left side appears disorderly, with words displaying uniform weights and lacking meaningful differentiation. These words are primarily noise rather than informative features. Conversely, the right side shows the word weights after ranking and selection, resulting in the removal of most of the words. Although this process might

PLM	Method	CoLA	SST-2	MRPC	QQP	MNLI-m	MNLI-mm	QNLI	RTE	WNLI	Avg.
BERT-base	FT.	57.35	93.42	90.03	84.36	84.54	83.22	90.81	70.86	74.41	81.00
	F&P.$_{(5)}$	57.52	93.63	89.18	83.20	83.12	82.26	91.25	71.82	75.01	80.78
	F&AP.$_{(5)}$	62.52	94.10	92.52	88.53	84.18	83.35	92.91	73.14	76.75	83.11 (+2.11)
BERT-large	FT.	61.90	93.62	88.57	85.50	86.13	85.25	93.65	71.16	75.31	82.34
	F&P.$_{(10)}$	62.74	93.27	89.34	84.14	86.04	87.31	93.92	72.53	77.04	82.93
	F&AP.$_{(10)}$	63.92	94.50	90.97	87.44	86.27	86.82	95.13	73.82	76.77	83.96 (+1.62)
RoBERTa-base	FT.	68.15	95.71	91.15	89.12	90.11	90.02	94.36	85.92	90.00	88.28
	F&P.$_{(30)}$	67.63	94.95	90.33	88.20	89.40	89.18	93.10	84.90	89.53	87.47
	F&AP.$_{(30)}$	68.42	96.62	91.51	91.05	90.25	91.65	95.82	86.66	91.47	89.27 (+0.99)
OpenAI GPT	FT.	37.18	93.50	87.55	69.17	81.65	80.20	84.35	63.74	72.73	74.45
	F&P.$_{(5)}$	46.17	93.46	89.14	76.60	81.23	81.42	83.70	66.28	73.08	76.79
	F&AP.$_{(5)}$	50.12	93.90	90.27	77.84	82.54	82.15	84.53	67.81	73.88	78.12 (+3.67)

Table 2: Results on the development set of GLUE benchmark. F1 score (%) is the metric used for MRPC and QQP, Matthew's Correlation for CoLA, and Accuracy (%) for the other tasks. The number in the bracket indict the number of words selected for each class for the verbalizer. , e.g., $_{[10]}$ means select top-10 words from each class. The number in red represents the improvements of F&AP over the fine-tuning.

involve some loss of information obtained from the training dataset, it significantly enhances the verbalizer's overall generality and effectiveness.

4.2.2 Prompts improve the distinctiveness of the model's output.

The performance analysis of F&AP revealed an improvement of approximately 2% compared to fine-tuning alone, suggesting that fine-tuning procedures may not fully exploit the inherent capabilities of PLMs. The inclusion of a prompt in the form of *"The sentence is [MASK]."* serves to constrain the output range of the PLM by introducing a fixed component within the context. This prompt requires the PLM's predictions to align with the given context, thereby encouraging the model to emphasize specific attributes crucial to the task during the fine-tuning process. This approach offers a method to enhance classification performance through context adjustment, complementing rather than contradicting traditional fine-tuning methodologies.

4.2.3 Verification on Chinese Dataset

We also validated the F&P method on CLUE, a Chinese dataset. The experimental results are shown in Table 3. Overall, the F&P method still outperformed traditional fine-tuning, with slight improvements across multiple models and tasks. This confirms the effectiveness of our approach not only in English but also in Chinese tasks.

However, the improvements on the Chinese dataset were not as significant as those on the English dataset. We attribute this mainly to suboptimal prompt designs for Chinese tasks. Since the AUTOPROMPT method was originally proposed for English data, although there is no evidence suggesting it only works for English, this experiment shows limited improvement on Chinese datasets. In the future, we will further tune this method to find optimal Chinese prompts for each task.

4.3 Explain the Verbalizer

Traditional classifiers typically involve a multitude of parameters whose complex interactions can obscure the decision-making process, even when the operations involved are purely linear. In contrast, prompting the PLM, mapping and aligning their outputs with specific classes through a verbalizer offers a stark contrast in transparency for human observers. As discussed by Molnar (2020), explainability refers to the degree to which a person can reliably anticipate the model's predictions. In this framework, the consistency of the verbalizer becomes paramount, ensuring a cohesive semantic alignment with the assigned class labels. For instance, if the term "favorable" is linked with the "Negative" class, such discrepancies highlight a breakdown in the verbalizer's coherence with human comprehension, thereby compromising interpretability.

4.3.1 Consistency Test Between Verbalizers and Humans

We evaluate the explainability of verbalizers using the SST-2 dataset, focusing on their consistency with human perception. To facilitate this evaluation, we utilize a manually curated list of sentiment words sourced from Hu and Liu (Hu and Liu, 2004). This curated list serves as a benchmark to assess

PLM	Method	TENWS	IFLYTEK	CLUEWSC2020	AFQMC	CSL	OCNLI	CMNLI	Avg.
BERT-base	FT	56.54	60.21	63.47	73.67	80.43	72.28	79.67	69.47
	F&P.$_{(10)}$	56.52	60.24	63.54	73.70	80.45	72.37	79.74	69.51
	F&AP.$_{(10)}$	**57.67**	**61.00**	**64.19**	**74.12**	**80.75**	**73.22**	**80.46**	**70.20** (+0.73)
BERT-wwm -ext-base	FT	56.81	59.33	62.50	74.00	80.65	74.41	80.38	69.73
	F&P.$_{(10)}$	56.90	59.28	62.49	74.02	80.61	74.31	80.39	69.71
	F&AP.$_{(10)}$	**57.43**	**59.65**	**62.99**	**74.67**	**80.86**	**75.37**	**81.04**	**70.29** (+0.56)
RoBERTa-wwm -ext-base	FT	56.88	60.30	72.13	73.97	81.07	74.66	80.44	71.35
	F&P.$_{(30)}$	56.87	60.23	72.12	73.95	81.10	74.68	80.46	71.34
	F&AP.$_{(30)}$	**57.21**	**61.26**	**72.54**	**74.19**	**81.64**	**74.87**	**80.69**	**71.77** (+0.42)
RoBERTa-wwm -ext-large	FT	58.55	62.90	81.37	76.61	82.21	78.28	82.19	74.59
	F&P.$_{(30)}$	58.45	62.87	81.43	76.57	82.18	78.22	82.19	74.56
	F&AP.$_{(30)}$	**59.28**	**63.36**	**82.22**	**77.75**	**83.16**	**78.68**	**82.93**	**75.34** (+0.75)

Table 3: Results on the development set of CLUE benchmark. Accuracy (%) is the metric used for all tasks. The number in the bracket indict the number of words selected for each class for the verbalizer. , e.g., $_{[10]}$ means select top-10 words from each class. The number in red represents the improvements of F&AP over the fine-tuning.

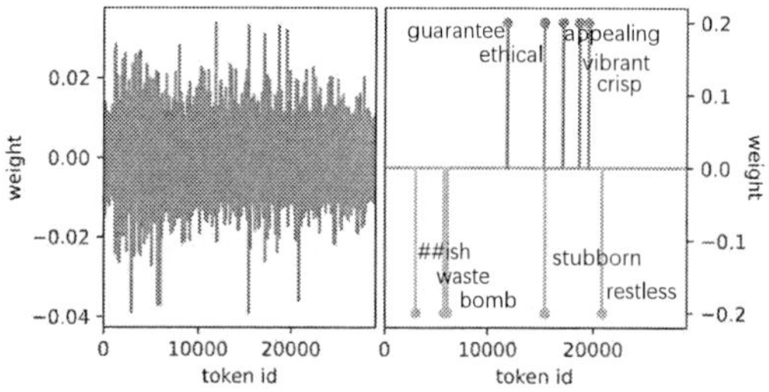

Figure 2: Denoise: left part shows all word weights, and the right shows the word weight after selection.

how well the verbalizers' vocabulary aligns with human sentiment understanding.

For the selection of verbalizers, we employ the F&P method, which identifies the top 50 words for each sentiment class based on their relevance to the dataset. The evaluation metric, depicted in the left part of Figure 3, measures the overlap between the manually curated word list and the verbalizer's selection, quantifying this as the "hit number."

Our findings indicate varying levels of consistency across different PLMs. Notably, GPT demonstrates higher consistency compared to RoBERTa-base. For instance, RoBERTa-base incorrectly categorizes certain words like *"addicted"* and *"odd"* as positive sentiments. This discrepancy partly stems from how these models' tokenizers segment words into smaller units (e.g., *"crazily"* segmented into [*"c, ##raz, ##ily"*]), which may not align with the intact sentiment words in the manual list, thus reducing the hit number.

To address the challenges posed by tokenizers, we undertook a detailed performance evaluation comparing the effectiveness of the original verbalizer against a manually curated alternative. Our approach involved meticulously identifying words shared between a manually compiled list and the vocabulary of the PLM. Subsequently, we employed a ranking methodology, selecting the top 50 words based on their classifier weights to establish the most suitable verbalizer. The outcomes of this evaluation are visually depicted in the right-hand section of Figure 3.

A smaller decrease in performance metrics indicates a closer alignment between the original and manually crafted verbalizers. Notably, the slight reduction observed in the performance of the GPT underscores the model's ability to maintain consistency and coherence with the verbalizer. This finding suggests that the verbalizer employed by GPT is inherently more transparent and interpretable, despite the challenges posed by tokenization processes.

4.3.2 Chinese Case Study

Table 4 provides real questions sampled from the OCNLI dataset. The task in OCNLI requires determining whether two given sentences are similar, which is a binary classification task. We manually constructed a template that includes two sentences for evaluation, a task description, and a [MASK] symbol. Models are tasked with predicting logits at the [MASK] position. Ideally, the token corresponding to the highest logit value should be 'yes' or another positively oriented word.

The bottom part of Table 4 displays a verbalizer obtained using the F&P method. We showcase 6 to-

Case Study
Input Demonstration:
句子 1: 一月份跟二月份肯定有一个月份有。
Sentence 1: One of January or February definitely has.
句子 2: 肯定有一个月份有。
Sentence 2: There must be a month has.
问题: 他们语义上相似吗?
Question: Are they semantically similar?
答案: [MASK]
Answer: [MASK]
Verbalizer:
1: 是, 像, 怡, ##贴, 忠, 净
1: yes, like, joy, ##paste, loyal, clean
0: 变, 败, ##糙, 罢, 讳, ##难
0: change, defeat, ##rough, cease, taboo, ##difficult

Table 4: Case study with a Chinese case. The upper part is a manual prompt provided to the model with its English translation. The [MASK] position in this prompt is reserved for the model to predict a logit. The lower part shows a verbalizer obtained using the F&P method, where 1 and 0 represent the positive and negative classes, respectively

kens for each class. Here, *1* represents the positive class, indicating similarity between two sentences, while *0* represents the negative class, indicating dissimilarity. It can be observed that the words in each class of the verbalizer generally correspond to the polarity expressed by that class. For instance, the list of words representing the positive class includes *yes, like, joy, ##paste, loyal, clean*. Although these tokens are not appropriate as answers to the question '*Are they semantically similar?*', their polarity aligns with human understanding.

4.4 Explain the PLM

Probing is an explainable task to detect the extent of encoded knowledge in the PLM. Linear probing (LP) (Conneau et al., 2018) is a method that only fine-tunes the linear classifier on top of the PLM on the downstream task. The predictive accuracy is interpreted as the volume of the task-related knowledge encoded in the PLM. However, during the fine-tuning, linear classifiers also encode knowledge, resulting in an overestimation in the probing results (Cao et al., 2021; Zhang and Bowman, 2018; Hewitt and Manning, 2019; Lasri et al., 2022).

As F&P does not include extra parameters, it prevents learning from fine-tuning. We freeze the PLM and only tune the linear classifier on top of the PLM. Then we construct the verbalizer according to the classifier's weight. This variant method

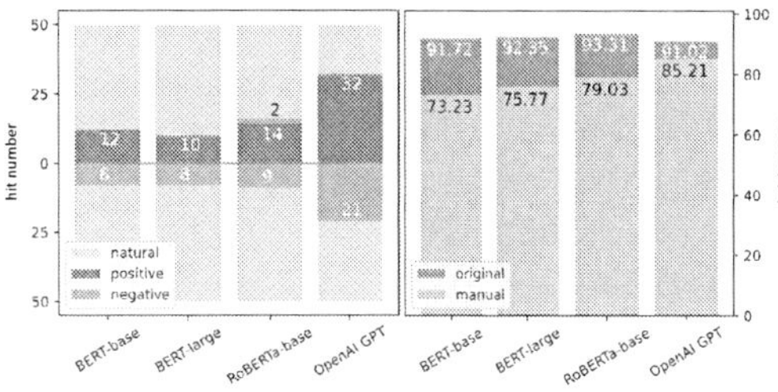

Figure 3: The left part shows how many words are both in the manual list also selected by verbalizers, i.e., hit number. The right part compares the performance of PLMs with the original verbalizer (grey) and the verbalizer constructed by the manual list (green).

is called **P**robing after **P**rompting (P&P). We conducted an experiment using the SST-2 dataset. We used AUTOPROMPT as both a baseline (Auto) and an enhancement to our approach (P&AP). The comparison results are presented in Tabel 5. The results indicate that P&P surpasses linear probing on all PLMs. This demonstrates that our method not only prevents interference from the tuning, but also maximizes the PLM's inherent potential. Furthermore, when enriched with prompts generated by AUTOPROMPT, P&AP achieved an average improvement of 7.92% over the linear probing method. The results show that combining prompting with probing is a more effective way to stimulate the most potential of PLMs.

Model	LP.	Auto.	P&P.	P&AP.
BERT-base	82.47	80.87	85.39	91.65 (+9.18)
BERT-large	84.97	82.75	86.59	91.24 (+6.27)
RoBERTa-base	85.27	91.33	86.87	92.61 (+7.34)
OpenAI-GPT	83.85	87.21	88.78	92.73 (+8.88)
Avg.	84.14	85.54	86.91	92.06 (+7.92)

Table 5: The probing result on SST-2 dataset. The number in red shows the improvements of F&AP over LP. We select the top 100 words from each class for the verbalizer in this experiment.

5 Conclusions

In this work, we propose an effective approach, referred to as F&P, which integrates fine-tuning and prompting to adapt PLMs for classification tasks. Our experimental results demonstrate that F&P yields performance comparable to fine-tuning, by employing prompts and verbalizers to replace the conventional classifier. Importantly, these prompts and verbalizers consist of real words that are easily understandable by humans. Additionally, we propose a method for assessing the explainability of verbalizers and a variation for probing tasks. We believe that F&P not only enhances classification performance but also plays a pivotal role in demystifying the inner workings of these models.

Limitations

We summarize the limitations in two points.

Despite the significant improvement in explainability compared to traditional fine-tuning methods, F&P does not show a significant improvement in performance. This observation is frustrating because while it is important to understand and explain the decisions made by PLMs, ultimately, the performance and accuracy of these models are crucial for practical applications.

In this work, we did not discuss the effectiveness of F&P on large language models (LLMs), though LLMs are currently a prominent trend in the field. Exploring the effects of F&P on LLMs would not only provide valuable insights into the potential benefits and drawbacks of using F&P in this context but also guide future research and development in a direction that aligns with the current trends and demands of the industry.

Acknowledgments

This research work is partially supported by CUHK direct grant No. 4055209 and CUHK Knowledge Transfer Project Fund No. KPF23GWP20.

References

Eyal Ben-David, Nadav Oved, and Roi Reichart. 2022. PADA: Example-based Prompt Learning for on-the-fly Adaptation to Unseen Domains. *Transactions of the Association for Computational Linguistics*, 10:414–433.

Tom Brown, Benjamin Mann, Nick Ryder, Melanie Subbiah, Jared D Kaplan, Prafulla Dhariwal, Arvind Neelakantan, Pranav Shyam, Girish Sastry, Amanda Askell, et al. 2020. Language models are few-shot learners. *Advances in neural information processing systems*, 33:1877–1901.

Steven Cao, Victor Sanh, and Alexander Rush. 2021. Low-complexity probing via finding subnetworks. In *Proceedings of the 2021 Conference of the North American Chapter of the Association for Computational Linguistics: Human Language Technologies*, pages 960–966, Online. Association for Computational Linguistics.

Xiang Chen, Ningyu Zhang, Xin Xie, Shumin Deng, Yunzhi Yao, Chuanqi Tan, Fei Huang, Luo Si, and Huajun Chen. 2022. Knowprompt: Knowledge-aware prompt-tuning with synergistic optimization for relation extraction. In *Proceedings of the ACM Web Conference 2022*, WWW '22, page 2778–2788, New York, NY, USA. Association for Computing Machinery.

Alexis Conneau, German Kruszewski, Guillaume Lample, Loïc Barrault, and Marco Baroni. 2018. What you can cram into a single $&!#* vector: Probing sentence embeddings for linguistic properties. In *Proceedings of the 56th Annual Meeting of the Association for Computational Linguistics (Volume 1: Long Papers)*, pages 2126–2136, Melbourne, Australia. Association for Computational Linguistics.

Yiming Cui, Wanxiang Che, Ting Liu, Bing Qin, Shijin Wang, and Guoping Hu. 2020. Revisiting pre-trained models for Chinese natural language processing. In *Proceedings of the 2020 Conference on Empirical Methods in Natural Language Processing: Findings*, pages 657–668, Online. Association for Computational Linguistics.

Jacob Devlin, Ming-Wei Chang, Kenton Lee, and Kristina Toutanova. 2018. Bert: Pre-training of deep bidirectional transformers for language understanding. *arXiv preprint arXiv:1810.04805*.

Ning Ding, Shengding Hu, Weilin Zhao, Yulin Chen, Zhiyuan Liu, Haitao Zheng, and Maosong Sun. 2022. OpenPrompt: An open-source framework for prompt-learning. In *Proceedings of the 60th Annual Meeting of the Association for Computational Linguistics: System Demonstrations*, pages 105–113, Dublin, Ireland. Association for Computational Linguistics.

Tianyu Gao, Adam Fisch, and Danqi Chen. 2021. Making pre-trained language models better few-shot learners. In *Proceedings of the 59th Annual Meeting of the Association for Computational Linguistics and the 11th International Joint Conference on Natural Language Processing (Volume 1: Long Papers)*, pages 3816–3830, Online. Association for Computational Linguistics.

Xu Han, Weilin Zhao, Ning Ding, Zhiyuan Liu, and Maosong Sun. 2021. Ptr: Prompt tuning with rules for text classification. *arXiv preprint arXiv:2105.11259*.

Benjamin Heinzerling and Kentaro Inui. 2021. Language models as knowledge bases: On entity representations, storage capacity, and paraphrased queries. In *Proceedings of the 16th Conference of the European Chapter of the Association for Computational Linguistics: Main Volume*, pages 1772–1791, Online. Association for Computational Linguistics.

John Hewitt and Christopher D Manning. 2019. A structural probe for finding syntax in word representations. In *Proceedings of the 2019 Conference of the North American Chapter of the Association for Computational Linguistics: Human Language Technologies, Volume 1 (Long and Short Papers)*, pages 4129–4138.

Minqing Hu and Bing Liu. 2004. Mining and summarizing customer reviews. In *Proceedings of the tenth ACM SIGKDD international conference on Knowledge discovery and data mining*, pages 168–177.

Shengding Hu, Ning Ding, Huadong Wang, Zhiyuan Liu, Juanzi Li, and Maosong Sun. 2021. Knowledgeable prompt-tuning: Incorporating knowledge into prompt verbalizer for text classification. *arXiv preprint arXiv:2108.02035*.

Zhengbao Jiang, Frank F Xu, Jun Araki, and Graham Neubig. 2020. How can we know what language models know? *Transactions of the Association for Computational Linguistics*, 8:423–438.

Diederik P Kingma and Jimmy Ba. 2014. Adam: A method for stochastic optimization. *arXiv preprint arXiv:1412.6980*.

Karim Lasri, Tiago Pimentel, Alessandro Lenci, Thierry Poibeau, and Ryan Cotterell. 2022. Probing for the usage of grammatical number. *arXiv preprint arXiv:2204.08831*.

Chengxi Li, Feiyu Gao, Jiajun Bu, Lu Xu, Xiang Chen, Yu Gu, Zirui Shao, Qi Zheng, Ningyu Zhang, Yongpan Wang, and Zhi Yu. 2021. Sentiprompt: Sentiment knowledge enhanced prompt-tuning for aspect-based sentiment analysis. *ArXiv*, abs/2109.08306.

Jiaoda Li, Ryan Cotterell, and Mrinmaya Sachan. 2022. Probing via prompting. In *Proceedings of the 2022 Conference of the North American Chapter of the Association for Computational Linguistics: Human Language Technologies*, pages 1144–1157, Seattle, United States. Association for Computational Linguistics.

Jiazheng Li, Runcong Zhao, Yongxin Yang, Yulan He, and Lin Gui. 2023. Overprompt: Enhancing chatgpt through efficient in-context learning. *Preprint*, arXiv:2305.14973.

Xiang Lisa Li and Percy Liang. 2021. Prefix-tuning: Optimizing continuous prompts for generation. *arXiv preprint arXiv:2101.00190*.

Xiao Liu, Yanan Zheng, Zhengxiao Du, Ming Ding, Yujie Qian, Zhilin Yang, and Jie Tang. 2021. Gpt understands, too. *arXiv preprint arXiv:2103.10385*.

Yinhan Liu, Myle Ott, Naman Goyal, Jingfei Du, Mandar Joshi, Danqi Chen, Omer Levy, Mike Lewis, Luke Zettlemoyer, and Veselin Stoyanov. 2019. Roberta: A robustly optimized bert pretraining approach. *arXiv preprint arXiv:1907.11692*.

Christoph Molnar. 2020. *Interpretable machine learning*. Lulu. com.

Fabio Petroni, Tim Rocktäschel, Sebastian Riedel, Patrick Lewis, Anton Bakhtin, Yuxiang Wu, and Alexander Miller. 2019. Language Models as Knowledge Bases? In *Proceedings of the 2019 Conference on Empirical Methods in Natural Language Processing and the 9th International Joint Conference on Natural Language Processing (EMNLP-IJCNLP)*, pages 2463–2473, Hong Kong, China. Association for Computational Linguistics.

Raul Puri and Bryan Catanzaro. 2019. Zero-shot text classification with generative language models. *arXiv preprint arXiv:1912.10165*.

Guanghui Qin and Jason Eisner. 2021. Learning how to ask: Querying lms with mixtures of soft prompts. In *Proceedings of the 2021 Conference of the North American Chapter of the Association for Computational Linguistics: Human Language Technologies*, pages 5203–5212.

Alec Radford, Karthik Narasimhan, Tim Salimans, Ilya Sutskever, et al. 2018. Improving language understanding by generative pre-training.

Timo Schick, Helmut Schmid, and Hinrich Schütze. 2020. Automatically identifying words that can serve as labels for few-shot text classification. In *Proceedings of the 28th International Conference on Computational Linguistics*.

Timo Schick and Hinrich Schütze. 2021. Exploiting cloze-questions for few-shot text classification and natural language inference. In *Proceedings of the 16th Conference of the European Chapter of the Association for Computational Linguistics: Main Volume*, pages 255–269.

Taylor Shin, Yasaman Razeghi, Robert L Logan IV, Eric Wallace, and Sameer Singh. 2020. Autoprompt: Eliciting knowledge from language models with automatically generated prompts. In *Proceedings of the 2020 Conference on Empirical Methods in Natural Language Processing (EMNLP)*, pages 4222–4235.

Ian Tenney, Patrick Xia, Berlin Chen, Alex Wang, Adam Poliak, R. Thomas McCoy, Najoung Kim, Benjamin Van Durme, Samuel R. Bowman, Dipanjan Das, and Ellie Pavlick. 2019. What do you learn from context? probing for sentence structure in contextualized word representations. In *International Conference on Learning Representations*.

Alex Wang, Amanpreet Singh, Julian Michael, Felix Hill, Omer Levy, and Samuel Bowman. 2018. GLUE: A multi-task benchmark and analysis platform for natural language understanding. In *Proceedings of the 2018 EMNLP Workshop BlackboxNLP: Analyzing and Interpreting Neural Networks for NLP*, pages 353–355, Brussels, Belgium. Association for Computational Linguistics.

Zezhong Wang, Luyao Ye, Hongru Wang, Wai-Chung Kwan, David Ho, and Kam-Fai Wong. 2023. ReadPrompt: A readable prompting method for reliable knowledge probing. In *Findings of the Association for Computational Linguistics: EMNLP 2023*, pages 7468–7479, Singapore. Association for Computational Linguistics.

Zihan Wang, Peiyi Wang, Tianyu Liu, Yunbo Cao, Zhifang Sui, and Houfeng Wang. 2022. Hpt: Hierarchy-aware prompt tuning for hierarchical text classification. *arXiv preprint arXiv:2204.13413*.

Albert Webson and Ellie Pavlick. 2021. Do prompt-based models really understand the meaning of their prompts? *arXiv preprint arXiv:2109.01247*.

Liang Xu, Hai Hu, Xuanwei Zhang, Lu Li, Chenjie Cao, Yudong Li, Yechen Xu, Kai Sun, Dian Yu, Cong Yu, Yin Tian, Qianqian Dong, Weitang Liu, Bo Shi, Yiming Cui, Junyi Li, Jun Zeng, Rongzhao Wang, Weijian Xie, Yanting Li, Yina Patterson, Zuoyu Tian, Yiwen Zhang, He Zhou, Shaoweihua Liu, Zhe Zhao, Qipeng Zhao, Cong Yue, Xinrui Zhang, Zhengliang Yang, Kyle Richardson, and Zhenzhong Lan. 2020. CLUE: A Chinese language understanding evaluation benchmark. In *Proceedings of the 28th International Conference on Computational Linguistics*, pages 4762–4772, Barcelona, Spain (Online). International Committee on Computational Linguistics.

Kelly W Zhang and Samuel R Bowman. 2018. Language modeling teaches you more syntax than translation does: Lessons learned through auxiliary task analysis. *arXiv preprint arXiv:1809.10040*.

Ningyu Zhang, Luoqiu Li, Xiang Chen, Shumin Deng, Zhen Bi, Chuanqi Tan, Fei Huang, and Huajun Chen. 2021. Differentiable prompt makes pre-trained language models better few-shot learners. *Preprint*, arXiv:2108.13161.

Runcong Zhao, Qinglin Zhu, Hainiu Xu, Jiazheng Li, Yuxiang Zhou, Yulan He, and Lin Gui. 2024. Large language models fall short: Understanding complex relationships in detective narratives. *Preprint*, arXiv:2402.11051.

Zexuan Zhong, Dan Friedman, and Danqi Chen. 2021. Factual probing is [mask]: Learning vs. learning to recall. In *Proceedings of the 2021 Conference of the North American Chapter of the Association for Computational Linguistics: Human Language Technologies*, pages 5017–5033.

Qi Zhu, Bing Li, Fei Mi, Xiaoyan Zhu, and Minlie Huang. 2022. Continual prompt tuning for dialog state tracking. In *Proceedings of the 60th Annual Meeting of the Association for Computational Linguistics (Volume 1: Long Papers)*, pages 1124–1137, Dublin, Ireland. Association for Computational Linguistics.

CausalBench: A Comprehensive Benchmark for Evaluating Causal Reasoning Capabilities of Large Language Models

Zeyu Wang
University of California, Los Angeles
zeyuwang@ucla.edu

Abstract

Causal reasoning, a core aspect of human cognition, is essential for advancing large language models (LLMs) towards artificial general intelligence (AGI) and reducing their propensity for generating hallucinations. However, existing datasets for evaluating causal reasoning in LLMs are limited by narrow domain coverage and a focus on cause-to-effect reasoning through textual problems, which does not comprehensively assess whether LLMs truly grasp causal relationships or merely guess correct answers. To address these shortcomings, we introduce a novel benchmark that spans textual, mathematical, and coding problem domains. Each problem is crafted to probe causal understanding from four perspectives: cause-to-effect, effect-to-cause, cause-to-effect with intervention, and effect-to-cause with intervention. This multi-dimensional evaluation method ensures that LLMs must exhibit a genuine understanding of causal structures by correctly answering questions across all four dimensions, mitigating the possibility of correct responses by chance. Furthermore, our benchmark explores the relationship between an LLM's causal reasoning performance and its tendency to produce hallucinations. We present evaluations of state-of-the-art LLMs using our benchmark, providing valuable insights into their current causal reasoning capabilities across diverse domains. The dataset is publicly available for download at https://huggingface.co/datasets/CCLV/CausalBench.

1 Introduction

Causal reasoning, the ability to understand and infer causal relationships between variables, is a fundamental aspect of human cognition and plays a crucial role in decision-making, problem-solving, and learning (Pearl, 2009). For large language models (LLMs), causal reasoning refers to the ability to accurately identify, represent, and reason about causal relationships described in text, mathematical equations, or code snippets (Pearl, 2009). Developing strong causal reasoning abilities in LLMs is essential for progress toward artificial general intelligence (AGI), as it enables models to understand not just correlations but the underlying mechanisms driving outcomes (Fridman and Pearl, 2022). This understanding is crucial for making accurate predictions, generating insightful explanations, and adapting to new situations, as core components of AGI.

However, existing causal reasoning benchmarks have several limitations that hinder their ability to comprehensively evaluate the causal reasoning capabilities of LLMs. First, current benchmarks often focus on a single perspective of causal reasoning, such as cause-to-effect, lacking a multifaceted assessment that considers effect-to-cause reasoning and the impact of interventions. This narrow focus allows models to correctly answer causal questions by chance without truly understanding the underlying causal relationships (Kaushik et al., 2020). Second, current benchmarks are primarily text-based, lacking diversity in problem types, such as mathematical and coding problems that can encapsulate causal dependencies. Incorporating these diverse problem formats would enable a more robust evaluation of LLMs' capacity to reason about causality across various modalities. Third, the limited scale of existing benchmarks may not provide a sufficiently comprehensive assessment of LLMs' causal reasoning abilities due to the limited scale of the benchmark dataset.

To address these limitations, we propose CausalBench, a comprehensive benchmark for evaluating the causal reasoning capabilities of LLMs. CausalBench comprises four perspectives of causal reasoning for each scenario: cause-to-effect, effect-to-cause, cause-to-effect with intervention, and effect-to-cause with intervention. This multi-perspective approach mitigates the potential for correct answers

Proceedings of the 10th SIGHAN Workshop on Chinese Language Processing (SIGHAN-10), pages 143–151
August 16, 2024 ©2024 Association for Computational Linguistics

by chance and provides a more accurate evaluation of LLMs' understanding of causal relationships. Moreover, CausalBench includes a diverse set of problem types spanning textual, mathematical, and coding domains, enabling a comprehensive assessment of causal reasoning abilities across different modalities. The benchmark consists of more than 60,000 problems and employs six evaluation metrics to measure LLMs' causal reasoning performance.

The major contributions of CausalBench are three-fold: (1) evaluating four causal reasoning perspectives per scenario to robustly assess causal understanding, (2) incorporating a diverse problem set spanning math, code, and natural language for cross-modal evaluation, and (3) implementing strict quality control measures, including a causal inference engine check and human expert review, to ensure the benchmark's validity and reliability. By addressing the limitations of existing benchmarks, CausalBench aims to provide a more comprehensive and accurate evaluation of the causal reasoning capabilities of LLMs, facilitating progress towards AGI.

2 Dataset Construction Process and Method

The construction of CausalBench involves three key steps: manual generation of initial test cases, scaling up using LLM such as GPT-4 Turbo, and quality control through causal inference engines together with human verification. Initially, we manually create a set of test cases covering four aspects of causal inference: (a) cause to effect, (b) effect to cause, (c) cause to effect with intervention, and (d) effect to cause with intervention to ensure a comprehensive evaluation of causal reasoning capabilities from different perspective. To expand the dataset, we then use GPT-4 Turbo with few-shot prompting, leveraging the model's ability to generate additional test cases that adhere to the desired format and cover the four causal inference aspects. The few-shot prompts are designed to guide GPT-4 Turbo in producing a diverse and extensive set of problems that maintain consistency with the manually generated cases. Afterward, we implement a quality control process involving validation through causal inference engines and review by human experts. The causal inference engines verify the logical consistency and correctness of the generated test cases, while human experts review and refine the dataset to maintain high standards of quality and relevance.

2.1 Workflow Overview

2.2 Manual Analysis and Generation

For the text problems of our Benchmark, we randomly selected 100 questions from the CLADDER dataset (Choshen et al., 2022) and manually analyzed them to determine their category within (1) inference from cause to effect, (2) effect to cause, (3) cause to effect with intervention, or (4) effect to cause with intervention. These perspectives represent different dimensions of causal reasoning: (1) Cause to the effect: Given the cause, what is the likelihood of the effect? (2) Effect to cause: Given the effect, what is the likelihood of the cause? (3) Cause to effect with intervention: If an intervention is added to the causal relationship, given the cause, what is the likelihood of the effect? and (4) Effect to cause with intervention: If an intervention is added to the causal relationship, given the effect, what is the likelihood of the cause?

After categorizing the selected cases from the CLADDER dataset, we expanded them by creating additional questions for the other three perspectives. For example, if a case was classified as "cause to effect", we generated corresponding questions for "effect to cause", "cause to effect with intervention", and "effect to cause with intervention" manually.

To correctly expand other perspective questions and their ground truths, we visualized the relationships between variables using causal diagrams and analyzed these relationships by calculating conditional probabilities. Causal diagrams represent variables as nodes and causal relationships as directed edges. For example, consider the following hypothetical scenario:

Imagine a self-contained, hypothetical world with only the following conditions, and without any unmentioned factors or causal relationships: Parents' intelligence has a direct positive effect on parents' social status and child's intelligence. Other unobserved factors has a positive direct effect on parents' social status and child's intelligence. If a child is intelligent, would it be more likely that this child had intelligent parents?

In this scenario, the causal diagram would have four nodes: Parents' intelligence, Parents' social status, Child's intelligence, and Other unobserved factors. There would be directed edges from Parents' intelligence to Parents' social status and

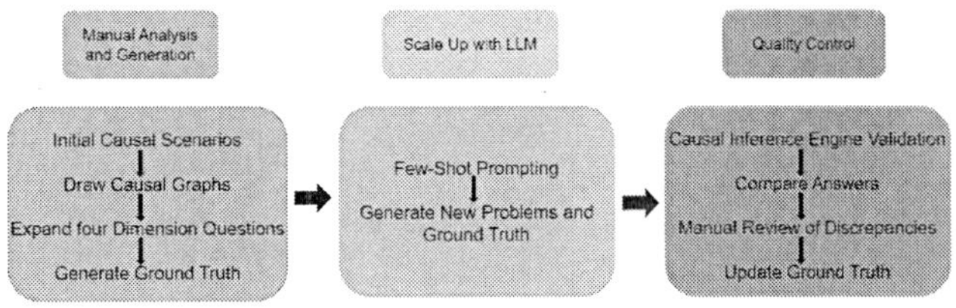

Figure 1: Workflow overview of the CausalBench dataset construction process.

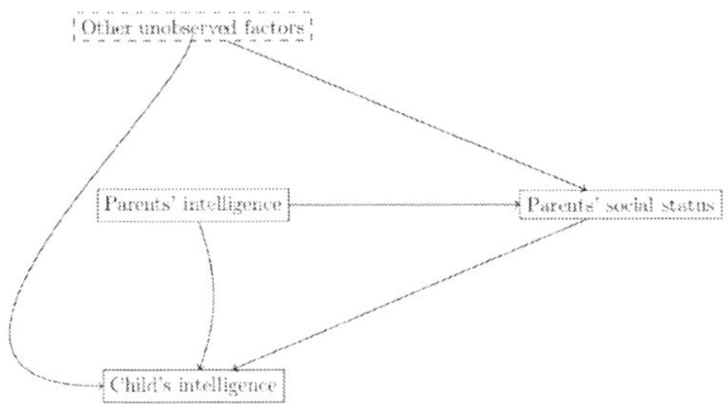

Figure 2: Causal Graph Example

Child's intelligence, from Other unobserved factors to Parents' social status and Child's intelligence, and from Parents' social status to Child's intelligence. Conditional probabilities can be estimated based on the causal graph.

Using the causal graph and conditional probabilities, we can categorized the original questions as effect-to-cause. The probability of the child being intelligent given that the parents are intelligent is higher than the probability of the child being intelligent given that the parents are unintelligent, so the ground truth is yes. Then extend the questions to cover four perspectives by adjusting the questioning logic and incorporating interventions into the causal path diagram, and calculate ground truth for each questions.(examples are provided in the Appendix)

Finally, we obtained 100 causal scenarios, with 400 causal questions. They serve as the foundation for our few-shot prompting approach, providing examples for GPT-4 Turbo on how to identify the type of the initial question and generate additional questions for the remaining perspectives. By using these examples in a few-shot prompting setting, we guide the model to generate additional perspective questions with answers for all other causal scenarios in the CLADDER dataset.

For coding and mathematical problems, we manually created 100 code scenarios and 100 math scenarios, each containing causal relationships, and designed four perspective questions for each scenario. These questions addressed causal issues based on the relationships described in the scenarios (examples are provided in the Appendix). We then used causal graphs and conditional probabilities to manually generate the ground truths and employed few-shot prompts with GPT-4 Turbo to generate additional code, math scenarios and questions with corresponding answers.

In summary, the manual analysis and generation process involved visualizing causal relationships using causal diagrams and calculating conditional probabilities for each scenario. We modified the questioning approach and added interventions to expand each problem into four forms, covering cause-to-effect, effect-to-cause, cause-to-effect with intervention, and effect-to-cause with intervention, and generated ground truths for each question. By the end of this section, we had created 100 sets of 400 text-based questions with ground truths, 100 sets of 400 coding questions with ground truths, and 100 sets of 400 math questions with ground truths. These manually generated samples serve as the foundation for our few-shot prompting approach, which utilizes GPT-4 Turbo to generate additional test cases.

2.3 Scaling Up with LLMs

After manually generating and verifying an initial set of questions, we employed GPT-4 Turbo to scale up the dataset. The scale-up process was divided into three parts: text problems, coding problems, and mathematical problems.

For the text problems, we provided GPT-4 Turbo with original CLADDER dataset(Choshen et al., 2022) questions with manually expanded questions along with their ground truths. By learning from these samples, GPT-4 Turbo was tasked with reading the remaining CLADDER scenarios (around 10,000 problems) and their corresponding questions, determining the question perspective, expanding the scenario into the other three perspectives, and generating the associated ground truths. This process ensures every text causal scenario has four dimension questions and corresponding ground truths.

In the case of coding problems, we supplied GPT-4 Turbo with the 100 manually created code examples containing causal relationships. Using these examples as a foundation, GPT-4 Turbo generated an additional 2,000 code snippets, each incorporating causal relationships. For each newly generated code snippet, GPT-4 Turbo created four perspectives of questions and provided the corresponding ground truths, ensuring a comprehensive evaluation of causal reasoning in the context of programming.

Similarly, for mathematical problems, GPT-4 Turbo was employed to generate 2,000 new mathematical scenarios across various domains, such as probability theory, mathematical statistics, differential equations, and complex analysis. For each mathematical scenario, GPT-4 Turbo generated four types of questions and their associated ground truths, assessing the model's ability to reason about causal relationships in mathematical contexts.

By leveraging the capabilities of GPT-4 Turbo, we were able to create a dataset across all three problem categories. The text problems were augmented by automatically generating additional question perspectives and ground truths based on the existing CLADDER scenarios. The coding and mathematical problems were scaled up by having GPT-4 Turbo create new scenarios containing causal relationships and generate the corresponding questions and ground truths. This scale-up process resulted in a more comprehensive and diverse dataset, enabling a thorough evaluation of causal reasoning abilities in large language models across various domains.

2.4 Quality Control

2.4.1 Causal Inference Engine Design

To ensure the accuracy and consistency of the generated questions and answers, we developed a causal inference engine. This engine utilizes causal diagrams and conditional probabilities associated with each question to compute the answers for all questions. The causal inference engine serves as a verification layer, comparing the answers generated by the language model. If the answer generated by the language model differs from the answer generated by the causal inference engine, the case will be manually inspected, and the ground truth will be generated by human experts. Here are the Causal Inference Engine design details:

Input

- A causal scenario described in natural language, code, or mathematical equations, including causal relationships among variables, known conditions, etc.
- A causal query, which is a question based on causal scenario

Steps

Causal Graph Extraction:

For natural language scenarios, we identify variables and causal relationships, and construct causal graphs (G := (V, E)) by implementing a pipeline consisting of semantic parsing and coreference resolution modules. The semantic parsing module first uses the Stanford Parser (Klein and Manning, 2003) to perform syntactic parsing and obtain the sentence structure. Then, it applies Compositional Semantics (Zettlemoyer and Collins, 2005) to recursively map the syntactic parse tree to a logical form, based on the principle of compositionality. The coreference resolution module uses techniques such as the mention-pair model (Soon et al., 2001) to determine which mentions refer to the same entity, and merges the variables corresponding to coreferent mentions. From the outputs of the semantic parsing and coreference resolution modules, the pipeline automatically extracts variables from nouns and noun phrases, and identifies causal relationships indicated by verbs and conjunctions expressing causality (Li and Mao, 2019). Finally, the causal graph construction module takes the extracted variables as nodes (V) and causal relationships as directed edges (E) to automatically build the causal graph (Pearl, 2009).

For code scenarios, we identify variables and their dependencies, and construct causal graphs by implementing a pipeline that analyzes the code structure, control flow, and data flow. The pipeline first uses a code parser, such as the ast module (Python Software Foundation, 2023) in Python, to generate an abstract syntax tree (AST). It then performs control flow analysis using techniques like control flow graphs (CFGs) (Allen, 1970) and program dependence graphs (PDGs) (Ferrante et al., 1987), and data flow analysis using def-use chains (Harrold and Rothermel, 1994) and static single assignment (SSA) form (Cytron et al., 1991), to identify execution paths, dependencies between statements, and variable dependencies. These analyses help automatically extract variables and their relationships from the code structure. Finally, the causal graph construction module takes the extracted variables as nodes (V) and their dependencies as edges (E) to build the causal graph based on the code semantics (Pearl, 2009), capturing the causal relationships between variables and enabling further reasoning and analysis.

For math scenarios, we identify variables and their functional relationships, and construct causal graphs by implementing a pipeline that parses and analyzes the mathematical equations. The pipeline first uses a math expression parser, such as the SymPy library (Meurer et al., 2017) in Python, to convert the equations into an abstract syntax tree (AST) representation. It then traverses the AST to identify variables and their functional relationships, such as dependencies and algebraic operations, using techniques like symbolic differentiation (Griewank and Walther, 2008) and expression simplification (Moses, 1971). These analyses help automatically extract variables and their relationships from the equation structure. Finally, the causal graph construction module takes the extracted variables as nodes (V) and their functional relationships as directed edges (E) to build the causal graph based on the equation semantics, similar to the approach in (Pearl, 2009). The resulting causal graph captures the causal relationships between variables in the mathematical equations, enabling further reasoning and analysis.

Query Classification: Classify the causal query into one of the three levels of the Ladder of Causation (Association, Intervention, Counterfactuals). Formalize the query into the corresponding causal language, as discussed in (Jin et al., 2023).

Estimand Derivation:

1. For text and math scenarios, we construct a module that uses causal inference algorithms (e.g., do-calculus (Pearl, 1995), counterfactual inference formulas (Pearl et al., 2000)) to derive the estimand based on the causal graph and query type.
2. For code scenarios, we use program analysis techniques (e.g., symbolic execution, data dependency analysis, control flow analysis) to derive the estimand based on the code structure and query type. This involve simulating interventions on code variables and analyzing the resulting program behavior.

Data Matching: Match the terms in the estimand with the available data or constraints in the scenario to obtain a computable estimand expression. Check the completeness and consistency of the data. Raise warnings or errors if critical data is missing. For code scenarios, this involve executing the code with specific inputs and observing the outputs. This step is similar to the data matching phase in (Jin et al., 2023).

Causal Effect Estimation:

1. Calculate the causal effect value based on the estimand expression and the available data, yielding the answer to the query.
2. For scenarios with unobserved confounders, use instrumental variable estimation (Angrist et al., 1996) or front-door adjustment (Pearl, 1995).
3. For code scenarios, this involve comparing program behaviors under different interventions.

This step is inspired by causal effect estimation phase in (Jin et al., 2023).

Output

- Answer to the causal query, including the estimated causal effect, confidence interval, and key assumptions.

In a summary, our Causal Inference Engine extends the original design presented in (Jin et al., 2023) by incorporating domain-specific graph extraction and estimand derivation techniques to handle causal inference problems in text, code, and math scenarios. The overall pipeline remains consistent with the one described in (Jin et al., 2023), but the internal methods are adapted to the specific structures and semantics of each domain.

2.4.2 Quality Control Process

After expansion with GPT4-Turbo, we obtained around 10000 x 4 text-based questions, 2000 x 4 math questions, and 2000 x 4 coding questions, along with their GPT-4 Turbo generated answers. To ensure the accuracy of the ground truth of each questions, we employed a strict quality control process as showing below:

We used the causal inference engine introduced above to independently solve the problems and generate its own set of answers. We compared the answers generated by GPT-4 Turbo and the causal inference engine. If two answers were the same, we updated the answer as ground truth. If any of the answers were inconsistent, we conducted a manual analysis of the question and answers to determine the correct answer and update ground truth accordingly.

This multi-step quality control process, involving the use of causal inference engine and human expert check, ensures that the final dataset contains accurate and reliable questions and answers. The manual review of inconsistent answers further enhances the quality of the dataset by addressing any discrepancies or edge cases that the models may encounter.

3 Benchmark Results

3.1 Baseline of Mainstream LLMs

We tested several state-of-the-art large language models, including GPT-4, Claude-3, LLAMA-3, and others, on our CausalBench. The evaluation metrics included: Four-Type Questions Group Correction Rate, Overall Correction Rate (Ignore Question Type), From Cause to Effect without Intervention Correction Rate, From Effect to Cause without Intervention Correction Rate, From Cause to Effect with Intervention Correction Rate, and From Effect to Cause with Intervention Correction Rate. For each causal scenario, there are four questions: cause-to-effect without intervention, effect-to-cause without intervention, cause-to-effect with intervention, and effect-to-cause with intervention. The Four-Type Questions Group Correction Rate represents the proportion of scenario cases where all four types of questions of one scenario are all answered correctly by the large language models. If any of the four questions of a scenario is answered incorrectly, the scenario is considered to be answered incorrectly by the LLM. The Overall Correction Rate (Ignore Question Type) is calculated by dividing the total number of correctly answered questions by the total number of questions, without categorizing the questions by type and scenario. The From Cause to Effect without Intervention Correction Rate is calculated by dividing the number of correctly answered "From Cause to Effect without Intervention" type questions by the total number of this type of questions. Similarly, the From Effect to Cause without Intervention Correction Rate is calculated by dividing the number of correctly answered "From Effect to Cause without Intervention" type questions by the total number of this type of questions. The remaining two metrics, From Cause to Effect with Intervention Correction Rate and From Effect to Cause with Intervention Correction Rate, follow the same calculation method as the previous two metrics, focusing on their respective question types.

Here are the tables showing LLMs' performance on text, math, and code problems.

3.2 Test Result Summary

The evaluation results of state-of-the-art large language models on CausalBench provide valuable insights into their causal reasoning capabilities across textual, mathematical, and coding problem domains:

Overall, the models achieved higher correction rates on mathematical problems compared to textual and coding problems. For instance, GPT-4 achieved an 88.7% overall correction rate on math problems, while scoring 73.3% and 71.0% on text and code problems, respectively. This suggests that causal reasoning in mathematical contexts is relatively easier for LLMs compared to natural language and programming domains.

The Four-Type Questions Group Correction Rate, which measures the proportion of scenarios where all four reasoning perspectives are correctly answered, was consistently lower than the Overall Correction Rate (Ignore Question Type) across all problem types. For example, GPT-4 achieved a 61.4% Four-Type Questions Group Correction Rate on math problems, compared to an 88.7% Overall Correction Rate. This indicates that LLMs often struggle to maintain a comprehensive understanding of causal relationships when questioned from multiple perspectives.

The introduction of interventions in the causal scenarios led to mixed results in correction rates across models and problem types. In the text domain, the correction rates slightly decreased for most models when interventions were introduced. However, in the math domain, the correction rates generally improved with interventions. For instance, GPT-4's performance increased from 78.6% to 91.7% on cause-to-effect questions with intervention in math problems. In the coding domain, the impact of interventions varied across models, with some showing improvements and others exhibiting a decline in performance.

Among the tested models, GPT-4 and Claude-3 consistently outperformed other large language models (LLMs) across most problem types and reasoning dimensions, achieving the highest cor-

Model	Four-Type Questions Group Correction Rate(%)	Overall Correction Rate(Ignore Question Type) (%)	From Cause to Effect without Intervention Correction Rate (%)	From Effect to Cause without Intervention Correction Rate (%)	From Cause to Effect with Intervention Correction Rate (%)	From Effect to Cause with Intervention Correction Rate (%)
GPT-4 Turbo	36.9	73.3	74.4	71.2	73.8	73.7
Claude3-Opus	36.8	72.6	74.1	70.9	73.2	72.2
Mistral-7B	25.5	63.6	58.7	66.5	64.2	65.0
Llama3-70B	21.8	61.5	62.6	59.6	63.8	60.1
Llama2-7B	20.7	62.1	62.8	64.0	56.4	65.4
GPT-3.5	16.7	57.8	57.6	58.5	56.2	58.7
Gemma-7b-it	12.8	50.7	50.0	46.9	53.6	52.1
Bloomz	4.2	41.7	41.0	40.7	41.7	43.6
AquilaChat	1.9	31.1	28.7	32.4	33.1	30.4

Table 1: LLM Performance on Text Problems.

Model	Four-Type Questions Group Correction Rate(%)	Overall Correction Rate(Ignore Question Type) (%)	From Cause to Effect without Intervention Correction Rate (%)	From Effect to Cause without Intervention Correction Rate (%)	From Cause to Effect with Intervention Correction Rate (%)	From Effect to Cause with Intervention Correction Rate (%)
Mistral-7B	62.0	87.2	78.9	85.6	85.3	98.9
GPT-4 Turbo	61.4	88.7	78.6	88.3	91.7	96.0
Claude3-Opus	54.6	85.9	74.7	87.1	86.5	95.4
Llama3-70B	40.8	80.7	56.8	86.8	82.0	97.1
Gemma-7b-it	38.3	79.2	50.4	82.8	91.1	92.0
AquilaChat	25.3	68.1	57.0	67.8	69.2	78.3
Bloomz	23.9	69.2	53.3	76.8	67.3	79.7
GPT-3.5	15.9	63.3	47.1	71.5	48.6	86.1
Llama2-7B	2.8	42.3	45.3	54.2	17.5	52.4

Table 2: LLM Performance on Problems.

Model	Four-Type Questions Group Correction Rate(%)	Overall Correction Rate(Ignore Question Type) (%)	From Cause to Effect without Intervention Correction Rate (%)	From Effect to Cause without Intervention Correction Rate (%)	From Cause to Effect with Intervention Correction Rate (%)	From Effect to Cause with Intervention Correction Rate (%)
Llama3-70B	43.8	77.0	82.0	75.7	73.9	76.0
Claude3-Opus	39.6	71.3	78.6	71.3	68.7	66.5
GPT-4	37.2	71.0	80.6	67.5	73.2	62.5
Gemma	32.3	68.4	74.1	67.7	66.0	65.4
Mistral	31.4	66.8	67.5	68.3	61.3	70.2
GPT-3.5	25.0	64.5	71.9	65.4	59.8	60.6
Llama2-7B	22.6	61.9	79.0	45.5	76.3	46.8
Bloomz	17.5	52.4	49.6	56.8	46.4	56.8
AquilaChat	14.7	47.3	36.8	56.4	38.9	57.2

Table 3: LLM Performance on Code Problems.

rection rates. Mistral demonstrated strong performance in mathematical problems but exhibited shortcomings in code-related tasks. Conversely, LLAMA-3 showed robust performance in code-related problems but faced challenges with text and mathematical tasks.

4 Correlation with Hallucination

To analyze the correlation between LLMs' causal reasoning ability and their hallucination rate, we referred to the LLMs' performance on hallucination datasets. The hallucination evaluation results were obtained from the Hallucination Leaderboard, developed by Vectara (Hughes and Bae, 2023). This leaderboard provides a comparison of LLM performance in maintaining a low hallucination rate and ensuring factual consistency when summarizing a set of facts.

The hallucination evaluation process involves measuring the hallucination rate, factual consistency rate, answer rate, and average summary length. These metrics provide a comprehensive understanding of each model's tendency to hallucinate and its ability to maintain factual accuracy (Hughes and Bae, 2023).

After comparing the LLMs' performance on CausalBench with their performance on the Hallucination evaluation leaderboard provided by Vectara on Huggingface (Hughes and Bae, 2023), we found that models with stronger causal reasoning abilities tend to exhibit lower hallucination rates. For instance, GPT-4 Turbo, LLAMA-3-70B, and Mistral-7B, which demonstrated superior performance on causal reasoning tasks, also had low hallucination rates. In contrast, models like Google Gemma-7b-it and LLAMA-2-7B, which showed weaker performance on our CausalBench, had higher hallucination rates of 7.5% and 5.6%,

Model	Hallucination Rate	Factual Consistency Rate	Answer Rate)	Average Summary Length (Words)
GPt-4 Turbo	2.5%	97.5%	100.0%	86.2
Llama3-70B	4.5%	95.5%	99.2%	68.5
Mistral 7B Instruct-v0.2	4.5%	95.5%	100.0%	106.1
Llama2-7B	5.6%	94.4%	99.6%	119.9
Claude3-Opus	7.4%	92.6%	95.5%	92.1
Google Gemma-7b-it	7.5%	92.5%	100.0%	113.0

Table 4: Performance of LLMs on the Hallucination Dataset.

respectively.

This trend indicates a potential link between a model's ability to understand and reason about causal relationships and its likelihood of not producing hallucinations. Further research is required to explore this correlation in more depth and to understand the underlying mechanisms driving this relationship.

5 Impact and Limitations

5.1 Impact

For the first time, we innovatively propose four types of questioning approaches for the same causal scenario: cause-to-effect, effect-to-cause, cause-to-effect with intervention, and effect-to-cause with intervention. We also calculate the proportion of cases where large language models correctly answer all four types of questions for a given causal scenario. This effectively avoids the situation where large language models coincidentally answer causal questions correctly without understanding the causal relationships embedded in the causal scenario, thereby improving the accuracy of the dataset's test results. By providing causal reasoning problems spanning multiple domains(text, code, math), it addresses the limitations of existing causal datasets and offers a more comprehensive and robust tool for assessing the causal reasoning abilities of language models. The findings in this paper suggest that models with stronger causal reasoning capabilities tend to exhibit lower hallucination rates, providing a new perspective on exploring the relationship between causal reasoning and reducing hallucinations. CausalBench has the potential to become a benchmark for driving progress in causal reasoning in artificial intelligence.

6 Conclusion

In this paper, we present CausalBench, a comprehensive benchmark dataset for evaluating the causal reasoning capabilities of large language models. CausalBench innovatively proposes four types of questioning approaches for each causal scenario: cause-to-effect, effect-to-cause, cause-to-effect with intervention, and effect-to-cause with intervention. By calculating the proportion of cases where models correctly answer all four question types, CausalBench effectively assesses whether LLMs truly understand the underlying causal relationships, mitigating the impact of models coincidentally providing correct answers without causal comprehension.

The dataset encompasses a diverse set of problems spanning textual, mathematical, and coding domains, addressing the limitations of existing causal reasoning benchmarks. Evaluated on CausalBench, state-of-the-art LLMs demonstrate stronger performance on mathematical problems compared to textual and coding tasks. Notably, models with superior causal reasoning abilities tend to exhibit lower hallucination rates, suggesting a potential link between the two capabilities.

Despite its contributions, CausalBench has several limitations, including the need for expanded domain coverage and deeper exploration of the intrinsic mechanisms connecting causal reasoning and hallucination reduction. Future work will focus on addressing these limitations, further refining the evaluation metrics, and providing insights to advance the development of causal reasoning abilities in large language models. CausalBench serves as a robust tool and an important step towards achieving artificial general intelligence.

Limitations

CausalBench has several limitations that need to be addressed in future work. These include the need for further expanding the domain coverage, increasing the scale of the dataset, incorporating causal discovery tasks and exploring the intrinsic mechanisms between causal reasoning and hallucinations through more empirical studies.

References

Frances E. Allen. 1970. Control flow analysis. *ACM SIGPLAN Notices*, 5(7):1–19.

Joshua D. Angrist, Guido W. Imbens, and Donald B. Rubin. 1996. Identification of causal effects using instrumental variables. *Journal of the American Statistical Association*, 91(434):444–455.

Leshem Choshen, Paarth Neekhara, Kyle Richardson, Lisa Xue, Madian Hou, Shehzaad Neekhara, Yao Chen, and Heike Adel. 2022. Cladder: A causal language model for causal reasoning. In *Proceedings of the 2022 Conference on Empirical Methods in Natural Language Processing*, pages 6205–6224.

Ron Cytron, Jeanne Ferrante, Barry K. Rosen, Mark N. Wegman, and F. Kenneth Zadeck. 1991. Efficiently computing static single assignment form and the control dependence graph. *ACM Transactions on Programming Languages and Systems (TOPLAS)*, 13(4):451–490.

Jeanne Ferrante, Karl J. Ottenstein, and Joe D. Warren. 1987. The program dependence graph and its use in optimization. *ACM Transactions on Programming Languages and Systems (TOPLAS)*, 9(3):319–349.

Lex Fridman and Judea Pearl. 2022. Causal reasoning, counterfactuals, and the path to agi. *Miniature Brain Machinery Webinar Review*.

Andreas Griewank and Andrea Walther. 2008. *Evaluating Derivatives: Principles and Techniques of Algorithmic Differentiation*. SIAM.

Mary Jean Harrold and Gregg Rothermel. 1994. Performing data flow testing on classes. In *Proceedings of the 2nd ACM SIGSOFT Symposium on Foundations of Software Engineering (SIGSOFT'94)*, pages 154–163.

Simon Hughes and Minseok Bae. 2023. Vectara hallucination leaderboard. `https://github.com/vectara/hallucination-leaderboard`.

Zhijing Jin, Jiarui Liu, Zhiheng Lyu, Spencer Poff, Mrinmaya Sachan, Rada Mihalcea, Mona T. Diab, and Bernhard Schölkopf. 2023. Can large language models infer causation from correlation? *CoRR*, abs/2306.05836.

Divyansh Kaushik, Eduard Hovy, and Zachary C Lipton. 2020. Learning the difference that makes a difference with counterfactually-augmented data. In *8th International Conference on Learning Representations, ICLR 2020, Addis Ababa, Ethiopia, April 26-30, 2020*. OpenReview.net.

Dan Klein and Christopher D. Manning. 2003. Accurate unlexicalized parsing. In *Proceedings of the 41st Annual Meeting of the Association for Computational Linguistics*, pages 423–430.

Pengfei Li and Kezhi Mao. 2019. Knowledge-oriented convolutional neural network for causal relation extraction from natural language texts. *Expert Systems with Applications*, 115:512–523.

Aaron Meurer, Christopher P Smith, Mateusz Paprocki, Ondřej Čertík, Sergey B Kirpichev, Matthew Rocklin, AMiT Kumar, Sergiu Ivanov, Jason K Moore, Sartaj Singh, et al. 2017. Sympy: Symbolic computing in python. *PeerJ Computer Science*, 3:e103.

Joel Moses. 1971. Algebraic simplification: A guide for the perplexed. *Communications of the ACM*, 14(8):527–537.

Judea Pearl. 1995. Causal diagrams for empirical research. *Biometrika*, 82(4):669–688.

Judea Pearl. 2009. *Causality: Models, Reasoning, and Inference*. Cambridge University Press.

Judea Pearl et al. 2000. *Causality: Models, reasoning and inference*, volume 29. Cambridge university press.

Python Software Foundation. 2023. ast — abstract syntax trees. `https://docs.python.org/3/library/ast.html`. Accessed: 2023-06-05.

Wee Meng Soon, Hwee Tou Ng, and Daniel Chung Yong Lim. 2001. A machine learning approach to coreference resolution of noun phrases. *Computational Linguistics*, 27(4):521–544.

Luke S. Zettlemoyer and Michael Collins. 2005. Learning to map sentences to logical form: Structured classification with probabilistic categorial grammars. In *Proceedings of the 21st Conference on Uncertainty in Artificial Intelligence*, pages 658–666.

PerLTQA: A Personal Long-Term Memory Dataset for Memory Classification, Retrieval, and Fusion in Question Answering

Yiming Du[1,2], **Hongru Wang**[1,2], **Zhengyi Zhao**[1,2], **Bin Liang**[1,2], **Baojun Wang**[3], **Wanjun Zhong**[3], **Zezhong Wang**[1,2], **Kam-Fai Wong**[1,2*]

[1] The Chinese University of Hong Kong, Hong Kong, China
[2] MoE Key Laboratory of High Confidence Software Technologies, China
[3] Huawei Noah's Ark Lab, Hong Kong, China
ydu@se.cuhk.edu.hk

Abstract

In conversational AI, effectively employing long-term memory improves personalized and consistent response generation. Existing work only concentrated on a single type of long-term memory, such as preferences, dialogue history, or social relationships, overlooking their interaction in real-world contexts. To this end, inspired by the concept of semantic memory and episodic memory from cognitive psychology, we create a new and more comprehensive Chinese dataset, coined as PerLTQA, in which world knowledge, profiles, social relationships, events, and dialogues are considered to leverage the interaction between different types of long-term memory for question answering (QA) in conversation. Further, based on PerLTQA, we propose a novel framework for memory integration in QA, consisting of three subtasks: **Memory Classification**, **Memory Retrieval**, and **Memory Fusion**, which provides a comprehensive paradigm for memory modeling, enabling consistent and personalized memory utilization. This essentially allows the exploitation of more accurate memory information for better responses in QA. We evaluate this framework using five LLMs and three retrievers. Experimental results demonstrate the importance of personal long-term memory in the QA task[1].

1 Introduction

Long-term memory is a crucial element in conversational communication, facilitate the consistent and personalized response generation(Xu et al., 2021b; Zhong et al., 2024). Previous studies, as shown in Table 1, have explored its various aspects, such as world knowledge(Kwiatkowski et al., 2019; Reddy et al., 2019; Chen et al., 2020), profiles (Zhang et al., 2018; Zheng et al., 2019; Xu et al., 2022), social relationships, events (Jang et al., 2023), and dialogue history (Zhong et al., 2024; Maharana et al., 2024; Xu et al., 2021a; Chen et al., 2021).

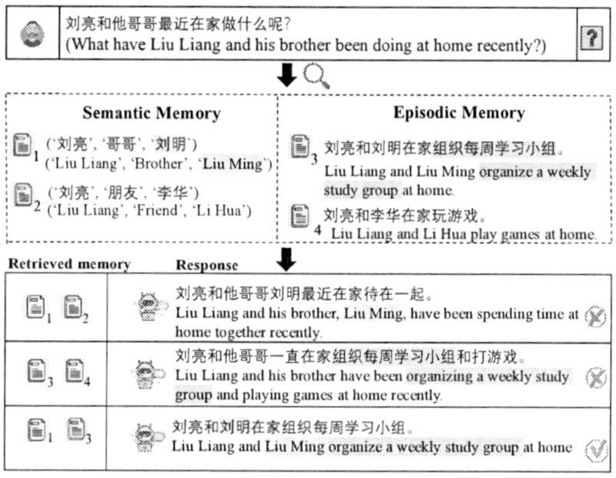

Figure 1: Example of external semantic and episodic memory used for QA in conversation.

However, existing research largely focused on a single type of long-term memory, ignoring the interaction of different types of memory, which are crucial for consistent and personalized response generation. As illustrated in Figure 1, with only event memory, the model cannot recognize social relationship *brother* in the query and fails to distinguish the event involving *LiuMing*. However, when integrating semantic and episodic memory, not only does it enhance the retrieval model (Izacard et al., 2021) to recall social relationships *LiuMing* but also aids generation model to accurately fuse the event *organize a weekly study group*. Based on the definition provided by cognitive psychology (Eysenck and Keane, 2020), long-term memory is categorized into semantic memory and episodic memory. Semantic memory encompasses structured data, including world knowledge, profiles, and relationships. In addition, episodic memory captures personal histories such as events and dialogues, typically represented as lengthy text. Combining these types of memory can enhance the retrieval of accurate memory, thus improving responses to user queries.

[1]Our code and dataset will be publicly released once accepted.

Proceedings of the 10th SIGHAN Workshop on Chinese Language Processing (SIGHAN-10), pages 152–164
August 16, 2024 ©2024 Association for Computational Linguistics

Dataset	Semantic Memory			Episodic Memory		Goal
	WK	PRO	SR	DLG	EVT	
Natural-QA (Kwiatkowski et al., 2019)	✓	✗	✗	✗	✗	QA on Wikipedia
CoQA (Reddy et al., 2019)	✓	✗	✗	✗	✗	Dialogue QA on world knowledge
HybridQA (Chen et al., 2020)	✓	✗	✗	✗	✗	Multi-Hop QA on world knowledge
OTT-QA (?)	✓	✗	✗	✗	✗	QA on tables and text
Multi-Woz (Budzianowski et al., 2018)	✗	✗	✗	✓	✗	Task-oriented Dialogue
Persona-Chat (Zhang et al., 2018)	✗	✓	✗	✓	✗	Consistent personality dialogue
DailyDialog (Li et al., 2017)	✗	✗	✗	✓	✗	Multi-turn dialogues on daily life
Personal-Dialogue (Zheng et al., 2019)	✗	✓	✗	✓	✗	Multi-turn personalized dialogues
MSC (Xu et al., 2021a)	✗	✓	✗	✓	✗	Long-Term open-domain conversation
DialogueSum (Chen et al., 2021)	✗	✗	✗	✓	✗	Dialogue summarization
Dulemon (Xu et al., 2022)	✗	✓	✗	✓	✗	Personal long-term Chinese conversation
HybridDialogue (Nakamura et al., 2022)	✓	✗	✗	✗	✗	Dialogue QA on tables and text
Topical-Chat (Gopalakrishnan et al., 2023)	✓	✗	✗	✗	✗	Knowledge-grounded open-domain conversations
ChatDB (Hu et al., 2020)	✓	✗	✗	✗	✗	Question answering with structured memory
MemoryBank (Zhong et al., 2024)	✗	✓	✗	✓	✗	Personal long-term memory dialogue
CONVERSATION CHRONICLES (Jang et al., 2023)	✗	✗	✓	✓	✓	Long-term multi-session open domain conversation
PerLTQA	✓	✓	✓	✓	✓	Question answering on personal long-term memory including semantic and episodic memory

Table 1: Typology of memories in QA/Dialogue datasets: Analysis of World Knowledge (WK), Profiles (PRO), Social Relationships (SR), Dialogues (DLG), and Events (EVT).

To establish a unified long-term memory bank, we leverage the in-context generation capabilities of large language models (LLMs) to generate various memory categories: world knowledge, profiles, social relationships, events, and dialogue history, as illustrated in Figure 2. The dataset consists of a memory database with 141 profiles, 1,339 semantic social relationships, 4,501 events, and 3,409 dialogues, and 8,593 memory-related evaluation questions.

In the realm of long-term memory research (Zhong et al., 2024; Stacey et al., 2024; Packer et al., 2023), retrieval models (Karpukhin et al., 2020; Izacard et al., 2021; Robertson et al., 1995) and generative models (Yang et al., 2023; Bai et al., 2023; Touvron et al., 2023; Zhang et al., 2023a; Jiang et al., 2023) are the two most commonly used modules to integrate external long-term memory. Furthermore, considering the variety of memory types examined in PerLTQA, classification models provide an effective means to refine the scope of retrieval and improve response consistency. Therefore, we propose three subtasks memory classification, memory retrieval, and memory fusion to evaluate the memory utilization capabilities of LLMs. We carry out experiments using five LLMs and three retrieval models.

The main contributions of this work are summarised as follows:

- We introduce a new personal long-term memory dataset, coined as PerLTQA, for QA. The PerLTQA provides a new research paradigm for the modeling of interaction between different memory types, paving the way for personalized question-answering systems and lifelong companion agents.
- We propose a new framework consisting of three subtasks memory classification, memory retrieval, and memory fusion to evaluate the memory utilization capabilities of LLMs.
- We carry out experiments using five LLMs and three retrieval models. The results demonstrate that a classification-based re-ranking mechanism improves the consistency of responses generated by LLMs when accessing unified long-term memory.

2 Related Work

The long-term memory differentiation is mirrored in the datasets like (Kwiatkowski et al., 2019; Chen et al., 2021; Zhong et al., 2024). In the realm of question answering, Natural-QA (Kwiatkowski et al., 2019) and CoQA (Reddy et al., 2019) both target Wikipedia-based knowledge, exemplifying the use of world knowledge as semantic memory. Within dialogue tasks (Wang et al., 2023b), MSC (Xu et al., 2021a) and Dulemon (Xu et al., 2022) consider dialogues as episodic memory. MemoryBank (Zhong et al., 2024) introduces a bilingual dataset using GPT-4 to summarize dialogues and personal data, effectively simulating episodic memory in multi-turn dialogues. However, existing datasets (Hu et al., 2020; Zhang et al., 2023b) lack comprehensive coverage of both memory types with detailed annotations on social relationships and events, highlighting a research gap for LLMs in personal long-term memory fusion.

Efficient retrieval methods for external mem-

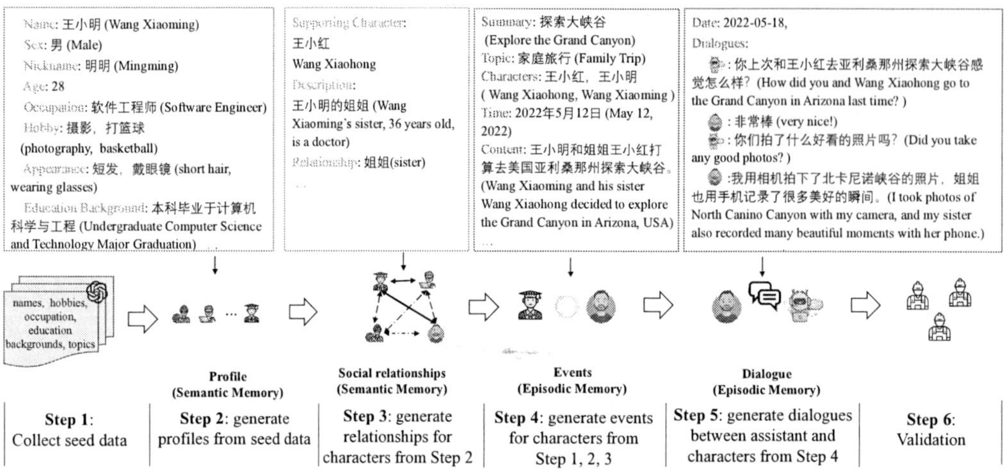

Figure 2: The process of PerLT Memory generation. A six-step process: Step 1. Seed data collection. Step 2. PRO generation. Step 3. SR generation. Step 4. EVT generation. Step 5. DLG generation and Step 6. Validation.

ory in dialogue system fall into two main categories: sparse retrieval method like BM25 (Robertson et al., 1995) and vector-based retrieval method like DPR (Karpukhin et al., 2020), Contriever (Izacard et al., 2021). The use of Retrieval-Augmented Generation (RAG) is increasingly enhancing retrieval tasks within large language models (LLMs). Within this framework, fine-tuned embeddings are employed for text similarity searches, such as REPLUG (Shi et al., 2023), OpenAI Embeddings [2]. This integration helps generate context-aware responses that consider personal memory, thereby improving the interaction quality in systems like those documented in recent studies (Wang et al., 2023a) and platforms like LangChain [3] and LlamaIndex [4].

With the aim of integrating the memories recovered in the responses, LLMs provide the consistent response generation method based on prompts (Zhang et al., 2023a; Yang et al., 2023; Bai et al., 2023; Zhang et al., 2023c; Touvron et al., 2023; Li et al., 2023). In dialogue systems, this approach incorporates memory directly into prompts, generating tailored responses that reflect individual memory (Zhao et al., 2023; Lee et al., 2023; Zhu et al., 2024; Zhong et al., 2024).

3 Dataset Collection

We detail the creation of the PerLTQA dataset, which involves collecting PerLT memories and generating and annotating PerLT QA pairs. Using an in-context technique, we build a memory database that encompasses profiles, social relationships, world knowledge, events, and dialogues. We then semi-automatically annotate components of memory-based Q&A, including questions, answers, reference memories, and memory anchors that connect answers to their respective memories.

3.1 PerLT Memory Generation

As shown in Figure 2, the generation of PerLT memories is decomposed into six steps:

Step 1. Diverse Seed Data Collection. We select ChatGPT and Wikipedia as initial world knowledge source for our seed dataset due to their comprehensive coverage of a wide range of occupations, educational backgrounds, hobbies, and event topics, essential for foundational world knowledge. It comprises professional backgrounds that span across 10 categories and 299 specialties, hobbies that are categorized into 7 groups with 140 items, and a comprehensive range of topics structured into 49 categories with 2442 subtopics. Complementing this approach, `gpt-3.5-turbo` is employed to generate 141 virtual names. We implement a manual review process, allowing us to avoid the unrealistic use for data generation.

Step 2. Profile (Semantic Memory) Generation. To study personalized memories, generating character profiles is essential. We leverage seed data, particularly occupations, educational backgrounds, hobbies inputs, within prompt templates that include descriptions of other attributes (gender, nickname, age, nationality, appearance,

[2]https://platform.openai.com/docs/api-reference/embeddings

[3]https://www.langchain.com/

[4]https://docs.llamaindex.ai/en/latest/index.html

achievements, education, profession, employer, awards, and role models). By utilizing ChatGPT (`gpt-3.5-turbo`), we generate random character profiles. The detailed prompts for this process is available in Appendix.A.1.

Step 3. Social Relationship (Semantic Memory) Generation. For the development of diverse social connections, we utilize structured prompts shown in Appendix.A.1 to craft 50 distinct categories of relationships. These categories span a wide array, including but not limited to family, friends, colleagues and neighbors, aiming to comprehensively cover social interactions.

Step 4. Event (Episodic Memory) Generation. Each character includes a series of narrative events, deeply embedded in their episodic memory and linked to interactions with others. The event generation starts by generating descriptions of background events chosen at random from the seed topics highlighted in Step 1. Following this step, we use prompts to help create detailed accounts of events that are deeply tied to these initial occurrences and the social networks. To ensure coherence between the dynamics of character interactions and the backdrop of events, few-shot learning techniques, as outlined by (Brown et al., 2020), are employed. This strategy aids ChatGPT (`gpt-3.5-turbo`) in achieving narrative consistency, weaving together individual events and relationships into a cohesive story for each character.

Step 5. Dialogues (Episodic Memory) Generation. Building on the events generated in Step 4, we craft historical dialogues between the AI assistant and the character. This process, anchored in historical events, ensures that conversations maintain relevance to past events. We utilize prompt templates that merge character profiles and event details to help dialogue generation, as detailed in Appendix.A.1. Furthermore, embedding the dialogues maintains a profound connection to the shared histories and relationships.

Step 6. Validation. We start with small batches for quality checks and scale up after ensuring error-free outputs. We conduct random sampling of the generated memory data, identifying types of issues as detailed in Appendix A.3, and then manually refine the memories. This refinement includes removing anomalies in profiles, discriminatory content, inconsistencies in character memories, and brief event narratives, enhancing the accuracy and consistency of the memory. Even so, there still be some biases as shown in Limitations.

3.2 PerLT Question Answering

To thoroughly assess each memory type for a character, we gather four QA-related metrics (*question*, *answer*, *reference memory*, and *memory anchor*) for evaluating the memory-based QA. The process of collecting PerLT QA items unfolds in three phases:

Question and answer generating. Utilizing ChatGPT, we generate questions and answers prompted by the memory sentences stored in PerLT Memory database. The answers are designed to align with the reference memories provided, adhering to the prompts we created, as shown in the Appendix.A.2.

Memory Anchor Annotation. The memory anchor, a key text segment in the answer that aligns with the referenced memory and question, is essential for memory evaluation in response generation. We employ exact match techniques and human verification to annotate the start and end positions of memory anchors, guided by the reference memory. Given the intensive labor involved in manual adjustments, we have annotated memory anchors for a limited set of 30 characters.

Validation on QA pairs and Memory Anchor. To ensure the integrity of PerLT QA pairs, we start with unbiased random sampling and a detailed error categorization in QA, references, and memory anchors, alongside pronominal reference checks for accuracy, with all errors cataloged in the Appendix.A. We employ LLMs to score QA pairs on a scale from 0 to 10, automatically accepting those scoring 10, reviewing scores between 6 and 9, and discarding scores below 6. This process includes automated validation to verify reference memory accuracy and remove irrelevant stopwords, followed by thorough manual corrections and alignment checks to guarantee the highest quality of QA items.

3.3 Dataset Statistics

The PerLTQA dataset, presented in Table 2, includes 141 character profiles with detailed occupations and relationships. With 50 relationship categories, an average of 9.5 social relationships per character, the dataset provides a vivid social relationship for semantic memory. Furthermore, PerLT Memory features 4,501 events, averaging 313 words each, which fuel 3,409 event-related historical dialogues, totaling 25,256 utterances. In the QA section, 8,593 question-answer pairs and

Dataset Statistics		
Profiles	# Character profiles	141
	# Jobs	98
Semantic Memory	# Relationship Descriptions	1,339
	# Relationship Categories	50
	# Average Social Relationships per Character	9.5
Episodic Memory	# Topics	49
	# Events	4,501
	# Average Words per Events	313
	# Event-related Historical Dialogs	3,409
	# Utterances	25,256
	# Average Words per Utterance	43.7
Memory QA	# Question Answer Pairs	8,593
	# Average Words per Question	16.7
	# Average Words per Answer	27.4
	# Memory Anchors	23,697
	# Average Anchors	2.8

Table 2: PerLTQA dataset statistics.

23,697 memory anchors average 16.7 and 27.4 words, respectively. This rich compilation of data supports the development of dialogue QA system with a profound understanding of human-like memory recall and fusion within a concise framework.

3.4 Task Definition

The PerLT memory database is formulated as $M = \{(S_i(l_1), E_i(l_2)) \mid i = 1, 2, \ldots, p\}$, where each tuple consists of semantic memories including profiles and social relationship and episodic memories including events and dialogs. Each $S_i(l_1)$ and $E_i(l_2)$ are defined to have l_1, l_2 elements, respectively, which are specific to the i-th character memory representation.

The PerLT QA dataset comprises a set of items $T = \{t_j\}_{j=1}^{N}$, where each item t_j is a tuple consisting of four elements: $t_j = (q_j, r_j, m_j, a_j)$. Here, q_j denotes the question, r_j the reference memory, m_j the memory anchor, and a_j the answer. The dataset spans various data types including semantic memory, and episodic memory, which are implicitly reflected in the construction of each t_j. The variable N represents the total number of QA items in the dataset.

As shown in Figure 3, to explore the integration of memory information in QA, we propose three subtasks: *memory classification*, *memory retrieval* and *memory fusion* for response generation. In particular, memory fusion is our ultimate goal.

Memory Classification. We introduce a classification model designed to assist queries in finding semantic memory or episodic memory. This model can operate through an instruction-based LLM, few-shot-based LLM, or BERT-based classifier. The classification model conforms to a unified formula as Eq.(1).

$$\pi = MC(q) \tag{1}$$

where π denotes the classification result, MC is the classification model, and q is the input query. The outputs from our classification model improve memory retrieval by assisting in the post-ranking of various types of retrieved memories, thereby reducing the over-reliance on memory classification. Further details are elaborated in Appendix.A.4.

Memory Retrieval. For each character, we perform memory retrieval for a given evaluation question from the PerLT memory database M separately, formalized as Eq.(2).

$$m, s = R(q, M, k) \tag{2}$$

where m is the retrieved memory with size k, s is the corresponding scores, R is the retrieval model.

Our method distinguishes itself by initially retrieving k memories from each category within the memory database, amassing $2k$ potential memory candidates. These candidates undergo a re-ranking process influenced by their classification scores, culminating in a composite score for each memory m_i, which is computed as follows:

$$s_i' = \alpha \cdot P(\pi|m_i) + \beta \cdot \text{sigmoid}(s_i) \tag{3}$$

where $P(\pi|m_i)$ represents the classifier's confidence that memory item m_i belongs to category π. Higher confidence indicates a greater likelihood of relevance to the queried category, which is vital for retrieval tasks. The weights α and β are both set to 0.5 to balance their contributions.

Memory Fusion. Memory fusion leverages LLM for response generation. This task uses a prompt template z (as illustrated in Appendix.8), an evaluation question q, and retrieved memories m as Eq.(4).

$$r' = LLM(z, q, m) \tag{4}$$

3.5 Evaluation Metrics

For the memory classification task, we use precision (P), recall (R), F1, and Accuracy to serve as metrics. For the memory retrieval task, we utilize Recall@K (Manning et al., 2008) as our metric. To

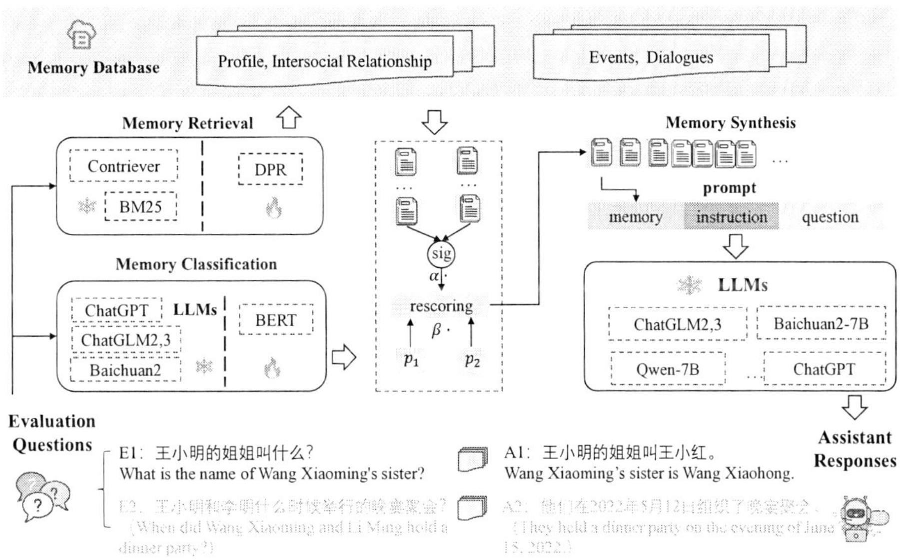

Figure 3: The framework of memory classification, memory retrieval and memory fusion in QA.

evaluate memory fusion for the response generation task, we measure the correctness and coherence of responses with `gpt-3.5-turbo`-based evaluation method (Zhong et al., 2024) and use MAP (mean average precision) of memory anchors as shown in Eq.(5) to evaluate memory fusion ability (Nakamura et al., 2022).

$$\text{MAP} = \frac{1}{N}\sum_{i=1}^{N}\frac{\text{EM}(q_i, mar_i)}{\text{NUM}(mar_i)} \quad (5)$$

where N represents the total number of questions in the evaluation dataset. mar denotes memory anchors, EM represents the tally of exact matches between answers and memory anchors, and $\text{NUM}(mar_i)$ is the count of memory anchors per question.

4 Experiments

4.1 Implementation details

In our work, we divide the data from the PerLT QA dataset into training (5155), validation (1719), and test sets (1719) for model training and evaluation. In the memory classification task, we fine-tune BERT-base model and compare the sentence classification performance on the test dataset with ChatGLM2, ChatGLM3 (Zhang et al., 2023a), Baichuan2-7B-Chat (Yang et al., 2023), Qwen-7B-Chat (Bai et al., 2023), and ChatGPT under instructional and few-shot settings. For the memory retrieval task, we employ three retrieval models - DPR (Karpukhin et al., 2020), BM25 (Robertson et al., 1995), and Contriever (Izacard et al., 2021) - to collect character memories. In the memory fusion task, we use the above five LLMs to generate responses of no more than 50 words, given reranked retrieved memories, employing in-context learning methods.

The memory fusion task is evaluated across three scenarios: with memory classification and retrieval (W-MC+R), without memory classification but with retrieval (W/o-MC+W+R), and without both classification and retrieval (W/o-MC+R). Experiment details are shown in the appendix.A.5

4.2 Memory Classification

BERT-based model provides better performance than LLMs for memory classification. As shown in Table 4, BERT demonstrates superior performance compared to other LLMs under instruction and few-shot settings. Specifically, in few-shot scenarios where an evaluation question is paired with corresponding examples for each type of memory, the performance of `gpt-3.5-turbo` declines in comparison to methods that rely solely on instruction-based classification. In summary, the BERT-base model achieves the highest weighted precision (95.96%), weighted recall (95.64%), weighted F1 score (95.74%), and accuracy (95.64%). Moreover, the high performance in memory classification reinforces confidence in the rescoring mechanism, as

	W-MC+R			W/o-MC+W-R			W/o-MC+R		
	MAP	**Corr.**	**Coh.**	**MAP**	**Corr.**	**Coh.**	**MAP**	**Corr.**	**Coh.**
ChatGLM2	0.688	0.483	0.963	0.688	0.481	0.962	0.128	0.054	0.960
ChatGLM3	0.704	0.517	0.971	0.695	0.517	0.969	0.130	0.060	0.962
Qwen-7B	0.729	0.535	0.960	0.720	0.532	0.959	0.131	0.057	0.957
Baichuan2-7B	0.736	0.535	0.966	0.728	0.522	0.968	0.132	0.051	0.953
gpt-3.5-turbo	0.756	0.573	0.969	0.745	0.562	0.969	0.156	0.088	0.961

Table 3: Comparison of MAP, Correctness (Corr.), Coherency (Coh.) across three settings: With memory classification and retrieval (W-MC+R), without memory classification but with retrieval (W/o-MC+W-R), and without memory classification and without retrieval (W/o-MC+R).

Models	P	R	F1	Acc
ChatGLM2-6B	0.749	0.712	0.729	0.712
ChatGLM3-6B	0.864	0.485	0.538	0.485
Qwen-7B	0.730	0.631	0.673	0.631
Baichuan2-7B	0.848	0.602	0.657	0.602
gpt-3.5-turbo	0.868	0.668	0.715	0.668
F+ChatGLM2-6B	0.770	0.806	0.785	0.806
F+ChatGLM3-6B	0.778	0.445	0.508	0.445
F+Qwen-7B	0.804	0.402	0.452	0.402
F+Baichuan2-7B	0.860	0.324	0.337	0.324
F+gpt-3.5-turbo	0.864	0.511	0.566	0.511
P+BERT-base	0.720	0.849	0.779	0.849
BERT-base	**0.960**	**0.956**	**0.957**	**0.956**

Table 4: Comparative performance of five LLMs and BERT in memory classification tasks under few-shot settings (F) and prompt-based training (P).

RM	R@1	R@2	R@3	R@5	T(s)
Contriever	0.486	0.674	0.737	0.792	0.070
DPR	0.602	0.803	0.862	**0.919**	2.960
BM25	**0.705**	**0.847**	**0.871**	0.895	**0.030**

Table 5: Performance of Recall@K (R@K) and average retrieval time (T) in memory retrieval using Contriever, BM25, and DPR models.

illustrated in Figure 3.

4.3 Memory Retrieval

Different retrieval models show variable Recall@K and time performance. In the memory retrieval task, Table 5 reveals that the unsupervised retrieval model Contriever significantly lags behind the statistic-based BM25 and the supervised DPR model. Moreover, as the top k values increase, DPR notably improves Recall@K performance, surpassing BM25 after k equals 3. However, the retrieval time cost of DPR is substantially higher than BM25 retrieval. This suggests that we need to balance the retrieval performance and time cost when deployment in dialogue QA tasks.

Models	NR		IR		CR	
	MAP	Corr.	MAP	Corr	MAP	Corr.
Baichuan2-7B	0.132	0.051	0.396	0.225	0.782	0.581
Qwen-7B	0.131	0.057	0.390	0.221	0.786	0.574
ChatGLM2	0.128	0.054	0.396	0.248	0.738	0.523
ChatGLM3	0.130	0.060	0.365	0.216	0.754	0.561
ChatGPT	0.156	0.088	0.375	0.252	0.842	0.609

Table 6: Performance of LLMs on MAP and Correctness (Corr.) under No Retrieval (NR), Incorrect Retrieval (IR) and correct retrieval (CR) settings.

4.4 Memory Fusion

Memory classification and retrieval significantly improve LLMs to integrate memory into responses. The results in Table 3 indicate LLMs enhanced with memory classification and retrieval models significantly improve the generation of personally consistent responses, with notable increases in precision (MAP peaking at 0.756) and correctness (up to 0.573). Without memory classification, robust scores decrease (MAP 0.688-0.745), underscoring the vital role of memory classification. Coherency remains consistently high across configurations, never falling below 0.953, highlighting the ability of LLMs to produce coherent text. Additionally, smaller-scale LLMs can achieve performance similar to ChatGPT, demonstrating that even less complex models can be optimized to deliver comparable output quality.

5 Analysis and Case Study

5.1 Ablation Study

Correct memory retrieval significantly enhances the accuracy of responses across various LLMs. The experimental results, as shown in Table 6, demonstrate the consistent ability of different LLMs to generate accurate memory based responses. This consistency underscores that LLMs experience a substantial improvement when they have access to accurate external memory. The find-

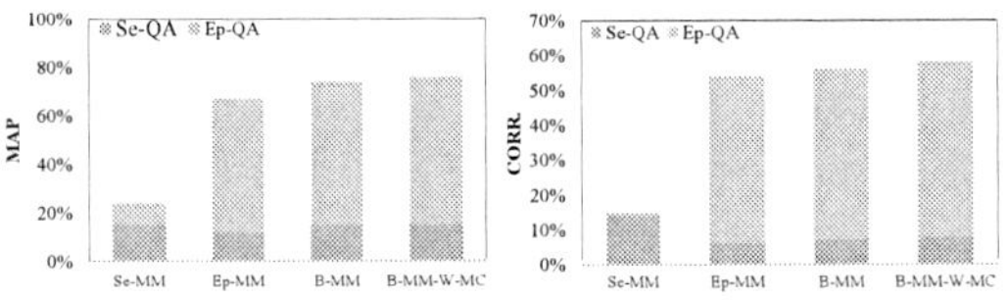

Figure 4: Evaluation results by memory type in Corr. and MAP metrics with different external memory configurations: Semantic Memory Only (Se-MM), Episodic Memory Only (Ep-MM), and Both (B-MM), Both with memory classifier (B-MM-W-MC).

ings further indicate that LLMs possess a degree of tolerance towards misinformation and are capable of leveraging accurate memory information to some extent. Despite incorrect memory retrieval, all models manage to sustain a reasonable degree of precision, with MAP scores from 0.365 to 0.396, underlining their robustness in less-than-ideal information conditions.

Episodic and semantic memories enhance each other and improve memory fusion performance. As shown in Figure 4, the results demonstrate that lacking any memory type significantly compromises the evaluation performance. Notably, even with only one memory type present like semantic memory, the system could still correctly address some questions related to the missing episodic memory, suggesting possible mutual enhancement between memory types. However, while including all memory types improves overall correctness and MAP, performance for individual memory types decreases compared to when only one memory type is used. This indicates that mixing memory types introduces additional noise, a prevalent issue with mixed interference. Compared to the mix retrieval, our soft classification mechanism improve performance for both memory types, emphasizing the importance of distinguishing memory features for better integration.

5.2 Case Study

We present specific cases in Figure 5 to evaluate the question *'What is Wang Wei's occupation?'* with the verifiable answer *'cameraman'*. Without memory retrieval, *gpt-3.5-turbo* generates a speculative response *'Wang Wei is a teacher'*, a common hallucination in most LLMs, or provides context-less responses. Introducing memory retrieval, we observe two cases. In case 2, the model response *'Wang Wei is an actor'* based on the dialogues retrieved. Despite higher accuracy due to analogous character experiences, case 2 still provides an incorrect answer. The key difference between cases 2 and 3 is the memory classification mechanism. While case 2 retrieves relevant dialogues, it fails to retrieve essential semantic memory as in case 3. With memory classification, our models retrieve accurate social relationship memory, yielding correct responses. In this evaluation, with *'cameraman'* as the memory anchor, only case 3 correctly incorporates the pertinent memory.

Question: What is Wang Wei's occupation?
Ground Truth Answer: Wang Wei is a cameraman.
Memory Anchor : cameraman

NR (W/o-MC+R) #case 1

R-1: Wang Wei is a teacher.
Memory Anchor Score: 0/1

IR (W/o-MC+WR) #case 2

Retrieved Memory:
AI Assistant: I heard that your cooperation with Wang Wei in the movie was very successful and received high praise. (episodic memory)
R-2 : Wang Wei is an actor.
Memory Anchor Score: 0/1

CR (W-MC+R) #case 3

Retrieved Memory: Wang Wei is a colleague of Xu Jia's film production company. He is 30 years old and a cameraman. They often work together on movies and TV series and have a very good rapport. Xu Jia and Wang Wei are colleagues. (semantic memory)
R-3 : Wang Wei is a cameraman.
Memory Anchor Score: 1/1

Figure 5: Comparative analysis of response performance without retrieval (NR), incorrect retrieval (IR), and Correct Retrieval (CR).

6 Conclusion

Our study introduces the PerLTQA dataset, which includes a memory database and memory-based question-answer pairs, covering personal long-term memory such as profiles, social relationships, events, and dialogues, categorized into semantic and episodic types. We outline three subtasks—memory classification, retrieval, and fusion—and report baseline experiments involving five large language models (LLMs) and three retrievers. Our findings indicate that Bert-based classifiers excel at categorizing memory types compared to other LLMs. Additionally, we observe significant variances among LLMs in producing accurate memory-based responses. We also discover that enhancing personalization and consistency in responses requires integrating the unique characteristics of various memory types with those of different retrieval models. Future research should focus on refining retrieval models to better manage complex memory structures and on minimizing irrelevant noise in the context, thus improving the quality of responses generated by LLMs.

Limitations

In this work, we utilize `gpt-3.5-turbo` to generate a memory-based dataset and evaluate its ability to generate responses based on memory in three distinct subtasks. However, we acknowledge the following limitations:

1. The process of generating memory data in the PerLTQA memory database could be varied. We have only implemented a step-by-step generation method based on memory types. Furthermore, the prompts used during the generation process still have room for optimization.

2. This dataset may exhibit certain biases, which are evident in several key aspects. Firstly, the range of names and nationalities included in the dataset is relatively limited, which may lead to potential discrepancies between the generated character events and the actual era, cultural background, and professional experiences of the characters. Secondly, due to the step-by-step generation process and the use of relatively uniform prompts, the diversity of the generated data remains constrained. Consequently, these biases make the dataset more suited for simulating personal narratives and science fiction scenarios, rather than accurately reflecting real-life situations. When utilizing this dataset, it is important to consider these limitations to avoid misinterpretations or inappropriate applications.

3. Our evaluations are limited to four open-source LLMs that are less than 10B in size and ChatGPT. We do not evaluate other LLMs of varying scales and types.

4. For the evaluation of the correctness and coherence of response generation, we adopted the evaluation methods of LLMs. However, this metric may still have uncertainties in accurately measuring the quality of responses.

Ethics Statement

The work presented in this paper introduces the PerLTQA dataset, which is generated from ChatGPT (`gpt-3.5-turbo`). This dataset does not violate any licenses or policies, nor does it infringe on privacy. The dataset can be utilized for academic exploration in memory-based QA, dialogue, and other related fields. To ensure the quality of the data, we have employed three researchers in the field of natural language who are proficient in both Chinese and English and possess excellent communication skills. Each researcher is paid $20 per hour (above the average local payment of similar jobs). The design, annotation, and review of the entire dataset took four months, costing approximately an average of about 200 hours per annotator. The annotators have no affiliation with any of the companies that are used as targets in the dataset, eliminating any potential bias due to conflict of interest.

Acknowledgement

Thanks for the reviewers for their valuable suggestions. This research work is partially supported by CUHK direct grant No. 4055209 and CUHK Knowledge Transfer Project Fund No. KPF23GWP20. We also wish to acknowledge the supports provided and contributions made by Huawei Noah's Ark Lab, Hong Kong, China.

References

Jinze Bai, Shuai Bai, and et al. 2023. Qwen technical report.

Tom Brown, Benjamin Mann, Nick Ryder, Melanie Subbiah, Jared D Kaplan, Prafulla Dhariwal, Arvind Neelakantan, Pranav Shyam, Girish Sastry, Amanda Askell, et al. 2020. Language models are few-shot learners. *Advances in neural information processing systems*, 33:1877–1901.

Paweł Budzianowski, Tsung-Hsien Wen, Bo-Hsiang Tseng, Inigo Casanueva, Stefan Ultes, Osman Ramadan, and Milica Gašić. 2018. Multiwoz–a large-scale multi-domain wizard-of-oz dataset for task-oriented dialogue modelling. *arXiv preprint arXiv:1810.00278*.

Wenhu Chen, Hanwen Zha, Zhiyu Chen, Wenhan Xiong, Hong Wang, and William Wang. 2020. Hybridqa: A dataset of multi-hop question answering over tabular and textual data. *arXiv preprint arXiv:2004.07347*.

Yulong Chen, Yang Liu, and Yue Zhang. 2021. Dialogsum challenge: Summarizing real-life scenario dialogues. In *Proceedings of the 14th International Conference on Natural Language Generation*, pages 308–313.

Michael W Eysenck and Mark T Keane. 2020. *Cognitive psychology: A student's handbook*. Psychology press.

Karthik Gopalakrishnan, Behnam Hedayatnia, Qinlang Chen, Anna Gottardi, Sanjeev Kwatra, Anu Venkatesh, Raefer Gabriel, and Dilek Hakkani-Tur. 2023. Topical-chat: Towards knowledge-grounded open-domain conversations. *arXiv preprint arXiv:2308.11995*.

Chenxu Hu, Jie Fu, Chenzhuang Du, Simian Luo, Junbo Zhao, and Hang Zhao. 2020. Chatdb: Augmenting llms with databases as their symbolic memory. *arXiv preprint arXiv:2306.03901*.

Gautier Izacard, Mathilde Caron, Lucas Hosseini, Sebastian Riedel, Piotr Bojanowski, Armand Joulin, and Edouard Grave. 2021. Unsupervised dense information retrieval with contrastive learning. *arXiv preprint arXiv:2112.09118*.

Jihyoung Jang, Minseong Boo, and Hyounghun Kim. 2023. Conversation chronicles: Towards diverse temporal and relational dynamics in multi-session conversations. *arXiv preprint arXiv:2310.13420*.

Albert Q Jiang, Alexandre Sablayrolles, Arthur Mensch, Chris Bamford, Devendra Singh Chaplot, Diego de las Casas, Florian Bressand, Gianna Lengyel, Guillaume Lample, Lucile Saulnier, et al. 2023. Mistral 7b. *arXiv preprint arXiv:2310.06825*.

Vladimir Karpukhin, Barlas Oğuz, Sewon Min, Patrick Lewis, Ledell Wu, Sergey Edunov, Danqi Chen, and Wen-tau Yih. 2020. Dense passage retrieval for open-domain question answering. *arXiv preprint arXiv:2004.04906*.

Tom Kwiatkowski, Jennimaria Palomaki, Olivia Redfield, Michael Collins, Ankur Parikh, Chris Alberti, Danielle Epstein, Illia Polosukhin, Jacob Devlin, Kenton Lee, et al. 2019. Natural questions: a benchmark for question answering research. *Transactions of the Association for Computational Linguistics*, 7:453–466.

Gibbeum Lee, Volker Hartmann, Jongho Park, Dimitris Papailiopoulos, and Kangwook Lee. 2023. Prompted LLMs as Chatbot Modules for Long Open-domain Conversation. In *Findings of the Association for Computational Linguistics: ACL 2023*, pages 4536–4554. ArXiv:2305.04533 [cs].

Jiazheng Li, Runcong Zhao, Yongxin Yang, Yulan He, and Lin Gui. 2023. Overprompt: Enhancing chatgpt through efficient in-context learning. *arXiv preprint arXiv:2305.14973*.

Yanran Li, Hui Su, Xiaoyu Shen, Wenjie Li, Ziqiang Cao, and Shuzi Niu. 2017. Dailydialog: A manually labelled multi-turn dialogue dataset. *arXiv preprint arXiv:1710.03957*.

Adyasha Maharana, Dong-Ho Lee, Sergey Tulyakov, Mohit Bansal, Francesco Barbieri, and Yuwei Fang. 2024. Evaluating very long-term conversational memory of llm agents. *arXiv preprint arXiv:2402.17753*.

Christopher D Manning, Prabhakar Raghavan, and Hinrich Schütze. 2008. *Introduction to information retrieval*. Cambridge university press.

Kai Nakamura, Sharon Levy, Yi-Lin Tuan, Wenhu Chen, and William Yang Wang. 2022. Hybridialogue: An information-seeking dialogue dataset grounded on tabular and textual data. *arXiv preprint arXiv:2204.13243*.

Charles Packer, Vivian Fang, Shishir G Patil, Kevin Lin, Sarah Wooders, and Joseph E Gonzalez. 2023. Memgpt: Towards llms as operating systems. *arXiv preprint arXiv:2310.08560*.

Siva Reddy, Danqi Chen, and Christopher D Manning. 2019. Coqa: A conversational question answering challenge. *Transactions of the Association for Computational Linguistics*, 7:249–266.

Stephen E Robertson, Steve Walker, Susan Jones, Micheline M Hancock-Beaulieu, Mike Gatford, et al. 1995. Okapi at trec-3. *Nist Special Publication Sp*, 109:109.

Weijia Shi, Sewon Min, Michihiro Yasunaga, Minjoon Seo, Rich James, Mike Lewis, Luke Zettlemoyer, and Wen-tau Yih. 2023. Replug: Retrieval-augmented black-box language models. *arXiv preprint arXiv:2301.12652*.

Joe Stacey, Jianpeng Cheng, John Torr, Tristan Guigue, Joris Driesen, Alexandru Coca, Mark Gaynor, and Anders Johannsen. 2024. Lucid: Llm-generated utterances for complex and interesting dialogues. *arXiv preprint arXiv:2403.00462*.

Hugo Touvron, Louis Martin, Kevin Stone, Peter Albert, Amjad Almahairi, Yasmine Babaei, Nikolay Bashlykov, Soumya Batra, Prajjwal Bhargava, Shruti Bhosale, Dan Bikel, Lukas Blecher, Cristian Canton Ferrer, Moya Chen, Guillem Cucurull, David Esiobu, Jude Fernandes, Jeremy Fu, Wenyin Fu, Brian Fuller, Cynthia Gao, Vedanuj Goswami, Naman Goyal, Anthony Hartshorn, Saghar Hosseini, Rui Hou, Hakan Inan, Marcin Kardas, Viktor Kerkez, Madian Khabsa, Isabel Kloumann, Artem Korenev, Punit Singh Koura, Marie-Anne Lachaux, Thibaut Lavril, Jenya Lee, Diana Liskovich, Yinghai Lu, Yuning Mao, Xavier Martinet, Todor Mihaylov, Pushkar Mishra, Igor Molybog, Yixin Nie, Andrew Poulton, Jeremy Reizenstein, Rashi Rungta, Kalyan Saladi, Alan Schelten, Ruan Silva, Eric Michael Smith, Ranjan Subramanian, Xiaoqing Ellen Tan, Binh Tang, Ross Taylor, Adina Williams, Jian Xiang Kuan, Puxin Xu, Zheng Yan, Iliyan Zarov, Yuchen Zhang, Angela Fan, Melanie Kambadur, Sharan Narang, Aurelien Rodriguez, Robert Stojnic, Sergey Edunov, and Thomas Scialom. 2023. Llama 2: Open foundation and fine-tuned chat models.

Hongru Wang, Minda Hu, Yang Deng, Rui Wang, Fei Mi, Weichao Wang, Yasheng Wang, Wai-Chung Kwan, Irwin King, and Kam-Fai Wong. 2023a. Large language models as source planner for personalized knowledge-grounded dialogue.

Hongru Wang, Lingzhi Wang, Yiming Du, Liang Chen, Jingyan Zhou, Yufei Wang, and Kam-Fai Wong. 2023b. A survey of the evolution of language model-based dialogue systems. *arXiv preprint arXiv:2311.16789*.

Jing Xu, Arthur Szlam, and Jason Weston. 2021a. Beyond goldfish memory: Long-term open-domain conversation. *arXiv preprint arXiv:2107.07567*.

Jing Xu, Arthur Szlam, and Jason Weston. 2021b. Beyond Goldfish Memory: Long-Term Open-Domain Conversation. ArXiv:2107.07567 [cs].

Ming Xu. 2023. Text2vec: Text to vector toolkit. https://github.com/shibing624/text2vec.

Xinchao Xu, Zhibin Gou, Wenquan Wu, Zheng-Yu Niu, Hua Wu, Haifeng Wang, and Shihang Wang. 2022. Long time no see! open-domain conversation with long-term persona memory. *arXiv preprint arXiv:2203.05797.*

Aiyuan Yang, Bin Xiao, Bingning Wang, Borong Zhang, Chao Yin, Chenxu Lv, Da Pan, Dian Wang, Dong Yan, Fan Yang, et al. 2023. Baichuan 2: Open large-scale language models. *arXiv preprint arXiv:2309.10305.*

Jing Zhang, Xiaokang Zhang, Daniel Zhang-Li, Jifan Yu, Zijun Yao, Zeyao Ma, Yiqi Xu, Haohua Wang, Xiaohan Zhang, Nianyi Lin, et al. 2023a. Glm-dialog: Noise-tolerant pre-training for knowledge-grounded dialogue generation. *arXiv preprint arXiv:2302.14401.*

Kai Zhang, Fubang Zhao, Yangyang Kang, and Xiaozhong Liu. 2023b. Memory-augmented llm personalization with short-and long-term memory coordination. *arXiv preprint arXiv:2309.11696.*

Pan Zhang, Xiaoyi Dong Bin Wang, Yuhang Cao, Chao Xu, Linke Ouyang, Zhiyuan Zhao, Shuangrui Ding, Songyang Zhang, Haodong Duan, Hang Yan, et al. 2023c. Internlm-xcomposer: A vision-language large model for advanced text-image comprehension and composition. *arXiv preprint arXiv:2309.15112.*

Saizheng Zhang, Emily Dinan, Jack Urbanek, Arthur Szlam, Douwe Kiela, and Jason Weston. 2018. Personalizing dialogue agents: I have a dog, do you have pets too? *arXiv preprint arXiv:1801.07243.*

Kang Zhao, Wei Liu, Jian Luan, Minglei Gao, Li Qian, Hanlin Teng, and Bin Wang. 2023. UniMC: A Unified Framework for Long-Term Memory Conversation via Relevance Representation Learning. ArXiv:2306.10543 [cs].

Yinhe Zheng, Guanyi Chen, Minlie Huang, Song Liu, and Xuan Zhu. 2019. Personalized dialogue generation with diversified traits. *arXiv preprint arXiv:1901.09672.*

Wanjun Zhong, Lianghong Guo, Qiqi Gao, He Ye, and Yanlin Wang. 2024. Memorybank: Enhancing large language models with long-term memory. In *Proceedings of the AAAI Conference on Artificial Intelligence*, volume 38, pages 19724–19731.

Qinglin Zhu, Runcong Zhao, Jinhua Du, Lin Gui, and Yulan He. 2024. Player*: Enhancing llm-based multi-agent communication and interaction in murder mystery games. *arXiv preprint arXiv:2404.17662.*

A Appendix

A.1 Memory Database Generation Prompts

The design of the PerLT memory dataset prompts are illustrated in Figure 7. The "Profile Generation" prompt creates character profiles using specified seed data and a prompt template. Following this, the "SR (Social Relationship) Generator" prompt produces social relationships based on ten provided seed relationships. Additionally, the "EVT (Event) Generator" prompt is employed to create events that align with the established social relationships between characters. Lastly, the "DLG (Dialogue) Generator" prompt facilitates the generation of event-based dialogues between a character and an AI assistant. Collectively, these prompts enable our model to generate raw memory data effectively.

Profile Generation Prompt

Please help me create a random profile for the above user? Include the following details: [name], gender, nickname, title, age, [occupation], nationality, physical features, [hobbies], achievements, ethnic background, [educational background], occupation, employer, awards and role models?

ISR Generation Prompt

Relationships between individuals include family, friends, romantic partners, acquaintances, colleagues, mentors/mentees, neighbors, community members, and strangers. Based on **[profile description],** can you help me randomly create relationships for **[name]** and provide their names? The answer should be in the JSON format like {relationship: {name:, description}})

EVT Generation Prompt

Given **[profile description]**, please integrate **[relationship description]**, and the relationship between **[name]** and **[s_name]** is **[relationship]**. Generate episodic memories related to the events with **[name]** and **[s_name]** , as much as possible while retaining the entity names. **[topic cases])** The generated response should conform to the following JSON format: {date | topic | supporting character name | relationship | event | detailed description}

DLG Generation Prompt

Please integrate **[episodic memory]** to generate a multi-turn, temporally related dialogue between **[name]** and the AI assistant. Requirements: Please note that the speakers are the AI assistant and [**name]** . Please use the appropriate titles. The dialogue should include entities such as time, characters, locations, and specific plot details. Please generate the JSON response in the following format:\n[{\"date\":,\"dialogue\":[[**name]** :, AI Assistant:, ...]}]

Figure 6: Prompts for PRO, SR, EVT, and DLG memory generator.

A.2 Memory QA items Generation Prompts

The design of the PerLT QA generation prompts are illustrated in Figure 6. The "Question and Answer Generation" prompt is designed to create questions and answers based on a provided reference memory and character name. Additionally, the "Memory Anchor Candidates Searching" prompt is utilized to identify key fragments that are crucial for crafting questions. These fragments are specifically chosen because they are present both in the generated answer and in the reference answer, ensuring relevance and coherence.

Question and Answering Generation Prompt
Based on the provided memory information, construct question-answer pairs and return them as a JSON array [{Q, A}], where Q and A are the keys that represent question and answering respectively.
Memory Anchor Candidates Searching Prompt
Based on the provided question-and-answer pair, identify the correct key answer word(s) from the response. Here is the given example: **Question**: When Zhou Ting's family was planning their summer vacation, who took the initiative to help arrange the itinerary? **Answer**: Zhang Tao took the initiative to help with the planning. **Memory Anchor Candidates**: ["Zhang Tao"] **Question**: [question] **Answer**: [answer] **Memory Anchor Candidates**:

Figure 7: Prompts for question answering generation, and memory anchor candidate searching.

A.3 Dataset Generation Error Types

In the dataset generation process for PerLT Memory and PerLT QA, several categories of errors are identified and corrected as shown in Table 7. Anomalies, such as missing information in profiles, are rectified by removing or emptying the faulty fields. Incorrect character relationships that do not provide sufficient event data are excluded from the dataset. Instances of brief event narratives without detailed information are eliminated. Referent errors, which include incorrect or ambiguous references, are replaced with accurate information to ensure clarity. Redundant answers are streamlined to avoid unnecessary repetition, ensuring concise and relevant data. Finally, blurred memory anchor boundaries are corrected to precisely reflect the intended memory cues. These steps are taken to enhance the accuracy and reliability of the dataset.

A.4 Optimizing Memory Retrieval with Memory Classification Re-Ranking

We devise a method in which the output probabilities of the classification model are utilized to furnish the retrieval model with classification insights, allowing for the re-ranking of candidate memories. This strategy minimizes the risks associated with memory retrieval based on specific memory bank classification results. Such risks primarily stem from potential classification inaccuracies that could lead to memory retrieval from an incorrect memory type, thereby unduly influencing the reliance on classification model precision within the framework. The introduction of a re-ranking strategy ensures the retrieval of a predefined number of memories across all memory types, regardless of the initial confidence levels of classification results. This is achieved through a weighted score re-ranking mechanism that effectively reduces the influence of classification inaccuracies on the ultimate ranking. For those instances with high classification confidence, revising their scores and reordering them accentuates their relevance, thereby optimizing the retrieval process.

Answer Generation Prompt:
Please answer the following question based on the provided memory information, ignoring any irrelevant memories. Keep the response under fifty words. **Memory Information**: [memories] **Question**: [question] **Answer**:

Figure 8: Prompts for answer generation.

A.5 Experiment Settings

Memory Classification settings. We conduct binary-class classification experiments on semantic memory, and episodic memory using BERT, Baichuan, ChatGLM2, ChatGLM3, and ChatGPT. For BERT, we employ fine-tuning with the evaluation questions to predict the memory type. For LLMs, we use instructions to guide LLMs in predicting the memory type. We also conduct instruction augmentation BERT experiments. Specifically, we train BERT-base classification models with 7,516 QA pairs. We finally evaluate the performance of memory type classification on a test set of 1,719 evaluation questions.

Memory Retrieval settings. We create unique memory banks for each character. In the case of DPR, we train the DPR model using 7516 evaluation questions. Contriever uses the text2vec model (Xu, 2023) from Hugging Face to calculate the similarity between memory sentences and questions.

Memory Fusion settings. In the W-MC+R setting, responses are generated using retrieved memories that are post-ranked based on memory classification outcomes. Conversely, in the W/o-MC+W+R scenario, responses are produced solely through memory retrieval, without the aid of memory classification for re-ranking. Meanwhile, in the W/o-MC+R framework, responses are generated directly without utilizing any external memory, relying solely on the inherent knowledge in LLMs. These configurations not only validate the effectiveness of each component but also underscore the importance of external memory. Due to limited re-

Error Type	Source	Error Example	Operation	Revision
Anomalies in profiles	PerLT Memory	{hobbies: "Not Provided"}	Remove	{hobbies: ""}
Invalid character relationship	PerLT Memory	Zheng Yong has a wife and girlfriend at the same time.	Remove	Remove the relationship wife or girlfriend which not provide enough events data.
Brief event narratives	PerLT Memory	Xiaoming's father used to participate in the activities.	Remove	-
Referent error	PerLT QA	When will Wang Xiaoming and the AI assistant plan to visit the exhibition?	Replace	When will Wang Xiaoming and Wang Xiaohong plan to visit the exhibition?
Redundant answer	PerLT QA	Who is the mentor of Wangxiaoming? Wangxiaoming's mentor is Zhangwen.	Reduce	Zhangwen.
Blurred Memory anchor boundaries	PerLT QA	Answer: They met at Bali Memory Anchor:["At Bali"]	Correct	Answer: They met at Bali Memory Anchor:["Bali"]

Table 7: The error types observed in PerLT Memory and QA items generation and revision by human.

sources, we only evaluated LLMs with fewer than 10 billion parameters. These models are prompted by retrieved memories. To ensure smooth operation on an Nvidia-3090 GPU with 24GB of memory, we have implemented a semi-precision inference setting.

Overview of the SIGHAN 2024 Shared Task for Chinese Dimensional Aspect-Based Sentiment Analysis

Lung-Hao Lee[1], Liang-Chih Yu[2], Suge Wang[3,4], and Jian Liao[3]
[1]Institute of Artificial Intelligence Innovation, National Yang Ming Chiao Tung University
[2]Department of Information Management, Yuan Ze University
[3]School of Computer and Information Technology, Shanxi University, Taiyuan, China
[4]Key Laboratory of Computational Intelligence and Chinese Information Processing of Ministry of Education, Shanxi University, Taiyuan, China
lhlee@nycu.edu.tw, lcyu@saturn.yzu.edu.tw, {wsg, liaoj}@sxu.edu.cn

Abstract

This paper describes the SIGHAN-2024 shared task for Chinese dimensional aspect-based sentiment analysis (ABSA), including task description, data preparation, performance metrics, and evaluation results. Compared to representing affective states as several discrete classes (i.e., *sentiment polarity*), the dimensional approach represents affective states as continuous numerical values (called *sentiment intensity*) in the valence-arousal space, providing more fine-grained affective states. Therefore, we organized a dimensional ABSA (shorted dimABSA) shared task, comprising three subtasks: 1) intensity prediction, 2) triplet extraction, and 3) quadruple extraction, receiving a total of 214 submissions from 61 registered participants during evaluation phase. A total of eleven teams provided selected submissions for each subtask and seven teams submitted technical reports for the subtasks. This shared task demonstrates current NLP techniques for dealing with Chinese dimensional ABSA. All data sets with gold standards and evaluation scripts used in this shared task are publicly available for future research.

1 Introduction

Aspect-Based Sentiment Analysis (ABSA) (Pontiki et al., 2014; 2015; 2016) is a critical NLP research topic that aims to identify the aspects of a given entity and analyze the sentiment polarity associated with each aspect. In recent years, considerable research has been devoted to ABSA, which can be categorized into different tasks based on the number of sentiment elements to be extracted. For example, the Aspect Sentiment Triplet Extraction (ASTE) task (Yuan et al., 2023; Chen et al., 2021; Mao et al., 2021; Peng et al., 2020; Wu et al., 2020; Xu et al., 2020; Zhang et al., 2020) extracts three elements in a triplet, including aspect/target term, opinion term and sentiment polarity (e.g., positive, neutral, and negative). Furthermore, the Aspect Sentiment Quadruple Prediction (ASQP) task (Cai et al., 2021; Gao et al., 2022; Mao et al., 2022; Peper and Wang, 2022; Zhang et al., 2021; Zhou et al., 2023) extracts the same three elements plus an additional aspect category to construct a quadruple.

However, compared to representing affective states as several discrete classes (i.e., *sentiment polarity*), the dimensional approach that represents affective states as continuous numerical values (called *sentiment intensity*) in multiple dimensions such as valence-arousal (VA) space (Russel, 1980), providing more fine-grained emotional information (Lee et al., 2022; Deng et al., 2022; 2023; Yu et al., 2016).

Therefore, we organized a Chinese dimensional ABSA shared task (dimABSA) in the 10th SIGHAN Workshop on Chinese Language Processing (SIGHAN 2024), providing fine-grained sentiment intensity prediction for each extracted aspect of a restaurant review. We have three subtasks: 1) Intensity Prediction, 2) Triplet Extraction, and 3) Quadruple Extraction. Participants are free to participate in any or all subtasks. Given a sentence with/without aspects, participating systems should be able to extract the

Proceedings of the 10th SIGHAN Workshop on Chinese Language Processing (SIGHAN-10), pages 165–174

Example	Version	Input & Output
Example 1 (subtask 1)	Traditional	Input: E0001:S001, 檸檬醬也不會太油，塔皮對我而言稍軟。, 檸檬醬#塔皮 Output: E0001:S001 (檸檬醬,5.67#5.50)(塔皮,4.83#5.00)
	Simplified	Input: E0001:S001, 柠檬酱也不会太油，塔皮对我而言稍软。 柠檬酱#塔皮 Output: E0001:S001 (柠檬酱,5.67#5.50)(塔皮,4.83#5.00)
Example 2 (subtask 2)	Traditional	Input: E0002:S002, 不僅餐點美味上菜速度也是飛快耶！！ Output: E0002:S002 (餐點, 美味, 6.63#4.63) (上菜速度, 飛快, 7.25#6.00)
	Simplified	Input: E0002:S002, 不仅餐点美味上菜速度也是飞快耶!! Output: E0002:S002 (餐点, 美味, 6.63#4.63) (上菜速度, 飞快, 7.25#6.00)
Example 3 (subtask 3)	Traditional	Input: E0003:S003, 這碗拉麵超級無敵霹靂難吃 Output: E0003:S003 (拉麵, 食物#品質, 超級無敵霹靂難吃, 2.00#7.88)
	Simplified	Input: E0003:S003, 这碗拉面超级无敌霹雳难吃 Output: E0003:S003 (拉面, 食物#品质, 超级无敌霹雳难吃, 2.00#7.88)

Table 1: Examples of the dimABSA task

sentiment elements with the corresponding valence-arousal rating values.

The rest of this article is organized as follows. Section 2 provides a description of the Chinese dimensional ABSA shared task. Section 3 introduces the evaluation data construction. Section 4 describes the performance metrics. Section 5 compares evaluation results from the various participating teams. Finally, we conclude this paper with findings and offer future research directions in Section 6.

2 Task Organization

This task aims to evaluate the capability of an automatic system for Chinese dimensional ABSA. The four sentiment elements are defined as follows:

- **Aspect Term** (shorted as **A**):

This denotes an entity indicating the opinion target. If the aspect is omitted without being mentioned clearly, we use "NULL" to represent the term.

- **Aspect Category (C)**

This represents a predefined category for the explicit aspect of the restaurant domain. We use the same categories defined in the SemEval-2016 Restaurant dataset (Pontiki et al., 2016). There are a total of twelve categories; each can be split into an entity and attribute using the symbol "#" as follows: 1) "餐廳#概括" / "餐厅#概括" (restaurant#general); 2) "餐廳#價格" / "餐厅#价格" (restaurant#prices); 3) "餐廳#雜項" / "餐厅#杂项" (restaurant#miscellaneous); 4) "食物#價格" / 食物#价格 (food#prices); 5) "食物#品質" / "食物#品质" (food#quality); 6) "食物#份量與款式" / "食物#份量与款式" (food#style&options); 7) "飲料#價格" / "饮料#价格" (drinks#prices); 8) "飲料#品質" / "饮料#品质" (drinks#quality); 9) "飲料#份量與款式" / "饮料#份量与款式" (drinks#style&options); 10) "氛圍#概括" / "氛围#概括" (ambience#general); 11) "服務#概括" / "服务#概括" (services#general); and 12) "地點#概括" / "地点#概括" (location#general).

- **Opinion Term (O)**

This describes the sentiment words or phrases towards the aspects.

- **Sentiment Intensity (I)**

This reflects sentiments using continuous real-valued scores in the valence-arousal dimensions. The valence represents the degree of pleasant and unpleasant (i.e., positive and negative) feelings, while the arousal represents the degree of excitement and calm. Both the valence and arousal dimensions use a nine-degree scale. Value 1 on the valence and arousal dimensions respectively denotes extremely high-negative and low-arousal sentiment, while 9 denotes extremely high-positive and high-arousal sentiment, and 5 denotes a neutral and medium-arousal sentiment. Valence-arousal values are separated by a hashtag (symbol "#") for a mark.

This dimABSA task can be further divided into three subtasks described as follows.

- **Subtask 1: Intensity Prediction**

The first subtask focuses on predicting sentiment intensities in the valence-arousal dimensions. Given a sentence and a specific aspect, the system should predict the valence-arousal ratings. The input format consists of ID, sentence, and aspect. The output format consists of the ID and valence-arousal predicted values that are separated with a 'space'. The intensity prediction is two real-valued scores rounded to two decimal places and separated by a hashtag, each respectively denoting the valence and arousal rating. Example sentences are presented in Table 1. In Example 1, a given sentence "檸檬醬也不會太油，塔皮對我而言稍軟" (The lemon curd is not too oily and the tart crust is a little soft for me.) and two aspects "檸檬醬" (lemon curd) and "塔皮" (tart crust) as an input, participating systems are expected to respectively predict valence-arousal ratings such as 5.67#5.50 for "檸檬醬" (lemon curd) and 4.83#5.00 for "塔皮" (tart crust).

- **Subtask 2: Triplet Extraction**

The second subtask aims to extract sentiment triplets composed of three elements. Given a sentence only, the system should extract all sentiment triplets (aspect, opinion, intensity). The output format consists of the ID and sentiment triplet that are separated with a 'space'. In Example 2, the input sentence is "不僅餐點美味上菜速度也是飛快耶！！" (The meals were not only delicious but were also served very quickly!!) and the output contains two tuples: the first triple contains "餐點" (meals) as an aspect term, "美味" (delicious) as an opinion term, with valence-arousal ratings as 6.63#4.63; the second triple consists of "上菜速度" (were served) as an aspect term and "飛快" (very quickly) as an opinion term, with valence-arousal ratings as 7.25#6.00.

- **Subtask 3: Quadruple Extraction**

The third subtask aims to extract sentiment quadruples composed of four elements. Given a sentence only, the system should extract all sentiment quadruples (aspect, category, opinion, intensity). The output format consists of the ID and sentiment quadruple that are separated with a 'space'. In Example 3, if the input sentence is "這碗拉麵超級無敵霹靂難吃" (This bowl of ramen is terribly unpalatable.), the expected quadruple includes "拉麵" (ramen) denoted as the aspect which belongs to an aspect category "食物#品質" (food#quality), along with an opinion term "超級無敵霹靂難吃" (terribly unpalatable) and a sentiment intensity value in terms of valence-arousal ratings of 2.00#7.88

3 Data Preparation

We first crawled restaurant reviews from Google Reviews and an online bulletin board system PTT. Then, we removed all HTML tags and multimedia material and split the remaining texts into several sentences. Finally, we randomly selected partial sentences to retain content diversity for manual annotation.

The annotation process was conducted in two phases. We first annotated the aspect/category/opinion elements and then V#A element. In the first phase, three graduate students majoring in computer science were trained to annotate the sentences for aspect/category/opinion. One task organizer led a discussion to clarify annotation differences and seek consensus among the annotators. A majority vote mechanism was finally used to resolve any disagreements among the annotators. In the second phase, each sentence along with the annotated aspect/category/opinion was presented to five annotators majoring in Chinese language for V#A rating. Similarly, one task organizer also led a group discussion during annotation. Once the annotation process was finished, a cleanup procedure was performed to remove outlier values which did not fall within 1.5 standard deviations (SD) of the mean. These outliers were then excluded from calculating the average V#A for each instance.

We provided two versions of all datasets with identical content, but one in traditional Chinese characters and the other in simplified Chinese characters. The participating teams could choose their preferred version for the task evaluation. The submitted results were evaluated with the corresponding version of the gold standard and ranked together as the official results.

This shared task is presented as an open test, and participating systems can use other publicly available data, but such data must be specified in the final system description paper. For example, we

Restaurant (REST) Domain									
Subtask	Dataset	#Sent	#Char	#Tuple	Aspect			Opinion	
					#NULL	#Unique	#Repeat	#Unique	#Repeat
ST1	Train	6,050	85,769	8,523	169	6,430	1924	-	-
	Dev.	100	1,109	115	0	115	0	-	-
	Test	2,000	34,002	2,658	0	2,658	0	-	-
ST2 & ST3	Train	6,050	85,769	8,523	169	6,430	1,924	7,986	537
	Dev.	100	1,280	150	0	78	72	143	7
	Test	2,000	39,014	3,566	52	1,693	1,821	3263	303

Table 2: Detailed data statistics

Scatter Plots of Valence-Arousal Distributions

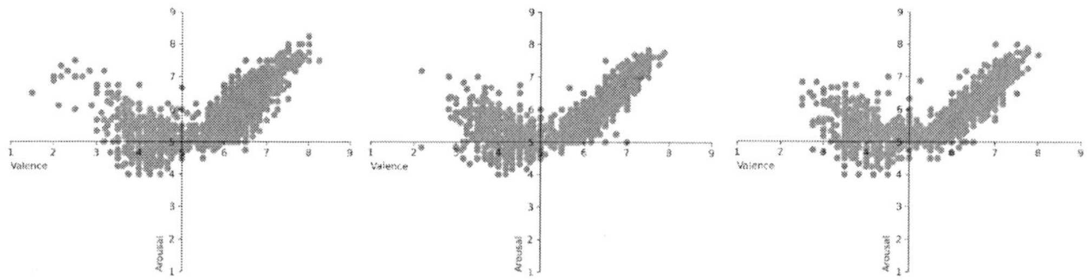

(a) Training Set for Subtasks 1, 2 and 3 (b) Test Set for Subtask 1 (C) Test Set for Subtasks 2&3

Figure 1: Scatter plots of valence-arousal distributions

also provide the Chinese EmoBank (Lee et al., 2022) as a potentially useful sentiment resource annotated with real-valued scores for both valence and arousal dimensions. This data set features various levels of text granularity including two lexicons called Chinese valence-arousal words (CVAW, 5,512 single words) and Chinese valence-arousal phrases (CVAP, 2,998 multi-word phrases), along with two corpora called Chinese valence-arousal sentences (CVAS, 2,582 single sentences) and Chinese valence-arousal texts (CVAT, 2,969 multi-sentence texts).

Table 1 presents detailed statistics for the mutually exclusive training, development and test sets, where #Sent, #Char, and #Tuple respectively denote the number of sentences, characters and tuples in the dataset. The training set provided for all three subtasks included 6,050 sentences (85,769 characters), annotated with 8,523 tuples. The development set only includes 100 sentences for output format validation. Two mutually exclusive test sets were prepared for system performance evaluation, each including 2,000 sentences. One was provided for Subtask 1 and the other was used for Subtasks 2 and 3.

We further analyzed the aspect types in the test set, including #unique and #repeat which respectively denote the number of aspects which occurred only one time or more than one time. For Subtask 1, a total of 2,658 aspects belong to the unique type, without the null and repeat cases. For Subtasks 2 and 3, 1821 aspects (51.1% out of total 3,566) occurred more than one time across all testing sentences. In addition, a very small portion (near 1.5%) of aspects belonged to the null cases. Similarly, we also analyzed the opinion terms, the repeat cases occupied about 8.5% (=303/3566). These findings revealed: 1) the aspect has a centered distribution, reflecting that users' opinion targets may be similar, and 2) the opinion has a diverse distribution, indicating that different affective words or phrases are used to express a user's feelings.

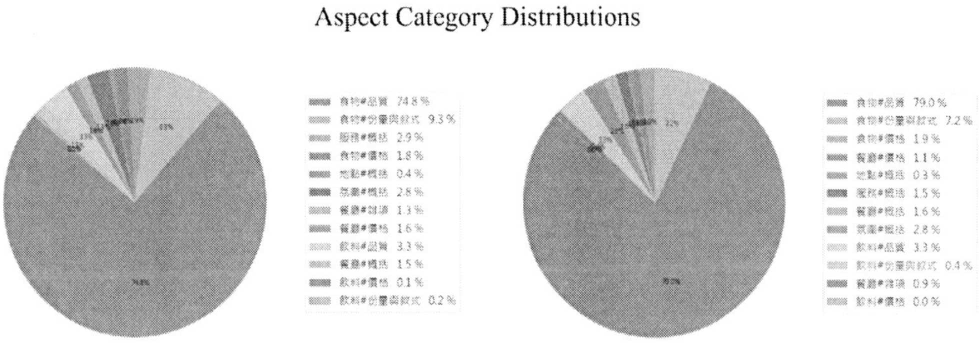

(a) Training Set for Subtasks 1, 2 and 3 (b) Test Set for Subtask 3

Figure 2: Aspect category distributions

Figure 1 shows the scatter plots of valence-arousal distributions. They presented similar curves for the training and test sets, indicating that both high-positive and high-negative opinion terms usually have high arousal values. Identical results were obtained from the Chinese EmoBank (Lee et al., 2022).

Figure 2 presents the aspect category distributions. The distributions are imbalanced for both the training and test sets for Subtask 3. This finding is the same as that for the SemEval-2016 Restaurant dataset (Pontiki et al., 2016). The most frequently occurring category was "食物#品質" (food#quality), followed by "食物#份量與款式" (food#style&options) and "飲料#品質" (drinks#quality). In the training set, these 3 categories accounted for 87.4% of the total, with the remaining 9 categories accounting for 12.6%. In the test set for Subtask 3, these 3 categories accounted for 89.5% of the total, with the other 9 categories accounting for the remaining 10.5%.

4 Performance Metrics

For Subtask 1, the sentiment intensity prediction performance is evaluated by examining the difference between machine-predicted ratings and human-annotated ratings using two metrics: Mean Absolute Error (MAE) and Pearson Correlation Coefficient (PCC), defined as the following equations.

$$\text{MAE} = \frac{1}{n}\sum_{i=1}^{n}|a_i - p_i| \tag{1}$$

$$\text{PCC} = \frac{1}{n-1}\sum_{i=1}^{n}\left(\frac{a_i-\mu_A}{\sigma_A}\right)\left(\frac{p_i-\mu_P}{\sigma_P}\right) \tag{2}$$

where $a_i \in A$ and $p_i \in P$ respectively denote the i-th actual value and predicted value, n is the number of test samples, μ_A and σ_A respectively represent the mean value and the standard deviation of A, while μ_P and σ_P respectively represent the mean value and the standard deviation of P.

Each metric for the valence and arousal dimensions is calculated and ranked independently. The actual and predicted real values should range from 1 to 9, so MAE measures the error rate in a range where the lowest value is 0 and the highest value is 8. A lower MAE indicates more accurate prediction performance. The PCC is a value between −1 and 1 that measures the linear correlation between the actual and predicted values. A lower MAE and a higher PCC indicate more accurate prediction performance.

For Subtasks 2 and 3, we use the F1-score as the evaluation metric, defined as:

$$F1 = \frac{2\text{xPxR}}{\text{P+R}} \tag{3}$$

where Precision (P) is defined as the percentage of triplets/quadruples extracted by the system that are correct. Recall (R) is the percentage of triplets/quadruples present in the test set found by the system. The F1-score is the harmonic mean of precision and recall.

Team	Subtask			Architecture		Data Augmentation
	ST1	ST2	ST3	PLM	LLM	
HITSZ-HLT	V	V	V	Erine-3.0-xbase-zg	deepseek-7B-instruct-v1.5	-
CCIIPLab	V	V	V	MacBERT-base	-	Chinese EmoBank
YNU-HPCC	V			BERT-wwm-ext	-	Merged-Train
DS-Group	V			-	GPT-4o	-
TMAK-Plus		V		-	GPT-4o	-
ZZU-NLP		V	V	BERT	Baichuan2-7B	-
JN-NLP			V		T5-base	

Subtask 3: Quadruple Extraction				
Team	Evaluation Metrics			Overall Rank
	V-Quad-F1	A-Quad-F1	VA-Quad-F1	
HITSZ-HLT	**0.567** (1)	**0.526** (1)	**0.417** (1)	**1**
CCIIPLab	0.555 (2)	0.507 (2)	0.389 (2)	2
ZZU-NLP	0.522 (3)	0.489 (3)	0.376 (3)	3
SUDA-NLP	0.487 (4)	0.444 (4)	0.336 (4)	4
JN-NLP	0.482 (5)	0.439 (5)	0.331 (5)	5
BIT-NLP	0.470 (6)	0.434 (7)	0.329 (6)	6
USTC-IAT	0.438 (7)	0.437 (6)	0.312 (7)	7

Table 6: Testing results of Subtask 3. V for valence, A for arousal, VA for valence-arousal, and Quad for quadruple. The best scores of each metric are in bold.

Each metric for the valence and arousal dimensions is calculated either independently or in combination. First, the valence and arousal values are rounded to an integer. Next, a triplet/quadruple is regarded as correct if and only if the three/four elements and their combination match those in the gold triplet/quadruple. All metrics range from 0 to 1. A higher Precision, Recall, and F1 score indicate more accurate performance.

5 Evaluation Results

5.1 System Summary

We received a total of 214 submissions from 61 registered participants during the evaluation phase. A total of eleven teams provided submissions to the leaderboard for each subtask and seven submitted their task technical papers. HITSZ-HLT (Xu et al., 2024) and CCIIPLab (Tong and Wei, 2024) participated in all three subtasks, ZZ-NLP (Zhu et al., 2024) team took part in two subtasks, and the remaining four teams only joined in one subtask.

Table 3 summarizes the participating systems, including involved subtasks, system architectures and additional data usage. HITSZ-HLT (Xu et al., 2024) integrated a BERT-based pre-trained language model (PLM) (i.e., ERNIE 3.0 (Sun et al., 2021)) and a code-style large language model (LLM) (i.e., deepseek (Guo et al., 2024)) to address this task, demonstrating promising performance in different scenarios. CCIIPLab (Tong and Wei, 2024) proposed a Contrastive Learning-enhanced Span-

Subtask 2: Triplet Extraction				
Team	Evaluation Metrics			Overall Rank
	V-Tri-F1	A-Tri-F1	VA-Tri-F1	
HITSZ-HLT	**0.589** (1)	**0.545** (1)	**0.433** (1)	**1**
CCIIPLab	0.573 (2)	0.522 (2)	0.403 (2)	2
ZZU-NLP	0.542 (3)	0.507 (3)	0.389 (3)	3
BIT-NLP	0.490 (4)	0.450 (4)	0.342 (4)	4
SUDA-NLP	0.475 (5)	0.448 (5)	0.326 (5)	5
TMAK-Plus	0.269 (6)	0.307 (6)	0.157 (6)	6

Table 5: Testing results of Subtask 2. V for valence, A for arousal, VA for valence-arousal, and Tri for triplet. The best scores of each metric are in bold.

based (CL-Span) framework based on MacBERT (Cui et al., 2021) to improve the performance of tuple extraction and sentiment intensity prediction. The Chinese EmoBank (Lee et al., 2022) was also incorporated as an auxiliary training resource to boost performance. YNU-HPCC (Wang et al., 2024) used a BERT-based encoder to generate aspect-specific representation and train linear predictors to jointly predict valence-arousal ratings. DS-Group (Meng et al., 2024) proposed an aspect-aware example selection method for in-context learning based on LLM. TMAK-Plus (Kang et al., 2024) presented a Multi-Agent Collaboration (MAC) model to assemble several GPT-based LLM for the dimensional ABSA task. ZZU-NLP (Zhu et al., 2024) proposed a two-stage contextual learning approach based on the Baichuan2-7B (Yang et al., 2023). JN-NLP (Jiang et al., 2024) used a paraphrase generation paradigm based on the T5 (Raffel et al., 2020) pre-trained model to address the dimABSA task.

5.2 Official Ranking

Tables 4, 5, and 6 respectively show the testing results for each subtask. Each metric in each individual subtask is ranked independently. (*) means the rank for each metric. A system's overall ranking is computed based on the cumulative rank. The lower the cumulative rank, the better the system performance.

The overall best results came from the HITSZ-HLT (Xu et al., 2024) team, achieving the best scores in all metrics across three subtasks, followed by the CCIIPLab (Tong and Wei, 2024), ranking second on the leaderboard for each subtask.

6 Conclusions and Future Work

This paper provides an overview of the SIGHAN-2024 dimABSA task for Chinese dimensional aspect-based sentiment analysis, including task descriptions, data preparation, performance metrics and evaluation results. We received a total of 214 submissions from 61 registered participants during the evaluation phase. Among eleven participating teams, seven presented their task technical reports. Regardless of actual performance, all submissions contribute to the development of an effective dimensional ABSA solution, and each task technical paper for this shared task also provides useful insights for further research.

We hope the data sets collected and annotated for this shared task can facilitate and expedite future development of Chinese dimensional ABSA. Therefore, the gold standard test set and evaluation scripts are made publicly available in GitHub repositories at: https://github.com/NYCU-NLP/SIGHAN2024-dimABSA

Future directions will focus on the development of Chinese dimensional ABSA models. We plan to build new language resources to develop techniques for the future enrichment of this research topic, especially for reviews in the other domains.

Acknowledgments

We thank all the participants for taking part in our shared task. We appreciate Tzu-Mi Lin, Zue-Yu Xu, Jian-Yu Chou, and all annotators for their efforts in data annotations and verifications. This work is partially supported by the National Science and

Technology Council, Taiwan, under the grants NSTC 111-2628-E-A49-029-MY3 and NSTC 113-2221-E-155-046-MY3. The works described in this paper are supported by the National Natural Science Foundation of China (62076158, 62376143), and CCF-Zhipu AI Large Model Foundation of China (CCF-Zhipu202310).

References

Hongjie Cai, Rui Xia, and Jianfei Yu. 2021. Aspect-Category-Opinion-Sentiment quadruple extraction with implicit aspects and opinions. In *Proceedings of the 59th Annual Meeting of the Association for Computational Linguistics and the 11th International Joint Conference on Natural Language Processing*. Association for Computational Linguistics, pages 340-350. https://doi.org/10.18653/v1/2021.acl-long.29

Shaowei Chen, Yu Wang, Jie Liu and Yuelin Wang. 2021. Bidirectional machine reading comprehension for aspect sentiment triplet extraction. In *Proceedings of the 35th AAAI Conference on Artificial Intelligence*. The Association for the Advancement of Artificial Intelligence. pages 12666-12674.

Yiming Cui, Wanxiang Che, Ting Liu, Bing Qin, and Ziqing Yang. 2021. Pre-training with whole word masking for Chinese BERT. *IEEE/ACM Transactions on Audio, Speech, and Language Processing*, 29:3504-3514. https://doi.org/10.1109/TASLP.2021.3124365

Yu-Chih Deng, Cheng-Yu Tsai, Yih-Ru Wang, Sin-Horng Chen, and Lung-Hao Lee. 2022. Predicting Chinese phrase-level sentiment intensity in valence-arousal dimensions with linguistic dependency features. *IEEE Access*, 10:126612-126620. https://doi.org/10.1109/ACCESS.2022.3226243

Yu-Chih Deng, Yih-Ru Wang, Sin-Horng Chen, and Lung-Hao Lee. 2023. Towards transformer fusions for Chinese sentiment intensity prediction in valence-arousal domains. *IEEE Access*, 11:109974-109982. https://doi.org/10.1109/ACCESS.2023.3322436

Tianhao Gao, Jun Fang, Hanyu Liu, Zhiyuan Liu, Chao Liu, Pengzhang Liu, Yongjun Bao and Weipeng Yan. 2022. LEGO-ABSA: A prompt-based task assemblable unified generative framework for multi-task aspect-based sentiment analysis. In *Proceedings of the 29th International Conference on Computational Linguistics*. International Committee on Computational Linguistics. pages 7002-7012.

Daya Guo, Qihao Zhu, Dejian Yang, Zhenda Xie, Kai Dong, Wentao Zhang, Guanting Chen, Xiao Bi, Y. Wu, Y. K. Li, Fuli Luo, Yingfei Xiong, and Wenfeng Liang. 2024. DeepSeek-Coder: When the large language model meets programming – the rise of code intelligence. *arXiv preprint*. arXiv:2401.14196. https://doi.org/10.48550/arXiv.2401.14196

Yunfan Jiang, Tianci Liu, and Hengyang Lu. 2024. JN-NLP at SIGHAN-2024 dimABSA task: Extraction of sentiment intensity quadruples based on paraphrase generation. In *Proceedings of the 10th SIGHAN Workshop on Chinese Language Processing*. Association for Computational Linguistics.

Xin Kang, Zhifei Zhang, Jiazheng Zhou, Yunong Wu, Xuefeng Shi, and Kazuyuki Matsumoto. 2024. TMAK-Plus at SIGHAN-2024 dimABSA task: Multi-agent collaboration for transparent and rational sentiment analysis. In *Proceedings of the 10th SIGHAN Workshop on Chinese Language Processing*. Association for Computational Linguistics.

Lung-Hao Lee, Jian-Hong Li and Liang-Chih Yu. 2022. Chinese EmoBank: Building valence-arousal resources for dimensional sentiment analysis. *ACM Transactions on Asian and Low-Resource Language Information Processing*, 21(4), Article 65, 18 pages. https://doi.org/10.1145/3489141

Yue Mao, Yi Shen, Jingchao Yang, Xiaoying Zhu and Longjun Cai. 2022. Seq2Path: Generating sentiment tuples as paths of a tree. In *Findings of the Association for Computational Linguistics: ACL 2022*. Association for Computational Linguistics, pages 2215-2225. https://doi.org/10.18653/v1/2022.findings-acl.174

Yue Mao, Yi Shen, Chao Yu and Longjun Cai. 2021. A joint training dual-MRC framework for aspect based sentiment analysis. In *Proceedings of the 35th AAAI Conference on Artificial Intelligence*. The Association for the Advancement of Artificial Intelligence, pages 13543-13551.

Ling-ang Meng, Tianyu Zhao, and Dawei Song. 2024. DS-Group at SIGHAN-2024 dimABSA task: Constructing in-context learning structure for dimensional aspect-based sentiment analysis. In *Proceedings of the 10th SIGHAN Workshop on Chinese Language Processing*. Association for Computational Linguistics.

Haiyun Peng, Lu Xu, Lidong Bing, Fei Huang, Wei Lu and Luo Si. 2020. Knowing what, how, and why: a near complete solution for aspect-based sentiment analysis. In *Proceedings of the 34th AAAI Conference on Artificial Intelligence*. The Association for the Advancement of Artificial Intelligence, pages 8600-8607. https://doi.org/10.1609/aaai.v34i05.6383

Joseph J. Peper and Lu Wang. 2022. Generative aspect-based sentiment analysis with contrastive learning and expressive structure. In *Findings of the Association for Computational Linguistics: EMNLP 2022*. Association for Computational Linguistics, pages 6118-6124. https://doi.org/10.18653/v1/2022.findings-emnlp.451

Maria Pontiki, Dimitrios Galanis, Haris Papageorgiou, Ion Androutsopoulos, Suresh Manandhar, Mohammad AL-Smadi, Mahmoud Al-Ayyoub, Yanyan Zhao, Bing Qin, Orphee De Clercq, Veronique Hoste, Marianna Apidianaki, Xavier Tannier, Natalia Loukachevitch. Evgeny Kotelnikov, Nuria Bel, Salud Maria Jimenez-Zafra and Gulsen Eryigit. 2016. SemEval-2016 Task 5: Aspect Based Sentiment Analysis. In *Proceedings of the 10th International Workshop on Semantic Evaluation*, Association for Computational Linguistics, pages 19-30. https://doi.org/10.18653/v1/S16-1002

Maria Pontiki, Dimitrios Galanis, Haris Papageorgiou, Suresh Manandhar and Ion Androutsopoulos. 2015. SemEval-2015 Task 12: Aspect Based Sentiment Analysis. In *Proceedings of the 10th International Workshop on Semantic Evaluation*. Association for Computational Linguistics, pages 486-495. https://doi.org/10.18653/v1/S15-2082

Maria Pontiki, Dimitrios Galanis, John Pavlopoulos, Haris Papageorgiou, Ion Androutsopoulos and Suresh Manandhar. 2014. SemEval-2014 Task 4: Aspect Based Sentiment Analysis. In *Proceedings of the 8th International Workshop on Semantic Evaluation*. Association for Computational Linguistics, pages 27-35. https://doi.org/10.3115/v1/S14-2004

Colin Raffel, Noam Shazeer, Adam Roberts, Katherine Lee, Sharan Narang, Michael Matena, Yanqi Zhou, Wei Li, and Peter J. Liu. 2020. Exploring the limits of transfer learning with a unified text-to-text transformer. *Journal of Machine Learning Research*, 21(140): 1-67.

James A Russel. 1980. A circumplex model of affect. *Journal of Personality and Social Psychology*, 39(6): 1161-1178.

Yu Sun, Shuohuan Wang, Shikun Feng, Siyu Ding, Chao Pang, Junyuan Shang, Jiaxiang Liu, Xuyi Chen, Yanbin Zhao, Yuxiang Lu, Weixin Liu, Zhihua Wu, Weibao Gong, Jianzhong Liang, Zhizhou Shang, Peng Sun, Wei Liu, Xuan Ouyang, Dianhai Yu, Hao Tian, Hua Wu, and Haifeng Wang. 2021. ERNIE 3.0: Large-scale knowledge enhanced pre-training for language understanding and generation. *arXiv preprint*. arXiv:2107.02137. https://doi.org/10.48550/arXiv.2107.02137

Zeliang Tong, and Wei Wei. 2024. CCIIPLab at SIGHAN-2024 dimABSA task: Contrastive learning-enhanced span-based framework for Chinese dimensional aspect-based sentiment analysis. In *Proceedings of the 10th SIGHAN Workshop on Chinese Language Processing*. Association for Computational Linguistics.

Zehui Wang, You Zhang, Jin Wang, Dan Xu, and Xuejie Zhang. 2024. YNU-HPCC at SIGHAN-2024 dimABSA task: Using PLMs with a joint learning strategy for dimensional intensity prediction. In *Proceedings of the 10th SIGHAN Workshop on Chinese Language Processing*. Association for Computational Linguistics.

Zhen Wu, Chengcan Ying, Fei Zhao, Zhifang Fan, Xinyu Dai, and Rui Xia. 2020. Grid tagging scheme for end-to-end fine-grained opinion extraction. In *Findings of the Association for Computational Linguistics: EMNLP 2020*. Association for Computational Linguistics, pages 2576-2585. https://doi.org/10.18653/v1/2020.findings-emnlp.234

Lu Xu, Hao Li, Wei Lu, and Lidong Bing. 2020. Position-aware tagging for aspect sentiment triplet extraction. In *Proceedings of the 2020 Conference on Empirical Methods in Natural Language Processing*. Association for Computational Linguistics, pages 2339-2349. https://doi.org/10.18653/v1/2020.emnlp-main.183

Hongling Xu, Delong Zhang, Yice Zhang, and Ruifeng Xu. 2024. HITSZ-HLT at SIGHAN-2024 dimABSA task: Integrating BERT and LLM for Chinese dimensional aspect-based sentiment analysis. In *Proceedings of the 10th SIGHAN Workshop on Chinese Language Processing*. Association for Computational Linguistics.

Aiyuan Yang, Bin Xiao, Bingning Wang, Borong Zhang, Ce Bian, Chao Yin, Chenxu Lv, Da Pan, Dian Wang, Dong Yan, Fan Yang, Fei Deng, Feng Wang, Feng Liu, Guangwei Ai, Guosheng Dong, Haizhou Zhao, Hang Xu, Haoze Sun, Hongda Zhang, Hui Liu, Jiaming Ji, Jian Xie, JunTao Dai, Kun Fang, Lei Sun, Liang Song, Lifeng Liu, Liyun Ru, Luyao Ma, Mang Wang, Mickel Liu, MingAn Lin, Nuolan Nie, Peidong Guo, Ruiyang Sun, Tao Zhang, Tianpeng Li, Tianyu Li, Wei Cheng, Weipeng Chen, Xiangrong Zeng, Xiaochuan Wang, Xiaoxi Chen, Xin Men, Xin Yu, Xuehai Pan, Yanjun Shen, Yiding Wang, Yiyu Li, Youxin Jiang, Yuchen Gao, Yupeng Zhang, Zenan Zhou, and Zhiying Wu. 2023. Baichuan 2: Open large-scale language models. *arXiv preprint*, arXiv:2309.10305. https://doi.org/10.48550/arXiv.2309.10305

Liang-Chih Yu, Lung-Hao Lee, Shuai Hao, Jin Wang, Yunchao He, Jun Hu, K. Robert Lai, and Xuejie Zhang. 2016. Building Chinese Affective Resources in Valence-Arousal Dimensions. In *Proceedings of the 15th Annual Conference of the North American Chapter of the Association for Computational Linguistics: Human Language Technologies*.

Association for Computational Linguistics, pages 540-545. https://doi.org/10.18653/v1/N16-1066

Li Yuan, Jin Wang, Liang-Chih Yu, Xuejie Zhang. 2023. Encoding Syntactic Information into Transformers for Aspect-Based Sentiment Triplet Extraction. *IEEE Transactions on Affective Computing*, 15(2): 722-735. https://doi.org/10.1109/TAFFC.2023.3291730

Chen Zhang, Qiuchi Li, Dawei Song, and Benyou Wang. 2020. A multi-task learning framework for opinion triplet extraction. In *Findings of the Association for Computational Linguistics: EMNLP 2020*. Association for Computational Linguistics, pages 819-829. https://doi.org/10.18653/v1/2020.findings-emnlp.72

Wenxuan Zhang, Xin Li, Yang Deng, Lidong Bing and Wai Lam. 2021. Towards generative aspect-based sentiment analysis. In *Proceedings of the 59th Annual Meeting of the Association for Computational Linguistics and the 11th International Joint Conference on Natural Language Processing (Short Papers)*. Association for Computational Linguistics, pages 504-510. https://doi.org/10.18653/v1/2021.acl-short.64

Junxian Zhou, Haiqin Yang, Yuxuan He, Hao Mou. and Junbo Yang. 2023. A unified one-step solution for aspect sentiment quad predication. In *Findings of the Association for Computational Linguistics: ACL 2023*. Association for Computational Linguistics, pages 12249-12265. https://doi.org/10.18653/v1/2023.findings-acl.777

Senbin Zhu, Hanjie Zhao, Xingren Wang, Shanhong Liu, Yuxiang Jia, and Hongying Zan. 2024. ZZU-NLP at SIGHAN-2024 dimABSA task: Aspect-based sentiment analysis with coarse-to-fine contextual learning. In *Proceedings of the 10th SIGHAN Workshop on Chinese Language Processing*. Association for Computational Linguistics.

HITSZ-HLT at SIGHAN-2024 dimABSA Task: Integrating BERT and LLM for Chinese Dimensional Aspect-Based Sentiment Analysis

Hongling Xu[1,3*], **Delong Zhang**[1,3*], **Yice Zhang**[1,3*], **Ruifeng Xu**[1,2,3†]
[1] Harbin Institute of Technology, Shenzhen, China
[2] Peng Cheng Laboratory, Shenzhen, China
[3] Guangdong Provincial Key Laboratory of Novel Security Intelligence Technologies
xuhongling@stu.hit.edu.cn, xuruifeng@hit.edu.cn

Abstract

This paper presents the winning system participating in the ACL 2024 workshop SIGHAN-10 shared task: Chinese dimensional aspect-based sentiment analysis (dimABSA). This task aims to identify four sentiment elements in restaurant reviews: aspect, category, opinion, and sentiment intensity evaluated in valence-arousal dimensions, providing a concise yet fine-grained sentiment description for user opinions. To tackle this task, we introduce a system that integrates BERT and large language models (LLM) to leverage their strengths. First, we explore their performance in entity extraction, relation classification, and intensity prediction. Based on preliminary experiments, we develop an integrated approach to fully utilize their advantages in different scenarios. Our system achieves first place in all subtasks and obtains a 41.7% F1-score in quadruple extraction.

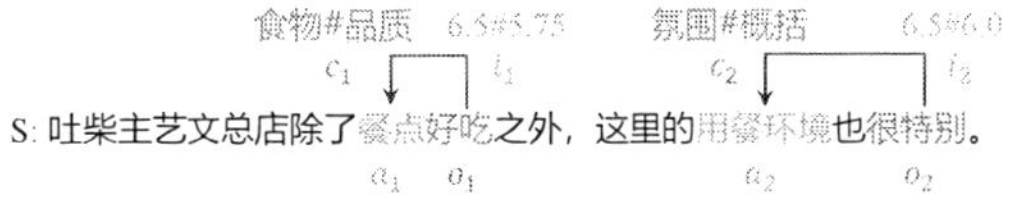

Subtask	Input	Output	Task Type
Intensity Prediction	S + a_1	$\{i_1\}$	Regression
	S + a_2	$\{i_2\}$	
Triplet Extraction	S	$\{a_1, o_1, i_1\}$ $\{a_2, o_2, i_2\}$	Extraction & Regression
Quadruple Extraction	S	$\{a_1, c_1, o_1, i_1\}$ $\{a_2, c_2, o_2, i_2\}$	Extraction & Classification & Regression

Figure 1: Illustration of three dimABSA subtasks.

1 Introduction

Aspect-based sentiment analysis (ABSA) is a fine-grained problem that aims to recognize aspect-level sentiments and opinions of users (Pontiki et al., 2016). ABSA generally involves four fundamental elements: (1) aspect term (a), the mention of the reviewed entity in the text; (2) aspect category (c), a predefined category of the evaluated aspect; (3) opinion term (o), the sentiment word or phrase towards the aspect; and (4) sentiment (Cai et al., 2021; Zhang et al., 2021). For example, in the review "*the sushi was delicious but the staff was unfriendly*", the quadruples are (*sushi*, food#quality, *delicious*, positive) and (*staff*, services#general, *unfriendly*, negative).

Existing ABSA works have typically treated sentiment as coarse-grained polarities, overlooking the complexity of sentiment dimensions. Pioneeringly, the SIGHAN-2024 dimABSA task (Lee et al., 2024) proposes to represent sentiment states as continuous real-valued scores in valence-arousal dimensions, referred to as intensity (i). Valence measures the positivity or negativity, and arousal evaluates the degree of emotional activation (Russell, 1980). As depicted in Figure 1, dimABSA consists of three subtasks: (1) Intensity Prediction, predicting the intensity of the given aspect; (2) Triplet Extraction, extracting the triplets composed of (a, o, i) from the given sentence; (3) Quadruple Extraction, extracting the quadruples composed of (a, c, o, i) from the given sentence.

To tackle these subtasks, we develop a system that integrates BERT and large language models (LLM), representing two leading paradigms for natural language understanding tasks. Specifically, we devise both BERT-based and LLM-based methods and evaluate them to highlight their respective advantages. The **BERT-based method** employs a pipeline approach that sequentially performs aspect-opinion extraction, pairing and classification, and intensity prediction. We implement three improvements to enhance performance: domain-adaptive pre-training (Gururangan et al., 2020), negative pairs construction, and removing dropout in intensity prediction. The **LLM-based method** transforms the three subtasks into text generation tasks and then fine-tunes a unified model using a multi-task learning strategy. We craft

* Equal contribution.
† Corresponding author.

Proceedings of the 10th SIGHAN Workshop on Chinese Language Processing (SIGHAN-10), pages 175–185
August 16, 2024

code-style prompts (Li et al., 2023) to enhance the extraction capabilities of LLMs and employ QLoRA (Dettmers et al., 2024) to reduce memory usage during training.

Through preliminary experiments, we make two observations: (1) in structure extraction (aspect-opinion extraction and pairing), the BERT-based method outperforms the LLM-based method; (2) in intensity prediction, the BERT-based method performs better with continuous values, while the LLM-based method excels in integer-level predictions. Therefore, for Subtask 1, we employ the BERT-based method. For Subtask 2 and 3, we utilize the BERT-based method to derive the aspect, category, and opinion, which are then fed into LLM to generate integer-level intensity predictions.

Our contributions are summarized as follows:

- We propose both BERT-based and LLM-based methods to address the dimABSA tasks and devise various strategies to enhance their performance.
- We analyze the strengths of BERT-based and LLM-based methods in different scenarios and develop an ensemble solution.
- Extensive experimental results demonstrate that our system achieves superior performance and validate the effectiveness of each module. Additionally, we conduct several discussions to provide further insights.

2 Related Work

2.1 Aspect-Based Sentiment Analysis

Aspect-level Sentiment Classification (ASC) is the most fundamental task in ABSA, aiming to identify the sentiment of specific aspect terms in a sentence (Pontiki et al., 2016). Early methods utilized LSTM with attention mechanisms to capture the interaction between aspects and their contextual relationships (Wang et al., 2016b; Ma et al., 2017). With the development of the fine-tuning paradigm, it became mainstream for ASC. Strategies such as interaction mechanism designs (Wu and Ong, 2021; Zhang et al., 2022b), post-training (Xu et al., 2019; Li et al., 2021; Zhang et al., 2023), graph neural networks (Wang et al., 2020; Chen et al., 2022), and contrastive learning (Liang et al., 2021; Cao et al., 2022) have been used to enhance fine-grained sentiment classification. With the advent of LLMs, recent work has explored the effect of LLMs, including in-context learning (Wang et al., 2023b; Xu et al., 2024), chain-of-thought prompting (Fei et al., 2023), and sentiment explanation (Wang et al., 2023a).

Aspect Sentiment Quad Prediction (ASQP) is the most comprehensive task in ABSA, aiming to extract all ABSA quadruples in a review (Cai et al., 2021; Zhang et al., 2021). Research can be categorized into three main types: discriminative methods, generative methods, and LLM-based methods. In the first stream, Cai et al. (2021) applied extract-classify techniques, and Zhou et al. (2023) involved table-based methods to extract aspect-category and opinion-sentiment pairs via simultaneous training. Generative methods, like Zhang et al. (2021), converted quad prediction into paraphrase generation, while Gou et al. (2023) used different permutations as prompts to generate quadruples in various orders for voting. Additionally, some methods enhanced ASQP performance through tree generation designs (Bao et al., 2022; Mao et al., 2022). In the third stream, LLM-based approaches mainly leveraged the rationale of LLMs to improve quad prediction (Kim et al., 2024).

However, early ABSA work solely modeled sentiment with three-class polarities. Our system predicts sentiment in valence-arousal dimensions, providing more fine-grained sentiment information.

2.2 Dimensional Sentiment Analysis

This task focuses on the multiple dimensions of emotional states, such as valence-arousal space (Russell, 1980). Valence measures positivity or negativity, while arousal evaluates excitement or calmness. Previous studies provided various multi-dimensional affective resources, such as lexicons (Warriner et al., 2013) and sentence-level corpora (Preoţiuc-Pietro et al., 2016; Buechel and Hahn, 2017). Meanwhile, some works developed multi-granularity Chinese dimensional sentiment resources, filling the gap in Chinese resources (Yu et al., 2016; Lee et al., 2022). To effectively predict dimensional scores, early approaches mainly used LSTM for modeling, including Densely Connected LSTM for phrase-level predictions (Wu et al., 2017), a relation interaction model for sentence-level predictions (Xie et al., 2021), and a Regional CNN-LSTM model for text-level predictions (Wang et al., 2016a, 2019). With the advancement of Transformer (Vaswani et al.,

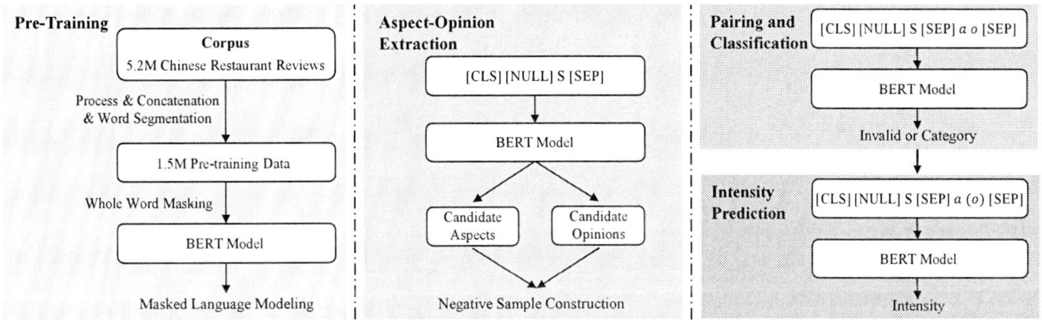

Figure 2: Overview of our BERT framework.

2017), researchers began leveraging PLMs for improvement. For instance, Deng et al. (2023) proposed a multi-granularity BERT fusion framework, and Wang et al. (2024) introduced soft momentum contrastive learning for pre-training. Different from them, our work further evaluates LLMs for dimensional score prediction, providing advanced exploration and analysis.

3 Methods

3.1 Task Definition

Given a sentence $S = [w_1, \cdots, w_T]$ and a pre-defined aspect term a (a substring of S), the objective of Subtask 1 is to predict the sentiment intensity val, aro, which are continuous values ranging from 1 to 9. For Subtasks 2&3, the input consists only of the sentence S, and the output includes all triplets $(a, o, val\text{-}aro)$ and quadruples $(a, c, o, val\text{-}aro)$, where c and o denote the aspect category and opinion term, respectively. In Subtasks 2&3, (1) the aspect term a and opinion term o can either be a substring of S or be implicit, in which case they are represented by 'NULL'; (2) the aspect category belongs to a pre-defined category set C.

3.2 BERT-based Method

As shown in Figure 2, our BERT framework is structured into four main steps: (i) Domain-adaptive Pre-training, (ii) Aspect-opinion Extraction, (iii) Pairing and Classification, and (iv) Intensity Prediction.

Domain-adaptive Pre-training. Pre-training on sentiment-dense corpus has been proven to enhance downstream sentiment analysis tasks (Xu et al., 2019; Zhang et al., 2023). We first collect 5.2 million open-source Chinese restaurant reviews and conduct data cleaning to remove duplicates and excessively short entries. Subsequently, we concatenate all data and split it according to the maximum length, resulting in 1.5 million pre-training corpora.[1] Moreover, we employ LTP (Che et al., 2010) for Chinese word segmentation and implement a dynamic whole-word masking strategy for masked language modeling (Cui et al., 2021), aiming at enhancing BERT's contextual understanding in the restaurant domain.

Aspect-Opinion Extraction. This step utilizes the pre-trained BERT model to extract aspect and opinion terms. To identify implicit terms, we augment the given sentence by prepending a special [NULL] token. We add this token to the vocabulary and initialize its embedding. Subsequently, we transform the extraction task into a `BIO` sequence labeling task. Using BERT, we predict the category of each token as follows:

$$\boldsymbol{h}_0, \boldsymbol{h}_1, \cdots, \boldsymbol{h}_T = \mathrm{BERT}(S'), \quad (1)$$

$$P(y_t) = \mathrm{softmax}(\mathrm{Linear}(\boldsymbol{h}_t)), \quad (2)$$

where $S' = [[\mathrm{NULL}], w_1, \cdots, w_T]$ denotes the augmented sentence, and y_t represents the tag for the t-th token in the sentence, belonging to {`BA`, `IA`, `BO`, `IO`, `O`}.

Pairing and Classification. This step pairs aspect and opinion terms and determines the corresponding aspect categories. In the BERT-based method, we frame the aspect-opinion pairing and category classification as a unified multi-class classification task. To achieve this, we input the sentence S' along with the aspect term a and opinion term o into BERT and feed the hidden vector at the

[1] Here, we set the maximum sequence length to 512 after adding [CLS] and [SEP] tokens.

[CLS] token position to a classifier, formulated as follows:

$$\boldsymbol{h}_{[CLS]} = \text{BERT}(S', a, o), \tag{3}$$

$$P(c) = \text{softmax}(\text{Linear}(\boldsymbol{h}_{[\text{CLS}]})), \tag{4}$$

where $c \in \{\text{Invalid}\} \cup C$.

In this step, we introduce **negative pairs construction** to mitigate error propagation. During training, the input aspect and opinion terms are true values. However, at the inference stage, these terms are predicted values obtained from the previous step. This discrepancy can lead the classifier to fail in rejecting those aspect and opinion terms with minor boundary errors, resulting in error propagation. To address this issue, we train the extraction model using k-fold cross-validation and incorporate incorrectly extracted aspect and opinion terms into the negative pairs, labeling them as invalid. These negative pairs, along with the true aspect and opinion terms, are then fed into the relation model during training to enhance its robustness against such errors.

Intensity Prediction. This step predicts the valence-arousal scores of an aspect term (for Subtask 1) or an aspect-opinion pair (for Subtask 2&3). We exploit two models for intensity prediction: a regression model and a classification model.

- The regression model obtains the valence and arousal scores s_{val}, s_{aro} by feeding the hidden vector at the [CLS] token position to two separate linear layers:

  $$\boldsymbol{h}_{[CLS]} = \text{BERT}(S', a, o), \tag{5}$$

  $$\hat{s}_{val} = \text{Linear}(\boldsymbol{h}_{[\text{CLS}]}), \tag{6}$$

  $$\hat{s}_{aro} = \text{Linear}(\boldsymbol{h}_{[\text{CLS}]}). \tag{7}$$

  We then compute two losses by mean squared error (MSE) and average them as the regression loss.

- The classification model first converts continuous scores into categories c_{val}, c_{aro} at fixed intervals and then predicts these two categories using two classifiers:

  $$\hat{c}_{val} = \text{softmax}(\text{Linear}(\boldsymbol{h}_{[\text{CLS}]})), \tag{8}$$

  $$\hat{c}_{aro} = \text{softmax}(\text{Linear}(\boldsymbol{h}_{[\text{CLS}]})). \tag{9}$$

  We use the cross-entropy function to compute two losses and average them as the classification loss.

Furthermore, for the regression model, we adopt the strategy of **removing BERT's internal dropout**. This approach was discussed in a Kaggle forum[2]. The rationale behind this strategy is that BERT's internal dropout may lead to inconsistencies in the variance of neuron activations between the training and inference phases, potentially affecting the numerical stability of the regression.

3.3 LLM-based Method

We transform the dimABSA tasks into text generation tasks and fine-tune a unified LLM using a multi-task learning strategy. To augment the extraction capabilities of the LLM, we employ code-style prompts, as suggested by Li et al. (2023). Additionally, we utilize QLoRA (Dettmers et al., 2024) to reduce memory usage during training. Our framework is illustrated in Figure 3.

Multi-task Learning. Recent work shows that LLMs exhibit excellent task generalization capabilities (Touvron et al., 2023). Inspired by this, we design a multi-task learning strategy for dimABSA to enable the LLM to acquire diverse sentimental knowledge across different tasks. Specifically, we manually construct 6 typical tasks from existing data and labels, including three target subtasks. These are aspect extraction, aspect intensity prediction, aspect-opinion-intensity triplet extraction, aspect-category-opinion triplet extraction, quadruple extraction, and aspect-opinion intensity prediction. These tasks encompass a variety of extraction, classification, and regression task types, thus allowing for a comprehensive learning of aspect-related sentiment knowledge.

Code-style Prompt. LLMs are general-purpose text generation models. To adapt them for specific tasks, it is necessary to craft prompts that direct their output to align with the specific requirements of these tasks. Following Li et al. (2023), we design code-style instructions as prompts. As shown in Figure 3, we formalize each task as Python code, explaining necessary information through comments and standardizing the output format or content via specific code to serve a more instructive role.

Optimization with QLoRA. After completing task selection and prompt design, we construct the task selection and prompt design, we construct the

[2]https://www.kaggle.com/competitions/commonlitreadabilityprize/discussion/260729

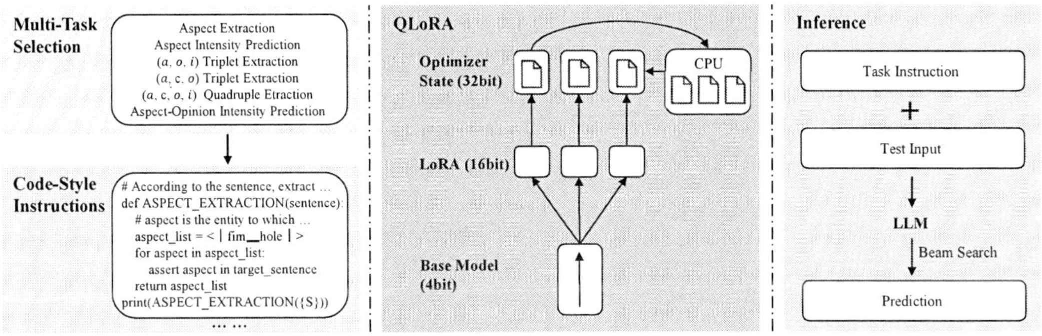

Figure 3: Overview of our LLM framework.

training data for fine-tuning the LLM. This fine-tuning approach is QLoRA (Dettmers et al., 2024). QLoRA is a typical parameter-efficient fine-tuning approach that integrates low-rank matrices into the architecture of LLMs and further quantizes the base model to 4-bit. QLoRA enables us to fine-tune most LLMs on a single 40G A100 GPU.

Inference. We load the parameters of the base model along with those obtained during the fine-tuning phase to perform inference. Utilizing code-style instructions as prompts for each task, we integrate these prompts with the test text inputs for model decoding. During decoding, we set the temperature coefficient to 1 and utilize the beam search strategy (Freitag and Al-Onaizan, 2017) with 'num_beams=2'.

3.4 Ensemble

We conduct preliminary experiments to compare the BERT-based and LLM-based methods. The results indicate that BERT performs better in continuous intensity predicting and aspect-opinion extraction. Conversely, the LLM shows superior per formance in integer-level intensity prediction tasks. We suppose this difference arises because LLMs, constrained by their natural language generation output format, may not ensure an accurate understanding of continuous values and extraction, but exhibit better results in coarse-grained predictions due to the larger parameter size.

To fully leverage the strengths of both models, we develop an integrated method. For Subtask 1, we average the predictions of the regression and classification models in the BERT-based method. For Subtasks 2 and 3, we use the BERT-based method to extract (a, c, o) tuples. Then, we input all valid aspect-opinion pairs into the LLM, employing the aspect-opinion intensity prediction

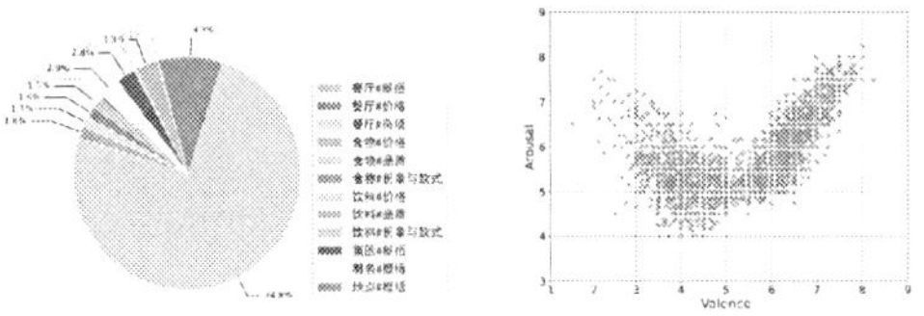

(a) Category distribution. (b) Intensity distribution.

Figure 4: Visualization of training data distribution.

prompt to output integer-level predictions of valence and arousal.

4 Experiments

4.1 Experimental Settings

Datasets. In experiments, we use the Chinese restaurant review dataset provided by the organizer, which includes 6,050 sentences for training, 2,000 sentences for Subtask 1 testing, and 2,000 sentences for Subtasks 2&3 testing. Specifically, the average sentence length, aspect length, and opinion length in the training set are 14.12, 3.14, and 3.07, respectively. Additionally, the training set contains 8,523 quadruples, with 22.81% of quadruples sharing the same aspect in one sentence, 6.10% sharing the same opinion, and 1.98% being implicit aspects. As depicted in Figure 4a, there are 12 predefined categories, with their specific distribution. The training set also includes valence-arousal annotations for aspect-opinion pairs, with real values ranging from 1 to 9. The distribution of valence-arousal annotations is visualized in Figure 4b.

Evaluation Metrics. For Subtask 1, the performance of sentiment intensity prediction is assessed using Mean Absolute Error (MAE) and Pearson Correlation Coefficient (PCC). These metrics evaluate the difference between model-predicted results and human-annotated scores for valence and arousal dimensions, respectively.

$$\text{MAE} = \frac{1}{n}\sum_{i=1}^{n}|y_i - \hat{y}_i| \tag{10}$$

where y_i is the actual value and $\hat{y}_i$ is the prediction.

$$\text{PCC} = \frac{\sum_{i=1}^{n}(y_i-\bar{y})(\hat{y}_i-\bar{\hat{y}})}{\sqrt{\sum_{i=1}^{n}(y_i-\bar{y})^2}\sqrt{\sum_{i=1}^{n}(\hat{y}_i-\bar{\hat{y}})^2}} \tag{11}$$

where $\bar{y}$ and $\bar{\hat{y}}$ are the means of the actual and predicted values, respectively. Lower MAE values indicate more accurate predictions, while PCC ranges from -1 to 1, with higher values indicating a stronger linear correlation. To evaluate Subtasks 2 and 3, the Precision (P), Recall (R), and F1-score (F1) are employed. Meanwhile, valence and arousal values are rounded to the nearest integer. A tuple is correct only if all elements and their combinations match the gold standard.

$$\text{F1} = \frac{2 \times \text{P} \times \text{R}}{\text{P} + \text{R}} \tag{12}$$

where P denotes the number of correct tuples divided by the total number of extracted tuples, and R denotes the number of correct tuples divided by the total number of standard tuples. Higher values of F1 indicate better performance. Additionally, each metric is calculated independently for valence and arousal dimensions or in combination.

Implementation Details. For BERT, we use *ernie-3.0-xbase-zh* (Sun et al., 2021) as the backbone encoder. The pre-training settings are as follows: batch size of 32, gradient accumulation steps of 12, bf16 mixed precision, 5 training epochs, initial learning rate of 1e-4, and a maximum sequence length of 512. During fine-tuning, we set the learning rate to 2e-5 and the batch size to 32. The fine-tuning epochs are 7 for aspect-opinion extraction, pairing-and-classification, and BERT_{CLS} models, and 6 for the BERT_{REG} model, using the AdamW optimizer. Besides, the interval l for classification is set to 0.25. All models are fine-tuned on five different random seeds and results are aggregated by voting. For LLM, we use *deepseek-7b-instruct-v1.5* (Guo et al., 2024) as the backbone. The training settings include the learning rate of 1e-4, 5 epochs, batch size of 4, bf16 mixed precision, and maximum sequence length of 2048. Besides, the rank of QLoRA fine-tuning is set to 8, and the scaler factor is set to 16. All implementations are based on the PyTorch framework, using NVIDIA A6000 GPUs.

Comparison. We apply different BERT models, LLMs, and the pipeline ensemble method for comparison, including: (1) $\textbf{BERT}_{\textbf{REG}}$, which utilizes regression method for intensity prediction; (2) $\textbf{BERT}_{\textbf{CLS}}$, which employs the interval-based classification approach to predict intensity scores; (3) $\textbf{LLM}_{\textbf{INT}}$, which trains LLM with integer-level intensity; (4) $\textbf{LLM}_{\textbf{DEC}}$, which uses one decimal place intensity and corresponding prompts for training; and (5) **Ensemble**, referring to the ensemble method described in Section 3.4.

4.2 Main Results

The main results are presented in Table 1, from which we can draw the following conclusions:

Firstly, the proposed ensemble method demonstrates obvious superiority, achieving the best results on the majority of metrics. For instance, in Subtasks 2 and 3, the Ensemble method shows improvements of 0.8% and 0.6% in VA-T-F1 and VA-Q-F1 compared to BERT_{CLS}. Compared to LLM_{INT}, these improvements even more achieve 4.1% and 3.8%. These results indicate that our ensemble method effectively leverages the respective strengths of both BERT and LLM in different scenarios, achieving better performance than single-model approaches.

Secondly, we find that the performance of LLM across various metrics is generally inferior to that of BERT. For example, the BERT_{CLS} outperforms LLM_{INT} by 1.1% on V-PCC and surpasses the LLM_{DEC} model by 3.2% on VA-Q-F1. This indicates that BERT is more suitable for predicting the intensity of continuous numerical scores. Additionally, further exploration reveals that although LLM underperforms in Subtasks 2&3, the performance is primarily constrained by aspect-opinion extraction. Conversely, LLM excels in predicting valence-arousal at integer levels, the superiority of Ensemble also supports this viewpoint.

Lastly, we compare different training methods within the same model. We observe that BERT_{CLS} significantly outperforms BERT_{REG} in Subtasks 2 and 3, indicating that the classification model is more suitable for coarse-grained evaluation. Furthermore, comparing LLM_{INT} and LLM_{DEC}, we find that LLM_{DEC} performs better in Subtask 1, whereas LLM_{INT} excels in Subtasks 2 and 3. We assume that in Subtasks 2 and 3, the joint extraction

Methods	Subtask 1				Subtask 2			Subtask 3		
	V-MAE	V-PCC	A-MAE	A-PCC	V-T-F1	A-T-F1	VA-T-F1	V-Q-F1	A-Q-F1	VA-Q-F1
$BERT_{REG}$	0.287	0.930	0.311	0.773	0.574	0.526	0.405	0.555	0.511	0.393
$BERT_{CLS}$	**0.279**	0.930	0.316	0.766	0.583	0.543	0.425	0.564	**0.527**	0.411
LLM_{INT}	0.367	0.884	0.394	0.683	0.530	0.498	0.392	0.512	0.482	0.379
LLM_{DEC}	0.294	0.919	0.331	0.738	0.457	0.437	0.312	0.443	0.426	0.302
Ensemble	**0.279**	**0.933**	**0.309**	**0.777**	**0.589**	**0.545**	**0.433**	**0.567**	0.526	**0.417**

Table 1: Main experimental results of our dimABSA system across three Subtasks. V for valence, A for arousal, T for Triplet, and Q for Quadruple. The best scores of each metric are in bold.

Methods	Type	V-Q-F1	A-Q-F1	VA-Q-F1
Voting	BERT	0.557	0.509	0.393
Co-Voting	BERT&LLM	0.563	0.526	0.413
Replace	BERT&LLM	0.565	**0.526**	0.416
Pipeline	BERT&LLM	**0.567**	**0.526**	**0.417**

Table 2: Results of different ensemble strategies for BERT and LLM on Subtask 3.

tasks require generating multiple tuples at once and generating more complex decimals may impact the overall extraction result.

4.3 Analysis of Ensemble

To further verify the effectiveness of the proposed ensemble method, we compare several different ensemble approaches on Subtask 3, including (1) Voting, where results from both types of BERT models are averaged; (2) Co-Voting, where votes are cast only for (a, c, o) tuples that are consistent between LLM and BERT while retaining BERT results for all other tuples; (3) Replace, using intensity results from LLM to replace those of BERT for consistent tuples; (4) Pipeline (ours), where extracted tuples from BERT are input into LLM for intensity prediction. Results are shown in Table 2. We observe that Voting performs poorest, highlighting the importance of combining LLM with BERT. Furthermore, when comparing the last three methods, we find that both Co-Voting and Replace underperform Pipeline. Since LLM excels in coarse-grained intensity prediction, the Pipeline method can more effectively leverage this advantage and achieve superior results.

4.4 Ablation Study

Ablation of BERT. To investigate the effectiveness of various components in BERT, we conduct ablation studies on $BERT_{REG}$, as shown in Table 3. We observe that removing pre-training (w/o pre-training) leads to a slight decline across all metrics, validating the effectiveness of domain-specific pre-training. Furthermore, eliminating the no-dropout strategy (w/o no-dropout) results in a substantial decrease in most metrics, confirming that dropout can introduce biases in the numerical outputs of regression models. Lastly, omitting the negative sample construction strategy during aspect-opinion pairing training (w/o construction) also degrades performance, proving that this strategy effectively reduces error propagation in the pipeline model.

Ablation of LLM. To explore the effectiveness of various strategies within the LLM framework, we conduct ablation studies on LLM_{INT}, specifically targeting code-style prompts, multi-task learning, and beam search. These modifications are denoted as w/o code prompt, w/o multi-task, and w/o beam search, respectively. The results, as shown in Table 4, indicate that replacing code-style prompts with standard natural language instructions significantly reduces performance in Subtasks 2&3, confirming the effectiveness of this method. Additionally, removing multi-task learning leads to a decline in all metrics, suggesting that LLM benefits from learning generalized emotional knowledge across tasks. Lastly, the performance also declines upon removing the beam search, highlighting the importance of decoding strategy design in LLM inference.

4.5 Effect of Pre-Trained Language Models

To compare the effectiveness of different PLMs on the dimABSA tasks, we conduct experiments on Subtask 1 using several types of models with varying parameter sizes. The results are presented in Table 5. Specifically, we employ our ensemble method to test five different Chinese language models, including *chinese-roberta-wwm-ext* and *chinese-roberta-wwm-ext-large* (Cui et al., 2021), *ernie-3.0-base-zh* and *ernie-3.0-xbase-zh* (Sun et al., 2021), and *erlangshen-deberta-v2-*

Methods	Subtask 1				Subtask 2			Subtask 3		
	V-MAE	V-PCC	A-MAE	A-PCC	V-T-F1	A-T-F1	VA-T-F1	V-Q-F1	A-Q-F1	VA-Q-F1
$BERT_{REG}$	**0.287**	**0.930**	**0.311**	0.773	**0.574**	**0.526**	**0.405**	**0.555**	**0.511**	**0.393**
w/o pre-training	0.294	0.924	0.313	0.771	0.565	0.520	0.401	0.544	0.502	0.386
w/o no-dropout	0.337	0.933	0.348	**0.779**	0.537	0.503	0.365	0.521	0.487	0.354
w/o construction	-	-	-	-	0.567	0.518	0.399	0.549	0.502	0.387

Table 3: Ablation study of $BERT_{REG}$.

Methods	Subtask 1				Subtask 2			Subtask 3		
	V-MAE	V-PCC	A-MAE	A-PCC	V-T-F1	A-T-F1	VA-T-F1	V-Q-F1	A-Q-F1	VA-Q-F1
LLM_{INT}	**0.367**	**0.884**	0.394	**0.683**	0.530	**0.498**	**0.392**	0.512	**0.482**	**0.379**
w/o code prompt	0.367	0.882	0.394	0.672	0.515	0.472	0.373	0.495	0.454	0.358
w/o multi-task	0.381	0.876	0.406	0.632	**0.535**	0.481	0.381	**0.514**	0.464	0.367
w/o beam search	0.377	0.880	**0.391**	0.670	0.531	0.489	0.388	0.511	0.472	0.374

Table 4: Ablation study of LLM_{INT}.

Model (Params)	Valence		Arousal	
	MAE	PCC	MAE	PCC
roberta-base (102M)	0.300	0.918	0.310	0.766
ernie-base (118M)	0.300	0.915	0.313	0.762
ernie-xbase (296M)	0.286	0.926	**0.309**	**0.776**
deberta-large (320M)	**0.284**	**0.930**	0.310	0.774
roberta-large (326M)	0.289	0.923	0.314	0.769

Table 5: Results of different pre-trained language models on Subtask 1 (using Ensemble strategy).

320m-chinese (Zhang et al., 2022a). The results indicate that larger models with more parameters tend to perform better than base models. Additionally, our backbone, ernie-xbase, with a moderate parameter size, demonstrates superior performance, ensuring both training efficiency and excellent results for our system.

5 Conclusions

In this paper, we describe our winning system in the SIGHAN-2024 dimABSA task, which involves identifying fundamental sentiment elements in restaurant reviews: aspect, category, opinion, and intensity. Our system integrates BERT and LLM, utilizing their strengths in entity extraction and intensity prediction across three subtasks. The experimental results not only validate the effectiveness of our methods but also underscore the potential of BERT-LLM ensemble strategies in advanced sentiment analysis, providing technical insights and a solid foundation for future research.

Acknowledgements

This work was partially supported by the National Natural Science Foundation of China (62176076), the Natural Science Foundation of Guangdong (2023A1515012922), the Shenzhen Foundational Research Funding (JCYJ20220818102415032), and the Guangdong Provincial Key Laboratory of Novel Security Intelligence Technologies (2022B1212010005).

Limitations

Despite proposing a novel approach that integrates BERT and LLM for the dimABSA task and achieves promising performance, our study has several limitations. Firstly, our exploration is confined to ensemble methods such as voting and pipeline approaches, leaving deeper integration strategies between BERT and LLMs unexplored. Methods such as knowledge distillation and designing hybrid architectures could potentially enhance performance by capturing more respect advantages. Secondly, our research is constrained by limited computational resources, preventing us from investigating the application of more advanced LLMs to this task. These advanced models might offer better performance in terms of both accuracy and generalization. Lastly, our work does not leverage existing dimensional sentiment resources, such as sentiment lexicons and annotated datasets, which we believe could further improve the prediction of sentiment dimensions. Future work should consider incorporating these resources to enhance the robustness and accuracy of sentiment predictions.

References

Xiaoyi Bao, Zhongqing Wang, Xiaotong Jiang, Rong Xiao, and Shoushan Li. 2022. Aspect-based sentiment analysis with opinion tree generation. In *IJCAI*, volume 2022, pages 4044–4050.

Sven Buechel and Udo Hahn. 2017. Emobank: Studying the impact of annotation perspective and representation format on dimensional emotion analysis. In *Proceedings of the 15th Conference of the European Chapter of the Association for Computational Linguistics: Volume 2, Short Papers*, pages 578–585.

Hongjie Cai, Rui Xia, and Jianfei Yu. 2021. Aspect-category-opinion-sentiment quadruple extraction with implicit aspects and opinions. In *Proceedings of the 59th Annual Meeting of the Association for Computational Linguistics and the 11th International Joint Conference on Natural Language Processing (Volume 1: Long Papers)*, pages 340–350.

Jiahao Cao, Rui Liu, Huailiang Peng, Lei Jiang, and Xu Bai. 2022. Aspect is not you need: No-aspect differential sentiment framework for aspect-based sentiment analysis. In *Proceedings of NAACL-HLT*, pages 1599–1609.

Wanxiang Che, Zhenghua Li, and Ting Liu. 2010. Ltp: A chinese language technology platform. In *Coling 2010: demonstrations*, pages 13–16.

Chenhua Chen, Zhiyang Teng, Zhongqing Wang, and Yue Zhang. 2022. Discrete opinion tree induction for aspect-based sentiment analysis. In *Proceedings of the 60th Annual Meeting of the Association for Computational Linguistics (Volume 1: Long Papers)*, pages 2051–2064, Dublin, Ireland. Association for Computational Linguistics.

Yiming Cui, Wanxiang Che, Ting Liu, Bing Qin, and Ziqing Yang. 2021. Pre-training with whole word masking for chinese bert. *IEEE/ACM Transactions on Audio, Speech, and Language Processing*, 29:3504–3514.

Yu-Chih Deng, Yih-Ru Wang, Sin-Horng Chen, and Lung-Hao Lee. 2023. Towards transformer fusions for chinese sentiment intensity prediction in valence-arousal dimensions. *IEEE Access*.

Tim Dettmers, Artidoro Pagnoni, Ari Holtzman, and Luke Zettlemoyer. 2024. Qlora: Efficient finetuning of quantized llms. *Advances in Neural Information Processing Systems*, 36.

Hao Fei, Bobo Li, Qian Liu, Lidong Bing, Fei Li, and Tat-Seng Chua. 2023. Reasoning implicit sentiment with chain-of-thought prompting. In *Proceedings of the 61st Annual Meeting of the Association for Computational Linguistics (Volume 2: Short Papers)*, pages 1171–1182, Toronto, Canada. Association for Computational Linguistics.

Markus Freitag and Yaser Al-Onaizan. 2017. Beam search strategies for neural machine translation. In *Proceedings of the First Workshop on Neural Machine Translation*, pages 56–60.

Zhibin Gou, Qingyan Guo, and Yujiu Yang. 2023. MvP: Multi-view prompting improves aspect sentiment tuple prediction. In *Proceedings of the 61st Annual Meeting of the Association for Computational Linguistics (Volume 1: Long Papers)*, pages 4380–4397, Toronto, Canada. Association for Computational Linguistics.

Daya Guo, Qihao Zhu, Dejian Yang, Zhenda Xie, Kai Dong, Wentao Zhang, Guanting Chen, Xiao Bi, Y Wu, YK Li, et al. 2024. Deepseek-coder: When the large language model meets programming–the rise of code intelligence. *arXiv preprint arXiv:2401.14196*.

Suchin Gururangan, Ana Marasović, Swabha Swayamdipta, Kyle Lo, Iz Beltagy, Doug Downey, and Noah A. Smith. 2020. Don't stop pretraining: Adapt language models to domains and tasks. In *Proceedings of the 58th Annual Meeting of the Association for Computational Linguistics*, pages 8342–8360, Online. Association for Computational Linguistics.

Jieyong Kim, Ryang Heo, Yongsik Seo, SeongKu Kang, Jinyoung Yeo, and Dongha Lee. 2024. Self-consistent reasoning-based aspect-sentiment quad prediction with extract-then-assign strategy. *arXiv preprint arXiv:2403.00354*.

Lung-Hao Lee, Jian-Hong Li, and Liang-Chih Yu. 2022. Chinese emobank: Building valence-arousal resources for dimensional sentiment analysis. *Transactions on Asian and Low-Resource Language Information Processing*, 21(4):1–18.

Lung-Hao Lee, Liang-Chih Yu, Suge Wang, and Jian Liao. 2024. Overview of the sighan 2024 shared task for chinese dimensional aspect-based sentiment analysis. In *Proceedings of the 10th SIGHAN Workshop on Chinese Language Processing*.

Peng Li, Tianxiang Sun, Qiong Tang, Hang Yan, Yuanbin Wu, Xuanjing Huang, and Xipeng Qiu. 2023. CodeIE: Large code generation models are better few-shot information extractors. In *Proceedings of the 61st Annual Meeting of the Association for Computational Linguistics (Volume 1: Long Papers)*, pages 15339–15353, Toronto, Canada. Association for Computational Linguistics.

Zhengyan Li, Yicheng Zou, Chong Zhang, Qi Zhang, and Zhongyu Wei. 2021. Learning implicit sentiment in aspect-based sentiment analysis with supervised contrastive pre-training. In *Proceedings of EMNLP*, pages 246–256.

Bin Liang, Wangda Luo, Xiang Li, Lin Gui, Min Yang, Xiaoqi Yu, and Ruifeng Xu. 2021. Enhancing aspect-based sentiment analysis with supervised contrastive learning. In *Proceedings of CIKM*, pages 3242–3247.

Dehong Ma, Sujian Li, Xiaodong Zhang, and Houfeng Wang. 2017. Interactive attention networks for aspect-level sentiment classification. In *Proceedings of the 26th International Joint Conference on Artificial Intelligence*, IJCAI'17, page 4068–4074. AAAI Press.

Yue Mao, Yi Shen, Jingchao Yang, Xiaoying Zhu, and Longjun Cai. 2022. Seq2Path: Generating sentiment tuples as paths of a tree. In *Findings of the Association for Computational Linguistics: ACL 2022*, pages 2215–2225, Dublin, Ireland. Association for Computational Linguistics.

Maria Pontiki, Dimitris Galanis, Haris Papageorgiou, Ion Androutsopoulos, Suresh Manandhar, Mohammed AL-Smadi, Mahmoud Al-Ayyoub, Yanyan Zhao, Bing Qin, Orphée De Clercq, et al. 2016. Semeval-2016 task 5: Aspect based sentiment analysis. In *ProWorkshop on Semantic Evaluation (SemEval-2016)*, pages 19–30. Association for Computational Linguistics.

Daniel Preoţiuc-Pietro, H Andrew Schwartz, Gregory Park, Johannes Eichstaedt, Margaret Kern, Lyle Ungar, and Elisabeth Shulman. 2016. Modelling valence and arousal in facebook posts. In *Proceedings of the 7th workshop on computational approaches to subjectivity, sentiment and social media analysis*, pages 9–15.

James A Russell. 1980. A circumplex model of affect. *Journal of personality and social psychology*, 39(6):1161.

Yu Sun, Shuohuan Wang, Shikun Feng, Siyu Ding, Chao Pang, Junyuan Shang, Jiaxiang Liu, Xuyi Chen, Yanbin Zhao, Yuxiang Lu, et al. 2021. Ernie 3.0: Large-scale knowledge enhanced pre-training for language understanding and generation. *arXiv preprint arXiv:2107.02137*.

Hugo Touvron, Thibaut Lavril, Gautier Izacard, Xavier Martinet, Marie-Anne Lachaux, Timothée Lacroix, Baptiste Rozière, Naman Goyal, Eric Hambro, Faisal Azhar, et al. 2023. Llama: Open and efficient foundation language models. *arXiv preprint arXiv:2302.13971*.

Ashish Vaswani, Noam Shazeer, Niki Parmar, Jakob Uszkoreit, Llion Jones, Aidan N Gomez, Łukasz Kaiser, and Illia Polosukhin. 2017. Attention is all you need. *Advances in neural information processing systems*, 30.

Jin Wang, Liang-Chih Yu, K Robert Lai, and Xuejie Zhang. 2016a. Dimensional sentiment analysis using a regional cnn-lstm model. In *Proceedings of the 54th annual meeting of the association for computational linguistics (volume 2: Short papers)*, pages 225–230.

Jin Wang, Liang-Chih Yu, K Robert Lai, and Xuejie Zhang. 2019. Tree-structured regional cnn-lstm model for dimensional sentiment analysis. *IEEE/ACM Transactions on Audio, Speech, and Language Processing*, 28:581–591.

Jin Wang, Liang-Chih Yu, and Xuejie Zhang. 2024. Softmcl: Soft momentum contrastive learning for fine-grained sentiment-aware pre-training. In *Proceedings of the 2024 Joint International Conference on Computational Linguistics, Language Resources and Evaluation (LREC-COLING 2024)*, pages 15012–15023.

Kai Wang, Weizhou Shen, Yunyi Yang, Xiaojun Quan, and Rui Wang. 2020. Relational graph attention network for aspect-based sentiment analysis. In *Proceedings of ACL*, pages 3229–3238.

Qianlong Wang, Keyang Ding, Bin Liang, Min Yang, and Ruifeng Xu. 2023a. Reducing spurious correlations in aspect-based sentiment analysis with explanation from large language models. In *Findings of the Association for Computational Linguistics: EMNLP 2023*, pages 2930–2941, Singapore. Association for Computational Linguistics.

Yequan Wang, Minlie Huang, Xiaoyan Zhu, and Li Zhao. 2016b. Attention-based LSTM for aspect-level sentiment classification. In *Proceedings of the 2016 Conference on Empirical Methods in Natural Language Processing*, pages 606–615, Austin, Texas. Association for Computational Linguistics.

Zengzhi Wang, Qiming Xie, Yi Feng, Zixiang Ding, Zinong Yang, and Rui Xia. 2023b. Is chatgpt a good sentiment analyzer? a preliminary study. *arXiv preprint arXiv:2304.04339*.

Amy Beth Warriner, Victor Kuperman, and Marc Brysbaert. 2013. Norms of valence, arousal, and dominance for 13,915 english lemmas. *Behavior research methods*, 45:1191–1207.

Chuhan Wu, Fangzhao Wu, Yongfeng Huang, Sixing Wu, and Zhigang Yuan. 2017. Thu_ngn at ijcnlp-2017 task 2: Dimensional sentiment analysis for chinese phrases with deep lstm. In *Proceedings of the IJCNLP 2017, Shared Tasks*, pages 47–52.

Zhengxuan Wu and Desmond C Ong. 2021. Context-guided bert for targeted aspect-based sentiment analysis. In *Proceedings of AAAI*, volume 35, pages 14094–14102.

Housheng Xie, Wei Lin, Shuying Lin, Jin Wang, and Liang-Chih Yu. 2021. A multi-dimensional relation model for dimensional sentiment analysis. *Information Sciences*, 579:832–844.

Hongling Xu, Qianlong Wang, Yice Zhang, Min Yang, Xi Zeng, Bing Qin, and Ruifeng Xu. 2024. Improving in-context learning with prediction feedback for sentiment analysis. *arXiv e-prints*, pages arXiv–2406.

Hu Xu, Bing Liu, Lei Shu, and S Yu Philip. 2019. Bert post-training for review reading comprehension and aspect-based sentiment analysis. In *Proceedings of NAACL-HLT*, pages 2324–2335.

Liang-Chih Yu, Lung-Hao Lee, Shuai Hao, Jin Wang, Yunchao He, Jun Hu, K Robert Lai, and Xuejie Zhang. 2016. Building chinese affective resources in valence-arousal dimensions. In *Proceedings of the 2016 Conference of the North American Chapter of the Association for Computational Linguistics: Human Language Technologies*, pages 540–545.

Jiaxing Zhang, Ruyi Gan, Junjie Wang, Yuxiang Zhang, Lin Zhang, Ping Yang, Xinyu Gao, Ziwei Wu, Xiaoqun Dong, Junqing He, Jianheng Zhuo, Qi Yang, Yongfeng Huang, Xiayu Li, Yanghan Wu, Junyu Lu, Xinyu Zhu, Weifeng Chen, Ting Han, Kunhao Pan, Rui Wang, Hao Wang, Xiaojun Wu, Zhongshen Zeng, and Chongpei Chen. 2022a. Fengshenbang 1.0: Being the foundation of chinese cognitive intelligence. *CoRR*, abs/2209.02970.

Kai Zhang, Kun Zhang, Mengdi Zhang, Hongke Zhao, Qi Liu, Wei Wu, and Enhong Chen. 2022b. Incorporating dynamic semantics into pre-trained language model for aspect-based sentiment analysis. In *Findings of ACL*, pages 3599–3610.

Wenxuan Zhang, Yang Deng, Xin Li, Yifei Yuan, Lidong Bing, and Wai Lam. 2021. Aspect sentiment quad prediction as paraphrase generation. In *Proceedings of the 2021 Conference on Empirical Methods in Natural Language Processing*, pages 9209–9219, Online and Punta Cana, Dominican Republic. Association for Computational Linguistics.

Yice Zhang, Yifan Yang, Bin Liang, Shiwei Chen, Bing Qin, and Ruifeng Xu. 2023. An empirical study of sentiment-enhanced pre-training for aspect-based sentiment analysis. In *Findings of the Association for Computational Linguistics: ACL 2023*, pages 9633–9651, Toronto, Canada. Association for Computational Linguistics.

Junxian Zhou, Haiqin Yang, Yuxuan He, Hao Mou, and JunBo Yang. 2023. A unified one-step solution for aspect sentiment quad prediction. In *Findings of the Association for Computational Linguistics: ACL 2023*, pages 12249–12265, Toronto, Canada. Association for Computational Linguistics.

Association for Computational Linguistics
209 N. Eighth Street
Stroudsburg, Pennsylvania 18360

ISBN 979-8-3313-0175-0

CURRAN ASSOCIATES INC.
proceedings.com